POVERTY MAPPING IN RAJASTHAN

About the Author

P.C. Bansil heads the Techno Economic Research Institute, New Delhi, founded by him in 1984. He belongs to the first batch of Indian Economic Service and has worked with the FAO for about 15 years in Sri Lanka, Thailand, Rome, Zambia and Libya. He has authored 28 books, besides a large number of reports and papers prepared for various governments. He has published over 400 papers in specialized technical journals. His work experience relates to the formulation, implementation, evaluation and regional plans for agriculture, statistics, marketing, livestock, irrigation, fisheries, forestry, wildlife, national parks, tourism, agro-industrial and social sectors like demography, health, education and housing, as well as project identification, formulation and evaluation in these fields.

Dr. Bansil was recently appointed by the Planning Commission as Chairman of the Tenth Plan Working Group on Animal Husbandry Economics and Statistics. He has just completed the study "Livestock in India 2000-2030" sponsored by the Food and Agriculture Organisation of the United Nations. During his FAO assignments in Sri Lanka, Zambia and Libya as Senior Planning Advisor, he undertook micro level studies on issues relating to water.

POVERTY MAPPING IN RAJASTHAN

P.C. BANSIL

CONCEPT PUBLISHING COMPANY, NEW DELHI-110059

Cataloging in Publication Data—DK
Courtesy: D.K. Agencies (P) Ltd. <docinfo@dkagencies.com>

Bansil, P. C. (Puran Chand), 1921-
Poverty mapping in Rajasthan / P.C. Bansil.
p. cm.
Includes index.
ISBN 8180693341

1. Rural poor—India—Rajasthan. 2. Rural poor—Government policy—India—Rajasthan. 3. Rural development projects—India—Rajasthan. I. Title.

DDC 339.460 954 4 22

ISBN-81-8069-334-1

First Published 2006

Published and Printed by
Ashok Kumar Mittal
Concept Publishing Company,
A/15-16, Commercial Block, Mohan Garden,
New Delhi-110059 (INDIA)

Phones : 25351460, 25351794
Fax : 091-11-25357103
Email : publishing@conceptpub.com

Preface

Poverty has been the bane of human society ever since its evolution, dispensed with a sense of Charity and Philanthropy in a mood of Sympathy. One, rarely, if at all, saw a focused, defined and definite effort to meet the situation arising out of it. (Un) Fortunately the Agenda for the State has always been determined by the Have's, whose primary concern has been to ensure visible development in terms of growth of their own assets. This style of Governance has changed very little with passage of time. When this Model left the crumbs from this approach to be picked up by the weaker and the poorer section of the society—it was termed the 'Trickle-down-effect' and a Theory of Development Hypothesis evolved on these lines, justifying and defending this Model as a valid one for all Developing Economies. This brings to our mind, rather cynically but perhaps realistically, what Prof. J.K. Gailbraith had to say "the problem is not economies; it goes back to a far deeper part of human nature. As people become fortunate in their personal well-being and as countries become similarly fortunate there is a common tendency to ignore the poor."

It was perhaps for the first time in mid-twenties of the twentieth century that Professor Arthur Lewis wrote a little noticed treatise on an investigation into the causes of poverty. This had little to do with the Great Depression as the treatise was penned earlier in time. For bringing the subject of Poverty in sharp focus, the credit rightly, richly and deservedly goes to Professor Gunnar Myrdal, whose visionary and analytical output in the form of Asian Drama in many respects is still valid and holds good.

'Garibi-Hatao' in this country was the offspring of given political compulsions – and not a little, on account of the sensitivity of the then leadership – that some time in 1972 a niche was sought to be created to address this question of Poverty Eradication in some measure. The measuring scale for the target group was the income levels by monetising the value of obtaining food items to provide for 2400 k-calories energy per person per day and a very small margin for other non-food items. This methodology and figure is held so sacrosanct that it is considered valid even today, at least, by the country's Planning Commission to determine the 'Great-Divide' that is, Poverty Line, in order to find out – in numbers/percentages –Below Poverty Line (BPL) and Above Poverty Line (APL) families. By and large the Ministry of Rural Development follows the same approach till recently, when they have added certain 'exclusion' criteria to determine this 'divide'.

Fundamental and obvious flaw in this scheme of things is that Food Security on the scale of k-calorie intake 'alone' is seen to be determining the Poverty line. Global experience and literature on the subject point out to many more additionalities required to be taken into consideration while determining poverty lines. Need is to look at the whole 'basket' of factors having a bearing on Poverty. An attempt has been made in this study not only to fill this gap, but also to present a document which can show the way for similar studies in other states. The study makes the first ever attempt to develop a Composite Index of Human Poverty in various Districts of Rajasthan. This will help the policy makers to develop location specific strategies for poverty alleviation.

The Institute undertook this 'Venture-Study' for which the Ministry of Rural Development, Government of India need to be thanked profusely for the co-operation and courageous support extended by them in ample measure. But for their support it would not have been possible for us to venture on this un-trodden path to find a secure place for the poor of this country. Both Mr. Welfred Lakra, Joint Secretary and Mr. S. Naik were available for discussions throughout the study period. Mr. Lakra was kind enough to spare time to personally visit the field in the interior of Rajasthan and acquaint himself with local ground situation. His valuable suggestions as a result of his field visit led to an improvement of the final report. Mrs. Asha Swaroop, the present Joint Secretary gave valuable comments on the first draft. This helped TERI to not only improve the final report, but also give new direction in a number of cases. The book as being presented now is a revised version of the report prepared for the Ministry of Rural Development.

The study is the result of a Team Work which comprised:

Dr. P.C. Bansil
Mr. B.K. Taimni
Dr. Padam Singh
Dr. P.K. Dikshit
Mr. K.R. Dasgupta

P.C. Bansil took over the total responsibility to organise and finalise the study. He is fully responsible for the final shape of the book which called for drastic revisions, additions and subtractions etc., made therein. Mr. B.K. Taimni who is a senior IAS Officer, retired as Union Food Secretary, Government of India. Besides his overall guidance throughout the period when the study was being carried out, his major contribution towards giving a new definition to poverty, developing a Composite Index and evolve a methodology for targeting the Poor, deserves special mention.

Dr. Padam Singh, Additional Director General, ICMR – an eminent statistician – was kind enough to guide at various stages on the methodology and data analysis. He also helped in making available ICMR data on demography, health, and nutrition. But for his contribution, it would have been rather difficult for the Institute to get meaningful results from a sea of primary and secondary data. His contribution is acknowledged with gratitude.

Mr. K.R. Dasgupta, Economic Adviser of the Institute, deserves special thanks. He was fully involved at every stage of drafting of the Report for submission to the Ministry of R & D. The book in its revised version as being presented now has a visible imprint of his untiring contribution which deserves special mention.

The contribution of Dr. P.K. Dikshit as Project Director deserves special mention. It was a feat to organize the field staff and complete the field survey of over 30,000 households in a short period of one month. Our thanks are also due to our faculty members – Dr. S.R. Mohnot, Dr. P.N. Radhakrishnan and Dr. M.L. Srivastava, in particular, for their invaluable support.

TERI staff members Mr. C.P. Sharma, Mrs. Ajitha Gangadharan and Mrs. Vasantha R. Pillai, who have contributed substantially to the project by adhering to time schedule and working under tremendous pressure deserve special thanks.

New Delhi **P.C. Bansil**

Contents

Acronyms

ADB	:	Asian Development Bank
AID	:	Assistance for International Development
AE	:	Agricultural Extension
APL	:	Above Poverty Line
BPL	:	Below Poverty Line
CAD	:	Command Area Development
CD	:	Community Development
CED	:	Chronic Energy Deficiency
CHPI	:	Composite Human Poverty Index
CRS	:	Catholic Relief Services
CRSP	:	Central Rural Sanitation Programme
CRY	:	Child Rights and You
CSO	:	Central Statistical Organisation
CSRE	:	Crash Scheme for Rural Employment
DANIDA	:	Danish International Development Agency
DDP	:	Desert Development Programme
DPAP	:	Drought Prone Area Programme
DRDA	:	District Rural Development Agency
DWCRA	:	Development of Women and Children in Rural Area
EAS	:	Employment Assurance Scheme
EGS	:	Employment Guarantee Scheme
FAO	:	Food and Agriculatural Organisation
FWP	:	Food for Work Programme
GDP	:	Gross Domestic Product
GKY	:	Ganga Kalyan Yojana
HDR	:	Human Development Report
HH	:	Household
HPI	:	Human Poverty Index
IAY	:	Indira Awaas Yojana
ICDS	:	Integrated Child Development Services
ICMR	:	Indian Council of Medical Research
IMR	:	Infant Mortality Rate
IRDP	:	Integrated Rural Development Programme

ISB	:	Inter Service & Business
ITI	:	Indian Technical Institute
JGSY	:	Jawahar Gram Samridhi Yojana
JRY	:	Jawahar Rozgar Yojana
kg	:	Kilogram
km	:	Kilometre
KVK	:	Krishi Vigyan Kendra
MFAL	:	Marginal Farmers and Agricultural Labourers
MMR	:	Maternal Mortality Rate
MWS	:	Million Wells Scheme
NAS	:	National Accounts Statistics
NDP	:	Net Domestic Product
NGO	:	Non-Government Organisation
NIRD	:	National Institute of Rural Development
NREP	:	National Rural Employment Programme
NRRDA	:	National Rural Road Development Agency
NSAP	:	National Social Assistance Programme
NSSO	:	National Sample Survey Organisation
ODI	:	Overseas Development Institute
PAP	:	Poverty Alleviation Programmes
PDS	:	Public Distribution System
PHC	:	Public Health Centre
PMGY	:	Pradhan Mantri Gramodaya Yojana
PMRY	:	Prime Minister's Rozgar Yojana
PMGSY	:	Pradhan Mantri Gram Sadak Yojana
REGP	:	Rural Employment Generation Programme
RGNDWM	:	Rajiv Gandhi National Drinking Water Mission
RLEGP	:	Rural Landless Employment Guarantee Programme
SAY	:	Samagra Awaas Yojana
SC	:	Scheduled Caste
SFDA	:	Small Farmers Development Agency
SEDI	:	Socio-Economic Development Index
SGSY	:	Swarnajayanti Gram Swarozgar Yojana
ST	:	Scheduled Tribe
TRYSEM	:	Training of Rural Youth for Self-Employment
UT	:	Union Territory
UNDP	:	United Nations Development Programme
VLW	:	Village Level Worker

Executive Summary

Blessed is he who considers the poor; the Lord delivers him on the day of trouble.

— *Psalm 41.1*

Introduction

Poverty has been the bane of human society ever since its evolution, and has been dispensed with a sense of Charity and Philanthropy in a mood of Sympathy. India which is no exception has been living with the evil of poverty for a very long time. The paradox of poverty amidst plenty existed in Pre-independent India and it exists even today in ample measure. During the Pre-independence period, poverty was largely attributed to colonial exploitation of the Indian economy by the British, coupled with feudal mode of agricultural production and overall economic stagnation. After independence, the Government felt obliged to undertake poverty alleviation programmes to enable the poor people to participate in democracy and development as equal partners. We have, however, no hesitation to say that 'Garibi-Hatao' in this country was the offspring of given political compulsions — and not a little, on account of the sensitivity of the then leadership – that some time in 1972 a niche was sought to be created to address this question of Poverty Eradication in some measure.

Background

A programme of Food for Work was launched in 1977 to provide opportunities of work for the rural poor particularly in slack employment periods for the year which would at the same time create durable community assets. Further, a Minimum Needs Programme was designed to secure to the rural areas within a reasonable time frame certain basic amenities in the field of education, health, drinking water, electrification, roads and house-sites.

It was realized in late seventies that there was a need for developing a strategy of direct attack on poverty through specific programmes of poverty alleviation as there was insufficient percolation of benefits to the poor from overall economic growth. Accordingly, various poverty alleviation programmes were initiated during the sixth and seventh plan periods for generating sufficient income among the rural poor so that they could cross the Poverty Line. There were self-employment programmes like Integrated Rural Development Programme (IRDP), and wage-employment programmes like National Rural Employment Programme (NREP) and Rural Landless Employment Guarantee Programme (RLEGP). These two similar wage-employment programmes were, however, later merged into one and rechristened as Jawahar Rozgar Yojana (JRY). All these programmes were again re-organized in recent years. The Swarnajayanti Gram Swarozgar Yojana (SGSY) was launched with effect from 1-4-1999 in place of IRDP with its allied programmes like TRYSEM, DWCRA, GKY, MWS, etc. Jawahar Gram Samridhi Yojana (JGSY) was also launched with effect from 1-4-1999 to ensure development of rural infrastructure by restructuring the Jawahar Rozgar Yojana (JRY). Again, the Sampoorna Grameen Rozgar Yojana (SGRY) was launched on 25th September, 2001, with the purposes of providing food security, additional employment to the rural poor and creating infrastructure in rural areas after merging SGSY and Employment Assurance Scheme (EAS). There are now a few other schemes which are in operation in the rural areas, viz. Pradhan Mantri Gram Sadak Yojana, Annapurna Yojana, National Mission for Rural Housing and Habitat, etc.

It cannot be denied that all these programmes had a salutary effect in removing poverty in the country at the aggregate level. In fact, in India, the proportion of people below the poverty line declined from 47.4 per cent in 1951-52 to 37.0 per cent in 1993-94 and 26 per cent in 1999-2000.

The Study

Two points led us to ponder and delve deeper into the whole question of poverty. One, that the basis of current estimation of poverty ratios was a certain monetary denomination largely including the consumption expenditure on food items. The measuring scale for the target group was the income levels by monetising the value of obtaining food items to provide for 2400 k-calorie energy per person per day in rural area and 2100 for urban area along with a very small margin for other non-food items.

Man does not live by bread alone, hence the very rationale was 'suspect' before us, and two, the imperatives of other factors having a bearing on poverty were never brought into sharp focus, thus leaving them outside the purview in the attempt to eradicate poverty. Man being both a social and economic animal – is a product of a combination of his own wherewithal – his access both physical and financial – to certain basic needs, as also the ethos, environment and infrastructure around him. They all need to be reckoned with while examining poverty.

The methodology adopted by Planning Commission uses the concept of poverty line in monetary terms in order to find out – in numbers/percentages – 'Below Poverty Line' (BPL) and Above Poverty Line (APL) families. The exercises made by the Planning Commission based primarily on NSSO consumption expenditure surveys are able to provide a comparative picture of BPL families at the State level, for estimating the magnitude of poverty or to be precise about the numbers involved.

While implementing poverty alleviation programmes, the main problem arises in identifying the poor based solely on income criterion. There are often complaints that number of APL families are being included and BPL families are excluded at the village level. Hence, it is necessary to evolve a new method of identification of the poor families in rural areas. It is necessary to look into the "very essential" Indicators, which have a cause and effect relationship. More particularly, it is necessary to identify the location specific nature and causes of poverty. Three clear questions arise in this exercise, viz. 'who are these poor', 'where are these poor' and 'why are they poor'. This will lead to a 'Triple A' approach on the part of the Policy Makers and Programme Administrators – which are:

- 'Assess' the situation
- 'Analyze' the situation, and take
- 'Action' to remedy the situation.

The aim of Poverty Mapping is to highlight the specific areas in the districts where concerted actions are needed to eradicate poverty and prepare development planning of a district keeping in view the inter-district variations in growth indicators, resource availability and status of capacity building strategies. Similarly, the purpose of constructing district-wise segmental stratum index and summative total index is to put emphasis on the urgency of planning at the grassroots level in terms of specific deprivation which varies significantly from district to district and need for formulation of different strategies for each component. Needless to say that the exercise of development planning necessitates realistic assessment of diversity in a district and participation of community, its representatives and other stakeholders, so that planning process for total Human Development lack or absence of which is indicative of poverty – becomes truly participatory and is in consonance with local realities.

Keeping the above aims in view, the State of Rajasthan was selected for the study. The State is physically divided into two major geographical units. The area to the west of Aravali ranges comprising nearly two-thirds of the total area of the state is almost arid and undulating, while the eastern part is relatively fertile. Intensive soil erosion and environmental degradation pose critical problems in many districts. Both human and livestock population in the state face lot of hardships due to unfavourable physiography and frequent natural calamity like draught.

The high rate of population growth (nearly 2.5 per cent per annum) with limited natural resources is impeding the rapid economic growth of the state. Though there has been significant improvement in the literacy rate during the nineties decade from 38.55 per cent in 1991 to 61.03 per cent in 2001, even now, almost two-fifths of the population is illiterate. In the per capita income, the state ranks tenth position among 14 major states in the country. With a share of nearly 32 per cent of the SDP, and 70 per cent of the workforce, agriculture plays an important role in the economy. With the cropping intensity below 25 per cent, farming in the state is primarily rainfed. Rajasthan occupies a place of pride in livestock. Of the total livestock population of 471 million in the country, the state accounts for over 10 per cent as against only 5.5 per cent of human population.

According to the Head-Count Ratio, the proportion of rural population below the poverty line in the state was only 13.7 per cent in 1999-2000 (using 30 days recall period), which was significantly lower than the national average of 27.1 per cent. But using other indicators of poverty and human development, Rajasthan would rank as one of the poorest regions. In general, low economic development and large number of pockets of poverty concentration in Rajasthan State is the consequence of low literacy, low status of women, large desert area, scarcity of water, weak industrialization, high IMR and MMR, higher rate of population growth and related social and cultural factors and forces.

The primary objective of this innovative study has, therefore, been to make an assessment in a comparative framework at inter-district level regarding the extent of deprivation in each segment of the selected indicators. Raw data often gives a picture at the level of generality; disadvantaged areas and disadvantaged social categories, within a district often become invisible. But when component and indicators are taken separately, deprivation for each stratum (sub-indicator) and segment (indicator) can be understood meaningfully. Hence, a serious thought has been given to the choice of number of components for each indicator and weights so that the values could be logically assigned.

The composite index which has been constructed raised certain other issues like relationship between different components of indicators and of index, and index which comprises of all the indicators. Inability to relate otherwise logical inter-linkages, no doubt, necessitates causality which, however, was beyond the scope of this study. However, our ability to identify the areas where there are concentration of poorer people and the reasons thereof will help immensely the policy makers to frame proper policies for removal of poverty.

Results

The present study has mapped out various districts of Rajasthan based on various indicators reflecting poverty and deprivation. It may be reiterated that unlike the Planning Commission or the Ministry of Rural Development which base their poverty assessment on income criterion alone, we have used here a much broader definition of poverty based on nine major indicators and a number of relevant sub-indicators that influence poverty. Besides, an effort has been made to identify who are poor and where are the poor people concentrated, but also why the poor people stay poor at macro and micro levels. The findings of the study are expected to help in prioritizing location specific investment strategies and programmes for poverty alleviation. Besides it would help in proper targeting of various programmes so that there is a visible impact of efforts made for poverty alleviation.

The study was based on both secondary data district-wise and primary data collected through household surveys in two blocks in two districts of Rajasthan. The selected districts include the relatively high poverty districts of Banswara and Chittorgarh. Further, two representative blocks, namely Rashmi and Sajjangarh from these two districts were selected for survey. A composite index of poverty was then developed at district, village and household levels, using appropriate weights assigned to various indicators, based on their relative contributions to poverty in the State.

The poverty ratio which is based on household income is not a sufficient indicator of deprivation. The composite human poverty index reflects a more realistic picture as it is based on 9 broad groups of indicators influencing poverty and deprivation. In developing CHPI the emphasis is more on outcome indicators having bearing on well-being as measured by health and nutrition. Rajasthan being a livestock based economy the same has also been given due importance. In contrast to this, poverty ratio is based on income criteria alone, whereas Human Poverty Index (HPI) considers many indicators under 11 groups including aspects of health and nutrition but not livestock.

The results of the district level and village and household level studies are presented in Chapters 7 and 8 respectively. Using the methodology as mentioned above a Composite Human Poverty Index (CHPI) for all the districts of Rajasthan has been developed. Table 7.11 presents the values of Composite Indices (CI) for different indicator groups as well as CHPI along with the ranks of the districts according to CHPI. The districts which had values of CIs higher than the average for different indicators are indicated in Table 7.11(a). The table would reveal that the number of districts showing higher deprivations vary from one indicator to another, the number ranging from 12 to 20. This will help the policy makers to formulate appropriate district-wise policies to alleviate poverty at the macro level. The CHPI had correlations with CIs ranging between 0.16 and 0.76 [Table 7.11(c)]. More important of these indicators influencing CHPI were Infrastructure (R = 0.76), Health (R = 0.66), Livestock (R = 0.65), Nutrition (R = 0.61) an Agriculture (R = 0.57).

Further, an analysis of poverty and deprivation have been undertaken to test the commonality of categorization of districts as high poverty districts by this innovative methodology and conventional poverty ratio approach and the results are presented in Table 7.12. It is observed that out of 13 high deprivation districts with CHPI, about 9 districts are common with that using poverty ratio. An attempt has also been made to estimate Poverty Ratio using CHPI by relating Poverty Ratio and CHPI through regression analysis based on districts data where ranks match by both methods, and the results are presented in Table 7.14.

In so far as the study at the village and household levels, is concerned, Sajjangarh block in Banswara district and Rashmi block in Chittorgarh district were selected. Altogether 267 villages in these two blocks were surveyed. The analysis of data in constructing composite index was carried out in the same manner as those of the secondary data at the district level. The overall poverty ratio was 85 per cent and 51 per cent in the selected villages in Sajjangarh and Rashmi blocks respectively. The Composite Human Poverty Index (CHPI) have been computed separately for village level data and household level data as well as for both giving 50:50 weight and results are given in Tables 8.7 to 8.10.

The correlation of CHPI with other indicators has been worked out using both village level data and household level data and the results are presented in Table 8.11. Using the village level data, for Banswara, the highest correlation of CHPI was observed with nutrition (R = 0.75) followed by infrastructure (R = 0.47), housing (R = 0.47) and development (R = 0.46). For Chittorgarh also nutrition had the highest correlation (R = 0.79), followed by health (R = 0.70), agriculture (R = 0.69) and infrastructure (R = 0.67).

Using household level data, for Banswara, the highest correlation of CHPI was observed with health (R = 0.64) followed by livestock (R = 0.46), literacy (R = 0.43) and nutrition (R = 0.30). In Chittorgarh, the household level data indicated highest correlation of CHPI with livestock (R = 0.59) followed by demography (R = 0.49) and housing (R = 0.43). This would mean that priorities for poverty alleviation differ from District to District and even village to village and therefore, the strategies will have to be location specific.

To sum up, findings of village and household level surveys

through this innovative method are revealing. It is conclusively proved that poverty measurement and identification of poor based on income criteria alone does not reflect the true picture of overall deprivation at the village/ household level. There are other indicators which determine the level of poverty quite significantly. Accordingly our conclusions and recommendations on the formulation of location-specific strategies for alleviation of poverty and deprivation are presented in Chapter 10.

The implication by inference is that if the costs of these are factored into figure of income levels determining the divide between BPL and APL, this figure shall necessarily work out to be much higher than at present. These changes, and challenges the very percept of measuring poverty as well as the focal points, at disaggregated level to address the question of poverty eradication. The study validates the necessity to measure poverty keeping in mind factors having a bearing on poverty as also the need for multi-dimensional approach, while flexibility at disaggregated levels to address the issues having a bearing on poverty. Overall poverty ratios go for change and usher us into a different reality with serious policy implications. The number of poor goes up overall. Current hypothesis of measuring poverty on the basis of income criteria alone gets de-throned heralding a new composite approach to the whole question of poverty, thus validating the *raison d'etre* of taking up this study.

1

Introduction

"Freedom from 'want' was one of the critical wants on which the world set its sight in the middle of last century—the goal and sincerity of purpose seem to have lost somewhere enroute"

India is living with the evil of poverty for a very long time. The paradox of poverty amidst plenty existed in pre-independent India and it exists even today in ample measures. No doubt, during the past five decades after independence, the country has achieved some measure of development in terms of green revolution, construction of sky scrapers and fly-overs especially in metropolitan cities. Yet, if one looks closely, one can see half naked hungry beggars all around. The slum dwellers as well as pavement dwellers exist side by side with the sky scrapers. The problem is much more serious in rural areas, as under employed, illiterate and unskilled persons swell the ranks of rural population. As many as 52 per cent of villages are getting non-potable water, 41.2 per cent villages do not have dispensaries within 5 km. The houselessness, or shelter in the form of *Kucha* house coupled with inaccessibility to roads, electricity, safe drinking water, toilet facilities etc. is widely prevalent in large parts of rural India. The small size of land holdings, low productivity, low wage rate and low level of non-farm employment opportunities compel a vast majority of the rural population to live under perpetual poverty trap. All this has resulted in widening the gap between rich and the poor.

During the pre-independence period, poverty was largely attributed to colonial exploitation of the Indian economy by the British, coupled with feudal mode of agricultural production and overall economic stagnation. Therefore, the people belonging to various social groups and classes joined the freedom movement with the hope that political independence would also bring home for them freedom from hunger, malnutrition and illiteracy, etc. After independence, the Government was thus under obligation to remove poverty to enable the poor people to participate in democracy and development as equal partners. Unfortunately, however, based on a simple head-count ratio, the absolute number of poor people in the country is reported to have increased from about 200 million in the 1950s to 260 million in 1999-2000, although the overall head-count poverty ratio declined from 47 per cent in 1951-52 to 26 per cent in 1999-2000 (Table 1.1). The state-wise number and percentage of population below poverty line during 1973-74, 1977-78, 1983-84, 1987-88, 1993-94 and 1999-2000 are indicated in Annexure 1.1. Though the overall poverty ratio recorded a sharp fall during 90s from 36 per cent in 1993-94 to 26 per cent in 1999-2000, there was wide disparity in poverty ratios between the states. While in Orissa and Bihar there were as high as 47 and 42 per cent respectively, in Jammu and Kashmir and Goa these were as low as 3 and 4 per cent respectively. In as many as 12 major states in the country the poverty ratios were significantly higher than that of the national average of 26 per cent. This phenomenon clearly indicates that affluence and poverty are still very close neighbours in India.

Considering other relevant indicators of poverty such as illiteracy, malnutrition and inaccessibility to certain basic amenities of life, the problem may be of even higher magnitude. These considerations are equally important, as man cannot live by bread alone. As a matter of fact, the continuing large incidence of poverty in many regions of the country, with its multi-dimensional character, poses a relevant question, whether our past policies and programmes of poverty alleviation were realistically designed to be effective, based on location specific analysis of the causes of poverty and proper assessment of the capabilities of the people, government and the local level institutions to meet the challenges of poverty. This calls for a fresh look at the strategies adopted in the past so that necessary corrective measures can be adopted in the near future. What

Table 1.1: Proportion of the rural people below the Poverty-line

Year	*Poverty Ratio*
1951-52	47.4
1952-53	48.2
1953-54	61.3
1954-55	64.2
1955-56	40.3
1956-57	58.9
1957-58	55.2
1958-59	53.3
1959-60	50.9
1960-61	45.4
1961-62	47.2
1963-64	48.5
1964-65	53.7
1965-66	57.6
1966-67	64.3
1967-68	63.7
1968-69	59.0
1969-70	57.6
1970-71	54.8
1972-73	59.4
1973-74	55.7
1977-78	50.6
1983	45.3
1986-87	38.8
1988-89	39.1
1989-90	34.3
1990-91	36.4
1992	43.5
1993-94	37.0
1999-2000	26.0

Source: Based on various rounds of NSS, Government of India.

is, however, lacking is political will. The country needs to work harder to create the policy environment, implement the programmes to allow people to overcome hunger and poverty. However, real development would involve the transformation of the human state to a higher level of being and living. Almost all versions of development accept that. However, such a transformation must have the participation and consent of those affected by it. Their involvement in the decision-making process. And the intrusion on their environment, culture, livelihood and tradition by that process should be minimal.

Land Reform: Green Revolution and Rural Poverty

At the dawn of independence, the National Planning Committee (1948) of the Indian National Congress made an important recommendation that the achievement of a National minimum standard in respect of the essentials of individual and social well-being within a reasonable period must be pursued as the practical goals of all schemes for economic development. This had set the basic tone of our economic policy since independence. During the first and second five year plan periods, especially in the 1950s and early 60s, a number of land reform measures were undertaken to remove the structural impediments to agricultural growth and poverty alleviation. All large intermediaries were abolished. Tenancy was either largely banned or regulated. A ceiling on land holding was imposed for re-distribution of surplus land to the landless persons. In Punjab, Haryana and Western Uttar Pradesh, even consolidation of land holdings was undertaken on priority basis, rightly hoping that it would promote agricultural growth and presuming that it will have 'trickle down' as well as 'spill over' effect on poverty alleviation.

No doubt, land reforms did yield some positive results. It removed the unproductive character of the agrarian economy. It also put in place some growth promoting forces. However, due to severe drought during 1965 and 1966, the country faced a famine like situation in many parts. It was at this juncture when the country was living from 'ship to mouth' that the Government decided to adopt High Yielding Varieties (HYV) of seeds for productivity growth in agriculture thinking that accelerated agricultural growth could alone prevent hunger and famine. There was thus more emphasis on adoption of HYV seeds and chemical fertilizers, particularly in irrigated areas for raising foodgrain production. As a result, the country achieved a remarkable success in raising foodgrain production in the late sixties in what came to be known as the Green Revolution.

Nevertheless due to growing incidence of landlessness and unemployment, there were land riots and naxalite movement in several parts of the country in late sixties and early seventies. Therefore, the Government lowered the ceilings on land holding with effect from April 1, 1971 and attempted to re-distribute the ceiling surplus land vigorously.

But the achievements were by no means substantial, as the vested interests embroiled the issue. It has been reported by the Ministry of Rural Development that only about 2 million hectares of land could be re-distributed among about 5 million poor families and in many cases, the land made available for re-distribution was of poor quality which required heavy investment in land improvement measures before being put to cultivation. Thus, both land reform and Green Revolution failed to contain rural poverty and tension. At best, these steps achieved some measure of success in limited areas. The success of land reform was largely confined to West Bengal and Kerala and that of Green Revolution to Punjab, Haryana and Uttar Pradesh. The rainfed areas which constitute the largest segment of our cultivated area remained outside the purview of Green Revolution and, therefore, poverty syndrome of these areas remained intact. Intra-state, interstate and regional imbalance in growth parameters are obvious on the face of it.

Special Area and Group Specific Programme

During the 1970s, the Government undertook some special area development programmes such as Drought Prone Area Programme (DPAP) and Desert Development Programme (DDP) etc. which were intended to counter endemic poverty caused by hostile agro-climatic conditions and degradation of natural resources. Since April, 1995, these programmes are implemented on "Watershed" basis. During the Fourth Five Year Plan (1969-73), group specific programmes like MFAL, SFDA and Food for Work were launched. These aimed at improving the socio-economic conditions of marginal and small farmers and landless labourer who constitute a vast majority of the rural poor. The Fifth Five Year Plan (1974-79) also launched Minimum Needs Programme (MNP) (which was designed to ensure certain basic amenities). The accelerated Rural Water Supply Programme, was introduced in 1972-73 to provide safe drinking water in rural areas. The National Rural Employment Programme (NREP) was launched in October, 1980 and became a regular Plan programme from April, 1981. The programme was expected to generate additional gainful employment in the rural areas, to the extent of 300-400 million mandays per annum, create durable community assets and improve nutritional status and living standards of the poor. The Rural Landless Employment Guarantee Programme (RLEGP) was introduced from 15th August, 1983 with the objective of improving and expanding employment opportunities for the rural landless with a view to providing guarantee of employment to at least one member of every landless household upto 100 days in a year and creating durable assets for strengthening the infrastructure so as to meet the growing requirements of the rural economy. In 1989, the above two programmes were merged into a single rural wage employment programme called Jawahar Rozgar Yojana (JRY). However, even these direct programmes did not yield much result because of both—faulty design and poor implementation.

Integrated Rural Development Programme

With this scenario, the Sixth Plan (1980-85), made an effort to integrate different schemes in a more cohesive manner. Various self-employment programmes were merged as Integrated Rural Development Programme (IRDP) and as stated above, the wage employment programmes like NREP and RLEGP were merged as Jawahar Rojgar Yojana (JRY) in 1989.

The Government of India also launched Indira Awas Yojana with effect from 1985-86 for providing assistance for construction of houses for the rural poor. The Central Rural Sanitation Programme (CRSP) was launched in 1986 with the objective of improving the quality of life of the rural people and to provide privacy and dignity to the women. However, the failure to integrate the poverty alleviation objective with the overall development strategy simply resulted in the proliferation of poverty alleviation programmes, leading to inefficient use of a large chunk of resources on account of weak linkages with growth, low potential for sustained employment generation and inefficient impact on social development and protection of environment. Although, the head-count ratio decreased from 56 per cent in 1973-74 to 37.3 per cent in 1993-94, still about 244 million people in rural India were reported to be below the income based poverty line (as per 50th round of NSSO).

Reorganisation of Rural Development Programmes in Recent Years

After a thorough review, the anti-poverty programmes were re-organized in recent years. The Swaranajayanti Gram Swarozgar Yojana (SGSY) was launched with effect from April 1, 1999 as a new self-employment programme. The earlier programme like IRDP, TRYSEM, DWCRA, GKY, MWS etc. are no longer in operation. The SGSY is intended to bring the assisted poor families above the poverty line by providing them income generating assets (Swarozgar) through a mix of Bank credit and Government subsidy. The emphasis is on establishment of a large number of micro enterprises in rural areas based on cluster approach. Jawahar Gram Samridhi Yojana (JGSY) was launched on April 1, 1999 to ensure development of rural infrastructure by restructuring the Jawahar Rozgar Yojana (JRY). Again, the Sampoorna Grameen Rozgar Yojana (SGRY) was launched on 25th September, 2001, with the purpose to take care of food security, additional wage employment and creating village infrastructure in rural areas after merging SGSY and Employment Assurance Scheme (EAS). Further more, the Pradhan Mantri Gram Saḍak Yojana was launched with effect from December 25, 2000 with the primary objective of providing rural road connectivity. It is proposed to connect about 1 lakh villages in the next seven years. It also envisages allocation of additional central assistance to the states and UT's for providing the basic minimum services, including rural shelter, primary education, primary health, rural drinking water and nutrition. A National Mission for Rural Housing and Habitat has been set up by the Ministry of Rural Development for providing convergence of technology, habitat and energy related issues, with a goal to provide affordable shelter for all in rural areas within a specified time frame and through community participation.

The Employment Assurance Scheme which was in operation since October 1993, has been restructured w.e.f. April 1, 1999 whereby Zilla Parishads have been designated as the implementing authority. The basic objective is to create additional wage employment opportunities during the period of acute shortage of wage employment in selected 5446 blocks of the country which are located in DPAP, DDP, tribal and hilly areas.

The government also launched the Annapurna Scheme w.e.f. April 1, 2000 for providing food security to those senior citizens who are eligible for Pension under National Old Age Pension Scheme, but are not getting the same. Under "Annapurna" Scheme, 10 kg of foodgrains per month per beneficiary are provided free of cost to the targeted beneficiaries. In addition, restructured Rural Sanitation Programme with effect from April 1999 claims to move away from the Principle of state-wise allocation primarily based on poverty criteria to a demand driven approach in a phased manner with a view to widening the coverage. Besides, the total sanitation compaign envisages a synergistic inter-action between the government machinery, active NGO participation and provision of an alternative delivery system and demand oriented construction norms.

Results of Various Anti-Poverty Programmes

The results of various anti-poverty measures discussed above remained far from satisfactory. While some schemes suffered from design fault, some others failed because of half-hearted and ad-hoc nature of implementation. Also in the absence of location specific strategies, involving either a big push or critical minimum effort in the locally desired direction, anti-poverty programmes have failed to break the vicious circle of poverty and underdevelopment, particularly when the traditional social structure and institutions and semi-feudal system of poor governance tend to chain the wheels of economic progress. It has been estimated that the proportion of people below the poverty line declined from 47.4 per cent in 1951-52 to 37.0 per cent in 1993-94 and 26 per cent in 1999-2000.

No doubt, the Central Government's spending on anti-poverty programmes increased from Rs. 62.59 billion in 1992-93 to Rs. 156.12 billion in 1997-98. During 2001-2002, the approved outlay on various rural development programmes worked out to be Rs.92.05 billion. However, this accounts for hardly 1 per cent of the country's total Gross Domestic Product (GDP) and 6 per cent of the total government expenditure. Even if the entire amount earmarked for these programmes reaches the poor, the total transfer to the poor is on an average only 5 to 7 per cent of the expenditure required to cross the poverty line. Given the high level of leakages of funds under these programmes, the task of poverty alleviation looks all the more challenging. On an average, IRDP provided assistance for self-employment at the rate of about 2 to 3 million rural families during 1990-91 to 1998-99. Similarly, the Jawahar Rojgar Yojana provided wage employment to the order of 80 to 102 crore of mandays annually. Number of mandays generated under JRY came down sharply from 21 days in a year in 1993-94 to 7 days in a year in 1998-99. Corresponding figure for EAS in 1998-99 was 9.13 days a year against a guaranteed employment of 100 days eligible families during off season. It has been widely recognised that these programmes failed to yield adequate impact on poverty alleviation. After review, therefore, these programmes were restructured with effect from April 1, 1999. The newly launched self-employment programme, called Swarnajayanti Gram Swarojgar Yojana (SGSY) has two key aspects, namely activity clusters and the group approach. Each block has to concentrate on 4 to 5 activities based on local resources, occupational skills of the people and availability of markets so that they can draw sustainable income from their investments. The SGSY also focuses on organization of self-help groups of the poor at the grassroots level of greater impact.

Similarly, the Jawahar Gram Samridhi Yojana has been launched by restructuring the erstwhile JRY, the main emphasis being on creation of rural infrastructure at the village level. During 1999-2000, about 9.3 lakh families were assisted under SGSY with per family investment of Rs.17,113. In the case of Rajasthan, about 34 thousand swarojgaris were assisted with an average per family investment of Rs. 25,556. Under JGSY, about 26.83 crore of mandays of employment were generated in 1999-2000 involving an expenditure of Rs. 2035 crores. In Rajasthan, nearly 10 million mandays of employment were generated under JGSY involving an expenditure of Rs. 81.5 crores in 1999-2000. In 2000-01 upto September only about 6.2 million mandays of employment were generated in Rajasthan, with an expenditure of Rs. 81.50 crores. Although it is too early to assess the impact of these two major restructured anti-poverty programmes, the available indications do not show much hope of their capabilities to make any significant dent on poverty. Particularly, everything-everywhere approach is bound to result in huge wastage of resources. Any poverty alleviation strategy based on income or calorie based definition of poverty would fall far short of bringing about the much desired socio-economic transformation in rural areas.

Literature Review

There is no dispute that Poverty has been with us since the beginning. Review of literature on the subject from early last century reveal that 'Development' route came to be accepted, with sops to the poor, as a long-term strategy to address the whole issue of Poor/Poverty. This concept was further strengthened immediately after the 'Great Depression' and the Keynesian Model dealing with 'Income' and 'Employment'.

Dealing with poverty *per se* drew attention only after middle of last century when large number of countries attained freedom and the biggest challenges confronting them were hunger, poverty and scarcities. There were two 'models' of development available – Soviet and the Market-led. India led others when it adopted what came to be known as Mixed Economy, i.e. a mix of both the 'models'.

International Studies

World Bank, as the largest multilateral lender led the pack by adopting the prevailing Development hypothesis with a trickle down effect to address the cause of poor. Soon this model was challenged – both at the theoretical and practical level. No wonder that countries were measured/ranked in terms of 'rate of growth' leaving its equitable distribution to the trickle down effect – which to say the least was not at all uniform.

Full credit has to be given to Mr. Robert McNamara, the then World Bank President who came to recognise 'Poverty' as the main enemy to be fought. To quote Prof. Paul Samuelson "I take off my hat to Robert McNamara for what has been its unique vision – has recognition that successful market forces alone cannot be relied on to mitigate flagrant inequality and abject poverty."

As a result of persistent and insistent introspection, World Bank brought out 'World Development Report – 1990' which for the first time accepted the traditional view of poverty "as encompassing not only material deprivation (measured by an appropriate concept of income or consumption) but also achievements in education and health."

While the World Bank continued to meander in the haze of traditional approach of measuring poverty in terms of income/consumption parameters and the social parameters of education, health, drinking water, etc., UNDP started the process of publishing 'Human Development Report' ranking countries on certain indicators. It is from 1997 onwards that the UNDP's 'Human Development Report' from early 1990s also came to have a chapter on 'Human Poverty Index (HPI)' developed on certain indicators; going from strength to strength HPI ranking was developed on following indicators:

- *Longetivity*: percentage of people not expected to survive to age 40
- *Knowledge*: Adult Literacy Rate
- *Decent Standard of Living*:
  1. Percentage of people without access to safe water,
  2. Percentage of people without access to health services, and
  3. Percentage of under weight children under five.

In the HDR of 2002, a further refinement has been attempted over and above the basic parameters referred to earlier for determining the HPI. The newly added dimensions are Demographic trends, Commitments to Health – access, services and resources, global health crisis and challenges dealing with issues on malnourishment and specific diseases, survival, commitment to Education—Literacy and Enrolment, Technology – diffusion and creation, Economic Performance, In-equality in Income or consumption, structure of trade, flow of aid, private capital and debt, priorities in public spending, energy and environment and Gender issues.

All these inputs, in spite of controversies surrounding the criteria measuring the poverty/poor between the approach adopted by UNDP and the World Bank, the leading organisations associated, involved on the subject – it is admitted position that whatever may be the merit of Income/ Consumption approach adopted to measure poverty, indicators like Health, Education/Literacy, Food/Nutrition, Security, Gender/Caste issues are *sin qua non*.

World Development Report 2000-2001 brought out by the World Bank captioned – "Attacking Poverty" accepts the need to move away from Income/Consumption approach and add Health, Education, Gender and Ethnicity factors to arrive at the poverty ratios.

"Choices for the Poor" – lessons from National Poverty Strategies brought out by UNDP last year was the result of

'Poverty Strategy Initiative' taken by UNDP emanating from UN Millennium Declaration of September 2000 through which International community unambiguously endorsed the goal of halving extreme poverty by the year 2015. In an unequivocal terms the thrust of UNDP's report is the outcome of its measurement of Human Development and Human Poverty as Indicators in addition to Income/Consumption alone.

In the publication of UNDP referred to above, one of the key and for us relevant conclusion is reproduced below:

"Despite some important commonalities among national studies, it is far from clear that a consensus on how poverty should be conceptualised and measured is emerging. The efforts in many countries to adapt and expand upon standard definitions and methodologies belie the notion of a budding consensus. Usage of poverty lines and income proxies is quite widespread. But at the same time, there is a much larger concern for the relationships and dynamics of poverty than is suggested by the international literature. This concern is informed by a desire to reflect local realities more accurately than conventional definitions would allow. Emphasis is placed on understanding the **social and relational dimensions of poverty**, as well as the **wider determinants of capability fulfilment, which money metric measures do not convey adequately. As the limits of economic definitions and measures are recognised, there is a corresponding search for viable alternatives.**"

In the World Development Report 2000-2001 brought out by the World Bank comprehensive evaluation of both approaches, i.e. the Head count ratios based on 'income/consumption approach' and measuring poverty on many dimensions has been gone into, at length. The conclusion arrived at was that – "Measurement of poverty thus must cover many dimensions. So far income and consumption dimensions has received most attention." Similar difficulties were faced in determining the 'poverty line'. It has area dimensions, intra-regional price dimensions, and time of recall dimensions. Another important lacuna noticed in this approach was that it failed to reflect the fact that among poor people there may be wide differences in income levels – with some people located just below the poverty line and allows experiencing for greater shortfalls.

Possible solution emerging from the past experience was succinctly put, as follows:

"Defining poverty as multidimensional raises the question of how to measure overall poverty and how to compare achievements in the different dimensions. One dimension might move in a different direction from another. Health could improve while income worsens. Or an individual might be "income poor" but not "health poor." Or one country might show greater improvement in health than in vulnerability – while another shows the converse.

This brings to the fore the relative value of the different dimensions: how much income are people willing to give up for, say, a unit of improvement in health or in voice? In other words, what weights can be assigned to the different dimensions to allow comparisons across countries, households, or individuals and over time? There are no easy answers.

One approach to addressing comparability is to define a multidimensional welfare function or a composite index. An alternative is to define as poor anybody who is poor in any one of the dimensions – without attempting to estimate tradeoffs among the dimensions – or anybody who is poor in all dimensions, and to define the intensity of poverty accordingly. This report does not try to define a composite index or to measure tradeoffs among dimensions. Instead, it focuses on deprivation in different dimensions and, in particular, on the multiple deprivations experienced by the income-poor. This is a necessary first step in developing a comprehensive multidimensional framework.

How should indicators be selected to monitor progress? The international development goals are a good starting point. But in practice, these goals will have to be adapted (by lengthening or shortening the time span, for example,) and modified (increasing the number of dimensions) depending on context. The specific goals will have to emerge from a participatory process in which governments and civil society agree on priorities. This process is already under way in many countries, and multilateral organisations are helping with resources and technical assistance.

Similar emphasis came to be focused in the 'World Bank Country Study' – "Reducing Poverty in India—Options for more effective Public services."

The GDP or income, in general, is a mean, though perhaps the most predominant one in obtaining valued outcomes in the course of development. On the other hand, the human development indicators are more appropriate in capturing desirable 'outcomes' for which the 'means' are ultimately engaged in the process of development. Some of these outcomes are desired because they are 'ends' in themselves and others because they extend opportunities available to people. Such an approach has not only made a useful distinction between means and the ends of development process, thereby highlighting the need to formulate and prescribe appropriate public policy and programmes, but it has also facilitated a move towards a more comprehensive evaluative and monitoring framework to guide the process of social change.

It is equally important to recognize that indicators and alternative criteria for evaluating the development process can be meaningful and effective in directing public policy and programmes only when they are rooted in the concerned context and also reflect its social valuation and priorities. For instance, in undertaking comparisons at regional level for a country like India, it may not be appropriate to use the same set of indicators/indices developed for facilitating cross-country comparisons spanning countries from the least developed to the industrially matured economies, as is the case with the UNDP HDRs. Similarly, the approach to build composite indices has to be different, if the objective is to map, on a set of human development indicators, the progress of a region or a country over time. It is these concerns and the need to build a state level database that has guided the preparation of the Human Development Report for India.

Following the UNDP's human development framework, the National Human Development Report seeks to put together indicators and composite indices to evaluate development process in terms of 'ex-post outcomes' rather than only in terms of available 'means' or 'inputs'. The Report, recognizing the broad based consensus that exists on the three critical dimensions of well-being, focuses on identifying the various contextually relevant indicators on each of them. These dimensions of well-being are related to:

- *Longevity* – the ability to live long and healthy life;
- *Education* – the ability to read, write and acquire knowledge; and
- *Command over resources* – the ability to enjoy a decent standard of living and have a social meaningful life.

For most individuals the choice to live a healthy life, free from illness and ailments, and of a reasonable life span are critical attributes in the notion of personal well-being. Longevity and a life free of morbidity is, thus, a valued end in itself and moreover, it is crucial for other valued human attainments. Similarly, apart from its intrinsic value, education in the present day context, is perhaps among the most important means for individuals to improve personal endowments, build capability levels, overcome constraints and in the process enlarge their available set of opportunities and choices for a sustained improvement in well-being. It is a critical means to empowerment and to bring about a social, economic and political inclusion of the marginalized segments in the mainstream of society. An individual's command over resources determines his/her sustenance, attainments on other aspects of well-being and the opportunities that these attainments facilitate.

The various indicators of these attainments and composite indices that they support could capture the process of development and well-being of people from two perspectives. The 'conglomerative perspective' – captures advances made by the society as a whole – and the 'deprivational perspective' assesses status of the deprived in a society. Both these perspectives are needed to adequately understand the process of development in any society. For the Report the compilation of indicators extends beyond the indicators on economic attainment; educational attainment; and health attainment and demographic concerns of the society to indicators on such aspects of the social environment that has a direct bearing on individual and collective well-being. This includes indicators on the state of the elderly; the working children; the disabled; and violence and crime against women. Besides the social context, the physical environment also has a bearing on the well-being of people. At the same time, the development process, as it unfolds, impacts the physical environment one way or the other, almost continuously. Attempt has, therefore, been made to include selected indicators to briefly highlight aspects of the physical environment having a direct bearing on the well-being of people.

The starting point for this Report has been the preparation of an extensive database. A State level database has been put together covering around 70 district indicators, in most cases, in terms of gender and rural-urban break-up and presented in over 150 tables. The entire data set has been compiled for, at least, two points of time, namely for early eighties (covering the period 1981-83), early nineties (covering the period 1991-93) and, where available, for the most recent year (including the available preliminary data from Census 2001). An important concern in building the database has been to also identify indicators that are readily available at sub-state level of disaggregation. This has prompted an extensive use of Census of India data. In addition, data from alternative sources, including the National Sample Survey Organization (NSSO), National Family Health Surveys (NFHS) and other official and some independent sources has also been used. The data has been presented for all States and Union Territories. This in some cases, has necessitated recourse to estimating data to fill-up gaps for a few States.

India Development Report 2002, IGIDR

The profile of rural poverty in India indicates that an R & D policy oriented to tackling specific problems of specific groups would have greater impact as compared to the generalized programmes, argues a paper titled Poverty and Agricultural Research by P.V. Srinivasan. It argues that the Green Revolution kind of strategy has to give place to a more locally sensitive programme aimed at increasing yields and income/food security for weaker groups.

Some pointers already emerge from this sort of profile for what policies would be better to alleviate poverty among labour; increase linkages and chains of value addition through transport, storage and marketing infrastructure building. Not only would this provide employment in the short-run, but also the subsequent usage of this infrastructure would create more lasting incomes and jobs.

Similarly, since a large proportion of the rural poor are small farmers, income-enhancement strategies like promoting animal husbandry become important, apart from research to improve crop yields and lower costs of production. Research would have to tackle two kinds of problems, chronic and transitory. Transitory problems of, say, access to adequate food, would have to be tackled by ensuring better management of food resources to smoothen temporary supply or price problems. If the problem is longer lasting, then one is looking at methods to increase yields in the kind of crops that grow best in those regions and have the greatest chance of enhancing incomes and ensuring a steady supply of food. For example, coarse cereals are a poor man's crop with a limited market.

If research at enhancing yields is made in these crops, it will help smaller farmers to use part of their holdings then for some other purpose. Considering the low productivity, as compared to international standards, in most Indian crops, there is clearly scope to improve yields. In fact the author says that considering the resource heavy practices in Green Revolution areas, efficiency improvements are possible there as well, apart from non-green revolution areas.

The much-documented lack of rural infrastructure itself points out that efficiency can be increased very substantially. Importantly, since there is now a move to greater free trade in agricultural commodities, private research may be increasingly channelled into export-crops while public research money can be set free to explore crop varieties and any other possibilities that have an explicit poverty-alleviation objective for small farmers.

State Level Studies

Human Development Report, Rajasthan

Society for International Development (SID-Rajasthan Chapter) in their report Human Development in Rajasthan, 1999 (the very first such Report) was based on the 3 indicators, viz.

(i) output indices,
(ii) process indices, and
(iii) input indices.

And constructed four indices:

(i) Human Development Index (HDI),
(ii) Gender Related Development Index (GDI),
(iii) Gender Related Health Index (GHI), and
(iv) Human Poverty Index (HPI).

The report has analyzed critically the development path of the State and has brought out both of its positive and negative aspects and provided a direction for the future.

Studies for Other States

In addition to Rajasthan, Human Development Reports of following States have been prepared – Assam, Punjab, Tamil Nadu, Maharashtra, U.P., M.P. and Sikkim. Further, the reports for the following states are under preparation—A.P., West Bengal, Orissa, H.P., Chattisgarh, Gujarat, Kerala and Arunachal Pradesh.

Other Relevant Studies

1. Food Insecurity Atlas of Rural India

The Food Insecurity Atlas of Rural India by the United Nations World Food Programme (WFP) and MS Swaminathan Research Foundation seeks to unfold the story at the level of Indian States. The story unfolds through the data to begin with. It is finally narrated with the help of the chosen indicators, indices and maps. Maps are used to enhance the awareness of the problem.

'Arc-view' Geographical Information System software has been used to detect the natural breaks in the series, so that the error in detecting natural breaks is minimized. Where necessary, the class limits have been adjusted slightly to suit the distribution of states more evenly between the two classes. Each class represents a typology, which is named as per the level of food insecurity. Class limits are rounded off to the nearest digit or two decimal points. This has been done to capture the typologies better. In the case of the Sustainability Index, the standard deviation method has been used. The ranges are one standard deviation and two standard deviations from the mean.

The mapping index of the composite maps gives the combined intensity of various factors. The state with severe problems in one aspect may be relatively problem-free in other aspects. Hence, the mapping index gives the relative position of a state *vis-à-vis* others as per the combined intensity of the problem of food insecurity. Unlike the Human Development Index, where the position of a state is measured against the total distance between the best and the worst, or a price index that measures the price position *vis-à-vis* the base year's position, the Mapping Index indicates the average position of the state with respect to others.

The inclusion or exclusion of certain indicators might change the final mapping index. Exclusion or inclusion of any one of the nineteen indicators changes the position of two to four states out of the total sixteen states just by one position.

The methodology as such does not give a special weight to any indicator. All indicators carry equal weight. The weighting is implicit in the number of parameters in each group. Out of the 19 indicators, five indicators represent food availability, eight represent food access and six represent food absorption. Thus, food availability gets an implicit weight of 26 per cent. Food access in terms of calories and livelihood access gets a weight of 42 per cent and the factors representing absorption get a weight of 32 per cent.

The atlas, released by the Planning Commission in April 2002, has identified Jharkhand, Gujarat, Rajasthan, Orissa and Chattisgarh as the most food insecure states in the country. The insecurity report includes detailed analyses of the five states in addition to a series of maps covering all states and districts in the country. The government's aim to move towards a hunger free India by 2007 could be given a definite direction by the contents of the atlas. According to WFP India country director Pedro Medrano, food insecurity of a region was determined not only by food production and food availability, but by various other factors like the number of malnourished people, average birth weight, infant mortality rate, stunted growth and proneness of an area to natural disasters.

The Report has identified about 20 indicators to help mark the kind of deficiency a particular region suffers from so that specific programmes could be devised to address their needs.

The series of maps in the atlas show areas with prevalent low birth rates, large anaemic population, high infant mortality rates, unbalanced gender ratio etc. The maps could be used as tools for planning and devising food security programmes and could help policy makers adopt an area-based approach. The objective of the detailed food insecurity reports on the five most vulnerable states was to identify districts which are more prone to food insecurity within the states. The analysis is intended to ensure that the interventions are directed to the most food insecure areas and thus improve the effectiveness of programmes. It is primarily based on secondary data from the Central and State government agencies.

2. *Food Insecurity Atlas of Urban India*

Compiled by the MS Swaminathan Research Foundation (MSSRF) in collaboration with the World Food Programme, the atlas claims to have done a ground-breaking survey of the country's hunger hot-spots by having done an analysis of the food security in urban areas. In fact, the atlas gives an indication of much more than just food security in urban areas in view of the wide range of indicators used by it to determine food security levels. Among them are the availability of safe drinking water, toilets, electricity, housing, as also the status of unemployed casual labour, poverty and literacy.

The atlas hopes that its findings will help in the formulation of policy which is decentralised in view of the wide variations in the nature of the problem of food security even within a particular class of towns, and not without reason. For instance, even Pune which has come out at the top in terms of food security does have its drawbacks. Access to housing and toilets remain problem areas in the city as also the high rate of unemployment among males.

3. *Dr. Sen's Concept of Poverty*

Doctoral thesis, "Choice of Techniques" is the first masterpiece that "delineated" the case which many developed nations faced – whether to adopt labour-intensive or capital-intensive techniques of production.

Dr. Amartya Sen in his thesis "Choice of Techniques" delineated the case which many developed nations faced – whether to adopt labour intensive or capital intensive techniques of production to tackle poverty. Influenced by J.B.S. Haldane's poem called "Cancer is a funny thing", Dr. Sen observed that "poverty is no less funny". He examined three broad aspects of poverty—subsistence, inequality and externality – and propounded the next as a first approximation, that "poverty is, of course, a matter of deprivation". The first concern of the concept of poverty is of a criterion – who should be the focus of the economist's concern. Part of the job is done by the specification of certain consumption norms, or of a "poverty line". The poor are those people whose consumption standards fall short of the norms, or whose incomes fall below that line. The second aspect is that of "primary poverty" popularized by S. Rowntree defining families in primary poverty "if their total earnings are insufficient to obtain the minimum necessities of the maintenance of merely physical efficiency".

The third is the "inequality approach" which believes that "transfers from the rich to the poor can make a substantial dent on poverty in most societies". The fourth is Dr. Sen's concept of relative deprivation which contrasts between the feelings of deprivation and conditions of deprivation. Accepting that the different issues related to the general notion of relative deprivation have considerable bearing on the social analysis of poverty, he came to the conclusion that "the approach of relative deprivation supplements rather than supplants the analysis of poverty in terms of absolute deprivation".

The close connection between evaluating poverty and assessing inequality (including inequality among the poor) has received much attention of the world economists in the mid-seventies. Dr. Sen made an attempt to integrate the two sets of concerns, namely poverty and inequality, and proposed a distributive-sensitive measure of poverty over the unidimensional indicator of the individual income, with poverty being seen as inadequately low income-labelled as poverty income. The poverty measure proposed in the mid-seventies is a direct combination of three distinctive characteristics of the interpersonal profile of poverty, namely the head-count ratio, which identifies the poverty of the community with the proportion of the poor people; the income-gap ratio wherein the depth of a poor person's poverty is measured by the "gap" between the poverty line and the person's income; and a measure of distribution of incomes among the poor, namely the Gini coefficient. The original derivation of the measure in Dr. Sen was based on welfare economic ideas rooted in the idea of relative deprivation.

By the mid-eighties the refinements in welfarism and utilitarianism on the one hand, and of the Rawlsian approach, on the other, tempted Dr. Sen to accept an alternative information perspective: the space of functioning, various things a person may value doing (or being). It was emphasized that "the valued functionings may vary from such elementary ones as being adequately nourished and being free from avoidable diseases, to very complex activities or personal states, such as being able to take part in the life of the community and having self-respect" almost analogous to Adam Smith's analysis of "necessities". This is termed the "capability approach" dealing with realized functioning or on the set of alternatives or real opportunities. In addition to the normal analysis or primary poverty defined in terms of lowness of incomes, economists emphasized secondary poverty influenced by relative deprivation in terms of incomes yielding absolute deprivation in terms of capabilities. This made sense to see poverty as capability deprivation.

It is apt to conclude, in the words of Dr. Sen, "How much further we can go in inequality analysis on the basis of ordinal comparisons alone remains to be seen. But it is definitely one of the possible routes through which the consideration of broader framework of advantages and capabilities can enrich the study of inequality and poverty.

4. NCAER Studies

A new element of controversy has been added by data on income and purchases (as well as ownership) of manufactured consumer goods from NCAER surveys as well as smaller sample surveys conducted by ORG-MARG, and IMRB as part of the Readership Surveys and other urban and rural surveys. These show that population proportions at the lowest levels of income have been falling. At higher levels population proportions have been rising. Even the population at the lowest income level seem to purchase large numbers of some select manufactured consumer goods.

The NCAER data for example, estimates the proportions and estimated numbers of the population at the lowest income level. This is higher than the poverty line. We can deduct the estimated numbers below the calorie poverty line from these numbers. The resultant numbers of the better-off within this lowest income group, could be said as being the buyers of these goods, if those below the poverty line are not assumed to be doing so. But this shows the better-off in the lowest level as buying disproportionate numbers of goods. It is more likely that some of the poorest of the poor also buy such manufactured goods. These poor may not have two full meals a day, but they buy such goods. Thus these recent other surveys raise questions as to how to define poverty and measure the numbers of the very poor.

It is quite possible that these new surveys might have some faults in method and execution. But the fact is that there is now trend data for at least ten years that appears to be remarkably consistent. Discarding it with abuse does not solve the question of whether poverty has been rising or falling especially in the 1990s. Accepting this new evidence supports the conclusion that moving away from an economy that was centrally directed and controlled, to one more subject to market forces, is in the interests of the very poor. Not accepting it enables a continuing hostility to such policies.

However, no one can deny that India is a society where there are too many vulnerable people with little opportunity for reducing their vulnerability. Central direction of the economy did not improve their condition or opportunities to the vulnerable. Our attack must be on changing this system so that it can deliver. It also lies in developing better measurements for vulnerability and opportunity, and monitoring them over time. Neither seem to have received enough attention.

Gross National Happiness

Gross National Happiness (GNH) is now being considered as a better indicator of National development than GDP, which doesn't really take into account the overall well-being of the people. As for all those who bicker over the word happiness and describe it to be a purely subjective state of being, this really amounts to selfishness. There is such a thing as common or public good, and it is indeed the task of governments to achieve that for its citizens. America's Founding Fathers took this richer meaning of the word happiness, and included the pursuit of happiness as a right.

An index of Gross National Happiness is now being prepared at the national and city levels. According to latest survey, India is happy – Happier than the UK and Canada. A survey by leading market research agency GfK-NOP has found that "India is fourth in the list of happiest populations in the world". The research, in which 30,000 people were interviewed in 30 countries, asked respondents how satisfied they were with their quality of live. Australia topped the chart with 46 per cent respondents saying they were "very happy" followed by the USA (40), Egypt (36) and India (34). The fifth spot was shared by the UK and Canada (32). On a global scale, 20 per cent claimed to be very happy, 62 per cent were "satisfied" 10 per cent "disappointed" and 4 per cent said they were "very unhappy". The research found intangible factors such as stability and family life ranked above money and possessions in making people happy. Good health, financial security, home ownership, happy marriage and children ranked high. This is where Indian scored over the West. The happiest age group was 13-19.

A survey of 127 cities by the Economist's Intelligence Unit gives New Delhi the unenviable rank of 108. Its virtual conclusion: we are living in a war zone. The survey on 'Liveability Ranking' is referred to by business houses as an authentic indicator about a city's liveability factor. It looked at about 40 indicators clubbed under five categories : stability, health care, culture and environment, education and infrastructure. Delhi fares badly on all counts. The worst-performance is recorded under 'stability'. Besides terrorism, civil unrest and military conflict, the survey found a high incidence of petty and violent crimes. 'Infrastructure' indicators – quality of water, road network and telecommunication are not up to the mark. The one good aspect of the Capital's infrastructure is the "availability of good housing".

The happiest Indians in all the world live in Pune and India's western seaboard is quite a happy lot compared to both Delhi and Silicon Valley down south in Bangalore, while Kolkata is our capital of cheerlessness, according to a survey of Gross National Happiness across the planet. The survey is published by GfK-NOP, the market research organization that happily boasts its figures among the top four journals world-wide with sales of EUR 672 million last year and operations in 63 countries. It reports that more than half of all pune residents say that they are "very happy with the overall quality of life". Pune is closely, if surprisingly, followed by its richer, sassier neighbour, Mumbai, which comes in at 42 per cent.

Hitherto unregarded Nagpur comes a close third with 39 per cent of its residents incredibly happy with the way they live. In contrast, just 26 per cent of Dilliwallahs say they are very happy and Bangalore's bits-and-bytes revolution still doesn't allow more than 27 per cent of its residents to describe themselves as very happy. Curmudgeonly Kolkata, meanwhile, has a happiness quotient totalling a mere 18 per cent of its harried people. GfK-NOP's European director of research Nick Chiarelli says this might be explained by "big city syndrome", which showed Londoners the unhappiest in all of Britain and Delhi deeply dolorous compared to smaller urban centres such as Pune. But Bengal's melancholic *bhadralok* have not managed to depress India's overall happiness ratings, with just over a third (34%) of all Indians everywhere cheerily claiming they are very happy with life, the survey says.

Bhutan Experiment

Bhutan's King Jigme Singye Wangchuck tossed the idea of Gross National Happiness in 1972. One of his most articulate ministers, Lyonpo Jigme Y. Thinley, elaborated it at an Asia-Pacific Conference in 1998. It seems that the world was waiting for a new mantra for salvation, and Bhutan provided it. At its simplest, it says that man needs more than mere economic development to be happy, and since human happiness is a universal desire although its meaning varies widely, the paradigm of Gross National Happiness, as opposed to GNP (Gross National Product), is the answer. Jigme Thinley defined it as an idea resting on four pillars: socio-economic development, a sustainable environment, good governance and a living culture. The truth is that happiness is a state of mind and the Bhutanese live in a unique environment of an abundance of nature's bounty, a set of beliefs that lays great stress on moderation and self-restraint and a culture sedulously preserved as a vibrant living institution.

The Bhutan 2020 vision document defines GNH's role as a single unifying concept to identify future directions of policy. The King's answer is that there are many concepts of development other than the GDP. The aim is to maximize happiness, rather than economic growth. The individual at the centre has material, spiritual and emotional needs. Consequently, development should not merely be defined as increased consumption of goods and services. The truth is that GNH is an almost intuitive idea to the Bhutanese and their King seeking to reconcile the need for development with preserving the essential ethos of Bhutanese spiritual and cultural life. In philosophical terms, the four pillars defined by Jigme Thinley would come naturally to them, living in an environment blessed by nature's bounty, pride in their culture and consciousness of the benefits of good governance.

Elsewhere, Jigme Thinley has suggested that in Bhutan inner spiritual development is as important as external material development. Enlightenment of the individual, not merely in the religious sense, is the blossoming of happiness. Such happiness is made more probable by consciously creating a harmonious psychological, social and economic development. At the very least, Bhutan's contribution has been to stir a new debate on what is happiness and on the limitations of the fashionable paradigms of seeking happiness by possessing more and more goodies.

If life expectancy can be taken to be one valid indicator of the success of GNH, then Bhutan has been a roaring success. From 1984 to 1998, life expectancy has increased by 19 years. There are other tangible indicators where the country has done well. Gross enrolment rate in primary schools has reached 72 per cent, and the literacy rate has grown from 17 per cent to 47.5 per cent. Higher GNH has "limited the social, cultural, ecological and human costs" of development. Bhutan has shown that people-centric development is a workable economic model. As Bertrand Russell put is, "man needs, for his happiness, not only the enjoyment of this or that, but hope and enterprise and change". GNH is a multi-dimensional measure that should take the place of GDP.

ANNEXURE 1.1

Poverty Ratios at State Level—1973-74 to 1999-2000

Name of the State	1973-74		1977-78		1983-84		1987-88	
	a(1)	b	a	b	a	b(2)	a	b
Andhra Pradesh	54.9	49.25	43.6	39.96	36.4	29.88	31.7	27.20
Arunachal Pradesh		51.96		58.55		41.40		37.47
Assam	47.0	51.23	47.3	57.63	23.5	40.86	22.8	36.84
Bihar	54.5	61.78	56.3	61.95	49.5	62.51	40.8	53.37
Goa		44.04		37.34		19.05		23.42
Gujarat	41.1	47.21	38.9	42.17	24.3	33.27	18.4	32.33
Haryana	23.1	35.24	25.2	29.48	15.6	21.24	11.6	16.63
Himachal Pradesh	15.1	26.40	27.0	32.45	13.5	16.39	9.2	15.46
Jammu & Kashmir	39.0	42.59	33.4	40.63	16.3	24.10	13.9	23.20
Karnataka	50.5	54.34	50.8	49.47	35.0	38.47	32.1	38.14
Kerala	56.9	59.71	48.4	52.93	26.8	40.91	17.0	32.08
Madhya Pradesh	58.6	61.90	58.9	62.43	46.2	50.13	36.7	43.40
Maharashtra	47.7	52.94	50.6	56.06	34.0	43.54	29.2	40.10
Manipur	24.7	50.01	28.7	54.83	12.3	38.08		32.93
Meghalaya	19.0	50.25	47.4	56.04	28.0	39.46		34.60
Mizoram		50.33		55.38		38.14		32.52
Nagaland		50.87		56.74		39.75		34.85
Orissa	68.6	66.24	65.1	70.35	42.8	65.32	44.7	55.61
Punjab	21.5	28.08	16.4	19.36	13.8	16.29	7.2	12.70
Rajasthan	46.0	46.33	33.6	37.99	34.3	35.02	24.4	34.60
Sikkim		50.91		56.69		39.62		34.67
Tamil Nadu	59.7	56.51	52.8	56.25	39.6	52.38	32.8	45.13
Tripura	39.9	51.03	60.5	57.41	23.0	40.79		36.84
Uttar Pradesh	52.8	56.98	49.7	49.19	45.3	47.19	35.1	41.99
West Bengal	56.8	63.39	52.2	60.65	39.2	54.72	27.6	43.99
Nagaland & all UTs	30.2		21.1		27.1		7.7	
Delhi		46.85		33.07		26.97		16.04
Andaman & Nicobar Islands		56.72		56.56		52.68		45.24
Chandigarh		27.68		27.64		23.86		12.91
Dadra & Nagar Haveli		46.65		37.32		15.64		18.71
Lakshadweep		59.61		54.09		43.48		37.26
Pondicherry		56.09		55.19		51.36		44.68
ALL INDIA	51.5	54.93	48.3	51.81	37.4	44.76	29.9	59.34

(Contd.)

Name of the State	*1993-94*					
	Rural		*Urban*		*Combined*	
	No. of Persons (Lakhs)	*% of Persons*	*No. of Persons (Lakhs)*	*% of Persons*	*No. of Persons (Lakhs)*	*% of Persons*
Andhra Pradesh	79.49	15.92	74.47	38.33	153.97	22.19
Arunachal Pradesh	3.62	45.01	0.11	7.73	3.73	39.35
Assam	94.33	45.01	2.03	7.73	96.36	40.86
Bihar	450.86	58.21	42.49	34.50	493.35	54.96
Goa	0.38	5.34	1.53	27.03	1.91	14.92
Gujarat	62.16	22.18	43.02	27.89	105.19	24.21
Haryana	36.56	28.02	7.31	16.38	43.88	25.05
Himachal Pradesh	15.40	30.34	0.46	9.18	15.86	28.44
Jammu & Kashmir	19.05	30.34	1.86	9.18	20.92	25.17
Karnataka	95.99	29.88	60.46	40.14	156.46	33.16
Kerala	55.95	25.76	20.46	24.55	76.41	25.43
Madhya Pradesh	216.19	40.64	82.33	48.38	298.52	42.52
Maharashtra	193.33	37.93	111.90	35.15	305.22	36.86
Manipur	6.33	45.01	0.47	7.73	6.80	33.78
Meghalaya	7.09	45.01	0.29	7.73	7.38	37.92
Mizoram	1.64	45.01	0.30	7.73	1.94	25.66
Nagaland	4.85	45.01	0.20	7.73	5.05	37.92
Orissa	140.90	49.72	19.70	41.64	160.60	48.56
Punjab	17.76	11.95	7.35	11.35	25.11	11.77
Rajasthan	94.68	26.46	33.82	30.49	128.50	27.41
Sikkim	1.81	45.01	0.03	7.73	1.84	41.43
Tamil Nadu	121.70	32.48	80.40	39.77	202.10	35.03
Tripura	11.41	45.01	0.38	7.73	11.79	39.01
Uttar Pradesh	496.17	42.28	108.28	35.39	604.46	40.85
West Bengal	209.90	40.80	44.66	22.44	254.56	35.66
Andaman & Nicobar Islands	0.73	32.48	0.33	39.77	1.06	34.47
Chandigarh	0.07	11.35	0.73	11.35	0.80	11.35
Dadra & Nagar Haveli	0.72	51.95	0.06	39.93	0.77	50.84
Daman & Diu	0.03	5.34	0.15	27.03	0.18	15.80
Delhi	0.19	1.90	15.32	16.03	15.51	14.69
Lakshadweep	0.06	25.76	0.08	24.55	0.14	25.04
Pondicherry	0.93	32.48	2.38	39.77	3.31	37.40
ALL INDIA	2440.31	37.27	763.37	32.36	3203.68	35.97

Sl. No.	State/UTs	1999-2000 Rural	Urban	Combined
1.	Andhra Pradesh	11.05	26.63	15.74
2.	Arunachal Pradesh	40.04	7.47	33.47
3.	Assam	40.04	7.47	36.09
4.	Bihar	44.30	32.91	42.60
5.	Goa	1.35	7.52	4.40
6.	Gujarat	13.17	15.59	14.07
7	Haryana	8.27	9.99	8.74
8.	Himachal Pradesh	7.94	4.63	7.63
9.	Jammu & Kashmir	3.94	1.98	3.48
10.	Karnataka	17.38	25.25	20.04
11.	Kerala	9.38	20.27	12.72
12.	Madhya Pradesh	37.06	88.44	37.43
13.	Maharashtra	23.72	26.81	25.02
14.	Manipur	40.04	7.47	28.54
15.	Meghalaya	40.04	7.47	33.87
16.	Mizoram	40.04	7.47	19.07
17.	Nagaland	40.04	7.47	82.87
18.	Orissa	48.01	42.83	47.15
19.	Punjab	6.35	7.75	6.16
20.	Rajasthan	13.74	19.85	15.28
21.	Sikkim	40.04	7.07	86.55
22.	Tamil Nadu	20.55	22.4	21.12
23.	Tripura	40.04	7.47	34.44
24.	Uttar Pradesh	31.22	30.89	31.15
25.	West Bengal	31.85	14.86	27.02
26.	Andaman & Nicobar Islands	20.55	22.11	20.79
27.	Chandigarh	5.95	7.75	5.75
28.	Dadra & Nagar Haveli	17.57	13.52	17.14
29.	Daman & Diu	1.35	7.52	4.04
30.	Delhi	0.40	9.42	3.73
31.	Lakshadweep	9.38	20.24	15.60
32.	Pondicherry	20.55	22.11	21.04
	ALL INDIA	27.07	23.62	26.10

Note: a. as per official released figures based a(1) relate to the year 1972-73

b. as per Expert Group Methodology b(2) relates to the year 1983.

Source: Planning Commission.

2

Rural Development and Poverty Alleviation Programmes

"Anyone who has ever struggled with poverty knows how extremely expensive it is to be poor".

James Baldwin

Hunger is often as much a cause as an effect of povery, and programmes to reduce chronic hunger could play an important role in the reduction of poverty especially extreme poverty.

Victoria Sekitoleko

Economic Planning may be stated as an action with a socio-economic purpose. In other words, the object of planning is not simply to achieve economic progress but also balance such progress with social justice. Social justice presupposes that opportunities in a greater measure must be provided to the poor so that they may become increasingly better off. The underprivileged class must get opportunities to rise to higher strata. Provision of basic minimum to all in respect of life and living and facilities for promoting one's own values and inner worth are essential content of social justice. In India, the main-stream political movement was deeply influenced by the Gandhian approach which emphasised the need to uplift the social and economic status of the poorest of the poor, or 'antyodaya'. Emphasis on an egalitarian social order was reflected in the policy documents which were produced by the Indian National Congress.

Economic Programme Committee appointed by the president of the Congress party, immediately after independence, in November 1947 also reiterated the national objective of economic justice. While stating the aims and objectives of the economic programme for independent India, the first recommendation of the Committee was: "A quick and progressive rise in the standard of living of the people should be the primary consideration governing all economic activities and relevant administrative measures of the Central and Provincial Governments. The achievement of a national minimum standard in respect of all the essentials of physical and social well-being within a reasonable period must be pursued as the practical goal of all schemes for economic development." This was really the birth of what may be called as 'Rural Development' although some stray experiments like those of Gurgaon Experiment had been tried earlier.

Developing countries have realized that the process of rural development is complex and multi-dimensional with diverse socio-economic and technological issues involved. The objective conditions, however, differ from one area to another. The specific goals to be achieved and strategies to be adopted vary from situation to situation depending on the circumstances. The complex and multi-dimensional process involving multilateral interactions on economic, political, social, technological and administrative decisions are often not properly visualized and perceived. However, rural development objectives can be sought in various ways once there is a firm commitment and people's participation. The critical elements in rural development, to be specific, are: (a) basic needs; (b) full employment and (c) local participation, all needing micro-level planning. In this chapter we will examine the various rural development programmes which have been formulated and implemented and the present status of rural poverty.

Rural Development – Concept

It may be stated that during more than fifty years of development planning in India, development of rural areas and rural people has been the central concern. However, the concept of integrated rural development is generally a phenomenon of a relatively recent origin in most of the developing countries coinciding with the realization by the national governments that the involvement of the rural people and particularly the rural poor majority, in their development is of utmost importance. Rural development is, in fact, a strategy to improve the economic and social life of a specific group of people – the rural poor.

Various other concepts of rural development have been propounded by various authors in the post-independence period. The former Union Finance Minister, late C. Subrahmaniam, who put forward the thesis of rural development at the All India Science Congress, Waltair, 1976, viewed it as a "systematic scientific use of all our natural resources and as a part of this process enabling every person to engage himself in a productive and socially useful occupation and earn an income that would meet at least the basic needs". According to him, application of science and technology for the use of natural resources was imperative. He emphasized that the functional linkages between the use of these resources, and the better use of natural resources should lead to full employment.

Uma Lele, a sociologist, defines rural development as "improving living standards of the masses of the low income population residing in rural areas and making the process of rural development self-sustaining". In this definition also we find that there is an emphasis on improvement of standard of living of the poor through opportunities for better utilization of their physical and human resources.

Many others, while enunciating the concept of rural development, have emphasized on effective participation of the rural people in achieving the objective of fuller utilization of available physical and human resources, and thus higher incomes and better living conditions. This may be termed as 'popular participation' and the need for popular participation should be recognized from the very beginning. In fact, it is now more intensively conceived that if we want to extricate ourselves from the quagmire of rural poverty which engulfs a large percentage of the rural population, proactive involvement of the people themselves in development programmes is a must.

Pre-Independence Initiatives

Long before independence, in the thirties, Rabindranath Tagore thought of rural development and launched a programme centred at Sriniketan in Birbhum district of West Bengal. Tagore's interest was in the all-round development of the village people, economically, educationally and aesthtically. Tagore aimed at inducing each villager to work to the limit of his capacity, and also to help his fellowmen. Tagore believed in both self-help and mutual help and was one of the first to recognize the need for a change in the outlook of villagers as pre-condition for improvement. He, therefore, urged that every villager and his family should be educated. Community action and collective endeavour, based on the intelligent and informed participation of all the members of the community, he realized, were essential for improving the condition of the villagers.

Around this time, another rural development programme in India was launched by Mahatma Gandhi. He was concerned simultaneously about the plight of persons in rural India and about developing a wholesome total pattern of rural life and work. The Gandhian approach to rural welfare emphasized the role of the people themselves in any constructive programme. The goal was the improvement of the inner man and the development of a sounder morality. According to him, self-help was the first step towards moral advancement. Hence, the material advancement of the village was, for him, merely the means to solving the social and economic problem of the villagers, but he was interested primarily in providing a moral and spiritual background for such secular activities as might be undertaken.

Early Experience

In formulating its Community Development Programme, India did have some rural development experience to draw on. There was Mahatma Gandhi's considerable experience with village uplift programmes. These Gandhian programmes contributed greatly in focusing national attention on the desperate plight of village people, especially Harijans, and therefore, contributed to the decision to initiate a national community development programme. The best known of the early experiments in village development was a project sponsored in Punjab by a Britisher, F.L. Brayne. The work of two missionary couples, Hatch and Wetser, contributed significant background as did the Etawah pilot projects conceived and led by an American, Albert Mayer. Finally, the two refugee settlement communities, Faridabad and Nilokheri, had considerable influence in the early days of the thinking and planning for community development.

The Etawah Project

The success attained at Etawah pilot project encouraged the government to experiment on a wider scale. The major objective of the Etawah Project was to see what degree of productive and social improvement, as well as of initiative, self-confidence, and co-operation can be achieved in the village of a district not the beneficiary of any set of special circumstances and resources such as hydro-electric development or large-scale industry or other non-typical high cost and high priority development. It was also considered necessary to ascertain how quickly those results may be obtainable consistent with their remaining permanent part of the people's mental, spiritual, and technical equipment and outlook after the special pressure is lifted.

While these several village development and pilot projects provided useful background information, India had no governmental experience to draw on in projecting its plans for launching a Government sponsored community development programme. What is significant is that the Government of new, independent India recognized the importance of establishing working relations with village cultivators and in assisting them in increasing their agricultural output and in establishing village institutions.

First Phase

Rural Development Programmes

After independence, the conquest of poverty and unemployment has been a major area of concern of the successive five year plans. The general objective of ensuring a certain rate of Economic Growth and the specific aim of building a socialistic pattern of society and reducing inequalities in income and wealth had been the refrain of all the plans. Rural India which encompasses three-fourth of the country's population is characterized by low income levels, not even adequate to ensure a quality of life compatible with physical well-being. The earlier five year plans had focused on the building up of productive capacities, infrastructures and social services as means, firstly, for the growth and development of the national economy and secondly, for making an impact on the problem of poverty, unemployment and under-employment. In more recent plans, poverty has been seen increasingly as the central problem calling for special action in relation to specified socio-economic groups which have remained weak and confined in essential services and opportunities.

While in the 1950s and the 1960s, the major concern was to induce rural people to substitute rational economic calculation for the dictates of custom and tradition, in the 1970s there concern was to achieve greater equity in the distribution of the gains from economic growth between urban and rural areas. Since the 1980s, the strategy of direct attack on poverty through specific poverty alleviation programmes has been adopted for rural development on account of insufficient percolation of benefits to the poor from overall economic growth. However, it has also been perceived that the strategy of direct attack on poverty cannot be sustained and would not yield the desired results, if the overall growth of the economy itself is slow and the benefits of such growth are inequitably distributed. Thus, the programmes for poverty alleviation are being regarded as supplementing the basic plan for overall economic growth, in terms of generating productive assets and skills as well as incomes for the poor, and the role of economic growth in providing more employment avenues to the population has been duly recognized. The growth-oriented approach has been reinforced by focusing on specific sectors which provide greater opportunities to the people to participate in the growth process. The various dimensions of poverty relating to health, education and other basic services have been progressively internalized in the planning process.

Attaining Objectives

Rural development objectives can be sought in various ways once there is a firm commitment. The World Bank considers that the effective planning and implementation of rural development programmes require the following elements:

- (i) A national plan or programme of action for rural development, together with supporting national and regional policies and adequate centre-local arrangements;
- (ii) A strong organization at the national level to co-ordinate vertically organized Central Government and sectoral departments;
- (iii) Greater decentralization with effective machinery at the regional and local level to co-ordinate the sectoral activities of national departments operating in the region and regional and local departments; and
- (iv) Participation by the rural poor in the planning and implementation process through local government, and other forms of group organizations/voluntary organizations.

Thus the discussions boil down to the assumptions that the critical elements in rural development are (a) basic needs, (b) full employment, and (c) local participation each handled at micro level. These have similarity with the goals of development as propounded by Mahatma Gandhi which are:

(i) satisfaction of basic need, but not everyman's greed; (ii) full employment, since work is not a disutility but is part of the living process; (iii) modes of employment which satisfy man's urge for fulfilment of personality through work; (iv) decentralization of government; and (v) a technology which serves social needs. However, the Gandhian concept of integrated rural development though have significant logical consistency, but there are elements which are difficult to translate into practice. In the Gandhian concept, there is emphasis on all-round development of the inner-man. Though India in her rural development programmes has not turned altogether a blind eye on this aspect of the development, the main thrust has been on economic development and removal of rural poverty. The present concern with rural development represents, in part, a response to distortions produced by the production-oriented development efforts of the 1960s – which were, in turn, a reaction against economic failures of rural development of an even earlier vintage.

The Strategies

During the fifties two great rural development programmes were sponsored by the Americans—community development (CD) and agricultural extension (AE). The former was newly fashioned by American sociologists, while the latter was an old product of the American land-grant colleges. Both CD and AE were generously supported and carefully supervised by American advisers. Rural Reconstruction Programmes of pre-independence period had two approaches—British view of the philosophy of F.L. Brayne and nationalist view of Gandhi. Brayne wanted to uplift the villagers by sending an official guide-philosopher-friend. Gandhi wanted to do that by sending a constructive worker. Following in the footsteps of Brayne and Gandhi, CD relied mainly on a government village-level worker (VLW) as the agent of change. Sending a missionary outsider was considered essential in every case. The VLW, like Brayne's guide, was advised to collaborate closely with the local gentry, the established or "natural" leaders. Evidently, the VLW came to help everybody, not by fighting for the weak against the strong, but by uniting all of them, weak and strong, into a fraternal community. This was the most significant development programme initiated during the First Five Year Plan to embody India's methods of approach to the problems of improving rural life under conditions of democratic planning. Community Development, in fact, was a concept, a movement and revolution. It had a crucial significance in our plans and from the point of view of both economic progress and social justice, its role was therefore of supreme importance.

Community Development Programme thus started almost simultaneously with the beginning of the First Five Year Plan on 2nd October, 1952 in a modest way. Community development was a comprehensive self-help movement which embraced multi-faceted development, viz. education, health, drinking water, roads, agricultural production and cottage industries. It was conceived as a people's programme with the avowed objective of harnessing the local resources, the energies of the masses for the socio-economic uplift of all, to create an urge among the rural people for better life and to show the way of satisfying this urge by means of self-help. Block Development Committees were constituted under the programme to provide local knowledge and local expertise and to decide in a spirit of co-operation and traditional consensus in the rural areas.

The community development programme was the first organized attempt to lift the centuries old stagnant rural economy from the morass and inertia of the proverbial fatalist outlook and to the extent it generated some awakening and visible changes in the social and cultural mores, it was successful. But the major roadblocks in the programme were the weight of the colonial traditions of government administration, and the lack of a sound technological base for improving productivity and incomes of the rural population. The programme, therefore, failed to provide the impetus for sustained growth of all-round rural scenario. The programmes so well conceived just floundered under the weight of over administration. By 1960 CD was demoted and the American concept of Agricultural Extension became the senior partner.

Second Phase

The second phase of rural development emphasized intensive agriculture as a strategy for the sixties since the country started facing acute food shortage. Frankly speaking, rural development became agricultural development in the form of Green Revolution. The strategy was to concentrate the flow of resources in the already better endowed areas. However, though paid dividend, thanks to the discovery of high yielding varieties of wheat and its spectacular productivity improvement, it also widened the hiatus between better endowed areas and the poorer areas. Second limitation was evolving suitable geno types for appropriate agro climatic regions as also access to other inputs led by chemical fertilizer and more importantly, ability to buy these high cost inputs. The latter was to come out of rural credit. We need not go into this as most of us know its status, its fate and its accessibility by small and marginal farmers who held over seventy per cent of the holdings. To say the least they did not profit much from this effort.

The regional imbalance magnified with its serious political and economic ramifications. It was also causing concern as there was no sign of decline in rural poverty in the country. In addition the case of Punjab—a major beneficiary of Green Revolution – would highlight the adverse results of the Revolution. Punjab realized around 1985 that the production of foodgrains in wheat-rice rotation was neither very remunerative in view of the totality of individual and social costs involved in their production nor it was sustainable in the context of resource endowments of the state. Above that, huge stocks of foodgrains had accumulated and there was no space in the godowns to accommodate additional stocks. There was, therefore, a need for diversification of the cropping pattern to improve stagnating incomes of the farmers on a sustainable basis and to check the over-exploitation of the production base in terms of water balance and soil degradation as well as negative agro-ecological externalities of the wheat-rice production system.

DPAP and DDP

A mode recognized to address the whole question of poverty–saw the country launching in mid-1970s what came to be called "Drought Prone Area Programme" (DPAP) and "Desert Development Programme" (DDP). DPAP was launched in 1973-74 and DPP in 1977-78. Another such programme "Integrated Watershed Development Programme" (IWDP) is under implement since 1989-90. This was the outcome of thinking on the part of some that 'drag' to rural development, more so in the agriculture development context, is coming from drought prone and desert areas. Suffice it to say that over a period, these programmes have undergone a change and modification profiting more the committees which went into its examination than the subject of discussion – the poor. Success or otherwise of these programmes could be gauged in the light of the fact these programmes since inception continue to fall prey to the same vagaries, which these programmes were designed to proof against.

These programmes were implemented on a sectoral basis until 1994-95. Since April, 1995, they are being implemented on watershed basis. As for DPAP, total number of the projects sanctioned was 2535, with funds released by the Centre at Rs. 295 crore. Under DDP, 1562 projects have been sanctioned with funds of Rs. 215 crore; and under IWDP, 190 projects with funding of Rs. 306 crore were sanctioned.

Crash Scheme for Rural Employment (CSRE)

This scheme came into operation during 1971-72. Under this scheme it was decided to execute essential labour intensive projects in all the districts of the country and implement these with utmost urgency. The scheme was conceived at a time when various special rural development programmes such as SFDA,

MFAL, DPAP, DDP, etc., had not spread out fully and a minimum effort was considered necessary to relieve distress caused by unemployment or underemployment. These programmes had by then operated for some time and were to be expanded and intensified.

As a part of this scheme, Pilot Intensive Rural Employment Programme (PIREP) were taken up during 1972-73 for a period of 3 years in 15 selected blocks. These had a limited objective to collect necessary data regarding the dimensions of the programme for providing full employment to everyone who was willing to work.

According to Fifth Five Year Plan the results achieved under CSRE were encouraging. The working of the programme showed that resources were spread thinly over a large number of comparatively small projects, Bulk of the expenditure (about 80 per cent) was incurred on road construction, despite the guidelines laid under the scheme that construction of roads should be given lowest priority. The Fifth Five Year Plan proposed a Minimum Needs Programme (MNP) which included massive schemes of construction of rural roads, drinking water supply, education and primary health centres.

During this period several State Governments also introduced innovative Poverty Alleviation Programmes (PAPs) in their states with a view to alleviating poverty. These include Employment Guarantee Scheme of Maharashtra (1972), Land Army Corporation of Karnataka (1974), further revamped in 1983, State Rural Employment Programme of Tripura (1981-82), Village Development Council of Nagaland (set up under the Village & Area Council Act of 1978) etc.

Food for Work Programme

The programme was started in the last year (1977-78) of the Fifth Plan as non-plan scheme to augment the funds of the State Governments for the maintenance of public works. The scheme was designed to offer gainful employment to the rural poor and improve their income levels through the development of infrastructure and durable community assets. In order to improve the nutritional standards of the rural poor, the scheme provided for payment of part of wages in kind by utilizing surplus foodstocks available in the country. The programme gained momentum in 1978-79. This programme besides creating substantial additional employment in the rural areas during lean periods, more particularly, in areas affected by widespread drought of 1978, did make a favourable impact on stabilization of wages in the rural areas as also helped check the rise in prices of foodgrains. However, the programme also suffered from severe limitations in respect of planning and supervision of works. The operation of this programme on year to year basis had resulted in uncertainty about its continuance for the full plan period. Hence, the State Governments were disinclined to build the needed technical and administrative supports to effectively plan, monitor and oversee the programme. No serious attempt also appeared to have been made by the State Governments to implement the programme at block level resulting in taking up works of low priority with dubious utility at several places. Nevertheless, quite a number of durable assets in the nature of irrigation tanks, school buildings, panchayat buildings, drinking water wells, etc. were created.

However, the Food for Work programme was reintroduced in 2000-01 as a component of the EAS (discussed later) in eight notified drought–affected states of Chattisgarh, Gujarat, Himachal Pradesh, Madhya Pradesh, Orissa, Rajasthan, Maharashtra and Uttaranchal. The programme aims at augmenting food security. In its new form as National Food for Work Programme which was launched on November 14, 2004 in 150 most backward districts with the objective to intensify the generation of supplementary wage employment, the programme is a part of the recently launched National Employment Guarantee Scheme.

Integrated Rural Development Programme

The concept of an Integrated Rural Development Programme was first mooted in the Central Budget of 1976-77, and a beginning was made. The programme was intended to assist the rural population to derive economic benefits from the development assets of each area. The programme with some modifications was introduced on an expanded scale in 1978-79, beginning with 2,300 blocks, of which 2000 were under coterminous coverage with SFDA, DPAP and CAD programmes. On 2nd October, 1980 all the blocks in the country were brought under IRDP. Besides the small and marginal farmers, this programme was more specific in regard to agricultural workers and landless labourers and additionally brought within its purview rural artisans also. The programme emphasized the family rather than individual approach in identification of beneficiaries.

The objective of IRDP was to enable identified rural families to augment their income and cross the poverty line through acquisition of credit based productive assets which would provide self-employment on a sustained basis.

This programme was implemented through District Rural Development Agencies (DRDA) and Development Blocks. At the State level, coordination committee headed by the Chief Secretary monitor and oversees all aspects of implementation of the programme. The Governing Body at the District level provides guidance and direction to the DRDAs. Representatives of the rural people such as Members of Parliament, Members of Legislative Assemblies, Chairman of Zila Parishad, heads of District Development Departments, representatives of SC/ST and women are intimately involved in planning and implementation of the programme. The overall guidance, policy making and monitoring of the programme is being done by the Department of Rural Development at the control level.

In a programme of the size of IRDP and given the size and diversity of the country, there are bound to be few shortcomings in its implementation. The major shortcomings which still persist in varying degree are, low percentage of people crossing the poverty line, leakages in the programme, wrong identification of the beneficiaries, low investment per family and lack of proper infrastructure linkages in some areas as well as limited after care. Taking note of the positive developments through implementation of this programme, these short comings have to be overcome by suitably restructuring the programme.

Development of Women and Children in Rural Areas (DWCRA)

This was a comparatively new scheme launched by the Department of Rural Development with effect from September 1982 as a sub-scheme of IRDP. The programme was initially launched on a pilot basis in 50 selected districts all over the country chosen on the twin criteria of low female literacy and high infant mortality rates. Thereafter there had been a phased expansion covering 161 districts up to 1980–90. It was proposed to continue the expansion strategy in the VIII Plan. To ensure coordination with ICDS programme of the Department of Women and Child Development, it was decided that the new districts under DWCRA should normally be those where ICDS projects were in operation in some blocks.

Through special efforts and provision of necessary inputs, the scheme sought to enable rural women to participate more effectively in the rural development programmes in general and IRDP in particular. Main features of the scheme included assistance to women members of rural households below the poverty line in suitable avenues for income generation according to their skills and local conditions. For better inter-communication women were organized in homogenous groups to take up economically viable activities on group basis. Provision of working conveniences, suitable appliances etc., to improve efficiency, reduce, drudgery, and to provide child care and health care facilities at the work sites also constituted part of the scheme.

The scheme is being implemented through concerned State Governments concerned by DRDA at the district level and by Block Agency at the Block level by suitably strengthening these agencies. One time grant of Rs. 15,000 is placed at the disposal of the group as revolving fund. The amount is shared equally by the Central/State Government and UNICEF. The fund can be used for purchase of raw materials, marketing, child care facilities etc. Multipurpose community centres are provided for the groups to carry on their activities.

TRYSEM

This programme was initiated with effect from 15th August, 1979. The main thrust of the scheme is on equipping rural youth in the 18-35 age group with necessary skills and technology to enable them to take vocations of self-employment and to an extent wage employments in any of the economic sectors. The scheme is an integral part of IRDP. The selection of beneficiaries is done from familiar families below the poverty line. Training is to be need based. It is provided at training institutions such as it is, polytechnics and institutes run by voluntary agencies or master craftsmen functioned from their own place of work. Duration of training is flexible and decided at the District level for courses upto 6 months and at state level for longer duration. TRYSEM trainees are provided financial assistance under IRDP on completion of the training programme. Every TRYSEM trainee is a potential IRDP beneficiary. Attempts have been made to associate bankers with TRYSEM from the selection stage itself. At least 30 per cent of trainees should belong to SC/ST and a minimum of $33\frac{1}{3}$ per cent should be women.

The scope of the TRYSEM scheme was widened with effect from June, 1993 to cover wage employment in the case of (i) project linkages, and (ii) decentralised rural industry sector including village and cottage industries, handicrafts and handlooms in rural areas. In order to get feedback on the field position of the scheme, independent institutions have been assisted by the Department in conducting concurrent evaluation studies.

Industries Services and Business Component of IRDP (ISBC)

The ISB was built into IRDP in February, 1979 with the objective of maximizing the employment opportunities in the secondary and tertiary sectors, as the absorption capacity of the farm sector was limited. All persons selected under ISB are entitled to subsidies under the IRDP pattern. A Central Coordination Committee on Rural Industrialisation has been set up under the Chairmanship of the Secretary Rural Development to coordinate the work between the different Ministries concerned with the ISB sector. This provides a common forum for coordination among the different Ministries dealing with the decentralized Industrial sector as also with the all-India bodies concerned with these sectors.

National Rural Employment Programmes

In the sixties, strategies for reducing poverty by providing the basic needs were pursued, at best, parallel to growth oriented concepts, or were even seen as competing with them. Employment considerations did play an important role in the development strategy debate, however, within the context of the analysis of the food and agriculture sector's key role in the development process. It was then identified that one of the main causes of rural poverty was the lack of purchasing power of the majority of the rural people in the absence of employment opportunities.

The NREP was considered to be a major programme being implemented to tackle unemployment and under employment in rural areas. This programme launched in October, 1980 replaced the earlier Food for Work Programme (FWP). It envisaged generation of additional employment opportunities in rural areas of the order of 300-400 million mandays every year. It also envisaged creating simultaneously durable community assets to strengthen the rural infrastructure and raising the nutritional standards of rural poor. The programme operated in close conjunction with the on-going development works ensuring that employment and development support each other and benefits flowing to the community were maximized.

Till 31st March, 1981, NREP was funded entirely by the Central Government. NREP became a regular plan programme from 1st April, 1981 and was being implemented as a centrally sponsored scheme on 50: 50 sharing basis between the Centre and States. It was essentially conceived as a programme to take care of that segment of the rural poor which largely depends on a wage employment and had virtually no other source of income during the lean agricultural periods. Its basic objectives were, generation of additional gainful employment for the unemployed and under employed persons, both men and women, in rural areas and creation of productive community assets for direct and continuing benefits to the poverty groups so as to strengthen rural economic and social infrastructure. In the ultimate analysis it envisaged rapid growth of rural economy, steady rise in the income levels of the rural poor, and improvement in the overall quality of life in rural areas.

Rural Landless Employment Guarantee Programme (RLEGP)

This was a totally Centrally financed programme introduced in 1983. While most of the objectives and stipulations under this were similar to those of NREP, it was to be limited only to the landless, with guaranteed employment of 100 days. Moreover, there was earmarking of funds specifically for certain activities – 25 per cent for social forestry, 10 per cent for works benefiting only the Scheduled Castes/Scheduled Tribes and 20 per cent for housing under Indira Awaas Yojana. In the Seventh Plan, Rs. 2412 crores were spent and 115 crore mandays were generated with an average expenditure of Rs. 21.00 per manday. Only 16 per cent had been spent on social forestry but 22 per cent had been spent on housing, with over 5 lakh houses created for SC/ST and freed bonded labourers. Rural roads accounted for 22 per cent while other construction, minor irrigation, soil conservation etc., each had a small share.

Anti-poverty Programmes Since 1980s

In the seventies itself, it was realized that the economic development programmes as such could not make much dent on the gigantic problem of rural poverty. "Trickle down effect" was the core aim of investment in agriculture, land development, terracing works, rural access roads, irrigation, soil and water conservation works, afforestation, etc. But as has been mentioned earlier, these created more inequalities in the rural areas and menacing rural poverty persisted unabatedly.

Removal of rural poverty, therefore, has become the key issue in the rural development programmes since the eighties onward. During the Sixth Plan, the government adopted a two-pronged strategy to deal with the problem of poverty. While laying emphasis on accelerated growth in agriculture with the hope that it would have a beneficial effect on raising the standard of living of the lower strata of the rural society, it was also decided to strengthen and expand the scope of beneficiary oriented anti-poverty programmes in rural areas. Consistent with this approach, the Seventh Plan laid emphasis on accelerated agricultural growth, increased productivity of various agricultural commodities, developing the potential of dry land agriculture, adoption of special measures to increase and expand irrigation facilities on the one hand and also included a number of anti-poverty and employment generation programmes especially designed to raise incomes and productivity of people below the poverty line, on the other.

We have already mentioned that providing additional employment opportunities to the rural poor has long been an integral part of the country's rural development programmes. During the Sixth Plan, the National Rural Employment Programme and the Rural Landless Employment Guarantee Programme (RLEGP) were implemented replacing the earlier Food for Work Programme. Evaluation studies of these programmes revealed that about half the villages in the country did not get benefit from any of these programmes. In order to intensify wage employment programmes in rural areas and to involve local people in planning and implementation of various works/schemes for the benefit of the rural poor, the NREP and RLEGP were merged into a single rural employment programme known as Jawahar Rozgar Yojana (JRY).

The new programme was taken up for implementation from 1st April, 1989. Under the programme it was aimed to cover all the village panchayats so that the benefits could flow to each and every village and at least one member of each family living below the poverty line could be provided fuller employment opportunities. The implementation of the programme was entrusted to village panchayats so as to involve local people in selection and execution of works/ schemes.

The primary objective of the JRY was to generate additional gainful employment for the unemployment and underemployed, men and women, in rural areas. The programme had other secondary objectives. These were: (i) creation of sustained employment by strengthening the rural economic infrastructure; (ii) creating community and social assets; (iii) creating assets in favour of the rural poor for their direct and continuing benefits; (iv) positive impact on wage levels; and (v) overall improvement in the quality of life in rural areas.

In 1993-94 the scheme was revised to be implemented in three streams. The first stream would consist of general work under the programme and the two sub-schemes, viz., the Indira Awaas Yojana (IAY) and the Million Wells Scheme (MWS). The second stream (also called Intensified Jawahar Rozgar Yojana) was implemented in 120 intensified backward districts with additional allocation. The third stream of JRY consisted of special and innovative projects. Since 1995-96 IAY and MWS are being implemented as separate schemes and no longer form part of the JRY. Later on, the centrally sponsored Rural Housing Scheme has also been merged with the IAY. A third stream of JRY was also introduced for taking up special and innovative projects aimed at preventing migration of labour, enhancing women's employment opportunities etc. JRY had two other sub-schemes. Million Wells Scheme (MWS) and Indira Awaas Yojana (IAY) to provide irrigation facilities to small/marginal farmers having land and yet living BPL, to enable them to improve their lot by adopting benefits of latest inputs/ agriculture research/practices. IAY provided houses to the houseless BPL families where land was made available under the scheme to help them build a house; funds were also available for developing the basic infrastructure like roads and facilities for drinking water etc. Both these schemes the Indira Awaas Yojana (IAY) and the Million Wells Scheme (MWS) were made into independent schemes in 1996.

Million Wells Scheme (MWS)

In India, though the small and marginal farmers, with holdings of less than 2 hectares, account for about 78 per cent of the total operation holdings, they only cultivate about 32.2 per cent of the cropped area (Agricultural Census 1990-91). To increase the productivity of these holdings they must be ensured an assured source of water supply. Ground water made available through wells is an important source specially in the remote areas of the countryside, where canal or tank irrigation is not feasible. Though the fixed capital investment in well irrigation is fairly high, it has many advantages such as flexibility in operation, dependability of source, timing of water deliveries and low conveyance losses.

The Million Wells Scheme (MWS) was launched as a sub-scheme of the National Rural Employment Programme (NREP) and the Rural Landless Employment Guarantee Programme (RLEGP) during the year 1988-89. After the merger of the two programmes in April 1989 into the Jawahar Rozgar Yojana (JRY), the MWS continued as a sub-scheme of JRY till December 1995. The MWS delinked from JRY and made into an independent scheme with effect from 1st January, 1996.

The scheme was primarily intended to provide open irrigation wells, free of cost, to individual, poor, small and marginal farmers belonging to Scheduled Castes/Scheduled Tribes and freed bonded labourers with a 20 per cent earmarking of JRY funds. Tubewells and borewells are not permitted under the Scheme. Where well are not feasible due to geological factors, other minor irrigation works can be undertaken such as irrigation tanks, water harvesting structures as also development of land belonging to small and marginal farmers. From the year 1993-94 the scope of the MWS has been enlarged to cover non–Scheduled Castes/

non-Scheduled Tribes small and marginal farmers who are below the poverty line and are listed in the IRDP register of the village. The sectoral earmarking which was 20 per cent upto 1992-93 had also been raised to 30 per cent from 1993-94 with the stipulation that the benefits to non-Scheduled Castes/ Scheduled Tribes would not exceed one-third of the total utilized during the year.

Indira Awaas Yojana (IAY)

The Government of India is implementing the Indira Awaas Yojana since the year 1985-86 with the objective of providing assistance primarily to the below poverty line (BPL) rural households belonging primarily to the Scheduled Castes, Scheduled Tribes and freed bonded labour categories. Under the Scheme, assistance upto 40 per cent of the IAY allocation can be provided to non-Scheduled Castes and Scheduled Tribes rural BPL households. Benefits of the scheme have also been extended to the families of the ex-servicemen of the armed and paramilitary forces killed in action. Upto 3 per cent of the funds are earmarked for the BPL, physically and mentally challenged persons within the SC/ST and other BPL families.

Upto 31st March, 2004, assistance per dwelling unit amounting to Rs. 20,000 in the plain area and Rs. 22,500 in the hilly/difficult areas was used to be provided. The same has been increased to Rs. 25,000 per unit for plain areas and Rs. 27,500 for hilly/difficult areas from 1st April, 2004. Similarly, the ceiling on upgradation of a *kutcha* house to semi-*pucca*/*pucca* house has also been enhanced from Rs. 10,000 to Rs. 12,500.

Allocation of funds under the Indira Awaas Yojana to the States/UTs is made based on the poverty ratios as approved by the Planning Commission and the rural housing shortage as per the Census 1991. Both parameters are given equal weightage.

Prime Minister's Rozgar Yojana (PMRY)

PMRY started in 1993 with the objective of making available self-employment opportunities to the educated unemployed youth by assisting them in setting up any economically viable activity. So far, about 20 lakh units have been set up under the PMRY, creating 30.4 lakh additional employment opportunities. The targets for additional employment opportunities under the Tenth Plan and in 2004-05 are 16.50 lakh and 3.75 lakh respectively. While the REGP is implemented in the rural areas and small towns (population up to 20,000) for is meant for educated unemployed youth with family income of up to Rs. 40,000 per annum, in both urban and rural areas, for engaging in any economically viable activity.

Rural Employment Generation Programme (REGP)

REGP, launched in 1995 with the objective of creating self-employment opportunities in the rural areas and small towns, is being implemented by the Khadi and Village Industries Commission (KVIC). Under REGP, entrepreneurs can establish village industries by availing of margin money assistance from the KVIC and bank loans, for projects with a maximum cost of Rs.25 lakh. Since the inception of RLEGP, up to 31st March 2004, 1,86,252 projects have been financed and 22.75 lakh job opportunites created. A target of creating 25 lakh new jobs has been set for the REGP during the Tenth Plan. 8.32 lakh employment opportunites have already been created during 2003-04. For 2004-05, a target of creating 5.25 lakh job opportunities has been fixed.

Jawahar Gram Samridhi Yojana (JGSY)

The JRY was revamped from April 1, 1999 as the Jawahar Gram Samridhi Yojana (JGSY). It was dedicated entirely to the development of rural infrastructure with employment generation as secondary objective. In fact, the primary objective of JGSY was creation of demand driven community village infrastructure including durable assets at the village level with a view to enabling the rural poor to have more opportunities for sustained employment. However, as mentioned, generation of wage employment for the unemployed poor remained as secondary objective.

Employment Assurance Scheme (EAS)

Though creation of employment opportunities has always been an important objective of developmental planning in India, the relatively higher growth of population and labour force has led to an increase in the volume of unemployment and under-employment from one plan period to another. The Sixth Five Year Plan aimed at bringing employment into a larger focus with the goal of reducing unemployment to a negligible level within the next ten years. Such an approach was necessary, because it was realized that larger and efficient use of available human resources was the most effective way of alleviating poverty, reduction of inequalities and sustenance of reasonable high pace of economic growth.

Accordingly, taking cue from Maharashtra's visibly successful Employment Guarantee Scheme (EGS), Employment Assurance Scheme (EAS) was launched on October 2, 1993 for implementation in 1778 identified backward Panchayat Samitis of 257 districts situated in the drought prone areas, desert areas, tribal areas and hill areas in which the Revamped Public Distribution System (RPDS) was in operation. The scheme was then extended to the remaining Panchayat Samitis of the country in phased manner and finally, universalized in 1997-98 to cover all the 5448 Rural Panchayat Samitis of the country. The EAS was designed to provide employment in the form of manual work in the lean agricultural season. Initially the scheme was demand-driven, but from 1999, resources were allocated to states based on the incidence of poverty.

Ninth Five Year Plan starting April 1997 saw a strategic shift. EAS was to be used as a main instrument for assuring wage employment for 100 days in a year while JRY, continuing to be largely labour intensive, would be aimed at infrastructure creation. Major departure/modification were made in IRDP. While the programme would continue to be the main plank for self-employment for BPL families, TRYSEM, supply of improved Tool kits to Rural Artisans, DWCRA and GKY were subsumed in IRDP as also signalling shift from individual beneficiary approach to Group/cluster approach.

Effective from 1st April, 1999, IRDP and Million Wells Scheme were merged into a single programme called Swarnjayanti Gram Swarozgar Yojana (SGSY) to help adopt a holistic approach of micro enterprise development in rural areas with emphasis on organizing rural poor into self-help groups, capacity building, infrastructure support, technology credit and marketing linkages. JRY was also rechristened as *Jawahar Gram Samridhi Yojana* (JGSY) without much change in content or format.

Swarnjayanti Gram Swarozgar Yojana (SGSY)

Integrated Rural Development Programme/Swarnjayanti Gram Swarozgar Yojana programme for self-employment of the poor has been an important component of the anti-poverty programmes implemented through government initiatives in the rural areas in India. The Swarnjayanti Gram Swarozgar Yojana (SGSY) is the major on-going programme for the self-employment of rural poor at present. The programme was started with effect from 1st April, 1999 after reviewing and restructuring of erstwhile Integrated Rural Development Programme (IRDP) and allied programmes, namely Training of Rural Youth for Self Employment (TRYSEM), Development of Women and Children in Rural Areas (DWCRA), Supply of Toolkits in Rural Areas (SITRA) and Ganga Kalyan Yojana (GKY), besides Million Wells Scheme (MWS). The earlier programmes are no more in operation with the launching of the SGSY.

Swarnjayanti Gram Swarojgar Yojana (SGSY) is a major on-going programme for providing opportunities of self-employment to the rural poor. The assisted families (Swarozgaris) may be individuals or Groups (Self-Help Groups). However, the emphasis is on Group approach. The basic objective of the SGSY is to bring the assisted poor families (Swarozgaris) above the Poverty Line by providing them income-generating assets through a mix of bank credit and governmental subsidy. The programme aims at establishing a large number of micro enterprises in rural areas based on the ability of the poor and potential of each area. It has been conceived as a holistic programme of self-employment and some of its salient features are:

- Organising the rural poor into Self-Help Groups (SHGs) through social mobilization.
- Key activity and development of activity clusters.
- Training and marketing support to the Swarojgaris.
- Involvement of NGOs/CBOs Animators in social mobilization and training and capacity building of Self-Help Groups.

In September 2001, the SGSY was merged into Sampoorna Gramin Rozgar Yojana (SGRY). The Government of India supplements efforts made by the States by providing financial and technical assistance under the two Centrally Sponsored programmes, namely the Accelerated Rural Water Supply Programme (ARWSP) and the Central Rural Sanitation Programme (CRSP).

Pradhan Mantri Gramodaya Yojana (PMGY)

The PMGY was launched in 2000-01 in all States and Union Territories (UTs) in order to achieve the objective of sustainable human development at the village level. This scheme envisages allocation of Additional Central Assistance (ACA) to the States and UTs for selected basic minimum services in order to focus on certain priority-areas. The PMGY initially had five components, viz., primary health, primary education, rural shelter, rural drinking water and nutrition. Rural electrification was added from 2001-02. For 2002-03 as well as 2003-04, the allocation of ACA for the PMGY was Rs. 2800 crore. Both financial and physical monitoring of the programme is being carried out by the Planning Commission.

Sampoorna Gramin Rozgar Yojana (SGRY)

Given the complementarity of the JGSY and EAS, and Food for Works Programme all aiming at the creation of employment opportunities in the rural areas, they were revamped and merged under the new Sampoorna Gramin Rozgar Yojana (SGRY) scheme from September, 2001. The basic aim of the scheme is not merely generation of employment, creation of durable economic infrastructure in rural areas and provision of food and nutrition security to the poor, but at the same time channellising its vast potential in nation building exercise through the development of human resource and economic infrastructure which may transform the rural face and give boost to the nation's economy.

With an Annual Outlay of Rs. 10,000 crore, the scheme envisages employment generation of 100 crore mandays annually.

The works taken up under the programme are labour-intensive and the workers are paid the minimum wages notified by the states. Payment of wages is done partly in cash and partly in kind – 5kgs of foodgrains and the balance in cash.

Besides above, a Samagra Awas Yojana (SAY) was taken up in 25 blocks for an integrated development of housing complexes for BPL families. A National Social Assistance Programme (NSAP) was also introduced in 1990s as part of social safety to cover aged, family losing a bread winner and pregnant women.

Other Rural Development Programmes

Rural Housing

Housing is one of the basic needs of mankind in terms of safety, security, self-esteem, social status, cultural identity, satisfaction and achievement. There is thus a clear correlation between the poverty and the housing condition. The poor person either does not have a house or lives in unserviceable *kutcha* house. According to the 1991 Census, around 3.1 million households were without shelter and another 10.31 million resided in unserviceable *kutcha* houses. Initiated in 1985-86, the IAY is the core programme for providing free housing to BPL families in rural areas and targets SC/ST households and freed bonded labourers. It was first merged with the JRY in 1989 and then spun off into a separate housing scheme for the rural poor in 1996. Operationalised from 1999-2000 it is the major scheme for construction of houses for the poor, free of cost. The Ministry of Rural Development (MORD) provides equity support to the Housing and Urban Development Corporation (HUDCO) for this purpose.

Considering the magnitude of the problem, the Government of India announced in 1998 a National Housing and Habitat Policy and setting up of Rural Building Centres (RBCs) which aimed at providing 'Housing for All' and facilitating construction of 20 lakh additional housing units (13 lakh in Rural Areas and 7 lakh in Urban Areas) annually with an emphasis on extending benefits to the poor and the deprived. Government is committed to the goal of ending all shelterlessness by the end of the Xth Plan period.

A National Mission for Rural Housing and Habitat has also been set up to address the critical issues of 'housing gap and induction of science and technology inputs into the housing/ construction sector in rural areas. Since inception (up to June 1, 2004), 113.96 lakh houses have been constructed/upgraded by incurring an expenditure of Rs. 19,869 crore.

Pradhan Mantri Gram Sadak Yojana (PMGSY): The Pradhan Mantri Gram Sadak Yojana (PMGSY) was launched on 25th September, 2000 to provide connectivity to all Unconnected Habitations (around 1.60 lakh) with all weather road. The programme envisages providing connectivity to all Unconnected Habitations with a population of 500 persons (or more) 250 in the case of hilly desert or tribal areas by the end of Tenth Plan Period (2007). The National Rural Roads Development Agency (NRRDA) registered under the Societies Registration Act, 1860 to extend support to programme through advice on technical specifications, project appraisal, appointment of part time Quality Control Monitors, etc.

The Asian Development Bank (ADB) has agreed to support the development of rural roads in Madhya Pradesh and Chhattisgarh, which have been identified as recipient states for the first tranche. The ADB Board has approved a loan of $ 400 million (in a project size of $571 million). The states of Assam, Orissa and West Bengal have been identified for the second tranche of ADB assistance of the order of $500 million. The third tranche of $400 million for funding projects in Himachal Pradesh, Jharkhand, Rajasthan and Uttar Pradesh is likely to be available from the World Bank by the end of 2004-05.

Two new schemes were launched in pursuit of search for Food Security for the rural poor. The National Rural Roads Development Agency (NRRDA) extends technical support to the programme at the central level. Rural Roads being a State subject, PMGSY works are executed by State Agencies. Most of the States have set up Rural Road Development Agencies (RRDA) for the purpose, which also serve to coordinate the execution of the programme in the field. Keeping in view the resource gap for the Programme, the Government have been taking steps to arrange additional funds for the Programme. After detailed studies, field visits, consultations and appraisal, Madhya Pradesh and Chhattisgarh were identified as recipient States for Asian Development Bank (ADB) assistance. ADB Board has approved a $ 400 million loan for PMGSY in November, 2003.

Urban Housing

Swarna Jayanti Shahari Rozgar Yojana (SJSRY): The Urban Self-Employment Programme and the Urban Wage Employment Programme are two special schemes of the SJSRY initiated in December 1997, which replaced various programmes operated earlier for urban poverty alleviation. Between the Centre and the States, SJSRY is funded on a 75 : 25 basis.

During 2002-03, the full allocation of Rs. 105 crore provided for various components of this programme was released. For 2003-04, an allocation of Rs. 94.50 crore plus Rs. 10.5 crore for North East and Sikkim was provided for various components of this programme.

Valmiki Ambedkar Awaas Yojana (VAMBAY): The VAMBAY was launched in December 2001 for the urban slum dwellers living below the poverty line without adequate shelter. The scheme has the primary objective of facilitating the construction and upgradation of dwelling units for slum dwellers and providing a healthy and enabling urban environment through community toilets under Nirmal Bharat Abhiyan, a component of the scheme.

The Central Government provides a subsidy of 50 per cent, the balance 50 per cent being arranged by the State Government. There are prescribed ceilings on costs both for dwelling units and community toilets. During 2003-04, central subsidy to the extent of Rs. 239 crore was released. Since inception up to May 2004, Rs. 522 crore have been released as subsidy by the Government of India for the construction/ upgradation of 246,035 dwelling units and 29,263 toilet seats under the scheme.

Antyodaya Anna Yojana

Launched on 25th December, 2000, by Ministry of Consumer Affairs, Food and Public Distribution, Government of India, it seeks to identify one crore families out of a total of 6.52 crore BPL families [under the Targeted Public Distribution System (TPDS) who are to be provided 35 kg. foodgrains per month at a highly subsidized rate of Rs. 2 per kg. (wheat) and Rs. 3 per kg. (rice) with the ardent hope that States shall ensure that retail issue price is kept at the same level, thus absorbing the intermediate overhead/costs. The scheme was further expanded in June 2003 by adding another 50 lakh BPL families.

Annapurna

Ministry of Rural Development also launched a new scheme almost at the same time called *'Annapurna'* to provide food security to those indigent senior citizens who were eligible for old age pension under the National Old Age Pension Scheme. Beneficiaries are to be given 10 kg. of foodgrains per month free of cost. This scheme has since been transferred to the States and there is no way to ascertain the impact of this scheme.

Swajal Dhara

A new initiative based on demand responsive strategy and community participatory approach in rural drinking water sector was launched in 1999. On a pilot basis Sector Reform Projects have been taken up in 67 districts of 26 States. Out of 62,909 water supply schemes taken up, 43,705 have been completed and 32,870 have been taken over by the community for operation and maintenance. Encouraged by the success of Sector Reforms Projects, a new initiative 'Swajal Dhara' has been launched on December 25, 2002. Under this initiative, as against the Districts under Sector Reforms, Panchayats, Blocks and other beneficiary groups have been empowered to formulate, implement, operate and maintain Drinking Water Projects. 90 per cent funds towards the project cost is provided by the Government and the beneficiary group has to contribute 10 per cent of the cost.

In order to further involve PRIs in the development process, a new initiative "*Hariyali*" has been launched on 27th January, 2003. Hariyali has been launched to strengthen and fortify Panchayati Raj Institutions for the implementation of Watershed Development Programmes, namely IWDP, DPAP and DDP. Under this initiative, the Gram Panchayats would execute watershed projects with technical support from the Block Panchayat Zilla Panchayat who would act as Project Implementation Agency (PIA) for all watershed projects in a particular Block. To provide encouragement to Panchayats to excel in performance of their role, the Ministry of Rural Development has also launched a scheme captioned 'Award for Best Panchayat' in April 2003.

Concept of sanitation connotes a comprehensive definition, which includes liquid and solid waste disposal, food hygiene, personal, domestic and environmental hygiene. Central Government supplements the efforts of the State in undertaking rural sanitation under Central Rural Sanitation Programme which was launched in 1986. CRSP aims at improving the quality of life of the rural poor and to provide privacy and dignity to women in rural areas. Since its inception and up to the end of the Ninth Plan, 94.5 lakh latrines were constructed for rural households under the CRSP as well as corresponding State Minimum Needs Programme.

In 1999, Total Sanitation Campaign (TSC) under restructured CRSP was launched to improve quality of life, and promote sanitation in rural areas. TSC follows participatory demand responsive approach, educating the rural households about the benefits of proper sanitation and hygiene. TSC is being implemented in 398 districts with an outlay of Rs. 3744 crore with Government of India share of Rs. 2214 crore, out of which Rs. 324.62 crore have been released. During 2003-04, 133 projects have been sanctioned.

Nirmal Gram Puraskar, an award scheme for achieving 100 per cent open defecation free environment has been launched on 2nd October, 2003 to encourage the Panchayati Raj Institutions. This has generated sufficient enthusiasm amongst the PRIs.

Information, Education and Communication

Information, Education and Communication (IEC) plays a vital role in creating awareness, mobilizing people and making the development participatory through advocacy and by transferring knowledge, skills and techniques to the people. Moreover, IEC plays two most important roles informative and persuasive. As such it is crucial for bringing about requisite social mobilization and facilitating participatory development.

Realizing the importance of communication, in mobilizing people towards participatory development, concerted efforts are being made by the Ministry of Disseminate Information and Message on Rural Development Programmes through most of the available modes of communication. The Information Education and Communication activities undertaken by the Ministry aim at:

- Primarily creating awareness amongst the target groups of the programmes of the Ministry and mobilizing them towards participatory development.
- Sensitizing opinion makers, urban elite about issues relating to rural development.
- Creating awareness amongst the general public.

National Employment Guarantee Scheme

It has long been realized that one of the major causes of rural poverty is lack of purchasing power following absence of gainful employment among the rural-masses. Hence since sixties one of the main strategies of poverty alleviation programmes is to give employment to the poor people. Rural Manpower Employment Programme initiated in 1960 was indeed the first such attempt as the Community Development Programmes of the fifties failed to a great extent to change the poverty scenario of the rural India. Thereafter the employment programmes like Crash Scheme for Rural Employment (CSRE) and Food for Work were implemented in 1970s. However, these programmes did not have the desired impact on the scurge of poverty.

In eighties it was decided to view poverty alleviation programmes in the wider perspective of socio-economic transformation in the country and a strategy of direct attack on poverty through specific poverty alleviation programmes was considered most suitable. In such a strategy, employment generation was given the utmost priority and during the Sixth Plan (1980-85) period two major employment generation programmes, namely National Rural Employment Programme (NREP) and then Rural Landless Employment Guarantee Programme (RLEGP) were implemented throughout the country replacing the earlier Food for Work Programme. The latter was the first such programme which provided a guarantee of employment to at least one member of every landless household upto 100 days in a year. However, this was to be fully financed by the central government and it was not backed by any statutory provision.

Since then there has been a plethora of changes in the nomenclatures and designs of the employment generation programmes which have been discussed quite elaborately early. Yet very little dent could be made in total eradication of rural poverty in the country. It is known to all that the employment elasticity of manufacturing has fallen sharply in the 1990s. It is only due to growth in services sector that employment is growing as rapidly as the labour force. But that has left the majority dependent upon India's slow-growing agriculture behind. Mention may be made that agriculture still accounts for 59 per cent of all employment. While in the medium run the transfer of labour out of agriculture is necessary, direct action by the government, in the form of employment guarantee may, it is reiterated, significantly reduce rural poverty within a short span of time.

Needless to say that the problem of unemployment, and the related problem of poverty has accentuated, in rural India in particular, since the introduction of the "reform". In such a situation the UPA's Common Minimum Programme (CMP) pledged to immediately enact the National Rural Employment Guarantee Act.

The Bill

The original proposal of Employment Guarantee was to give a statutory right to 100 days a year of employment at the minimum wage in each state to one person per household both in rural and urban areas of the country. The new draft Bill namely, the National Rural Employment Guarantee Bill, 2004 was introduced in the Parliament on 21st December, 2004. It promises a minimum of 100 days of employment to every poor household whose adult members volunteer to do unskilled manual work in rural India. If an eligible applicant is not provided with such an employment within 15 days of receipt of his application, he shall be entitled to a daily unemployment allowance, the rate of which will be specified by the State Governments.

Most poor families in the country are in casual employment or self-employed, while those with regular employment are least likely to be poor. The EGS will ensure at least 100 days a year of regular employment to the poor-eliminating a basis of poverty. Based on a minimum wage for all states of Rs.60 per day, 100 days work will raise incomes by Rs.6000 a year for poor households, raising two-thirds of India's poor above the poverty line. The scheme is modelled closely on the EGS of Maharashtra except that the proposed national one is to be vested with Panchayats.

As the Act comes into force, all State Governments will have to prepare a scheme to give effect to guarantee the provisions under the legislation. Some of the works identified for providing employment include water conservation and harvesting, drought proofing, irrigation canals, including micro and minor irrigation works, renovation of traditional water bodies, including desilting of tanks, land development, flood control and rural connectivity. The bill provides for establishing National Employment Guarantee Fund at the central level and a State Employment Guarantee Fund to implement the employment guarantee scheme. The standing committee of the District Panchayat, District Programme Coordinator, Programme Officers and Gram Panchayats have been given responsibilities in implementing the scheme. Four crore rural households are expected to benefit from the scheme. The total cost for implementation of the scheme is estimated to be Rs.1,20,500 crore.

Deviation

As mentioned above in India, many overlapping employment generation programmes have been in operation over a considerable period with varying degree of effectiveness. The original proposal would have given a statutory right to 100 days a year of employment at the minimum wage in each state to one person per household. But the present Bill, unfortunately contains no time horizon for the scheme to cover the entire country and even undermines the government to withdraw the legal guarantee in particular districts at any time. However, it will initially cover the 150 poorest districts in the country.

National Rural Employment Guarantee Bill, 2004 – Salient Features

- State Governments to provide at least 100 days of guaranteed wage employment in every financial year to every household whose adult members volunteer to do unskilled manual work.
- Sampoorna Grameen Rozgar Yojana (SGRY) and National Food for Work Programme to be subsumed with in the Scheme once the Act is in force.
- Until such time as a wage rate is fixed by the Central Government, the minimum wage for agricultural labourers shall be applicable for the scheme.
- An applicant not provided employment within fifteen days, to be entitled to a daily unemployment allowance as specified by the State Government subject to its economic capacity, provided such rate is not less than a quarter of the wage rate for the first thirty days during the financial year and not less than a half of the wage rate for the remaining period of the financial year.
- Central Employment Guarantee Council to be constituted to discharge various functions and duties assigned to the Council. Every State Government to also constitute a State Council for this purpose.
- Panchayat at the district level to constitute a Standing Committee of its members to supervise, monitor and oversees the implementation of the Scheme within the district.
- For every Block, State Governments to appoint a Programme Officer for implementing the Scheme.
- Gram Panchayat to be responsible for identification of the projects as per the recommendations of the Gram Sabha and for executing and supervising such works.
- Central Government to establish a National Employment Guarantee Fund. State Governments to establish State Employment Guarantee Funds for implementation of the Scheme.
- The Scheme to be self-selecting in the sense that those among the poor who need work at the minimum wage would report for work under the scheme.

Draft Employment Guarantee Act (dEGA) *vs* Maharashtra Employment Guarantee Act (MEGA)

Many economists and votaries of UPA Government's CMP have welcomed tabling of this Draft Employment Guarantee Act (dEGA) bill in parliament on two counts. First, they think of the proposed national Employment Guarantee Act as one of a range of the potential methods of transferring income to the poor. Secondly, they are enthusiast looking at the 'success' of the Maharashtra Employment Guarantee Act (MEGA). Loosely based on MEGA, it is an effort to combine the dual goals of providing unskilled work and generating productive assets. MEGA came into force in 1977 and has now been operational for close to three decades.

The differences between the dEGA and the MEGA are significant. Formally, and to a significant degree in practice, the Maharashtra Scheme, guarantees unlimited employment to all rural adults, provided there is a recognized need to the locality and people are willing to appear for work regularly. By contrast, the dEGA limits employment to one member from each BPL (below the poverty line) family as identified by the gram panchayat for a maximum period of 100 days in each year. The MEGA applies to all rural areas in the State, whereas the dEGA will be implemented, at least initially, only in the poorest 150 districts in the country. In Maharashtra, wages under the MEGA are tied to the minimum wages in the relevant agricultural zone. By contrast, the dEGA makes no reference to minimum wages. The scheme that follows from the MEGA is funded through a set of hypothecated taxes imposed on the urban population, and a matching grant from the State Government. The funding sources for the dEGA are still under consideration.

Some have also expressed that the current dEGA has serious weaknesses. First, the provision that the beneficiaries will be chosen on BPL criteria will result in the loss of the benefits that come from the self-targeting nature of the scheme. In particular, there will be little incentive for activists to mobilize the poor to access their rights; and the scheme is vulnerable to exclusion of the deserving. Secondly, there is no reference in the dEGA to tying wages to the legal minimum wage; if very low rates are offered, the programme will have no taker. Thirdly, the 'national' dEGA is to be implemented initially in only the poorest 150 of India's 593 districts, without a commitment to a timetable for extension to the whole country. Finally, the provision for unemployment allowance if work is not provided within the time period specified is likely to be meaningless if the experience of a similar allowance in Maharashtra is anything to go by. In more than 25 years since the MEGA's operation in Maharashtra, the unemployment allowance has not been paid even once.

Critics' Observations

The proposed Employment Generation Scheme is being hotly debated at various forums throughout the country. The critics point out that the Bill was dilution of what was promised by the United Progressive Alliance in the CMP on three counts. Now, the burden of implementing the scheme is on the states which are already facing a financial crunch, the scheme is, by and large, an extension of the Rural Development Programmes, and its application is limited to rural areas. The critics also raise the question of arranging such a huge fund for implementation of the scheme, though others opine that financing a universal EGS is far from being a daunting task. The annual expenditure on such a scheme is unlikely to exceed Rs.25,000 crores at present, or 1 per cent of GDP. This would not be a difficult to arrange. However, there are differences on who would foot the bill. According to them, the three players – the Planning Commission, the finance and rural development ministries do not see eye to eye on it. In fact, the differences on this issue have come into sharper focus with how the Budget treats two food-for-work programmes – an old one, the Sampoorna Gramin Rozgar Yojana (SGRY), and a new National Food for Work (NFW). Programme launched in November last for 150 backward districts. The new programme is supposed to be a precursor to the work guarantee Bill. Some say the two may eventually be merged. But some jugglery has already begun. Chidambaram's Budget gives less on paper in the coming year to SGRY and more to NFWP – about Rs. 4,000 crore for the first, down from this year, and Rs. 54,000 crore for the second. This is the cash component for both. The figures hide a battle. Rural Development Ministry sources say when the NFW programme was launched in 150 districts, there was an attempt to subsume the SGRY in those districts. The rural development ministry, administering both, protested the logic of this, SGRY functions through panchayats, the new programme doesn't I, says a source.

The noted economist Jean Dreze of Delhi University states that the Bill allows both the employment guarantee and the unemployment allowance to be restricted to "poor households". He raises the question about how the "poor households" are to be identified. The Bill defines poor households as those below the poverty line (BPL) in the relevant financial year. According to him this is little more than tautology, devoid of any practical guidance. He believes that in practice, state governments are likely to restrict the employment guarantee schemes to household with BPL card. But the BPL list is known to be highly unreliable, and this restriction, in his view, is bound to exclude many poor households from the scheme defeating the main purpose of employment guarantee, namely, to protect rural households from economic insecurity. Further, he apprehends that this approach is likely to intensify the pernicious social division between BPL and non-BPL households.

The EGS implementation would however not obviate the need for transfer of labour out of agriculture in the medium-term, where few have regular employment, most are self-employed or casual labourers. Much of the new regular jobs should be for low-skilled workers. This implies a growth strategy of manufactured exports requiring low-skilled labour and producing low-skill intensity goods for the domestic market. But with 222-million work force in agriculture, even a fast transfer out of agriculture will not pull all the working poor out of poverty. Hence direct employment creation through EGS is an essential component of policy.

Finally, Noble Laureate Prof. Amartya Sen, a supporter of

Maharashtra's employment guarantee programme, says "employment by itself does not add to the productive capabilities of people. Education, healthcare as well as expansion of physical infrastructure are needed to enhance the productivity". Hence the centre has to ensure first how resources will be generated and what will be the burden on the state.

It has been realized that India can sharply cut poverty in this decade with an employment guarantee. While the economic growth rate increased in the 1990s in the country, it was a process of jobless growth. It is believed that unless this pattern of growth changes, the momentum on poverty reduction may slow down in future and only employment intensive growth may make continued poverty reduction possible. There is also plenty of evidence that unemployment has many far-reaching effects other than loss of income leading to abject poverty, including psychological harm, loss of work motivation, skill and self-confidence, increase in ailments and morbidity (and even mortality rates), disruption of family relations and social life, hardening of social exclusion and accentuation of gender asymmetries.

Most significantly, the point is that employment generation schemes, if imaginatively conceived and properly implemented, can have very substantial effects in terms of creating conditions for much higher levels of economic activity and therefore growth, especially in the rural areas. To begin with, there are the obvious multiplier effects of such spending. Wage employment puts money in the hands of rural workers who are therefore able to spend on basic consumer items, which will play an important role in reviving local markets and rural industries. Since the entire rural economy is in severe depression, such a positive effect is very important, since it will create conditions for the further expansion of private economic activity in rural India. In addition, since the EGS will ensure public employment of a certain level for a continuous period, it will allow local authorities to plan and put such labour to the best possible use. These uses can include creating durable rural assets, water management and watershed development, activities designed to increase land productivity and create more sustainable agriculture with less chemical use, providing essential public services such as sanitation and mobilization for health purposes, providing mid-day meals in schools, and the like. All these not only ensure a better quality of life for rural residents; they also have critical effects in enabling future economic growth on a sustainable basis.

Ultimately, the EGS is a major move in the right direction. It can provide much-needed employment for the rural poor and can become the basis for the necessary regeneration of the rural economy, without which sustainable aggregate growth is not possible.

Budget 2005-06

The growth rate of the economy though high at nearly 7 per cent a year in recent years has not been generating enough jobs (at 1.5 per cent a year when the labour force is growing at 3 per cent) to progressively reduce the unemployment backlog, absorb excess farm labour into industry, and provide for the new entrants in the labour force. Moreover, the productivity of labour and capital is not growing fast enough. Answering the criticism of reforms ushering in such a type of a jobless growth, the Budget has announced concessions for industries that create employment. Job prospects are maximum in areas like IT, textile, food processing, construction and irrigation works. The existing Food-for-Work programme will get a boost as it will be covered under the National Rural Employment Guarantee Scheme.

As part of "Bharat Nirman" the government plans to provide additional 10 million hectare of irrigation, build 60 lakh houses for the rural poor and connect all villages with at least 1,000 residents in the plains and 500 in the hill areas with roads. There is a daring proposal to use part of the foreign exchange reserves, estimated at $ 132 billion, for developing infrastructure. For this the Budget proposes the creation of a special purpose vehicle, which can borrow up to Rs. 100 billion. This is the brainchild to Planning Commission Deputy Chairman Montek Singh Ahluwalia.

Where New Jobs Lie

- Nearly 12 million new jobs in textile sector by 2009.
- Additional 10 million irrigated hectares to create 10 million jobs.
- IT sector to create 70 lakh jobs over the next four years.
- Food processing to create 2.5 lakh jobs annually.
- Construction sector to create lakhs of jobs annually.
- Additional jobs in pharma, education and health sectors.

Land Reforms

Globally, nearly three-quarters of the poor live in rural areas and derive their livelihoods from agriculture and allied activities. In India, almost 60 per cent of the population is dependent on agriculture, and land is the primary resource on which agriculture is based. The initial assault on poverty even before independence was attempted to be made by ushering in Land Reforms by way of Zamindari Abolition Act. Ceiling on holding laws, Tenancy Legislation and distribution of Surplus land to landless poor. This could be said to be the first phase of Rural Development. It is a different point that the objective of Land to the Tiller, at best, had only a marginal success.

At the dawn of independence, the National Planning Committee (1948) of the Indian National Congress made an important recommendation that the achievement of a national minimum standard in respect of the essentials of individual and social well-being within a reasonable period must be pursued as the practical goals of all schemes for economic development. As land is the primary resource on which agriculture is based, the pattern of ownership of this has to be just and rational if we are to secure growth with social justice. The structure of land ownership is central to the well-being of the people. The objectives of the land reforms policy over the successive plans have been to remove such impediments to agricultural development as arise from the agrarian structure inherited from the past and to eliminate exploitation and social injustice within the agrarian system so as to ensure equality of tenurial status and opportunity for all. The main elements of land reforms policy have been five-fold, viz. (i) abolition of intermediary tenures; (ii) tenancy reforms comprising regulation of rent, security of tenures and conferment of ownership rights on tenants; (iii) ceiling on land holdings and distribution of surplus land; (iv) consolidation of holdings; and (v) compilation and updating of land records.

The Department of Land Resources in the Ministry of Rural Development has, therefore been playing a crucial role in evolving a national consensus for initiating effective land reforms which included abolition of zamindari system and all intermediaries since the beginning of the fifties, introduction of family ceiling in the mid-fifties, reduction of the ceiling limit, consolidation of land holdings and monitoring of the progress of the distribution of ceiling surplus land as part of the 20 point programme of the Government of India.

Land is a critically important national resource. Its efficient management is vital for economic growth and development of rural areas. Concerted efforts are being made through Area Development Programmes of Department of Land Resources such as Integrated Wastelands Development Programme (IWDP), Dorught Prone Areas Programme (DPAP) and Desert Development Programme (DDP) to regenerate and rejuvenate wastelands and degraded lands. All the Area Development Programmes are being implemented through the Watershed Development approach.

Presently, 972 Blocks of 182 Districts in 16 States are covered under DPAP. Similarly, 235 Blocks of 40 Districts in 7 States are covered under DDP. The coverage under Integrated Wastelands Development Programmes (IWDP) extends generally to Blocks that are not covered in the above Programmes.

In addition, it has been administering the Land Acquisition Act, 1894. For the purpose of strengthening of Survey and Settlement Operations and updation of land records and other allied matters, a Centrally Sponsored Scheme of Strengthening of Revennue Administration and Updating of Land Records is under implementation in collaboration with the State Governments.

The Department of Land Resources of the Ministry has brought out a new initiative on 27th January, 2003 called

'Haryali' with an objective of empowering PRIs, both financially and administratively, in implementation of Watershed Development Programmes in the country. Under this new initiative, all ongoing area development programmes, namely IWDP, DPAP and DDP would be implemented through the PRIs. New Projects under the on-going area development programmes are being implemented in accordance with the guidelines for "Haryali" w.e.f. 1-4-2003.

Agrarian reforms have been a core issue for Rural Reconstruction, ensuring social justice to actual tillers and landless rural poor, thereby creating a sustainable base for the overall growth of the industrial and tertiary sectors of our economy. Generating greater access to landless rural poor to land is considered an important component of poverty alleviation. The abolition of intermediaries immediately after Independence, in spite of its many well-documented shortcomings and lack of implementation in certain parts of the country, was significant and covered close to 40 per cent of the cultivated area (*vide* Tenth Five Year Plan Document, Vol. II).

However, the lack of progress in the other components of the land reforms programme, viz., implementation of land ceiling laws, security of tenure to tenants and consolidation of land holdings, remains yet a matter of concern. The SC/STs, who constitute the bulk of the labour force, do not have either the assets or the skills to participate in the limited but emerging employment opportunities in different sectors of the economy. The problem is further compounded by the fact that though the contribution of agriculture to GDP has nearly halved from over 50 per cent in 1951 to around 25 per cent in 2000-01 and 20 per cent during 2003-04, a similar transformation of employment opportunities has not taken place. The number of people dependent on agriculture and allied activities has fallen only 12 percentage points – from 71 per cent of the population in 1951 to 59 per cent in 2001 (*vide* Tenth Five Year Plan Document, Vol. II).

It is distressing to point out that since 1990s land reforms appear to have been relegated to the background. Lately, initiatives of State Governments have related to liberalization of land laws in order to promote large scale corporate farming. This is in sharp contrast to the policy environment created soon after Independence when land reforms were meant to provide ownership rights to small and marginal farmers on equity considerations. Though the pressure of populations has led to further sub-division and fragmentation of land holdings, thereby considerably weakening the case for further lowering of land ceilings, the need for effective implementation of the existing land ceiling laws cannot be over-emphasized. The Ninth Plan had laid strong emphasis on agrarian restructuring to make agriculture more efficient leading to increased "output and employment". However, progress of different components of the land reforms package during the Plan has been extremely limited. There has also been no progress in the detection of concealed land and the distribution to the landless rural poor.

Status of progresses in respect of a few components of land reforms till 31st March, 2002 is shown in Annexures 2.I to 2.IV. Various Rural Development and Poverty Alleviation Programmes implemented by the Ministry of Rural Development Government of India and their year-wise outlays and expenditures are also indicated in Annexures 2.V and 2.VI

Panchayati Raj as a Developmental Vehicle and Food Security

Having a close link with the rural fabric, Panchayats with their network are most suited to undertake responsibility not only in enhancing agricultural production, but also ensuring food security by streamlining the PDS – a most abused system as at present. The 11th Schedule of the Constitution has recommended vital areas of agricultural operation to be brought under the panchayats: (1) Agriculture, including agricultural extension, (2) Land, improvement, implementation of land reforms, land consolidation and soil conservation, (3) Minor irrigation, water management and watershed development, (4) Animal husbandry, dairying and poultry, and (5) Fisheries.

They are also entrusted with the responsibility of preparing plans for economic development and social justice in respect of these areas and are expected to act as the implementation agencies of schemes and plans related to these areas. Such institutions can serve as an effective medium for bringing about technology transfers in the areas of agriculture. Being in close contact with ground realities they can ensure that inputs meet local requirements. Also they can provide valuable feedback for agricultural universities and research institutes to help develop technology and inputs suited to regional variations.

The importance of land reforms in ensuring higher production and thus contributing to food security cannot be overstated. Land reforms provide the rural poor (small and marginalized farmers) with greater income and consequently enhanced purchasing power. The State of West Bengal is the best example. The land reforms through the famous operation barga was successful because of "pressure from below", i.e., the Panchayati Raj Institutions. PRI's in West Bengal were crucial in sustaining grassroots pressure in favour of the reforms during their first term (1978-1983). The extent of land reforms in West Bengal can be gauged from the fact that while Bengal has only 3.5 per cent of the country's cultivable land, it contributed 20.77 per cent of the total ceiling surplus land distributed in the country. The beneficial impact of land reforms on agriculture is evident from the significant improvement in agricultural production in the post-1983 period, when panchayati raj had established itself. If the growth of rice production in West Bengal in 1950-60 was 1.01 per cent, it reached 6.41 in 1980-81[1]. A visit to West Bengal country side is a refreshing experience where one can see the linkage between increased agricultural production, land utilization and relatively self-content village population dependent on agriculture related activities and vibrant Panchayati Raj system. Functions performed by line departments are now brought under the gram panchayats and in close proximity with community problems, giving space for constructive activity.

Greater involvement of Panchayati Raj Institutions with the PDS can again help in ensuring food reaching the needy and that is why the PDS has been explicitly included in the list provided in the 11th Schedule. In order to actualize this provision there is a need for furthering experiments like that attempted in the Keonjhar district of Orissa. Under section 44 (1) (x-3) of Orissa Gram Panchayat Act, 1965; PDS is an obligatory function of the gram panchayat, within the limits of funds, to undertake control, administer and be responsible for the PDS in the village. Making use of this provision the gram panchayats in Keonjhar were entrusted with the retail of the goods through the PDS by replacing private retailers. Observers argue that this not only helped generate funds for the panchayats but also brought down corruption drastically by bringing in greater transparency and accountability[2].

In the case of Rajasthan, the government has been utilizing the Gram Sabha as a public forum for selecting people below poverty line (BPL) for the purpose of the Integrated Rural Development Programme (IRDP). Under the "Annapurna" scheme Gram Panchayats are to identify, prepare and display a list of beneficiaries after wide publicity. It has been observed that the BPL identification process by the Gram Sabha has been generally fair and in conformity with the programmatic guidelines.

The recently published report of the Task Force on Devolution of Powers and Function upon Panchayati Raj Institutions has identified the various functions that can be performed by different tiers of PRIs[3]. The report sought to give concrete share to activities to be performed by PRIs under the PDS. They are: (1) Availability and movement of essential commodities and demand assessment under the PDS programme; (2) Transport, storage and delivery system; (3) Vigilance and enforcement aspects; (4) Linking PDS with poverty alleviation programmes. Within these broad activity areas the report seeks to identify tasks that can be performed by each tier. An analysis of these taks reveals that District Panchayats have been generally deemed to be suitable for performing overall planning and assessment tasks. Thus, for instance, District Panchayat has been assigned the task of preparing a district map of PDS outlets and deciding the opening of new shops. Intermediate level panchayats can assist in the performance of these planning and assessment tasks by undertaking these activities in the areas under their jurisdiction and also providing a link between District Panchayats and Gram Panchayats.

The task assigned to Gram Panchayats are more related to supervision and control of functioning of Fair Price Shops (FPS). Being closest to the people, it seems as crucial in identifying the beneficiaries as well as eliminating bogus ration cardholders. The Report of the Task Force contains no major surprises. As early as January, 2000 the Ministry for Consumer Affairs and Public Distribution had released a six-point action plan empowering the Gram Panchayats to supervise and regulate the working of Fair Price Shops. The Report of the Task Force is, however, a comprehensive attempt at giving shape to the activities of the PRIs while also delineating the various powers and sources of finance which need to be devolved with each activity. In that sense the latest report in some ways represents the collective wisdom gained by the afore mentioned initiatives and experiments as well as the critical role of the local self government institutions in this vital area.

Access to Food

Increased income generation amongst the rural poor is a *sine qua non* for ensuring food security. For it is only if the people have adequate purchasing power can they have economic access to the food requirements. The recent starvation deaths in Kashipur, Orissa highlight the disastrous consequences of inadequate purchasing power amongst the rural poor. It also highlights the failure of welfare and development schemes initiated from above without giving power to the people through the panchayats. The PRIs can help break the nexus between the corrupt local officials and the rural elite by both empowering the weak and marginalized sections of society and bringing in greater accountability and transparency. As is well known PRIs provide an excellent opportunity for ensuring greater participation of the hitherto marginalized sections of society. Panchayati Raj Institutions can further ensure accountability of Fair Price Shops and the PDS system through effectively implementing the right to information and by conducting social audit.

The Finance Minister, Mr. P. Chidambaram, in fact argued in favour of replacing the PDS with "food-for-work" programmes run by panchayats[4]. These programmes are crucial for ensuring the food security of the rural poor who have neither work nor food. However, in order to ensure that these programmes are effectively implemented Mr. Chidambaram had called for a greater role for panchayats than that has been hitherto assigned to them. He argued that adequate quantity of wheat or paddy should be transported to the drought-affected areas and the stock should be entrusted to the panchayats. The panchayats should then decide what works they should take up and fix the wage for each unit of work in terms of wheat or rice. Thus, the goals of rural development and food security would be met simultaneously by the panchayats.

Rajiv Gandhi Grameen Vidyutikaran Yojana

On 4th April, 2005, the Government of India has launched a new scheme for rural electricity infrastructure and household electrification under the above Yojana. The scheme aims at:

- Electrifying all villages and habitations;
- Providing access to electricity to all households; and
- Providing electricity connection to BPL families free of charge.

The above goals to be achieved within a period of 5 years through creation of:

- Rural Electricity Distribution Bone (REDB);
- Village Electrification Infrastructure (VEI); and
- Decentralised Distributed Generation (DDG) Systems.

The scheme, once implemented, is anticipated to accelerate rural development through:

- Irrigation Pumpsets,
- Village Industries,
- Cold Chains,
- Healthcare,
- Education and Information Technology.

The National Rural Health Mission (NRHM)

The National Rural Health Mission (NRHM) is a response to the verdict of the May 2004 general elections which led to the conceptualization of a set of pro-poor policies under the Common Minimum Programme (CMP). This mission, launched by the Union Government on April 12, 2005 could help correct the gross neglect of the healthcare needs of the rural people. It has, however, begun on a rather tentative note. For a long time a need has been felt for volunteers to mobilize communities to prevent diseases, promote health and thus improve the quality of life. The Community Health Workers (CHWs) Scheme launched in 1978 was seen as an option to fulfill this need. However, the scheme failed to achieve its objectives and was discontinued in most states. Many states have attempted to fill in the void by having different variants of CHWs such as the Jan Mangal Volunteers in Rajasthan, Jan Swasthya Rakshaks in Madhya Pradesh, Mitanins in Chattisgarh and Pada Workers in Maharashtra. Several NGOs are also organsing comprehensive health programmes putting into optimum use local human resources.

Indian Health System is perhaps guilty of many sins of omissions and commission ... that we have grievously erred in the design of our many health programmes. A fatal flaw in the approach had been that comprehensive health care and a public health perspective had been gradually abandoned for focused attention on selective diseases. NRHM would address the absence of a residential healthcare provider in every village. Patients have to travel to a nearby PHC for even minor problems like a small wound, ordinary diarrhoea or fever. People tend to stay at home and seek help only when the situation deteriorates. It aims to provide healthcare facilities to the poor by making architectural correction in the basic healthcare delivery system.

In order to avoid the same fate as of the 1978 CHW scheme, the Government of India (GOI) is in the process of supporting a band of community-based women volunteers known as ASHAs (Accredited Social Health Assistants). It has been envisaged that each village in the Empowered Action Group and other states will have an ASHA. Scheme guidelines are being finalized to reflect their roles and responsibilities, selection criteria and process, and training and support systems for ASHA's.

Bharat Nirman Scheme

The Prime Minister cleared Rs. 1,74,000 crore to be spent over four years to build rural infrastructure including telecom connectivity (May 2005). The Bharat Nirman Project focuses on six critical areas such as irrigation, roads, water supply, housing and rural electrification besides telecom.

Bharat Nirman will bring an additional 10 million hectares under assured irrigation, connect all villages with a population of 1,000 (or 500 in hilly/tribal areas) with a road; construct 60 lakh houses for the poor, provide drinking water to over 74,000 new habitations; reach electricity to 1,25,000 villages that still do not have electricity and offer electricity connection to 2.3 crore households; and give telephone connectivity to the remaining 66,822 villages.

'Bharat Nirman' is the most important initiative of the UPA government this year, offering a new deal to rural India, the Prime Minister was quoted as saying in an official statement. It will emphasize outcomes and not just outlays. The system should not become a constraint on ability to deliver. Bharat Nirman should be implemented with a sense of urgency.

Decentralised Planning – Fortifying Food Security

The preceding discussion highlights the numerous ways in which PRIs can contribute to ensuring food security. These are, however, unlikely to materialize or lead to long-term benefits if unaccompanied by a genuine empowerment of the people at the grassroots levels. It is impossible to imagine starvation deaths in a community where local bodies have the autonomy and the power to decide their development priorities, projects and their implementation and the entitlements of the poor. For no sensitive community today is likely to condemn its members to starvation. Empowerment of local communities through grassroots democracy, decentralized planning is, therefore, the best guarantee of food security. The experience of Kerala in the last five years highlights the fact that if there is scientific, participatory planning from below, decentralization is the best means of ensuring the development of the people including enhanced food production.

In 1996 the LDF government in Kerala, for the first time in the country decided to earmark 35-40 per cent of the outlay of the states Ninth Five Year Plan for the local bodies. Moreover, in order to ensure maximum autonomy for local bodies it decided to provide 75 per cent of the funds in the form of grant-in-aid as 'united'. The only restriction was that the local bodies should spend at least 40 per cent on productive sector (agriculture and allied activities, industries and self-employment, etc.). Through peoples plan campaign a decentralized approach to planning was developed which highlighted the differences that existed between the peoples perception of their needs and priorities and those perceived by a centralized bureaucracy. A comparative analysis of the decentralized plan prepared by the panchayats with that of the state that existed earlier, reveals the shift in priorities. Local bodies gave a much higher priority to agriculture than the state plan – 19 per cent of the local outlay compared to 10.5 per cent in the state plan[5].

Animal husbandry received a greater share (7.57%) which is significant considering that dairy farming in Kerala is not undertaken on a large scale commercial basis[6]. It was found that ideally it suited raising of income of small and marginal farmers. Numerous case studies are indicative of how agricultural productivity can be boosted through the efforts of PRIs. For instance, the Kanjikuzhy Panchayat (Alappuzha, Kerala) has successfully revived the traditional vegetable cultivation. Technical input and guidance was provided by the Krishi Bhavan while the panchayat provided the funds and mobilized the community through an awareness and mass contact programme. The programme was a resounding success. A drop in the local prices of vegetables to the extent of 20-30 per cent was observed during the 3 month harvest period. Similarly, minor irrigation projects and other infrastructural support for agriculture received greater attention. This illustrates the priority people place on food security. Thus, given a chance they can to a large extent ensure food security for the local community provided the local government institutions are empowered to plan and execute projects required to meet their needs and priorities. At the implementation stage, in order to ensure accountability and transparency several measures were taken up resulting in less corruption and "leakages". Thus, decentralization ensured that development programmes not only reflected people's priorities to a greater extent but also increased their efficacy. This is significant for, as shift in priorities discussed above indicated, food security is a priority area for the people, particularly the rural poor.

Epilogue

All said and done, poverty eradication from the country has still remained an unfinished task, though there has been laudable progress after more than five decades of implementation of various poverty alleviation programmes. Starting from the first poverty estimates of 1972-73 when 51.5 per cent of the population was estimated below the poverty line, this came down to 35.97 per cent by 1993-94. According the latest estimate of 1999-2000 (55th round), this number has further been reduced to 26.10 per cent on a 30 day recall method (Annexure 2.VII) and 23.33 per cent on a 7 day recall method (Annexure 2.VIII). Thus nearly a quarter of the population is still below the poverty line which is a sad commentary on our five decade effort of elimination of poverty. The latest estimate is, however, being contested by many economists about which we have discussed in the next chapter.

The undying myth of development, that it will remove all poverty for ever from all corners of the world, now lies shattered. It is surprising that so many people believed it for so many years with such admirable innocence. Even societies that have witnessed unprecedented prosperity during the last five decades, such as US, have not been able to exile either poverty or destitution from within their borders. The world GNP has grown many times in the last 50 years; even more spectacular has been the growth of prosperity in the US. Yet, more than 11 per cent of its citizens—the figure, according to some, rose to something like 18 per cent a decade ago—have more or less consistently stayed in poverty throughout almost the entire period of American hyper-prosperity.

In this context, it may also be stated that no per capita income figures, no indices of calorie consumption can however capture the wretchedness that is lot of the poor, whether destitute amidst the dust of rural India or begging the side-walks of its teeming cities. To be poor is to be born of a malnourished mother in conditions where his survival is uncertain; to survive with inadequate food, clothing and shelter, without the stimulation of learning or play; to grow unequipped intellectually or physically to be productive member of a striving society. We have failed in many cases to identify the real poor and why they are poor and many of our poverty alleviation programmes have only benefited the contractors and bureaucrats.

ANNEXURE 2.I

Consolidation of Land Holdings—State-wise as on March 2002

(*Area in Lakh Acres*)

Sl. No.	*States/UTs*	*Area Consolidated*
1.	Andhra Pradesh	8.18*
2.	Bihar	96.05*
3.	Gujarat	69.98*
4.	Haryana	104.38
5.	Himachal Pradesh	29.91
6.	Jammu & Kashmir	1.37*
7.	Karnataka	26.76#
8.	Madhya Pradesh	95.53
9.	Maharashtra	526.50$
10.	Orissa	26.74
11.	Punjab	121.81
12.	Rajasthan	42.30@
13.	Uttar Pradesh	481.63
14.	Delhi	2.33
	TOTAL	1633.47

* Scheme has been discontinued (in Andhra Pradesh from 1966, in Bihar and Gujarat from 1992).

Consolidation of holding Act, 1966 has been repealed in 1991.

@ Scheme discontinued from 1965.

$ Implementation of the scheme stopped w.e.f. 1.4.1993.

Source: Annual Report 2002-2003, Government of India, Ministry of Rural Development.

ANNEXURE 2.II

Alienation and Restoration of Tribal Lands

Sl. No.	*States*	*No. of cases filed in the court*	*Area*	*Cases Disposed of by the Court*	*Area*	*Cases Rejected*	*Area*	*Cases Decided in favour of Tribals*	*Area*	*Cases in which land was restored to tribals*	*Area*	*Cases pending in Court*	*Area*
1	*2*	*3*	*4*	*5*	*6*	*7*	*8*	*9*	*10*	*11*	*12*	*13*	*14*
1.	Andhra Pradesh	65875	287776	58212	256452	31737	150227	26475	106225	23383	94312	7663	31324
2.	Assam	2042	4211	50	19	–	–	50	19	50	19	1992	4192
3.	Bihar	86291	104893	76518	95151	31884	49730	44634	45421	44634	45421	9773	9742
4.	Gujarat	47926	140324	40400	120691	119	497	40281	120194	39503	118259	7526	19633
5.	Himachal Pradesh	NEGLIGIBLE											
6.	Karnataka	42582	130373	38521	115021	16687	47159	21834	67862	21834	67862	4061	15352
7.	Madhya Pradesh	53806	158398	29596	97123	29596	97123	NR	NR	NR	NR	24210	61275
8.	Maharashtra	45634	NR	44624	99486	24681	NR	19943	99486	19943	99486	1010	NR
9.	Orissa	1431	1712	594	816	152	204	442	612	212	455	837	896
10.	Rajasthan	651	2300	240	774	53	187	187	587	187	587	411	1526
11.	Tripura	28926	25295	28888	25274	20084	18366	8804	6908	8551	6732	38	21
	TOTAL	375164	855282	317643	810807	154993	363493	162650	447314	158297	433133	57521	143961

Source: Annual Report 2002-2003, Government of India, Ministry of Rural Development.

ANNEXURE 2.III

Alienation and Restoration of Tribal Lands

(Area in acres)

Sl. No.	*States/UTs*	*Area Declared surplus*	*Area Taken possession benef.*	*Area Distributed to indv.*	*Total No. of benef.*	*SC/ST Beneficiaries*				*Other Beneficiaries*	
						SC Beneficiaries		*ST Beneficiaries*			
						No.	*Area*	*No.*	*Area*	*No.*	*Area*
1	2	3	4	5	6	7	8	9	10	11	12
1.	Andhra Pradesh	799663	641655	582319	540344	225932	231179	83688	121085	230724	230055
2.	Assam	613400	575377	545870	445848	43720	86068	42361	58985	359767	400817
3.	Bihar	415447	390752	306964	379528	234861	182045	43050	39978	101617	84941
4.	Gujarat	227404	160801	139853	32308	14915	84467	13267	29608	4126	25778
5.	Haryana	107487	103017	102123	29228	12522	43405	NA	NA	16706	58718
6.	Himachal Pradesh	316556	304895	6167	6259	3912	2727	329	245	2018	3195
7.	Jammu & Kashmir	455575	450000	450000	450000	NA	NA	NA	NA	450000	450000
8.	Karnataka	268478	161834	123204	33610	20285	73991	1248	4331	12077	44882
9.	Kerala	141427	96851	68745	166814	70853	26619	8990	7248	86971	34878
10.	Madhya Pradesh	298763	260323	186942	74705	21904	49542	28138	73379	24663	64021
11.	Maharashtra	740002	670449	642835	140850	42128	163742	29528	98675	69194	380418

(Contd.)

(Contd.)

Sl. No.	States/UTs	Area Declared surplus	Area Taken possession benef.	Area Distributed to indv.	Total No. of benef.	SC/ST Beneficiaries				Other Beneficiaries	
						SC Beneficiaries		ST Beneficiaries			
						No.	Area	No.	Area	No.	Area
1	2	3	4	5	6	7	8	9	10	11	12
12.	Manipur	1830	16885	1682	1258	96	128	72	97	1090	1457
13.	Orissa	179176	167253	156948	139595	48059	49975	51390	65682	40146	41291
14.	Punjab	223115	105834	104232	28574	11351	44247	NA	NA	17223	59985
15.	Rajasthan	611096	569211	461847	81808	29656	144357	11586	49957	40566	267533
16.	Tamil Nadu	200920	191628	181295	143683	64239	68704	204	274	79240	112317
17.	Tripura	1995	1944	1598	1424	256	217	359	448	809	933
18.	Uttar Pradesh	374125	341464	258698	294062	200320	180193	699	1195	93043	77310
19.	West Bengal	1383852	1294739	1064044	2651619	983829	365283	512156	221365	1155634	477396
20.	D & N Haveli	9406	9305	6851	3353	30	53	3321	6795	2	3
21.	Delhi	1132	394	394	654	495	277	NA	NA	159	117
22.	Pondicherry	2326	1209	1070	1464	858	640	NA	NA	606	430
	TOTAL	7373175	6500620	5393681	5646988	2030221	1797859	830386	779347	2786381	2816475

Source: Annual Report 2002-2003, Government of India, Ministry of Rural Development.

ANNEXURE 2.IV

Number of Tenants Conferred Ownership Rights (or Rights Protected) and Area Accrued to Them (As on 31-3-2002)

Sl. No.	*States*	*No. of Tenants (in lakhs)*	*Area Accrued (lakh acres)*
1.	Andhra Pradesh	1.07	5.95
2.	Arunachal Pradesh	System not prevalent	
3.	Assam	29.08	31.75
4.	Bihar*	NR	NR
5.	Gujarat	12.76	25.92
6.	Goa	NR	NR
7.	Haryana	Tenancy not prevalent	
8.	Himachal Pradesh	4.01	NR
9.	Jammu & Kashmir	6.10	NR
10.	Karnataka	6.05	26.32
11.	Kerala	28.42	14.50
12.	Madhya Pradesh #	Tenancy not prevalent	
13.	Maharashtra	14.92	42.90
14.	Manipur	NR	NR
15.	Meghalaya	Nil	Nil
16.	Mizoram	Nil	Nil
17.	Nagaland	NR	NR
18.	Orissa	1.65	0.98
19.	Punjab	NR	NR
20.	Rajasthan	0.18	NR
21.	Sikkim	NR	NR
22.	Tamil Nadu	4.98	6.95
23.	Tripura	0.14	0.39
24.	Uttar Pradesh@	NR	NR
25.	West Bengal	14.60	NR
	Union Territories		
26.	Andaman and Nicobar Island	Nil	Nil
27.	Chandigarh	NR	NR
28.	D & N Haveli	0.26	0.64
29.	Delhi	NR	NR
30.	Daman and Diu	NR	NR
31.	Lakshadweep	Neg	Neg
32.	Pondicherry	Neg	Neg
	ALL INDIA	124.22	156.30

NR: Not reported.

*Including Jharkhand, # Including Chhattisgarh @ Including Uttaranchal.

Source: Annual Report 2002-2003, Government of India, Ministry of Rural Development.

ANNEXURE 2.V

Poverty Alleviation Programme

			year
1.	National Extension and Community Development Programme	CDP	Oct. 1952
2.	Village Housing Scheme	VHS	1957
3.	Rural Manpower Employment Programme	RMEP	1960
4.	Drought Prone Area Programme	DPAP	1970-71
5.	Crash Scheme for Rural Employment	CSRE	1971-72
6.	Rural Water Supply Programme	RWS	1972-73
7.	Pilot Intensive Rural Employment Programme	PIREP	1972-73
8.	Minimum Needs Programme	MNP	1974-75
9.	Food for Work Programme	FWP	1977-78 Merged into NREP & RLEGP
10.	Desert Development Programme	DDP	1977-78
11.	Training for Rural Youth for Self-Employment	TRYSEM	15th Aug. 1979 Employment. Merged with SGSY in April 1999
12.	Integrated Rural Development Programme	IRDP	1980 Merged with SGSY in April, 1999.
13.	National Rural Employment Programme	NREP	1980 Merged with JRY from April 1989.
14.	Distribution of Surplus Land	DSL	1980
15.	Development of Woman and Child in Rural Area	DWCRA	1982-83 Merged with SGSY in April 99
16.	Rural Landless Employment Guarantee Programme	RLEGP	1983 merged with JRY from April 1989

(*Contd.*)

			year
17.	Council for Advancement of Rural Technology	CART	1983
18.	People's Action for Development of India	PADI	1983
19.	Rural Roads Programme	RRP	During 5th Plan
20.	National Wasteland Development Board	NWDB	1985
21.	Council for Advancement of Peoples Action for Rural Technology	CAPART	1986 By merging PADI & CART
22.	Central Rural Sanitation Programme	CRSP	1986
23.	National Drinking Water Mission	NDWM	1986
24.	Jawahar Rozgar Yojana	JRY	April 1989 Merged with JGSY
25.	Integrated Watersheds Development Programme	IWDP	1989-90
26.	Supply of Improved Tool Kits to Rural Artisans	SITRA	July 1992 Merged with SGSY In April 1999
27.	National Social Assistance Programme	NSAP	1990
28.	Rajiv Gandhi National Drinking Water Mission	RGNDWM	1991 (NDWM renamed)
29.	Employment Assurance Scheme	EAS	1993
30.	Intensified JRY	IJRY	1993 Merged with EAS in 1996.
31.	Rural Employment Generation Programme	REGP	1995
32.	National Old Age Pension Scheme	NOAPS	15th Aug.1995
33.	National Family Benefit Scheme	NFBS	15th Aug.1995
34.	National Maternity Benefit Scheme	NMBS	15th Aug.1995
35.	Indira Awaas Yojana (Sub-Scheme of IRDP)	IAY	Jan.1996 (Merged with SGSY)
36.	Million Wells Scheme	MWS	Jan.1996
37.	Ganga Kalyan Yojana	GKY	1997

(*Contd.*)

			year
38.	Swarn Jayanti Shehari Rozgar Yojana	SJSRY	Dec. 1997
39.	National Housing and Habitat Policy	NHHP	1998
40.	National Mission for Rural Household	NMRHH	1998
41.	Rural Building Centres	RBCs	1998
42.	Swarnajayanti Gram Swarojgar Yojana	SGSY	April 1999
43.	Jawahar Gram Samridhi Yojana	JGSY	April 1999
44.	Pradhan Mantri Gram Sadak Yojana	PMGSY	Dec. 2000
45.	Annapurna Yojana	AY	2000
46.	Antyodaya Anna Yojana	AAY	2000
47.	Pradhan Mantri Gramodaya Yojana	PMGY	2000-01
48.	Sampoorna Gramin Rozgar Yojana	SGRY	Sept. 2001
49.	Valmiki Ambedkar Awaas Yojana	VAMBAY	Dec. 2001
50.	Swajal Dhara	SD	Dec.25, 2002
51.	Hariyali	H	Jany. 27, 2003
52.	National Food for Work Programme	NFWP	Nov. 2004
53.	National Employment Guarantee programme	NEGP	Proposed-2005
54.	Rajiv Gandhi Grameen Vidyutikaran Yojana	RGGVY	April-2005

ANNEXURE 2.VI

Expenditure on C.D./Rural Development Programme

(*Rs. Crores*)

	C. Development/ RDP		*Land Reforms*		*Special Area Programme*		*Total*
	Outlays	*Actual*	*Outlays*	*Actual*	*Outlays*	*Actual*	
1951-56		116					116
1956-61		197					197
1961-66	288						288
1966-69	99						99
1969-74		115.2					115.2
1974-78		99.3		126.7			226.0
1978-79		40.8		47.0			87.8
1979-80	58.6		48.3				106.9
1980-81		887.8		44.6		206.4	1138.8
1981-82		919.9		52.9		258.5	1231.3
1982-83		1076.2		62.3		335.1	1473.6
1983-84		1263.6		66.6		356.9	1687.1
1984-85		1845.8		77.5		423.6	2346.9
1985-86		2151.20		74.90		447.30	2673.40
1986-87		2586.80		80.80		627.60	3295.20
1987-88		3049.10		97.40		677.10	3823.60
1988-89		2875.01		107.33		926.51	3908.85
1989-90		4079.30		144.69		791.86	5015.85
1990-91		4007.43		142.51		986.33	5136.27
1991-92		3984.91		156.68		1067.28	5208.87
1992-93		4830.58		179.39		1153.91	6163.88
1993-94		6860.74		172.62		1363.59	8396.95
1994-95		8506.31		210.79		1428.24	10145.34
1995-96		9225.67		248.61		1780.18	11254.46
1996-97	10756.67		285.65		1824.66		12866.98
1997-98	6805.20	9759.08					
1998-1999	7280.99	10322.55					
1999-2000	7517.00		324.00				
2000-2001	6760.00		900.00				
2001-2002	9205.00		900.00				
2002-2003	10270.00		1000.00				
2003-2004	10270.00		1050.00				

* Anticipated.

Note: This represents only the expenditure incurred under the Ministry of Rural Development under the above heads. Assuming Rs. 13000 crore as the budget for 1997-98, the total upto the 8th Plan and works out to Rs. 90,000 crores.

ANNEXURE 2.VII

Number and Percentage of Population Below Poverty Line by States, 1999-2000 (7-day Recall Method)

Sl. No.	*States*	*Rural*		*Urban*		*Combined*	
		No. Persons (Lakhs)	*% of Persons*	*No. Persons (Lakhs)*	*% of Persons*	*% of Persons*	*% of Persons*
	(1)	*(2)*	*(3)*	*(4)*	*(5)*	*(6)*	*(7)*
1.	Andhra Pradesh	48.14	9.15	55.96	24.48	104.10	13.79
2.	Arunachal Pradesh	3.23	34.00	0.15	6.29	3.38	28.41
3.	Assam	78.27	34.00	2.00	6.29	80.27	30.64
4.	Bihar	322.96	38.00	43.64	29.23	366.60	36.69
5.	Goa	0.23	2.80	0.40	5.03	0.62	3.90
6.	Gujarat	36.87	12.20	24.80	13.76	61.66	12.78
7.	Haryana	11.13	7.71	4.33	8.02	15.46	7.79
8.	Himachal Pradesh	4.63	7.61	0.24	3.95	4.88	7.27
9.	Jammu & Kashmir	3.10	4.14	0.42	1.70	3.52	3.53
10.	Karnataka	47.02	13.64	39.35	22.23	86.36	16.58
11.	Kerala	18.20	8.14	17.73	17.91	35.93	11.14
12.	Madhya Pradesh	202.78	34.58	74.93	35.46	277.70	34.81
13.	Maharashtra	109.25	20.71	96.81	25.23	206.05	22.61
14.	Manipur	5.54	34.00	0.56	6.29	6.10	24.21
15.	Meghalaya	6.70	34.00	0.29	6.29	6.99	28.75
16.	Mizoram	1.19	34.00	0.38	6.29	1.57	16.50
17.	Nagaland	4.42	34.00	0.24	6.29	4.66	27.73
18.	Orissa	131.63	43.98	23.92	40.33	155.55	43.38
19.	Punjab	8.53	5.31	4.03	5.40	12.56	5.34
20.	Rajasthan	48.97	12.22	25.36	18.80	74.33	13.88
21.	Sikkim	1.70	34.00	0.04	6.29	1.74	31.03
22.	Tamil Nadu	73.19	18.68	45.81	20.27	119.00	19.26
23.	Tripura	10.64	34.00	0.41	6.29	11.05	29.24
24.	Uttar Pradesh	379.41	28.75	110.82	29.04	490.23	28.82
25.	West Bengal	154.04	27.24	31.06	13.83	185.10	23.43
26.	Andaman & Nicobar Islands	0.52	18.68	0.22	20.27	0.75	19.13

(Contd.)

Sl. No.	*States*	*Rural*		*Urban*		*Combined*	
		No. Persons (Lakhs)	*% of Persons*	*No. Persons (Lakhs)*	*% of Persons*	*% of Persons*	*% of Persons*
	(1)	*(2)*	*(3)*	*(4)*	*(5)*	*(6)*	*(7)*
27.	Chandigarh	0.06	5.40	0.42	5.40	0.48	5.40
28.	Dadra & Nagar Haveli	0.26	15.31	0.02	10.89	0.28	14.84
29.	Daman & Diu	0.02	2.80	0.04	5.03	0.05	3.92
30.	Delhi	0.12	0.63	6.52	5.38	6.64	4.75
31.	Lakshadweep	0.02	8.14	0.07	17.91	0.10	13.72
32.	Pondicherry	0.58	18.68	1.62	20.27	2.20	19.83
	ALL INDIA	1713.35	24.02	612.57	21.59	2325.92	23.33

Notes: Poverty Ratio of Assam is used for Sikkim, Arunachal Pradesh, Maghalaya, Mizoram, Manipur, Nagaland and Tripura.

Poverty Line of Maharashtra and expenditure distribution of Goa is used to estimate poverty ratio of Goa.

Poverty Line of Himachal Pradesh and Expenditure distribution of Jammu & Kashmir is used to estimate poverty ratio of Jammu & Kashmir.

Poverty Ratio of Tamil Nadu is used for Pondicherry and A & N Island. Urban Poverty Ratio of Punjab used for both rural and urban poverty of Chandigarh. Poverty Line of Maharashtra and expenditure distribution of Dadra & Nagar Haveli is used to estimate poverty ratio of Dadra and Nagar Haveli. Poverty Raio of Goa is used for Daman & Diu Poverty Ratio of Kerala is used for Lakshadweep.

Urban Poverty Ratio of Rajasthan may be treated as tentative.

Source: Planning Commission.

ANNEXURE 2.VIII

Number and Percentage of Population Below Poverty Line by States, 1999-2000 (30-day Recall Method)

Sl. No.	*States*	*Rural*		*Urban*		*Combined*	
		No. Persons (Lakhs)	*% of Persons*	*No. Persons (Lakhs)*	*% of Persons*	*No. Persons (Lakhs)*	*% of Persons*
	(1)	*(2)*	*(3)*	*(4)*	*(5)*	*(6)*	*(7)*
1.	Andhra Pradesh	58.13	11.05	60.88	26.63	119.01	15.77
2.	Arunachal Pradesh	3.80	40.04	0.18	7.47	3.98	33.47
3.	Assam	92.17	40.04	2.38	7.47	94.55	36.09
4.	Bihar	376.51	44.30	49.13	32.91	425.64	42.60
5.	Goa	0.11	1.35	0.59	7.52	0.70	4.40
6.	Gujarat	39.80	13.17	28.09	15.59	67.89	14.07
7.	Haryana	11.94	8.27	5.39	9.99	17.34	8.74
8.	Himachal Pradesh	4.84	7.94	0.29	4.63	5.12	7.63
9.	Jammu & Kashmir	2.97	3.97	0.49	1.98	3.46	3.48
10.	Karnataka	59.91	17.38	44.49	25.25	104.40	20.04
11.	Kerala	20.97	9.38	20.07	20.27	41.04	12.72
12.	Madhya Pradesh	217.32	37.06	81.22	38.44	298.54	37.43
13.	Maharashtra	125.12	23.72	102.87	26.81	227.99	25.02
14.	Manipur	6.53	40.04	0.66	7.47	7.19	28.54
15.	Meghalaya	7.89	40.04	0.34	7.47	8.23	33.87
16.	Mizoram	1.40	40.04	0.45	7.47	1.85	19.47
17.	Nagaland	5.21	40.04	0.28	7.47	5.49	32.67
18.	Orissa	143.69	48.01	25.40	42.83	169.09	47.15
19.	Punjab	10.20	6.35	4.29	5.75	14.49	6.16
20.	Rajasthan	55.06	13.74	26.78	19.85	81.83	15.28
21.	Sikkim	2.00	40.04	0.04	7.47	2.05	36.55
22.	Tamil Nadu	80.51	20.55	49.97	22.11	130.48	21.12
23.	Tripura	12.53	40.04	0.49	7.47	13.02	34.44
24.	Uttar Pradesh	412.01	31.22	117.88	30.89	529.89	31.15
25.	West Bengal	180.11	31.85	33.38	14.86	213.49	27.02
26.	Andaman & Nicobar Islands	0.58	20.55	0.24	22.11	0.82	20.99
27.	Chandigarh	0.06	5.75	0.45	5.75	0.51	5.75
28.	Dadra & Nagar Haveli	0.30	17.57	0.03	13.52	0.33	17.14

(Contd.)

Sl. No.	States	Rural		Urban		Combined	
		No. Persons (Lakhs)	% of Persons	No. Persons (Lakhs)	% of Persons	No. Persons (Lakhs)	% of Persons
	(1)	(2)	(3)	(4)	(5)	(6)	(7)
29.	Daman & Diu	0.01	1.35	0.05	7.52	0.06	4.44
30.	Delhi	0.07	0.40	11.42	9.42	11.49	8.23
31.	Lakshadweep	0.03	9.28	0.08	20.27	0.11	15.60
32.	Pondicherry	0.64	20.55	1.77	22.11	2.41	21.67
	ALL INDIA	1932.43	27.09	670.07	23.62	2602.50	26.10

Notes: Poverty Ratio of Assam is used for Sikkim, Arunachal Pradesh Maghalaya, Mizoram, Manipur, Nagaland and Tripura.

Poverty Line of Maharashtra and expenditure distribution of Goa is used to estimate poverty ratio of Goa.

Poverty Line of Himachal Pradesh and Expenditure distribution of Jammu & Kashmir is used to estimate poverty ratio of Jammu & Kashmir.

Poverty Ratio of Tamil Nadu is used for Pondicherry and A & N Island. Urban Poverty Ratio of Punjab used for both rural and urban poverty of Chandigarh. Poverty Line of Maharashtra and expenditure distribution of Dadra & Nagar Haveli is used to estimate poverty ratio of Dadra and Nagar Haveli. Poverty Ratio of Goa is used for Daman & Diu Poverty Ratio of Kerala is used for Lakshadweep.

Urban Poverty Ratio of Rajasthan may be treated as tentative.

Source: Planning Commission.

REFERENCES

1. Bandyopadhaya, D. (2000); Land Reforms in West Bengal, *Economic and Political Weekly*, May 27.
2. Chidambaram, P., "Problem of Plenty", *India Today*, September 24, 2002.
3. Garg, Saurabh, "Gram Panchayats as Retailers of Public Distribution System Commodities" (2000-2001) *Compass*, Monsoon Issue.
4. *Ibid*. p. 8, p. 206.
5. Report of the task force on Devolution of Powers and Function upon Panchayati Raj Institutions, Government of India, Ministry of Rural Development, Department of Rural Development (Panchayati Raj Division) (2001), Krishi Bhavan, New Delhi, August.
6. Thomas Isaac, T.M. and Franke, Richard W.: *Local Democracy and Development – People's campaign for decentralized planning in Kerala (2000)*, Left Word Books, New Delhi,p.205.

3

Definition and Measurement of Poverty: A Critical View

....Panting in sweltering summers,
Shivering in winter nights, drenched in monsoon rains,
I turned poorer.
But you were tireless: you came again,
'Poverty is a meaningless term...
You have suffered deprivation all your life...'
My suffering was endless...
But you did not forget me;
This time, hand knotted into a fist, you said in a rousing voice.
'Wake up, wake up, you the dispossessed of the world...'
...Many years passed, by now you were cleverer...
You brought a blackboard and carefully chalked a neat, long line on it;
Your strain showed; wiping sweat from your forehead, you said.
'This line you see, below it, much below it you live.'
Fabulous!...
Thank you for my poverty, deprivation, dispossession...
Above all, thank you for the neat, long line, that luminous gift.
...My profound well wisher, thank you many times over.

—From Tarapada Roy, 'The Poverty Line'.

What Does Poverty Mean?

Being poor means lacking access to good health and skill to make most of the economic opportunities for development and growth. It means, nearly fifty per cent of these children under five years of age are suffering from malnutrition and later in life the other effects of this status, thus affecting his physical ability to perform. Being poor in rural India also means as much as forty per cent probability of being illiterate. For example, in the States of Bihar, Rajasthan, Madhya Pradesh, and Orissa where barely half of the rural population can read and hardly one-third of all women are literate; this percentage is dropping to 27 per cent in Rajasthan and 30 per cent in Bihar.

The incidence of poverty and the poor's access to social services varies considerably over inter and intra State. Poverty in rural Orissa and Bihar at 48.01 and 44.30 per cent respectively in 1999–2000 was more than four times than in Andhra Pradesh, Himachal Pradesh and Kerala at 11.05, 7.94 and 9.38 per cent respectively. Even within a single State, the variance can be striking as for example in Southern and Northern parts of Orissa and Eastern and Western parts of Madhya Pradesh. Better health status of the poor in Kerala and Himachal Pradesh could be explained by these State's better education, water and sanitation and basic infrastructure services. Even more noticeable than the geographical differences in poverty, social indicators and inequality persist across gender, caste and ethnic groups. The size of the gender gap seen in the enrolment/attendance in schools varies significantly across states but clearly and definitely works to the disadvantage of female child—wherever they live.

Being a baby boy puts one in an advantage to go and attend the school. Being a poor pregnant woman means risking death. The country's Maternal Mortality Rate is so high (MMR is 407 per 100,000 births) that this nation accounts for one in almost four maternal deaths worldwide. Similarly members of the scheduled castes particularly their children are likely to die prematurely. What is sadly consistent is this higher risk of poverty amongst women, illiterate, the landless and members of the scheduled castes and tribes. The fundamental fact remains that India's pervasive poverty, predominantly rural, is reflected in Health, Education and Nutrition indicators. They remain too low even accounting for the country's low per capita income.

Rural poverty in India does not have a uniform face. Many of the poor manage to provide for themselves a steady subsistence levels of income for themselves and their families, while others – truly destitute – are often without any means of livelihood. Most inherit low socio-economic status and remain its prisoners. They have no land, no productive assets, no knowledge of reading or writing or technical skills. They have only ill nourished bodies which make them prey to frequent illness. Unfortunately for the families belonging to SC/ST, the social stratification based on caste, ethnicity and gender impedes their mobility in search of better avenues outside their present environment.

A typical 'poor' household as per one study of World Bank, carried out in U.P. and Bihar, is one at the low end of caste hierarchy. SC/ST households are usually grouped in a separate hamlet at the end of a village, landless, lack of homestead plot, ending as a bonded labourer in its formal or informal sense. In purely tribal villages, life veers around collecting wood from the jungle most of the time and selling it in the market, leading to a subsistence level of living. Women headed households are the most vulnerable amongst all.

Measures of poverty have remained a matter of controversy and subject of hot debate among the scholars and policy makers. Poverty is also often related with inequality. In fact, the relationship between poverty and inequality is neither clear nor direct. Nevertheless, they are of interest to both social theory and social policy, and they have received attention from social scientists in Britain, the United States, India and other countries for more than hundred years. This study is however confined to poverty only. Betelle (2003) states that poverty studies go back to the late 19th and early 20th centuries in Britain where they are closely associated with the beginning of empirical sociology. The two great pioneers of poverty studies in Britain, Charles Booth (1840-1916) and Seebohm Rowntree (1871-1954), were both men of wealth who were guided by philanthropic motives. Their work did not enter the mainstream of sociological theory but influenced both directly and indirectly the development of welfare state. Further, the traditions of survey research initiated by Booth and Rowntree influenced later sociological enquiries, including the monumental work on poverty by Peter Townsend in the second half of the 20th century (Townsend, 1979, Abel-Smith and Townsend, 1965).

Seebohm Rowntree (1871-1954) in his book "*Poverty: A Study of Town Life* (1901)" defined poverty as a condition in which earnings were insufficient to meet the minimum requirements of a healthy and productive life. Nutritional data made up the core of his index to which were added data relating to clothing, fuel and other household sundries in addition to rent. Rowntree (*Poverty and Progress*, 1941) published a second study 40 years after the first. He came to feel that a single, invariant and unchanging definition of poverty would not do justice to the social reality which varied across space and changed over time. He may be said to have laid the groundwork for the 'relative' as against the 'absolute' conception of poverty.

It is often mentioned that unlike in Britain or the US, poverty studies in India have been the preserve of economists rather than sociologists (Bardhan and Srinivasan, 1974; Dantwala, 1973; Krishnaswamy, 1990). They have been driven by the preoccupation with development planning in which economists have played a leading part. One of the major objectives of development planning has been the reduction if not the removal of poverty and inequality. In independent India, its concern has been not simply with growth but also with distribution, and the control of poverty has always been viewed as an important test of its success. In the early years of economic planning, poverty appeared to be increasing rather than decreasing.

It may be said with a little simplification that in India students of poverty study have been concerned less with its definition than its measurement. Over the last 50 years an impressive data set has been created with the National Sample Survey (NSS) playing a leading role. Volumes have been written about the reliability, the comparability and the accuracy of these data. The data relate mainly to household expenditure and income, and they have been used for constructing indices to determine the number and proportion of households and individuals below the poverty line. It would appear in retrospect that the magnitude of poverty was at first somewhat overestimated. Present indications are that there has been a decline in poverty, in both proportion and absolute terms, in the last decade of the 20th century, although even on this issue one cannot say there is full agreement among the experts.

In this context it may be highlighted that in India much of the research on poverty in the period since independence was concern for growth and development. As a matter of fact, the research and debates over the interpretation of its result continue to this day. The Planning Commission, set up soon after independence, played a leading part in initiating, stimulating and organizing the research on poverty. The economists were in the forefront of the work both within and outside Planning Commission that sought to relate poverty and inequality to growth and development. However, in course of time it became increasingly evident that development and growth were not the synonym. Where growth led to an increase of poverty and inequality, it could hardly be called development in any meaningful sense of the term. However, definition of poverty remained a controversial issue among the economists, sociologists and administrators.

The controversy persisted on the definition of poverty, as it could be defined in either absolute or relative terms. Each conception has its attractions. The concept of absolute poverty has an obvious advantage as a guide to policy and as a test of it. One starts with a certain poverty line and then, holding that constant, finds out whether over a particular period of time the number and proportion of those below that line rose or fell. In fact, it was felt that a scientific definition of poverty line was a prerequisite for both estimation of number of poor as well as for identification of beneficiaries under various poverty alleviation programmes.

Measuring Poverty

Broadly speaking, the poor people are those who are deprived of certain goods and services which are considered essential or basic for a minimum acceptable standard of well-being. However, such a definition raises the question of how basic needs are determined. What is acceptable?. What is an accepted minimum standard of living and who determines it. In fact, poverty has never been defined as such except through its measurement parameters, which were in terms of monetised value of a basket of commodities required to meet the kilo calorific value. In the context of India, the first effort to measure poverty was attempted in 1962 by a Working Group set up by the Planning Commission on the suggestion of Indian Labour Conference for the seminar on some aspects of Planning. It was anchored in the minimum normative food basket. Apparently, this was used by the Perspective Planning Division in its planning exercises for working out the implications of ensuring a minimum standard of living, over a fifteen year planning horizon[1]. We say apparently as this was not indicated in the Perspective Planning Division study which used it. In fact, there exists no report of the Expert Group, published or unpublished, which explicitly suggests this. Based on the recommendations of Nutritional Advisory Committee of ICMR (ICMR, 1958), regarding a balanced diet, the Working Group suggested that the expenditure needed to obtain 2400 calories per capita per day in rural areas and 2250 calories per capita per day in urban areas plus 20 per cent of the expenditure on non-food items to meet other basic requirements would be the criteria for identification of poor households. Translated into money terms, the national minimum recommended was Rs.20 per month per person for rural areas and Rs.25 per month per person for urban areas at 1960-61 prices.

Using the medical and nutritional criteria, the minimum normative food basket was specified in the commodity space in terms of quantities on a per capita basis. Let the quantities be denoted by the vector q and the corresponding price vector by p. The prices used were 1960-61 prices. The normative minimum per capita food expenditure is the product of the vectors p and q. The (implicit) per capita per month expenditure on non-food needs is derived on the basis of observed consumer behaviour as follows. From the general purpose sample survey of consumer expenditure, we have the observed relationship for a cross-section (*f*) and the PCTE per month (*e*) was single-valued and monotonic. By inverse interpolation we find that value of the PCTE, say z_1, which corresponds to $f = pq$. This z_1 is taken to be the absolute poverty line anchored in the minimum normative food basket.

The other track, of anchoring the absolute poverty line in the normative minimum calorie intake, was adopted by the later Task Force [2]. This group accepted the calorie intake norms recommended by the Nutrition Expert Group (1968), according to fourteen age-sex activity categories. The census based activity pattern, according to age and sex (differing for rural and urban populations), was super-imposed on the (projected) rural and urban population [3]. This provided the age-sex activity specific composition of the rural and urban population. These specific calorie norms (assumed to be uniform for the rural and urban population) were then weighted by the corresponding composition of the rural and urban population separately, to derive the rural and urban average uniform calorie norms.

The daily calorie requirements per person worked out, on the average, to 2435 for rural and 2095 for urban. The National Sample Survey (NSS) data on consumer expenditure relating to the 28th round (1973-74) had provided information on the average quantities of food items consumed per capita, as well as, on the PCTE for the households grouped into pre-specified PCTE class intervals. The average per capita quantities of food items consumed within each PCTE class interval were converted into calories using appropriate conversion factors. Thus, a relationship between average daily calorie consumption per capita and the associated PCTE was obtained separately for the rural and the urban populations. Given the average calorie norms per capita for rural and urban sectors[4], the Task Force once again used the inverse interpolation method to get the associated PCTE, or the poverty line, Z_2. For the rural sector, the poverty line turned out to be Rs. 49.09 at 1973-74 prices; for the urban sector, the corresponding figure was Rs. 56.64.

We have noted that the food basket underlying the poverty line of Rs. 20 PCTE per month at 1960-61 prices could not be traced, even though the procedure leading up to it has been described.

Dandekar and Rath (1971) in their work on poverty used caloric norm of 2,250 calories per capita per day for both rural and urban areas, as a criterion to define the poverty line. On the basis of National Sample Survey data on consumer expenditure, the study revealed that, in rural areas, the households with an annual per capita expenditure of Rs. 170.80 (or Rs. 14.20 per capita per month) at the 1960-61 prices consumed on an average food with caloric equivalent of 2250 per capita per day together with such non-food items as they chose. The corresponding figures in the urban area were Rs. 271.70 or Rs. 22.60 per capita per month at 1960-61 prices. In comparison with the recommendations of the Working Group (1962), the authors observed that the rural minimum determined by the Group was considerably below, while the urban minimum was a little above the level recommended by the Group. In view of this, they decided to revise the rural minimum slightly upwards to Rs. 180 per annum or Rs. 15 per month. Similarly, they rounded off the urban minimum to Rs. 270 per annum or Rs. 22.50 per month, both at 1960-61 prices. This was also used by Bardhan (1973), Rudra (1974) and later by many others

Task Force

The Planning Commission then constituted a Task Force in 1977 on projections of minimum needs and effective consumption demand, which submitted its report in 1979. The Task Force by taking into consideration the caloric consumption requirement for different groups like children of certain age, heavy workers, moderate workers and sedentary workers, arrived at an average caloric intake of 2435 in rural areas and 2095 for urban areas. Using the 28th round (1973-74) of NSS data, relating to household consumption, the Task Force also computed the monetary equivalent of these caloric norms, which is known as the poverty line. Using the poverty line and the state-wise distribution of persons by expenditure classes, estimation was made of the percentage of persons below the poverty line. It was estimated that consumer expenditure/per capita per month of Rs. 49 in rural areas and Rs. 56 in urban areas would meet the requirements. Thus for that year Rs. 3000 p.a. per family income was determined as the dividing line, i.e. BPL/APL. The poverty line so defined was updated from time-to-time to compensate for the changes in the price levels.

In order to appreciate the dichotomy on which the methodology for determining the poverty ratios is based needs to be explained somewhat. National Sample Survey Organisation (NSSO) collects data on monthly per capita expenditure (MPCE) for both food and non-food items for given income groups state-wise for both rural and urban areas: Food items under each income group are then converted into its equivalent calorie value: calorie intake, this level becomes the dividing line, non-food expenditure is neither discussed nor touched under the generic explanation of being normative or behavioural. This is then deflated to 1973-74 prices and poverty ratios for the State/Country are arrived at a simple average. The report of the Task Force does appreciate the need, requirement for arriving at the poverty ratios taking into calculation the norms for non-food components and monetising it but leaves it to be studied further; thus leaving a much desired sector of social security like education, health, clothing and shelter to be taken care of by the ghosts, choking the very issues associated with the cause and effect relationships of poverty. At 1976-77 prices corresponding figures were worked out at Rs.61.8 and Rs.71.3 per capita per month respectively. It is an admitted fact that the Government accepted these recommendations which were based on expenditure purely on food items. The estimation of poverty for the year 1973-74 and 1977-78 for both rural and urban poor was made on the above totally unacceptable rationale of determining the poverty line on the basis of a certain money value to meet a given calorie energy intake per capita per day/month/year.

Expert Group 1993

The implicit private consumption deflator from NAS was used for adjusting the poverty line for the years 1977-78, 1983-84 and 1987-88. However, the Task Force methodology was often criticized mainly for application of the same poverty line in all the States, use of a fixed consumption basket over time and the uniform consumption basket for all the States. The Planning Commission constituted an Expert Group in 1989 to look into the methodology for estimation of poverty, which submitted its report in July 1993. The Expert Group estimated separate poverty lines for each State, using regional level consumer price index. It also gave up the system of adjustments of NSS data, using the implicit CSO private consumption deflator. In March, 1997, the Expert Group methodology was approved by the Planning Commission. Since then, we have poverty estimates of rural poverty of various regions, based on regional level consumer price index for agricultural labourers.

Thus, the most used widely data base for poverty studies at the all-India level is the household consumer expenditure data collected by the National Sample Survey Organization (NSSO). However, we are aware that throughout the 1990s, the NSS results on household consumption expenditure generated much interest in both academic and policy circles. Though official estimate of the number or percentage of poor persons based on NSS data shows sharp decline during 1990s, many independent researchers, using the same data, have come to the conclusion that rural poverty at the all-India level does not show any declining trend during 1990s. The enormous and ridiculous controversy that have generated with the 55th round National Sample Survey results is now well documented. The endless debate continues among the academicians and bureaucrats about efficacy of methodology adopted by the NSSO in the 55th round and inconsistency in the comparison of the latest estimate with earlier estimate.

Simultaneously the Ministry of Rural Development have undertaken income based poverty measurements in rural areas. While the Planning Commission's poverty estimates are used for allocation of Central resources between States, the estimates by the Ministry of Rural Development are used for better targeting of various anti-poverty programmes. (For a detailed critical analysis, please see Chapter-9 Targeting the Poor).

Lesson from China

Over the past 25 years China has transformed its economy into one of the most dynamic in the world and it made huge strides in its battle against poverty. China's poverty rate today is probably slightly lower than the average for the world as a whole, which was one of the highest in the world around 1980 (*vide* Chen, Shaohua and Martin Ravallion, 2004a, "How Have World's Poorest Fared Since the Early 1980" World Bank Research Observer, Vol. 19, No.2, pp. 141-70).

The preceding observation from Martin Ravallion and Shaohua who in their article ["Learning from Success – Understanding China's (uneven) progress against poverty" published in the quarterly publication – Finance & Development of the International Monetary Fund for the quarter ending December 2004, Vol. 41, number 4] highlighted the fact that poverty lines were designed to have a fixed real value over time and between urban and rural areas. These can be interpreted as "absolute poverty lines," rather than a "relative poverty line" that tends to rise with overall living standards. Region-specific food bundles are used, with separate food bundles for urban and rural areas. The bundles are scaled to reach 2,100 calories per person per day, with 75 per cent of the calories from foodgrains. Allowance for spending on items other than food is factored in separately, by looking at the non-food spending of people who can just afford the food component of the poverty line.

One interesting point is that about three-quarters of the overall reduction in poverty in the 1980s and 1990s came from gains to the rural poor, stemming from growth within rural areas and remittances from urban areas. Growth in the primary sector (primarily agriculture) did much more to reduce poverty and inequality than growth in either the secondary or tertiary sectors. From their empirical analysis, they assert that "promoting agricultural and rural development is crucial to pro-poor growth in most developing countries". Further, macro economic stability (notably avoiding inflationary shocks) has also helped in reducing poverty. But the most important lesson which we can learn from China's experience consistent with the view from much of the past research is that promoting agricultural and rural development is crucial to pro-poor growth in most developing countries. It would be of interest to have some idea about the yardsticks of 'measuring poverty' in China where over the 20 year period 1980-2001, the proportion of the population living in poverty fell from 53 to 8 per cent. However, there were some setbacks for China's poor. Poverty reduction stalled in the late 1980s and early 1990s, recovered pace in the mid-1990s, but showed signs of stagnating again in the late 1990s. About half of the decline in poverty came in the first few years of the 1980s.

Adjusted Head Count Ratios

For estimating the number of poor, the Planning Commission had been making adjustments in the NSS consumer expenditure data. This was justified by them on the grounds that the aggregate final consumption expenditure estimates obtained from the NSSO was less than that from the NAS.

Although, such an adjustment of the NSS data have been severely criticized, this practice had been followed by the Commission till very recently. The exact methodology of computation of the adjustment factor is not reported in detail. All that we know is that it was derived using NAS (New Series) data on Aggregate Private Final Consumption and the same variable derived from the NSS data. For 1987-88 the adjustment factor is 1.26 obtained from the Report of the Expert Group (1993). For the 50th round we calculated this to be 1.332. From the NAS literature we got the total private consumption expenditure to be Rs. 4,79,586 crores for 1993-94. From the NSS data of the 50th round, rural average per capita expenditure came out to be Rs. 281.37 per month for 1993-94. For the urban sector this was Rs. 458.58 per month. The population projection for January 1994 was 639.08 million and 259.58 million for the rural and urban sectors, respectively. The total consumption expenditure for the rural sector was Rs. 21321.184 crores and for the urban sector this was Rs. 1,42,845.835 crores, both for 1993-94. So the total all India consumption expenditure was Rs. 3,60,167.019 crores. Dividing the NAS estimate of total private consumption expenditure by the NSS estimate (both at current prices), we got the adjustment factor to be 1.33.

Controversies on Poverty Line and Poverty Ratios

In a spatial context one would appreciate that the Expert Group did not specifically address the non-food items as 1960s were times of food distress, manifested in hunger, food shortages and the like although the Task Force had no such shackles to bind themselves. They seemed to have committed a historic blunder by not taking into account what it would cost to make a man, a human being. Non-food items were left untouched, leaving them to take its own course and again sticking to base the dividing line between BPL and APL on the monetised value of food items to provide 2400 calorie intake. This could possibly be attributed to the current context in which many multilateral agencies were looking at poverty largely concentrating on GDP growth rate hoping against hope on the 'trickle' down-effect. The various World Organizations/Institutions were looking at food security in terms of cereal led security. In this regard, led by one of the super powers on account of its own internal compulsions, the aspiring followers followed suit. One sees no vision – no perception for or of the poor or poverty. Many of the studies and material relied upon by the Task Force also suffered from the same. Presumption perhaps was that if people could be given a bread basket, rest would take care of itself. The Expert Group fell in this trap. It failed the posterity by assuming that this national minimum "excludes expenditure on health and education, both of which are expected to be provided by the State in accordance with the provision of the Constitution and in the light of its commitments". The Task

Force report recorded that a few additional points also emerged in the course of their discussions, such as:

(i) Need for developing norms in respect of non-traded public goods like housing primary education, drinking water, clothing and medicines.

(ii) Distribution policy that should be adopted regarding food, sugar, clothing, housing, education, health and miscellaneous civil services.

Yet the report was sublimely silent on what it would cost to the poor especially access to health facility. Ensconced in secure surroundings, need was not felt to monetise what it would cost to get these services along with food items to determine the dividing line of APL from BPL.

The same mistake–some would call it informed blunder – was repeated by the Expert Group after deliberating on this issue for four long years. Very conveniently they also were in line with the report of Task Force on the basic methodology of arrival at the poverty rates to the extent they also held in the year 1973-74 as sacrosanct for 'deflator' purpose. However, one of the major departure they made from the Task Force report was to rely upon the data generated by NSSO only. Recommendation of the Expert Group has already been reproduced earlier.

Based on this normative approach, poverty line/ratios/ incidence is arrived at and reworked for the past years in comparison with the same arrived at by using this methodology recommended by the Task Force.

Three other features referred to in these recommendations need special mention:

(i) The poverty line defines on an average the level of per capita per day expenditure which meets a normative minimum standard of living, deemed reasonable. Calorie intake is but one of the ingredients, though an important one, of the minimum standard, but the poverty line makes an allowance for non-food consumption needs as well, on the basis of observed consumer behaviour. The Group realizes the desirability of defining the normative standard of non-food consumption and its constituents without references to actual behaviour but until this is done, the existing basis seems to be the most practical and reasonable (para 4.4).

(ii) The concept of poverty line incorporating the norm of minimum living standard has to be kept distinct from the concept of malnourishment and under nourishment. The incidence of malnourishment and under nourishment is indeed an important indicator of well-being of population (para 4.5).

(iii) Having decided to accept the minimum standard level for defining poverty line normatively, we feel that it should be applied to all parts of the country for assessing poverty (para 4.6).

Both the Reports have one common feature. Largely self-serving and self-promoting, that is more studies need to be carried out on certain issues. If any work has been done between 1979 and 1993, and again between 1993 till date, at least it is not known to the public as the poverty line continues to be worked out on the basis of these two reports for the relevant periods. In chapter 5 of its report the Expert Group goes on to suggest the need to supplement the estimates of the definition of the poor with the assessment of Nutrition Status, Health Status, Educational Status and Living Environment. The data on nutrition was available with National Institute of Nutrition and NNMB for certain states: Data on health status had already been generated by National Family Health Survey carried out in 1991, Data on education and living environment especially on housing was available from census data – yet no attempt is made to make use of it. A realistic view would be to fiddle a little with the existing methodology without really tampering much with the basis, as that could have jacked up the poverty incidence by an ample measure. This would suite noone—Planners; government and perhaps the academia, as it would have sent a wrong signal to public and more so to the multilateral institutions. Poor in any case had in fact, never any voice. There was no one to speak for them as to what poverty means! This brings to our mind an old dictum "Pursuit of knowledge is essential in search of solutions to the problems but jinx sets in when pursuit of knowledge becomes an end in itself".

On the basis of these recommendations, Poverty rates arrived at were as follows:

Estimates of Poverty

Year	*Poverty Line (Income Rs. per capita per month)*		*Poverty Ratios (in %)*			*BPL Population in crores*		
	Rural	*Urban*	*Rural*	*Urban*	*Combined*	*Rural*	*Urban*	*Combined*
1973-74	49.63	56.75	56.44	49.01	54.88	26.13	6.00	32.13
1977-78	56.84	70.33	5.07	45.24	51.32	26.42	6.46	32.83
1983	89.50	115.65	45.65	40.79	44.48	25.19	7.09	32.39
1987-88	115.20	162.16	39.09	38.20	38.86	23.19	7.52	30.70
1993-94	205.84	281.35	37.27	32.26	35.37	24.40	7.63	32.04
1999-2000	327.56	454.11	27.09	23.62	26.10	19.32	6.70	26.10

Not available 2004-05.

Source: The Expert Group on Identification of Household below BPL (BPL Census 2002) – Ministry of Rural Development, New Delhi.

Conclusion

Official estimates published by the Planning Commission (2001) suggests that India recorded one of the developing world's fastest reduction in poverty. On this, however, there has been an active and acrimonious debate regarding the accuracy of the official numbers, as well as the accuracy of the various alternative estimates offered in place of the official figures. According to official estimates, poverty fell from 36 per cent of the population in 1993-94 to nearly 26 per cent at the end of the decade (1999-2000). Needless to reiterate that these estimates were derived from successive rounds of the National Sample Survey, which had collected household level data for over 50 years. The NSS provides the basis for one of the longest continuous time series of poverty estimates in the world. But, of late, concerns have been raised regarding the comparability of the latest poverty estimates (based on the NSS 55th round, 1999-2000) with estimates based on earlier rounds of the NSS. Changes in the survey methodology used to calculate household welfare (measured in terms of per capita consumption) have rendered the most recent official poverty estimates not comparable to the earlier official estimates.

In view of the controversies, many authors take a different approach to check the results of the 55th round. They have developed an econometric model for projecting poverty in India after 1993-94. In constructing the model, they have built on past research indicating that the key determinants of poverty in India at state level are economic growth and its sectoral composition (depending on state's initial conditions), development spending, and inflation. From this starting point they calibrate the model to the time series data by state upto 1993-94 and then forecast forward and compare the results to those of the 55th round.

REFERENCES

1. Bardhan, P.K. and T.N. Srinivasan (eds.) (1974), *Poverty and Income Distribution in India*, Statistical Publishing House, New Delhi.
2. Betelle, Andre (2003), 'Poverty and Inequality', *Economic and Political Weekly*, October 18, 2003.
3. Dandekar, V.M. and N. Rath (1971), *Poverty in India*, Indian School of Political Economy, Poona.
4. Dantwala, M.L. (1973), *Poverty in India*, Macmillan, Delhi.
5. Krishnaswamy, K.S. (ed.) (1990), *Poverty and Income Distribution*, Sameeksha Trust and Oxford University Press, Bombay.
6. Rowntree, B.S. (1941), *Poverty and Progress*, Longman, Green, London.

4

The Study

I was scornful of the poverty at first; Now, I admire the courage to smile despite adversity.

—Mahatma Gandhi

"As people become fortunate in their personal well-being and as countries become similarly fortunate, there is a common tendency to ignore the Poor."

—J.K. Galbraith

In order to have a more realistic approach for identification of poor, it was felt necessary to look into the 'very essential' Indicators, which have a cause and effect relationship. Most of the Indicators developed for the purpose have either been considered or gone into, but in isolation by various agencies/ministries/departments. It is no-one's case that nothing is being done, but the point being made is that, 'Look' at poverty as emanating from several factors and not from food insecurity alone. The main objective of the study is to identify the poor—individually or in a group/regional basis so that specific remedial measures could be directed to address the 'laggard-factor' in that region or for that group or a combination of both.

One factor haunted us interminably and that is related to the inherent contradiction in the Transfer-of-Income approach under Public Distribution System (PDS); theoretical Models on the subject speak of this largely in terms of helping a family meet its food requirements, yet not saying a word in the same breath, about what are now considered very significant and over-bearing factors like skills, education, health, rural infrastructure, etc. If any indirect co-relationship exists in a substantial measure between the two, it does not appear to be visible or established in this country. It is our effort to bring a balance to this rather lopsided approach by looking at poverty not as a 'Bundle' of food insecurity alone but as a 'Basket' of factors having a direct and indirect bearing on poverty and address them all in a combination. It is also well realized by now that 'reforms' tend to leave out the poor, in the short-term, as they do not have the requisite skills and the capability to profit from the technology driven, efficiency led economic reforms. These factors prompted us to take this initiative.

We have discussed in the previous pages efforts being made in India to alleviate poverty and the methodology adopted to implement the programme. What we have done so far is to work on a narrow definition of poverty primarily based on income criteria to meet basic food needs? The fundamental and obvious flaw in this scheme of things is that Food Security on the scale of k-calorie intake 'alone' is seen to be determining the Poverty line. Global experience and literature on the subject point out to many more additionalities required to be taken into consideration while determining poverty lines. Therefore, there is a need to look at the whole 'basket' of factors having a bearing on Poverty.

The very fact that deprivation means something more than deprivation of income and food consumption, definition of poverty would have to be much broader. It is true that to be poor is to be unable to manage the basic elements of human subsistence. No per capita income figures, no indices of calorie consumption can capture the wretchedness of the poor. To be poor is to be born of a malnourished mother, to survive with inadequate food, clothing, shelter and without the stimulation of learning or play; to grow unequipped intellectually or physically as a member of a striving society.

With this broader approach on the definition of Poverty, efforts have been made by the international agencies to enlarge the scope of poverty. In 1995, the UNDP introduced methods of calculating a gender related development index (GDI) and a gender empowerment measure (GEM). In the Human Development Report 1997, a methodology was introduced for calculating a Human Poverty Index (HPI) based on deprivations in basic human needs.

The Human Development Report, 1999 adopted four criteria to arrive at Human Poverty Index, i.e. (i) percentage of people not expected to survive beyond the age of 40 years, (ii) functional literacy rate, (iii) percentage of people below the nationally defined income poverty line, and (iv) long term unemployment rate. This was partly modified in the Human Development Report, 2000 which adopted the following criteria:

(i) percentage of people not expected to survive beyond the age of 40 years,
(ii) Adult illiteracy rate,
(iii) Percentage of people without access to safe drinking water,
(iv) Percentage of people without access to health services and sanitation,
(v) Percentage of under weight children,
(vi) Percentage of people below the nationally defined poverty line (Human Development Report UNDP, 2000).

Based on these criteria, India has been ranked 128, i.e. one of the poorest countries in the world.

The World Development Report – 2000-2001, defined poverty to mean not only material deprivation as measured by an appropriate concept of income or consumption, but also low achievements in education and health. It also broadened the notion of poverty to include vulnerability and exposure to risk and their voiceless and powerless, based on the assumption that all these forms of deprivation severely restrict what Amartya Sen calls the capabilities that a person has, i.e. the substantive freedom he or she enjoys to lead the kind of life he or she values. As indicated in the World Development Report (2000-2001), increasing poor peoples' voice and participation not only addresses their sense of exclusion, but it also leads to better targeting of health and education services to their needs.

The poverty assessment of India, as indicated in the World Development Report is given in Box-1.

Box 1: Poverty Assessment of India

1. India suffers severe deprivation in education and health – especially in the Northern Region where caste, class and gender inequities are strong.
2. Poverty reduction in India lagged behind that of East Asia because of slower growth of mass education and basic health.
3. Accelerated poverty reduction will require development of social infrastructures such as education and health through better fiscal management and diversion of more funds to these sectors. Besides, the higher spending will have to be matched by better service provision.
4. Poverty reduction would also require empowering women and members of lower castes.

Source: World Development Report, p.34, World Bank 2000-2001.

However, while it is relatively easy to measure income, health and education related variables, the measurement of vulnerability, voicelessness and powerlessness become often very difficult. For example, a measure of either household assets or social safety nets may not necessarily reflect the peoples' exposure to risk. Similarly, the measurement of voicelessness and powerlessness which are generally attempted by using polls and surveys on the extent of civil and political liberties poses numerous methodological and accuracy of data collecting efforts. Nevertheless, it is obvious that poverty is multi-dimensional in nature. A mere income based poverty approach will not reflect true poverty. Hence, one needs to develop either a physical quality of life index as Morris did in 1979 (combining the literacy rate, the infant mortality rate and life expectancy) or a composite index of poverty, on the line of Ravallion (1997) and the UNDP reports on Human Development for the years 1999 and 2000. While the above mentioned papers and reports assigned equal weights to each component on arbitrary basis, there is a need to calculate weights on reasonably scientific basis.

Thus, the present 'Study' which attempts to map out poverty in Rajasthan based on a scientifically weighted composite index of poverty would make a real methodological contribution to the measurement of poverty. Besides, the study tries to incorporate as many as 9 variables which measures factorized deprivation, which can be easily measured and for which either data were available or could be scientifically collected using household survey technique.

Need for the Study

It becomes clear from the foregoing discussion that there is a need for a critical study of both poverty situation and implementation of anti-poverty programmes. It is particularly necessary to identify the location specific nature and causes of poverty and suggest appropriate measures for poverty alleviation.

Objectives

The present study makes an humble attempt to analyse the location specific causes of poverty in Rajasthan, using both district-wise secondary data and primary data collected through an extensive household survey in two 'Blocks' in two districts of Rajasthan. The study is intended not only to identify 'who' are poor and 'where' are the poor people concentrated, but also 'why' the poor people stay poor, at macro and micro levels. The findings would help in prioritising location specific investment strategies and programmes for poverty alleviation. It would also help in proper targeting of various programmes so that there is a visible impact of efforts made for poverty alleviation. Unlike earlier studies which considered only a few indicators, this study has a comprehensive coverage of nine main indicators and several sub-indicators.

In order to have a more realistic approach, it was felt necessary to look into the 'very essential' Indicators, which have a bearing on poverty. Most of these Indicators developed for this purpose have been considered but in isolation by separate agencies/ministries/departments. What has been attempted here is to look at poverty from a much broader angle than to look at it merely from a single point of view for income or food security. The objective is to identify the poor—individually or in a group/regional basis to enable taking specific remedial measures directed to address the 'laggard-factor' in that region or for that group or a combination of both.

Triple 'A' Approach

Improved Management of resources at all levels through better use of the available information is an important factor for the success of any intervention. Therefore, strategies to prevent and control a given situation should aim at attacking the underlying immediate and basic causes simultaneously. Identification of the problem, its spread, affected population and related details are essential for effective utilisation of scarce resources.

It is not enough to collect information and build a data base unless integrated with ability and opportunity to analyse the root causes at the earliest to initiate positive or preventive action.

Triple 'A' approach lays down the following principle:

Assess a situation
Analyse the situation for getting at the underlying causes
Act once the causes are established to remove or fight the underlying causes.
No one single component can have relevance in isolation.

A comprehensive Triple 'A' approach comprising Assessment of the problem, Analysis of the causes of the problem and Action to address the causes help attain the set goal in a comprehensive manner.

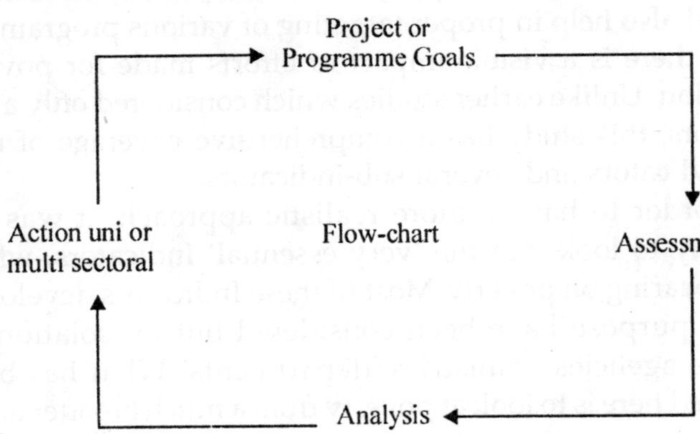

Output

(i) The key expected output of this study will be its contribution towards an 'understanding' to find out:—

- *Who* are these poor?
- *Where* are these poor? and
- *Why* are they poor?

so as to enable the Policy-makers and Programme Administrators to work on a 'Triple A' approach –

- *'Assess'* the situation
- *'Analyze'* the situation; and take
- *'Action'* to remedy the situation.

Plan of the Study

After the introduction in Chapter 1, Chapter 2 is devoted to highlighting in detail the various policy prescriptions for rural development and poverty alleviation programmes initiated and implemented in the country including pre-independence initiatives. The broad elements of the strategies hitherto adopted are macro economic framework consistent with the objective of poverty reduction and direct attack on poverty through increasing investment of both self-employment and wage employment. Further, since land is the primary resource on which agriculture is based, the pattern of ownership of this resource has to be just and rational if we are to secure growth with social justice. With this realization, policy on land reforms has also been considered as one of the strategies of poverty reduction and a section in this chapter deals with Land Reforms also.

As the main focus of attention of the study is poverty reduction through construction of poverty index and identification of poverty stricken areas in Rajasthan state, the Chapter 3 deals with defining poverty and criteria of poverty measurements including the various controversies involved in this sphere.

The next chapter, i.e. Chapter 4 elaborates the objectives and design of the study and net outcome expected of the study. Chapter 5 is devoted to giving details about the introducing the State of Rajasthan, its physical features, demographic profile, economic profile and magnitude of poverty. The methodology of undertaking this pioneering study has been outlined in Chapter 6. The 7th and 8th Chapters have been devoted to identification of who are the rural poor, where they are located and why they are poor, both at district level and at village and household levels respectively. These have been indicated by maps for easy comprehension.

The study then takes a forward looking rational approach in targeting the poor and highlights the taxonomy of poverty, etc. in Chapter 9. Finally, in Chapter 10 the findings of the study have been summarized and a number of recommendations have been made for poverty reduction policy formulation purpose.

RAJASTHAN
District Map
N
State Capital
State Boundary
PUNJAB
HARYANA
UTTAR PRADESH
MADHYA PRADESH
GUJARAT
Ganganagar
Hanumangarh
Bikaner
Churu
Jhunjhunu
Sikar
Alwar
Bharatpur
Dausa
Jaipur
Karauli
Tonk
Nagaur
Ajmer
Jodhpur
Jaisalmer
Barmer
Jalor
Pali
Sirohi
Rajsamand
Bhilwara
Udaipur
Dungarpur
Banswara
Chittaurgarh
Bundi
Kota
Baran
Jhalawar

5

Rajasthan—An Overview

India of my dreams—An India in which the poorest shall feel that it is their country in whose making they have an effective voice.

—*Mahatma Gandhi*

Historical Background

Rajasthan represents the ultimate confluence of history, chivalry romance, rugged natural beauty and colour. In the words of celebrated author Col. James Todd, Rajasthan exhibits "the sole example in the history of mankind of a people withstanding every outrage barbarity can inflict or human nature sustain." Today, long years after the last bugle was sounded and the warring kingdoms of erstwhile Rajputana sheathed their swords, the desert appears romantic – its arts, the expressions of a brave yet sensitive race, its architecture the embodiment of strength and grace. It is as if in celebration of life itself. Again in the words of Col. Todd, the land bends "to the earth, yet rising buoyant from the pressure and making calamity a whetstone to courage".

Go to any village or city in Rajasthan, the land of sand dunes and forts, it is common to see and listen to an old man with a *hookah* tell tales of royal grandeur—Maharana Pratap and his favourite horse Chetak—to his grandchildren. The tales are not what they are – they are tales that give an outsider an opportunity to delve deeper into the Rajasthani psyche. How entrenched he or she still is in the hoary past but, at the same time making an effort to come out of it. To an extent, it is not only the people who live in the past. Today the state of affairs in present-day Rajasthan, a long cry from the pre-colonial era, is quite pathetic.

Situated in North Western India stretching over 3.42 lakh sq. kms, Rajasthan is the second largest state in the country accounting for about 10 per cent of its area and 5.5 per cent of its population, but has only one per cent of the country's water resources of which agriculture consumes 83 per cent. Rajasthan state was constituted in 1949 by merger of 19 princely states and 3 chiefs hips which varied in size, population, administrative efficiency and socio-economic development. Late, in 1956, Ajmer was merged with it. Administratively, the state presently is divided into 32 districts, 105 sub-divisions, 241 tehsils and 237 development blocks (Panchayat Samitis) with 39,810 inhabited villages.

Rajasthan has a population of 5.65 crore (2001 census), of which 23.38 per cent live in the urban areas, and 61 per cent are literate. For the record, Rajasthan, a treasure trove of minerals, holds a share of about 24 per cent in the total national production of non-metallic minerals. The state contributes around 90 per cent of the national output of rock phosphate, 100 per cent of natural gypsum output and 10 per cent of the output of limestone. The other minerals found here include feldspar, dolomite, china clay etc. The largest state of India is now also rich in petroleum products – if the recent discoveries in the desert area are anything to go by then Rajasthan in true sense of the word can be called rich. Rail infrastructure to and from Rajasthan is excellent, with a total track length of 5,926 km.

The rail route length per 1,000 sq. m of area is 17.3 km as against 19.2 km in the country. Road network in the State is over 1.52 lakh km, including 4,665 km of National and 8,601 km of State Highways. Rajasthan is an archaeologist's dream come true, with its forts and palaces and heritage buildings. To give a fillip to tourist inflow, the Government had thought of coining a brand name for Rajasthan; akin to Kerala's God's own country. But nothing much has been done in that field. Naturally endowed to rake in the moolah from foreign tourists, the Government, of late has initiated served innovative programmes.

Rajasthan has a fine tradition of visionary planning as is evident in the layout of the capital city of Jaipur itself. Plato dreamt of an ideal state in which philosophers would be kings and kings would be philosophers. Sawai Jai Singh, who founded the city of Jaipur in 1727, was an astronomer-king who left behind an exquisite example of the planned city, pleasing to look at and comfortable to live in. It is built around geometrical squares and circles with broad highways interconnecting them. Running water supply from the Ramgarh lake was provided way back in 1875, and gas street lighting in 1878. Conscious of the needs of education and health for the people, even an attempt, though abortive, was made in 1872 to start a medical school. The famous walled city from which Jaipur, capital of Rajasthan, derives its name 'Pink City' is surrounded by an ancient 20 ft. high wall and eight gates. Situated 261 kms away from Delhi, it was a state of warring factions locked in deadly warfare, thousands of royal ladies consigning themselves to flames, preferring death to dishonour. Jaipur is a part of famed Golden Triangle tourist circuit of India with Delhi and Agra. The best time to visit Jaipur is winter (mid-September to March).

Udaipur, once the capital of Mewar, is another important tourists attraction lies nearly 2,500 ft. above the sea level. The city has a healthy climate and the heat is never excessive. The winter months are delightful for visiting the beautiful city. Cupped by soft green hills, the opiate beauty of Udaipur is like a miracle in the dusty wind-blown heat of Rajasthan. The city combines beauty with picturesque association of a glorious past. It stands in a valley amid green hills on the banks of the steel-blue Pichola lake. Udaipur was named after its founder Maharana Uday Singh. This 16th century bastioned city is unique in the feminine quality among the masculine citadels of Rajasthan. With Pichola, Fateh Sagar, Swaroop Sagar and Udai Sagar lakes adorning it, Udaipur is also known as the city of lakes. Crowning the ridge is the palace of Maharana known as the city palace. Within the palace is the magnificence of the east peacocks in mosaic on the walls, floors laid with tiles of rare beauty and roof gardens, which give a thrilling view of the panorama below. The building is of soft cream colour and its octagonal towers are crowned with cupolas. The Krishna vilas is the finest enclosure with its remarkable miniature. The museum has the armour of Maharana Pratap.

Location

The State of Rajasthan sprawls over the major part of North-west India between 23° 3′ and 30° 12′ north longitude and 69° 30′ and 78° 17′ East latitude. It is flanked by International boundary with Pakistan in North-west, Punjab and Haryana in the North, Uttar Pradesh in the North-east, Madhya Pradesh in the South-east and Gujarat in the South-west.

Topography

The state is physically divided into two major geographical units. The area to the west of Aravali ranges, comprising nearly two-thirds of the total area of the state is almost arid and undulating, while the eastern part is relatively fertile. Moreover, the intensive soil erosion and environmental degradation pose a critical problem of formation and spread of ravines in districts like Chittorgarh, Jhalawar, Bundi, Kota, Sawai Madhopur and Dholpur. In short, both human and livestock population have to face lot of hardships due to unfavourable physiography as much as natural calamity like drought.

The topography of Rajasthan is dominated by the Aravali system of hill ranges. The Aravali range of hills and mountains, from Delhi to Gujarat, runs through the state and divides it into South-east and North-west. The North-west region covers nearly two-thirds of the state and consists of a series of sand dunes. It covers the area formed by Bikaner, Jaisalmer, Jodhpur and Shekhawati area of Sikar and Jhunjhunu districts.

On the other hand, large tracts of state lying to the east of the Aravallis are fertile and there are several rivers in this area. There are hills and valleys in this region and some forests as well. It becomes a flat plain towards Bharatpur. Apart from the Aravali hills there are also some other hills going down from Delhi in a South-Westerly direction. The peaks of Bahai Raghunathgarh and

Taragarh are 787 metres to 1047 metres in height respectively. Mount Abu in the Sirohi district is the highest mountain in Rajasthan and its tallest peak of Gurushikhar is 1717 metres high. It is cool for most parts of the year and attracts a large number of tourists, especially from nearby Gujarat state.

Climate and Rainfall

Extreme climate prevails in many parts of the state where the day temperature rises very high in summer. The desert areas are terribly hot by day but cool down considerably by nightfall. Hot winds, called loo, blow in a south-westerly direction in the districts of Bikaner, Jodhpur and Jaisalmer. The day temperatures here range from 45 to 48 degree Celsius and in the remote desert it often goes up to 52 degree. But by night the mercury begins to drop and the nights are often pleasant and cool. The hot months are May and June. The winter is quite pleasant and the maximum temperature goes upto 24.5 degree falling to as low as 8.5 degree at night but it could go down to freezing point on occasions.

The areas in the south-east are comparatively less hot although the difference could be only one of degree. The north-eastern part adjoining Haryana is also less hot but the nights are not so cool as in the desert areas. Scanty rainfall and the hot climate have taught the people the art and technique of preserving water which is scarce in many areas. The impounding of water in vast man-made lakes, called 'samunds', is one such device which helps in drinking water being preserved and also vegetation being encouraged in a big way around the storages. Water is also stored in tanks in houses and sometimes this is kept under lock and key. The camel which is a sturdy animal and can live for hours without water is thus the main beast of burden which is also used in agriculture. It is appropriately called the ship of the desert.

The average annual rainfall in the state is 536 mm. But districts like Barmer, Bikaner, Churu, Ganganagar, Hanumangarh, Jaisalmer, Jalore, Jhunjhunu, Jodhpur, Nagaur, Pali and Sikar get very scanty rainfall and belong to the arid zone. In the second category of semi-arid districts are Bharatpur,

Alwar, Dausa, Ajmer, Jaipur, Karauli, Sawai Madhopur, Bhilwara and Tonk. Thirdly, Banswara, Dungarpur, Jhalawar, Baran and Kota form the humid zone, while Sirohi, Udaipur, Rajsamand, Bundi and Chittorgarh are in the sub-humid zone.

Drought

Desert has been a dead-weight on the economy of Rajasthan. A major portion of the state is covered by the Thar desert. Sand dunes sprawl across 2.88 lakh square metres in 11 districts out of the total 32. Droughts occur almost once every three years and sometimes they are continuous as during 1984, 1985 and 1986 – the worst in this century. Of the total 39,810, 26,725 villages belonging to 170 tehsils are famine-hit. Nearly 21.8 million people and 34 million head of cattle have been affected by drought in an area of 9.1 hectares. Solution to the recurring droughts lies in the development million of irrigation and agriculture facilities.

Amongst all the constituent units of the country, Rajasthan with its scanty, low and irregular rainfall is highly susceptible and vulnerable to drought conditions. The spectre of famine due to failure of monsoon constantly looms large over the state. Human and cattle population have to undergo severe hardships due to droughts since it leads to loss of work (employment), and scarcity of fodder, drinking water, etc. The people have to be employed as casual labour on famine relief works to provide them with minimum of subsistence livelihood. Barring a few exceptions, year after year, drought and famine conditions have prevailed in some or the other districts. Particulars about drought conditions in Rajasthan from 1967-68 onwards are in Table 5.1.

During the 2002 drought, the people of Rajasthan faced the fifth successive year of hunger – a situation comparable to the worst the state has been in the past 100 years. Cereal production did not exceed 30 lakh tonnes compared to 110 lakh tonnes in a normal year. According to official estimates, 76 lakh landless households in addition to small and marginal farmers and farmers with a single crop holding, were with chronic hunger. What is more, their survival strategy, of migration for casual labour; also offered a setback, thanks to drought in the neighbouring states. With nowhere else to go, they looked to the state to provide them food in exchange for work. But the response was far from enough.

Table 5.1: Information on Drought in Rajasthan

Year	*No. of Districts affected*	*No. of Villages affected*	*Population affected (Lakh)*
1967-68	12	2365	15.16
1968-69	26	22799	131.63
1969-70	23	10877	72.84
1970-71	8	503	3.29
1971-72	12	4510	30.00
1972-73	26	18768	140.23
1974-75	25	20073	148.99
1977-78	18	12251	92.37
1978-79	24	5609	NA
1979-80	26	31095	240.00
1980-81	26	21395	167.79
1981-82	26	23246	200.12
1982-83	26	22606	171.62
1984-85	21	10276	92.02
1985-86	26	26859	218.18
1986-87	27	31936	252.70
1987-88	27	36252	317.37
1988-89	17	4497	43.45
1989-90	25	14024	120.67
1991-92	30	30041	289.00
1992-93	12	4376	34.66
1993-94	25	22586	246.81
1995-96	29	25478	273.82
1996-97	21	5905	55.29
1997-98	24	4633	14.91
1998-99	20	20039	215.07
1999-2000	26	23406	261.79

Note: The total number of Districts in the State are 32.

Desert Development Programme

Rajasthan has taken yet another grant step forward to tame the Thar in western part of the State. The State has in fact launched a multipronged battle to subdue the Thar to make it possible for the people to live in this hostile tract in a respectable manner. The magnitude of the problem can be judged from the fact that roughly three-fifths of Rajasthan, lying north-west of the Aravalies, falls within the limit of arid zone. It comprises Barmer, Bikaner, Churu, Ganganagar, Jaisalmer, Jalore, Jodhpur, Nagaur, Jhunjhunu, Pali and Sikar.

Of the total classified area of the desert reported to be 2,25,000 square km affecting a population of about 18.2 million, 2,09,000 square km, 89 per cent lies in Rajasthan inhabiting 13.5 crores of people. To tackle problems of this area on an enduring basis, the State formulated the project profile of a long-term master plan with a total outlay of Rs. 560 crore in the Seventh Plan. The plan covers the forestation, drinking water facilities for livestock, agriculture and irrigation sector, groundwater, sheep development, animal husbandry and industries. State district level coordination which includes monitoring, supervision and project planning fisheries and desert control in fringe areas outside these Districts.

Demographic Profile

According to 2001 census, the population of the State is 56.47 million constituting nearly 5.5 per cent of the country's population. Rural sector accounts for 77 per cent of the population, majority of which is poor. The male population is 29.38 and female 27.09 million. The sex ratio in the State is only 922 which is lower than that of India's average of 933. However, over the decade there has been a significant improvement in the sex ratio as in 1991 it was only 910. In the two selected districts under the Project, the sex ratio is considerably higher than that of the state average, being 978 in Banswara district and 966 in Chittorgarh district.

Due to hostile topography and climatic condition, the density of population in the State is still very low being only 165 persons per square kilometre as against the country's 324 persons. The State ranks 24th in this regard among all the states and union territories in the country. However, due to average annual exponential growth rate of 2.49 per cent during the 1990s the density in 2001 was much higher than that of 1991 when it was only 129 persons per square kilometre. It may be mentioned in this context that about 57.5 per cent of the state consists of the Great Indian Desert (THAR). This arid region of the state is very sparsely populated. In the Jaisalmer district (which is the largest district on area basis) the density was only 9 persons per sq km. In 1991, the population density in Banswara and Chittorgarh districts was 229 and 137 persons per sq/km respectively.

Rajasthan is projected to have huge increase in its population even if there is a substantial reduction in the fertility rates in the coming days. The State which registered one of the highest population growth rates in the country in the 2001 census, holds tremendous growth potential because 40 per cent of its present population is under 15 years of age and 47 per cent of the female population are in the reproductive age.

The 2001 census has shown that Rajasthan has a 2.5 per cent annual growth rate of population. With an estimated population of 56.5 million on March 1, 2001 the State has 9.6 million couples in the reproductive age (between 15 and 49 years). This figure was 7.5 million in 1991 and 5.8 million in 1981. The number is estimated to increase by 2.3 million by 2011. This growth is estimated to result in a population of 69.8 million in Rajasthan by 2011 and 81.9 million by 2021. It means that the population that is expected to be added in Rajasthan during the next 20 years is 25.4 million which is almost equal to the population of the State in 1971.

Literacy

In 2001 the literacy in the State was 61.03 per cent which was a significant improvement over 1991 when it was only 38.55 per cent. The literacy rate in the State was still lower than that of all-India average of 65 per cent. The male literacy rate was much higher being 76 per cent than that of female which was only 44 per cent. Thus, almost two-fifths of the population in the State was still illiterate. This is considered to be one of the major reasons for the economic backwardness of the state.

Per Capita Income

State domestic product is an important indicator for measuring the level of development and highlight regional disparities. Rajasthan state as per contents of the table given below is ranked at tenth position amongst 14 major states of the country in terms of per capita income (Table 5.2).

Table 5.2: Per Capita Income of States – 1995-96

Sl. No.	*State*	*Per Capita Income*			
		Constant (1980-81) Prices		*Current Prices*	
		Rs.	*Rank*	*Rs.*	*Rank*
1.	Andhra Pradesh	2407	8	9274	7
2.	Bihar	986	14	3524	14
3.	Gujarat	3375	4	11977	4
4.	Haryana	3679	3	13573	3
5.	Karnataka	2551	7	9384	6
6.	Kerala	2200	9	9004	8
7.	Madhya Pradesh	1791	11	6518	11
8.	Maharashtra	4598	1	15457	2
9.	Orissa	1608	13	6192	12
10.	Punjab	4176	2	16053	1
11.	Rajasthan	1974**	10	7523*	10
12.	Tamil Nadu	2820	5	10222	5
13.	Uttar Pradesh	1654	12	5872	13
14.	West Bengal	2707	6	8409	9
	ALL INDIA	2573		10525	

* Provisional ** Revised

Source: Economic Review 1998-99, Directorate of Economics & Statistics—Rajasthan.

Some Equality in Inequality

In a positive indication to the status of women's education in Rajasthan, the Gender Related Educational Development Index (GEDI) of the State has registered an increase by 3.6 times during 1991-2000 and the index of deprivation (IOD) has come down simultaneously. The indices were worked out by an appraisal at the panchayat samiti level on the basis of the methodology adopted for preparation of the Human Development Report by the United Nations Development Programme (UNDP). The study incorporated the changing relative status of panchayat samitis and took into account their growth trends.

The research was conducted by Hemlata Joshi, Professor of Geography, Mohanlal Sukhadia University, Udaipur, for the Jaipur-based Institute of Development Studies (IDS). GEDI had been introduced by the UNDP to measure inequality in educational achievement between women and men and its methodology imposed a penalty for inequality. GEDI falls when the achievement levels of both women and men go down or when the disparity between their achievements increases. The phenomenal increase in GEDI, from 0.192 to 0.693, combined with the decline in IOD from 0.808 to 0.307, was an explicit illustration of an improvement in the socio-educational status of women.

There are seven major factors that have affected the GEDI level in Rajasthan during the past decade. They are the State's physiography, level of educational amenities, economic development, socio-cultural traditions of a given area, political climate, distance from the nearest urban centre, and proximity to prosperous States, such as Punjab, Haryana, Delhi and Gujarat.

In 1991, when the GEDI of the State was only 0.192, 59 per cent of the panchayat samitis had GEDI value below average and no panchayat samiti, except Nimrana and Behror in Alwar district, had even achieved 0.4 level. Jaipur was the only district where more than 75 per cent of panchayat samitis had GEDI above 0.2.

During the decade of 1991-2000, 13 panchayat samitis maintained their first rank while 15 maintained the last rank. The study revealed that Udaipur district was at the top in the GEDI range and was followed by Alwar, Jalore, Jaipur and Ajmer. On the other side, Jaisalmer was at the bottom, followed by Jhunjhunu, Dhaulpur, Karauli and Churu.

In an interesting finding, the study had discovered that with a few exceptions, the districts belonging to deprived areas such as the western desert, southern hilly, south-eastern plateau and the central regions have registered higher growth rate when compared to other areas. Prominent among these districts are Barmer, Sirohi, Rajsamand, Bundi and Nagaur.

Among the 32 districts in the State, all panchayat samitis of seven districts and more than half of eight others registered improvement in both GEDI value and their ranks. At the end of the decade, as many as 234 panchayat samitis had GEDI level above 0.4; and only Kota remained at the below 0.3 level. Another trend of increase in the GEDI level from south and south-west to north and north-east directions had indicated that "winds of change" had swept through the State and helped remove the gender bias in education.

Agriculture

With a share of nearly 32 per cent in State GDP, and 70 per cent of workforce, agriculture plays an important role in the economy. Of the total gross cropped area of over 22 million hect., nearly half is devoted to foodgrains. Bajra and wheat among the cereals, gram among pulses, rape and mustard and soybean among the oilseeds and cotton as a cash crop are important. The State has a place of pride in the production of oilseeds particularly rapeseed and mustard, although cotton and wheat are primarily irrigated. With the cropping intensity of below 25 per cent, farming in the State is primarily rainfed. Kota, Ganganagar, Bundi and Dausa are the major districts with high percentage of irrigated area.

According to Report by the Central Groundwater Department, groundwater in 86 of Rajasthan's 236 blocks has been over-exploited, 21 are critical and 80 in the semi-critical category. Only 49 blocks can safely dig into groundwater reserves.

With less than one-third irrigated area, the Rajasthan agriculture consumes 83 per cent of water resources. Increased water scarcity and frequent droughts plague the State. The

Rajasthan water sector restructuring project (a $140 million World Bank Sponsored Project) aims to promote more sustainable development and use of the state's limited water resources by improving its management, particularly in the irrigation sector. By improving agricultural productivity, the project would generate additional jobs in the rural sector. Productivity would be enhanced by increasing the involvement of farmers and through the development of partnerships with the public and private sector. The project is expected to generate additional employment for 22,000 rural farm families per year, which represent a 24 per cent increase in rural farm employment.

Irrigation

Urgent steps are needed to grapple with the growing menace of water-logging in the Indira Gandhi Canal command area along the Ghaggar depressions. Official admit that in over 8,600 hectares of command area in the grip of the problem. The problem in some of the areas is so acute that water level up to 1.5 metre below the ground level could be located. As a result no cultivation in the area is possible.

Liberal use of the canal waters is aid to be the main reason for the area turning water-logged. The problem has further been accentuated by the groundwater recharge due to the Ghaggar flood inflows. It is learnt that the average rate of water use for the irrigated areas, measured in terms of water released at the head of the feeder canal was 1,500 mm as against the designed value of 723 mm.

In the neighbouring project areas of the Ganga and Bhakra the average rate of water used were 526 and 462 mm only, respectively. The average annual inflow in the head reach of stage-I due to the Ghaggar floods was 715 mm, which also contributed to the groundwater recharge. The only redeeming feature is that in certain areas of the canal the intensity of the problem may be come less with the reduction in the water availability due to the opening of more and more areas in stage-II. Even in stage-II of the project the area so far hit by water-logging is 1,000 hectares and it is located along the main canal.

Investigations for minimizing the losses from canals have been taken up in the right earnest by Sanyu Consultants Inc and Wapcos.

In Stage-II much would depend on the time required for the natural aquifer to get saturated. The monitoring of the ground water system has also been taken up. A net work of 500 piezometres was contemplated in 1996-97. Groundwater system model studies have also been undertaken with the assistance from Canadian International Development Agency (CIDA). To solve the problem Wapcos, the project consultants, have recommended 560 km interceptor drains and 896 shallow tubewells along the main canal and feeder.

The Rajasthan Canal is a supreme example of a project which is supposed to make the desert bloom. There are other lesser examples. But environmental studies now suggest that such canals can, unwittingly, become a major cause of desertification. Desertification is the sustained decline of biological productivity of soil, ending in dead desert sand with virtually no capacity to support plant life. Natural erosion and misuse of land by locals speed up desertification. There have, long been fears that the Thar desert is advancing towards Delhi, and that Sahara desert is creeping south into countries like Nigeria. However, studies by the Central Arid Zone Research Institute in Jodhpur have failed to detect a forward march by the Thar desert. The real problem lies elsewhere.

A study by David Steeds of West Africa shows that the threat of desertification is not greatest on the fringe of the Sahara desert. It is greatest in semi-arid areas well away from the desert where population is growing fast, thanks to expanding livestock and crops. The study has divided the area into six climatic belts with increasing rainfall, stretching south from the Sahara desert into the Sahel and beyond. It has estimated the maximum population that each belt can support on a long-term basis using traditional agricultural and livestock practices. It has also estimated the maximum population each belt can support on the basis of the natural growth of fuelwood from trees. In every case without exception, the land can support far more people on the basis of agriculture than of fuelwood.

The danger is obvious. Population will tend to keep rising because agriculture is still viable. But there is not enough fuelwood to sustain a rising population, and so trees are cut. The gap between the capacity of the land to support agriculture and yield fuel keeps worsening as trees are hacked down. Deforestation leads to soil erosion, and the process is accelerated by overgrazing caused by a rising animal population. The carrying capacity of the soil begins to fall, and the descent to desertification begins.

The Steeds' study shows that, from the viewpoint of fuelwood sustainability, the excess population in the two belts on the fringe of the Sahara desert is only 1.7 million. But the excess population is 3.7 million in the third belt and 7.1 million in the fourth belt, where agriculture is expanding. Given the strident growth of population in Africa, the excess population in these belts will double in a short time, putting unbearable pressure on local fuelwood. Thus desertification appears to be taking the shape of neo-deserts in the Sahelian heartland, not a southward creep of the Sahara desert.

Irrigation and modern agricultural techniques can greatly increase the carrying capacity of the lad with respect to agriculture. But this will simply attract a large flow of migrants, worsening the problem of deforestation and erosion. What looks good for crops and livestock may be disastrous for fuelwood and ultimately for the soil which is the basis of agriculture. The Steeds' study does not address this problem directly, but it logic points clearly in this direction.

What are the implication for a desert State like Rajasthan? It is well known that population in the State is rising fast. Thanks in fair measure to the Rajasthan Canal, population growth in the desert districts has been among the fastest anywhere in India, according to the 1981 census. It is also well known that the State has suffered from rampant deforestation and that the Aravali Hills have been denuded at an unprecedented rate. However, few people so far have seen any connection between the spread of the Rajasthan Canal and the spread of deforestation. The logic of the west African study suggests that there could indeed be a connection, perhaps a strong one. Research is needed to throw more light on the issue.

The demand for wood is much higher in a newly-opened area like the Rajasthan Canal than in old settled areas. Wood is used in rural areas for construction as well as fuel. Houses, fences, ladders, farm implements and a host of other items need poles. The demand for poles is strongest when a new area is being settled and new houses and structures are coming up. Twigs may be good enough for fuelwood but strong poles and roof beams can be obtained only from tree trunks or very large branches. Hence the incentive to cut trees is huge Rajasthan, and the government machinery is too weak and corrupt to check illegal felling.

The Rajasthan Canal has brought under crops large areas which once used to be grazing lands. Pastures in other parts of the State have also been brought under the plough because of rising population pressure. As a result grazing lands shrank from 11.3 million hectares in 1951-52 to 8.7 million hectares in 1977-78. At the same time the livestock population shot up. The net result has been extensive overgrazing, denuding once green pastures. When the soil loses its cover of grass and shrubs, the intense heat of the sun wreaks havoc on the exposed ground and erosion follows rapidly. Herders are progressively shifting from cattle to goats to overcome the shortage of animal feed. In 1951 Rajasthan had twice as many cattle as goats, but by 1983 there were 14 goats for every 10 cattle. In the short run goats can give desperate herders a living. But they eat anything in sight and in the ling run will devastate the environment. Even cattle are undergoing spontaneous mutation which enable them to eat shrubs which were once fatally poisonous, denuding the land further.

Livestock

With a major part of its arid area, Rajasthan occupies a place of pride in livestock. Of the total livestock population of 471 million, Rajasthan accounts for over 10 per cent. Although the share of buffaloes is only 9 per cent, camels, sheep and goat are quite prominent in Rajasthan in the livestock economy of the country (Table 5.3).

Table 5.3: Livestock in Rajasthan, 1992

(Number in millions)

	India	*Rajasthan*	*%Share in India*
Total	470.9	48.4	10.29
Cattle	204.6	11.7	5.72
Buffaloes	84.2	7.7	9.15
Sheep	50.8	12.5	24.61
Goat	115.3	15.3	13.28
Camels	1.0	0.7	72.65

White Revolution Takes a Big Leap

The White Revolution launched in Rajasthan more than a decade back has transformed the State's rural economy. The ambitious dairy development programme, commonly referred to as 'Operation Flood' is a revolution comparable in scale to the Green Revolution in agriculture. From the modest beginnings in the early seventies when the dairy programme was oriented towards supplying milk to the urban consumer, 'Operation Flood' today has brought a flood of benefits to the rural folk reducing in its wake, employment and pressure on milk supplies. The success of the integrated dairy development programme rests largely on efforts at setting up dairies and an organized marketing structure for milk products. More than that it is the outcome of a sustained programme of breed improvement and cattle health.

The Rajasthan Cooperative Dairy Federation, the apex body, plays an important role in the farmer's economy by processing and marketing of milk and milk products to ensure a remunerative price for the producers. Besides, it provides producers with inputs for cattle management and carries out intensive extension and training programme. Rajasthan occupies a significant place in the county for its fairly large number of milch cattle and production of milk. Despite this, prior to August, 1975 due to the lack of proper marketing facilities for milk, the cattle breeders had hardly any option except to convert the milk into *ghee* or *khoa* which used to yield them a meagre return. As a result, the cattle breeders remained poor which in turn affected their cattle breed.

To ameliorate the condition of the cattle breeders, an ambitious and multi-pronged programme of dairy development was taken up to increase the productivity of the milch animals with the aid of latest scientific techniques and to ensure a remunerative market. Besides ensuring increased production of milk and milk products, i.e. milk powder, butter, *ghee*, cheese and tetrapacked milk etc., the programme also envisages improvement in cattle breed and provision of balanced cattle feed. A chain of veterinary dispensaries and mobile medical units set up under the programme have also ensure proper treatment facilities.

Rural Poverty

According to Head-count Ratio, the proportion of the rural population below the poverty line in Rajasthan, based on Expert Group Methodology, declined from 44.8 per cent in 1973-74 to 33.5 per cent in 1983, 26.5 per cent in 1993-94 and 13.7 per cent in 1999-2000 (using 30 day recall period). No doubt, based on this measure of poverty alone, the existing poverty ratio in Rajasthan (15.3 per cent) is significantly lower than the national average rural poverty ratio of 26.1 per cent. But using other indicators of poverty and human development, Rajasthan would rank as one of the poorest regions. As it has been already indicated, income based poverty ratio is an inadequate measure of poverty. Low levels of land productivity, per capita income, literacy, health services etc. would increase the overall poverty index of the state.

Further, in 1997, the State Government of Rajasthan had undertaken a major exercise in all the villages of the State and collected particulars of families having annual income below Rs.20,000. According to this survey, nearly 30.1 per cent of families in rural areas were poor. In other words, estimation and procedures and methods also, matter. According to this survey, districts like Banswara, Chittorgarh, Dungarpur, Karauli and Udaipur had 40 to 70 per cent of families below the poverty line. Moreover, about 55 per cent of the poor people are reported to belong to the category of marginal farmers and agricultural labourers (HDR, 1999, p.38). Using the head-count ratio, India Rural Development Report (NIRD, 1999), observed about 45.9 per cent rural poverty ratio in southern Rajasthan comprising of Banswara, Udaipur and Dungarpur districts and 34.8 per cent in South Eastern Rajasthan, comprising Kota, Chittorgarh, Jhalawar and Bundi Districts. About 16 per cent rural population in these two regions of the State are also considered to be extremely poor. It has been further observed that about 55.6 per cent agricultural labourer in South-Eastern Rajasthan and 73.5 per cent agricultural labourers in Southern Rajasthan live below the poverty line. The incidence of poverty was comparatively low among those who were self-employed in agriculture, in all regions of the State. The Human Development Report of Rajasthan (1999) has further indicated that the total number of houseless households in Rajasthan is 25,076, of which 69 per cent are in rural areas. The number of such persons in rural area is 84,000. Nearly two-thirds of the population are deprived of electricity. Eighty per cent are deprived of toilet facilities. The total length of roads in Rajasthan was 42.6 km per 100 sq. km of area and 332.5 km per lakh of population. Besides, more than 50 per cent villages, (ranging from 50 to above 70 per cent), in Jhalawar, Udaipur, Baran, Chittorgarh, Dausa, Tonk, Alwar, Bundi, Ganganagar and Kota were not connected by roads.

Human Development Report And Panchayats

Rajasthan is the first State to formulate a human development report at the Panchayat Samiti level on the basis of development status index worked out with the United Nations Development Programme (UNDP) methodology. The three factors taken into account for the report are education, health and economy. The project has been undertaken by the Jaipur based Institute of Development Studies, which has completed an in-depth analysis of education and economic aspects in two phases and will take up the study of the health factor in the final phase. The appraisal of economic development index was completed recently.

The report has measured economic development at the Panchayat Samiti level with the help of income index, gender-related income index and human poverty index, going beyond the conventional per capita income concept. Besides making extensive analyses, the study has also pointed to possible actions on the economic development front. Despite a 43 per cent increase in income index 11 per cent rise in gender-related income index during 1991 to 1998 the constant prices, the index of deprivation remained high and Rajasthan had to go a long way to achieve the targeted value. The per capita income of rural areas in the State during the period rose from Rs. 4,523 to Rs. 6,432.

The changing relative status of Panchayat Samitis was brought out through indices, special distribution pattern, division-wise and district-wise classification, and distribution of areas having very high, high medium, low and very low indices. A great deal of spatial variation was seen in the income index among the 237 Panchayat Samitis spread over 32 districts and six divisions in the State. The economic development status increased from south-west and south to north-east, north and south-east direction. Prof. Joshi said the regional disparity in economic development had increased during the period of study.

While Sangod Panchayat Samiti in Kota district in 1991-92 and Sanganer in Jaipur in 1998-99 secured the top rank in the State, Aspur in Dungarpur district was the most deprived Panchayat Samiti and maintained its bottom rank. The poverty across the State decreased marginally during the 1990s with the human poverty index coming down from 57 per cent in 1991 to 55 per cent in 2001. As many as 157 Panchayat Samitis in the State had human poverty index measuring more than 50 per cent during 2001.

An analysis of the available 2001 census and other data throws an interesting side light on the place of the 32 districts of Rajasthan in 569 districts in the country as at present (Table 5.4).

Table 5.4: Ranks of Districts of Rajasthan Out of Total Districts in the Country

Percentage current user of family planning method	*Percentage of girl marrying below 18 years of age*	*Sex Ratio (females per 1000 males)*	*Percentage of women during pregnancy*	*Percentage of children getting complete immunisation*	*Female literacy rate (per cent)*	*Estimated percentage of village not connected with pucca road*	*Estimated percentage of safe drinking water (habitation)*	*Estimated percentage of Birth registered*	*Estimated percentage of death registered*	*Ranking of State/UTs on the basis of composite index*
341	493	328	269	478	336	254	272	322	96	337
290	420	453	416	447	405	343	469	452	305	456
399	517	135	278	506	540	364	392	425	330	477
308	489	396	245	264	432	471	253	399	368	403
514	460	434	309	551	407	411	520	468	487	555
407	445	518	387	505	403	345	540	376	290	504
377	558	187	374	275	510	407	385	450	285	449
332	499	451	306	402	436	303	393	418	269	428
358	566	400	279	322	485	454	273	396	275	438
492	479	179	332	448	487	458	270	439	279	439
356	531	246	502	495	276	360	448	426	276	460
395	548	424	357	435	417	362	305	402	379	478
507	436	555	403	446	429	300	514	421	383	530
365	273	31	298	444	523	305	318	417	299	382
99	377	485	385	378	292	283	384	477	304	371

(Contd.)

Percentage current user of family planning method	*Percentage of girl marrying below 18 years of age*	*Sex Ratio (females per 1000 males)*	*Percentage of women during pregnancy*	*Percentage of children getting complete immunisation*	*Female literacy rate (per cent)*	*Estimated percentage of village not connected with pucca road*	*Estimated percentage of safe drinking water (habitation)*	*Estimated percentage of birth registered*	*Estimated percentage of death registered*	*Ranking of State/UTs on the basis of composite index*
106	415	438	449	412	291	282	383	519	272	396
247	356	431	274	380	240	363	306	395	346	384
506	403	561	517	501	520	421	350	378	464	553
402	382	172	408	383	541	320	422	362	301	432
320	556	341	320	475	450	498	446	387	226	464
201	385	260	247	414	187	231	387	374	354	332
378	455	401	346	440	462	224	292	420	376	433
467	449	514	293	502	389	423	516	492	509	542
309	490	439	246	265	173	472	254	297	373	364
383	528	229	335	443	448	403	468	424	266	467
388	404	117	352	376	486	326	391	372	338	407
413	394	69	318	285	474	385	339	359	251	376
468	450	450	294	503	497	424	517	380	256	488
328	336	230	261	297	236	331	359	405	323	357
433	374	270	287	436	478	228	260	444	462	423
371	561	313	397	313	519	497	403	437	270	496
400	541	159	321	507	411	384	338	413	241	446

6

Methodology

"True Economics stands for Social justice. It promises the good of all equally including the weakest and it is indispensable for decent life."

—Mahatma Gandhi

The study was organised at the district level from secondary sources and village/household level from primary sources.

Collection of secondary data at District Level:—The secondary data of the districts from various State departments were collected on the indicators likely to influence poverty. Following State departments had been consulted:

1. Department of Rural Development
2. Department of Economics and Statistics
3. Department of Agriculture
4. Department of Animal Husbandry
5. Department of Medical and Health
6. Department of Agricultural Marketing
7. Rajasthan Cooperative Milk Federation
8. State Census Office, Jaipur.

Besides above, a number of Central Government Departments, autonomous organizations and NGOs were consulted to obtain secondary data of the districts. The names of such notable organizations are as given below:

1. Ministry of Health and Family Welfare
2. Registrar General Census, Ministry of Home Affairs
3. ICMR
4. Food and Nutrition Board, Ministry of Human Resource Development

5. Planning Commission
6. UNICEF
7. Harish Chand Mathur Institute of Management
8. Vatsalya, an N.G.O.
9. Institute of Human Resources
10. I.D.S. Jaipur

Collection of Primary Data

A Basic data sheet was prepared for all the 32 districts giving broad information about total rural families, those Below the Poverty Line and average number of farm families per village (Table 6.1).

2. In consultation with the Government of Rajasthan, two districts—Chittorgarh (49%) and Banswara (72.9%)—one with high and the other with medium BPL ratio were selected for the study. In Rajasthan, a Panchayat Samiti represents the concept of the Block. Two Panchayat Samities—Rashmi (Chittorgarh) and Sajjangarh (Banswara) were selected on the basis of highest poverty ratio within the districts. Draft questionnaires for collecting primary data from village households and villages were developed and discussed with the Ministry officials. The suggestions put forward by the officials were incorporated. The final questionnaires were then put for field testing in the month of July, 2001 in one of the tentatively identified Panchayat Samities of Chittorgarh district. A few modifications suggested by the field functionaries were incorporated with the approval of the Ministry. Table 6.2 gives details of the number of villages and families where a structured questionnaire was canvassed both at the village and household levels.

In the selected blocks, one-third of the villages were completely surveyed and in remaining two-third of the villages only BPL families as identified by the state government were covered. The number of villages covered from two blocks were 186 in Sajjangarh (Banswara) and 81 from Rashmi (Chittorgarh). The total number of families surveyed were over 30,000.

Field Survey: The questionnaires so finalized were got printed for collection of data. Rajasthan being a Hindi speaking

Table 6.1: District Level Basic Data

Sl. No	*Districts*	*Total No.*	*No. of B.P.L. Families*					*Per cent B.P.L*
			Households	*Total*	*S.C.*	*S.T.*	*O.B.C.*	*Others*
1.	Ajmer	237514	62932	16064	4003	33782	9083	26.4
2.	Alwar	358621	78911	21168	6503	21120	24120	22
3.	Banswara	732657	169792	8875	149242	4914	6761	72.9
4.	Baran	140172	45684	12934	13177	15805	3768	32.5
5.	Barmer	273750	78603	20082	9050	16745	32726	28.7
6.	Bharatpur	249257	45869	17200	1327	12402	14937	18.3
7.	Bhilwara	301451	104663	27253	21727	44025	11658	34.7
8.	Bikaner	151505	53811	19426	621	10754	23010	36.8
9.	Bundi	121938	43918	12958	9993	17015	3952	25.5
10.	Chittorgarh	271184	133253	28411	48016	36650	20176	49.1
11.	Churu	224261	64191	30646	402	11499	21644	28.5
12.	Dausa	172585	40345	12983	9818	13016	4528	35.8
13.	Dholpur	89060	31047	9697	1815	13899	5636	34.8
14.	Dungarpur	182900	130459	7249	106457	6380	10373	71.3
15.	Ganganagar	189467	40281	26023	63	8058	6137	20.2
16.	Hanumangarh	173138	37878	20099	151	8671	8957	21.8
17.	Jaipur	396800	61631	18071	9321	21108	13131	16.3
18.	Jaisalmer	72217	18857	3332	1607	3367	10551	26.1
19.	Jalore	179058	67150	21889	10664	20224	14373	37.5
20.	Jhalawar	166203	55190	16205	9671	18071	11243	33.2
21.	Jhunjhunu	238401	25202	10675	1034	7430	6063	10.5
22.	Jodhpur	255480	34744	10492	3577	7596	13079	13.1
23.	Karuli	148473	60599	18520	14707	16906	10466	40.8
24.	Kota	117934	37867	13134	4921	15682	4130	32.1
25.	Nagaur	339825	56772	27820	297	13597	15058	16.5
26.	Pali	268280	64414	22443	10439	23979	7553	24
27.	Rajsamand	162062	57961	10037	15355	24055	8514	35.7
28.	S. Madhopur	138336	51840	15306	9666	19002	7866	37.4
29.	Sikar	248931	28460	12281	1636	6937	7606	10
30.	Sirohi	116265	36060	10176	17940	5894	2050	30.9
31.	Tonk	166625	54876	16316	10857	19404	8299	32.9
32.	Udaipur	384185	222915	13579	157539	22409	29388	58

state, care was taken to get the questionnaires translated in Hindi before printing so that the functionaries in the Panchayat Samities and even the villagers could read and understand them properly. Sufficient number of copies of the questionnaires were also printed in English for the use of Investigators, Supervisors and Block and District Coordinators. To understand each and every column of the questionnaires a guideline was developed both for household and village survey and got printed in Hindi as well as in English. To create awareness amongst the local residents posters were pasted in the notice boards of the gram panchayats and other prominent places in the villages indicating the date of survey and the object of survey.

Table 6.2: Survey Sample Frame

	Banswara (Sajjangarh)	*Chittorgarh (Rashmi)*
Villages	186	81
Total Households	33243	13374
% B.P.L.	85.6	50.5
Household Surveyed		
BPL	19043	6752
APL	1989	2394
Total	21032	9146
Investigators	186	100
Supervisors	19	10
Samiti Supervisor	1	1
Senior Supervisor	1	1

Human Resource: For collection of primary data and its proper scrutiny, a five tier system was developed under which a State coordinator was made responsible at State level to organize work in the State, provide logistic support, training, survey material and coordinate the work of the field functionaries. At District level a district coordinator was appointed to organize survey work, train supervisors and investigators and develop liaison with State coordinator. He was also made responsible to scrutinize the filled in formats, collect forms and pass on the same to appropriate persons for computerization and analysis. To supervise the survey work of investigators, one supervisor on every ten investigators was attached to guide and supervise the work of investigators. They were also made responsible for test checking of the surveyed household forms and to collect secondary information of the villages under their charge in the Panchayat Samiti. Besides, a block coordinator was made responsible to provide support to the field functionaries in obtaining secondary information from different sources of Panchayat Samiti, block and district. The investigators were so placed that none of them had to survey more than hundred families. While developing the human resource, care was taken to give respective responsibility to the persons who were friendly to the village families and had worked in the same area for a long time.

Accordingly district coordinators collected the basic information on number of villages in the Panchayat Samities and list of families both APL and BPL in the villages. Before start of the survey, one day training was organized in both the Panchayat Samities on 29th July 2001 for supervisors and investigators in which they were got acquainted with the object and necessity of the study apart from methodology to be used for household survey and method of filling up the questionnaires. As per the methodology, 30 per cent of the villages were surveyed for 100 per cent households, whereas 70 per cent villages were surveyed only for BPL families.

The survey in both the Panchayat Samities started on 1st August 2001 and continued at Rashmi up to 21st August, 2001, whereas at Sajjangarh it continued till 31st August, 2001. During the course of the survey, physical appraisal was undertaken by Shri Willfred Lakra, Joint Secretary, Department of Rural Development, Ministry of Rural Development, Government of India. He visited the villages of Panchayat Samiti Rashmi of Chittorgarh district on 15th August, 2001 and discussed with the villagers and pointed out some discrepancies in survey which was later rectified to the satisfaction of the Joint Secretary. He was also of the view that some modifications needed to be done in collection of data and asked to include some more information in the format. The information were later collected from the villages. Similar information were also collected from villages of Sajjangarh Panchayat Samiti. The field data were computerised, cleaned and processed.

Composite Index

These variables that could generally influence poverty, either directly or indirectly were grouped under nine major blocks namely: (i) demography, (ii) housing and sanitation, (iii) literacy, (iv) health, (v) nutrition, (vi) agriculture, (vii) live stock, (viii) infrastructure, and (ix) development. These were subjected to statistical regression analysis for estimating the relative role of each of the significant variables in determining poverty. The estimates of elasticity to measure the relative role of various factors in influencing poverty was found out by estimating a log-linear regression.

The indicators considered at district, village and household level were in consonance with each other. These are presented in Table 6.3.

Table 6.3: Indicators at District, Village and Household Level

District Level	*Village Level*	*Household Level*
Agriculture		
Per cent irrigated Area		Agricultral land per household
Cropping intensity		
Per cent Small holdings	Per cent irrigated area	Irrigated land per household
Per cent Marginal holdings		Owned land per household
Average area per holding — hec	Per cent area under rice and wheat	Kharif land per household
Average area per holding (SC) — hec	Per cent Irrigated Area under rice and wheat	Kharif irrigated land per household
Average area per holding (ST) — hec	Dependable source of irrigation (%)	
Production in 000′ tonnes Cereals/lakh population	Use of diesel pump (%)	Rabi land per household
Production of Oilseeds/lakh population	Distance of Mandi Yard (km)	Rabi irrigated land per household
Production of Cash Crop/lakh population		Zayad land per household
	Distance of Agri Centre (km)	Zayad irrigated land
	Panchayat resources allocation for Agriculture	
Demography		
Per cent of urban population	SC (%)	Female Headed households (%)
SC/ST population	ST (%) as	S.C./S.T. (%)
Sex Ratio	Workers (%) of total population	Sex ratio (%)
Agricultural Labour/Rural Population	Population density	
Living Children (M)		

(Contd.)

(*Contd.*)

District Level	*Village Level*	*Household Level*
Living Children (F)		
Population density		
Development		Wage Rate
NDP/capita (1991-92)		Agricutural — Male
Annual growth rate (81-92)		
BPL families/rural population	Per cent beneficiaries covered	—Female
BPL families engaged in Agri.	Per cent Crossing Poverty Line	Non-Agricultural — Male
BPL families Registered under I.A.Y –Number	Receiving Pension (%)	—Female
JGSY Number		
JRY Number	Drought (%)	
Women getting employment in Swarojgar/JGSY	Per cent population effected	
No. of people regd. under TRYSEM/JGSY	Flood (%)	
	Per cent population effected	
Average Market Price (Wheat) Rs. per quintal	Self-Help Group (%)	Training under TRYSEM
Average Market Price (Rice) Rs. per quintal		
	DWCRA	Help from IRDP
Crop loss due to drought (%)	Wage rate (Rs.)	
	ssSkilled Male	Increase in Income from IRDP
No.of Self Help Groups	Unskilled Male	Drought Effected (%)
Persons covered under old age pension upto 2001	Skilled Female	Flood Effected (%)
	Unskilled Female	Both

(*Contd.*)

(Contd.)

District Level	*Village Level*	*Household Level*
	Panchayat allocation of resources for Development	Loss in days due to drought/flood
		Loss in Rs. due to drought/flood
		Income
		Economic Activities
		Days allocation
		Male — Agricultural
		Non-Agricultural
		Others
		Female — Agricultural
		Non-Agricultural
		Others
		Migration
		Duration (Days)
		Distance (kms)
Housing and Sanitation		
Pucca House		
Owned House		Electricity available in the house (%)
House less families	Regular Supply of Electricity (%)	Tap (%)
Toilet	Safe Drinking Water (%)	Type of House (*Pucca*)—Own (%)
Safe Drinking Water		Rented (%)
		Given Free (%)
		Indira Awaas Yojna (%)

(Contd.)

(*Contd.*)

District Level	*Village Level*	*Household Level*
	Is village Electrified (%)	
Infrastructure		
No. of branches of co-operative banks	Access to cooperatives/Government for	
Access to *pucca* road (%)	Loan for — Seed	Sources of Loan
No. of branches of commercial banks	Fertilizer	Cooperative for Agriculture (%)
No. of Regulated Markets	Medicine	—For non-Agricuture (%)
Fair Price shop	Access to *Pucca* Road (%)	
No. of Milk Co-operative/lakh population	Distance of *Pucca* Road (km)	
Electricity (%)	Distance of Ration Shop (km)	
	Distance of Railway Station (km)	
	Distance of Post Office (km)	
	Panchayat resources allocation to Infrastructure (%)	
Live Stock		
Cows- Cross bred	Cows (miltch) per Capita	
Cows-Indigenous	Buffaloes (miltch) per Capita	Miltch Cow
Buffaloes		Miltch Buffaloes
Draught Cattle above 3 years	Live Stock per Capita	
Milk Cooperatives	Distance of Vaternary Hospital	Other Animals
	Panchayat allocation of resources to Live Stock(%)	

(*Contd.*)

(Contd.)

District Level	Village Level	Household Level
Nutrition		
Per capita availability of milk kg/day		Consumption (kg)
Annapurna Benificiaries/lakh population	ICDS villages (%)	Cereals
Access to Anganwadi Centres/lakh population`		Milk & Milk Product
Protein Deficient (%)		Edible Oil
Calorie Deficient (%)		Pulses
Severely Mal. Nut. Child (M) (%)		Fruits
Severely Mal. Nut. Child (F) (%)		Vegetables
CED (M) (%)		Sweetener
CED (F) (%)		Egg
		Fish/Meat
		Rice
		Wheat
		Others
Literacy		
Literacy (Male)		
Literacy (Female)	Literacy Rate (%)	Literacy rate (%)
Children Attending school I-XII (Male)	Primary School Boys	
Children Attending school I-XII (Female)	Primary School Girls	
Drop-out rate (Male)	Primary School Children	
Drop-out rate (Female)	Panchayat resources allocation for Literacy and Culture	
Children attending primary school (Male)		
Children attending primary school (Female)		

(Contd.)

(*Contd.*)

District Level	*Village Level*	*Household Level*
Health		
No. of Doctors/lakh population		Disabled persons per 1,00,000
No.of beds/ lakh population	Trained Dai (%)	
Complete ANC (%)	Disabled (%)	
Safe Delivery (%)	Distance of PHC (km)	
Complete Immunisations (%)	Distance of Sub-Centre (km)	
Current User of Family Planning Methods (%)	Distance of Private Practitioner (km)	
3rd & Higher Order Births (%)	Panchayat resources allocation for Health (%)	
Girls marrying after 18 years of age (%)		
IMR		
Exp. Life (Male) — Yes		
Exp. Life (Female) — Yes		

In working out the composite index following methodology was adopted. To start with, all variables were categorised as positive or negative. Positive variables are those whose higher values are measures of prosperity (such as *pucca* house, electricity availability) and negative variables are those for which higher values are indicative of deprivation such as houseless families, IMR etc. Further (for each district in case of secondary data and village in case of primary data) the values of each variable were converted into indicators as under:

$$\text{Indicator (I)} = \frac{X_{max} - X}{X_{max} - X_{min}} \text{ for positive variables}$$

$$= \frac{X - X_{max}}{X_{max} - X_{min}} \text{ for negative variables}$$

where X_{max} = maximum value of the variable in the districts

X_{min} = minimum value of the variable in the districts

X = value of the variable for the district

Thereafter the Composite Human Poverty Index (CHPI) was computed using the indicator values and weights as explained below:

$$\text{CHPI} = \frac{\Sigma WI}{\Sigma W}$$

where *W* is the weight and *I* is the value of the indicator.

The composite index has been worked out using the data at the district, village level and household levels after grouping the variables into broad heads and giving suitable weights. For each broad group Composite Index (C-I) has been worked out and that combined for all groups a Composite Human Poverty Index (CHPI) has been calculated.

Mapping

Based on the Composite Index (CI) for each indicator as well as combined CHPI, the districts are categorised in the following groups and mapped using a different scheme. Same uniform pattern and scheme has been followed and districts are mapped accordingly.

Groups
1. Around the state average (within 5% of average value)
2. Between 5 to 10% below the state average
3. Below 10% of state average
4. Between 5 to 10% of above the state average
5. More than 10% of state average

Poverty Ratio Estimation

Ideally the Composite Index (CI) value and CHPI values should be used only for ranking purposes for inter-district/ inter-village comparison. But it is desirable if estimation of poverty ratio could also be attempted even with all its limitations. With this a relationship of poverty ratio and CHPI was worked out based on the data of the districts for which the ranks broadly matched. Making use of this and adjusting for intercept and slope corresponding to the district average the estimation of poverty ratio has also been attempted. The results though crude are the best which could be attempted in the study.

7

Rural Poor — Who, Where and Why District Level Analysis

Question often posed, for which groping for answer is:

Does anyone believe that the weakest and smallest and least developed economies—the poorest people in the world—can look to the twenty first century with confidence in the future.

It becomes clear from the earlier discussion that poverty is a much broader concept than what is generally thought of. A simple head-count ratio, derived from income based poverty line is not, cannot and does not reflect the true nature of human deprivation. Therefore, this study, developed a composite poverty index for different districts of Rajasthan, using elasticities of various indicators and their relative importance as weights. The list of variables considered at the district level along with group level weights are as under:

Table 7.1: Variables considered for District mapping along with Group weights

		Indicator/group	*Weight*
(i)	Demography	Urbanisation	
		SC/ST population	
		Sex Ratio	
		Agricultural Labour/Rural Population	
		Living Children (Male)	
		Living Children (Female)	
		Group weight	6.0
(ii)	Housing & Sanitation	*Pucca* House	
		Own House (%)	
		Houseless families	
		Toilet	
		Safe Drinking Water	
		Group Weight	8.0

(*Contd.*)

(Contd.)

	Indicator/group	*Weight*
(iii) Literacy	Literacy Rate (Male)	
	Literacy Rate (Female)	
	Children attending school (Male)	
	Children attending school (Female)	
	Drop-out rate (Male)	
	Drop-out rate (Female)	
	Primary school attendance (Male)	
	Primary school attendance (Female)	
	Group Weight	15.0
(iv) Health	No. of Doctors/lakh population	
	No. of beds/lakh population	
	Complete Antenatal Care (%)	
	Safe Delivery (%)	
	Complete Immunisations (%)	
	Current User of Family Planning Methods (%)	
	3rd and Higher Order Births (%)	
	Girls marrying after 18 years of age (%)	
	Infant Mortality Rate (IMR)	
	Expectation of life (Male)	
	Expectation of life (Female)	
	Group Weight	12.0
(v) Nutrition	Per capita availability of milk kg/day	
	Annapurna Beneficiaries/lakh population	
	Access to Anganwadi Centres/lakh population	
	Protein Deficiency (%)	
	Calorie Deficiency (%)	
	Severely Malnourished Children (Male) (%)	
	Severely Malnourished Children (Female) (%)	
	Chronic Energy Deficiency (CED) – Adult Male (%)	
	Chronic Energy Deficiency (CED) – Adult (Female)(%)	
	Group Weight	13.0
(vi) Livestock	Cows—Cross bred per capita	
	Cows—Indigenous per capita	
	Buffaloes per capita	
	Draught Cattle Above 3 years per capita	
	No. of Milk Cooperatives per capita	
	Group Weight	10.0

(Contd.)

(*Contd.*)

	Indicator/group	*Weight*
(vii) Agriculture	Irrigated Area (%)	
	Cropping intensity	
	% small holding	
	% marginal holding	
	Average area per holding	
	Average area per holding (SC)	
	Average area per holding (ST)	
	Production in '000 tonnes of Cereals/lakh population	
	Production in '000 tonnes of Oilseeds/lakh population	
	Production of Cash Crop in '000 tonnes/lakh population	
	Group Weight	10.0
(viii) Infrastructure	No. of branches of co-operative bank/lakh population	
	No. of branches of commercial bank/lakh population	
	No. of Regulated Markets/lakh population	
	No. of Fair Price Shops/ lakh population	
	No. of Milk Co-operatives/lakh population	
	Access to *pucca* road (%)	
	Electricity availability (%)	
	Group weight	12.0
(ix) Development	NDP per capita (1991-92)	
	Annual growth rate of NDP per capita (81-92)	
	BPL families /rural population	
	BPL families engaged in agriculture (%)	
	No. of BPL families registered under IAY (%)	
	No. of BPL families registered under JGSY (%)	
	No. of BPL families registered under JRY (%)	
	No. of Women getting employment in Swarojgar/JGSY (%)	
	No. of people registered under TRYSEM/JGSY (%)	
	Average Market Price(Wheat)	Rs. per quintal
	Average Market Price (Rice)	Rs. per quintal
	Crop loss due to Drought (%)	
	No. of Self-Help Groups	Per lakh population
	Persons covered under old age pension (%)	Per lakh population
	Group Weight	14.0
	Total	**100**

FACTORS INFLUENCING RURAL POVERTY IN RAJASTHAN

Out of the seventy four sub-indicators considered (as mentioned in Table 7.1) about one-third turned out to be statistically significant in terms of correlation with poverty ratio. However, the relative importance of these variables differed from district to district. Therefore, a detailed group specific as well as indicator specific discussion would be in order. Composite indices for different indicator groups are presented in Tables 7.2 to 7.10 and Composite Human Poverty Index (CHPI) combining all Indicators in Table 7.11.

Demography and Rural Poverty

This study considered six demography related variables or sub-indictors which could influence poverty either directly or indirectly. These are level of urbanisation, proportion of agricultural labour population, proportion of SC/ST population, sex ratio, the number of living male children and living female children. Of these, the first three indicators were statistically significant. However, we analysed the other variables also because in Rajasthan male/female ratio was reported to be unfavourable to females because of sex bias against female children, due to poverty. Similarly, the number of living male and female children reflected whether appropriate child care was taken and also whether there was any gender dimension in this.

(a) Level of Urbanisation and Rural Poverty.

The level of urbanisation turned out to be a significant determinant of rural poverty.

The elasticity co-efficient of urbanisation as a determinant of rural poverty was 0.67, which meant that 1 per cent rise in the proportion of urbanisation resulted in 0.67 per cent decline in the rural poverty ratio. Relatively poor districts with high CHPI had also low levels of urbanisation.

(b) Agricultural Labour and Incidence of Rural Poverty

It has been generally observed from NSS data that rural poverty is largely concentrated among agricultural labour households. Therefore, the relationship between agricultural labour household and rural poverty (CHPI) was examined. The elasticity co-efficient of proportion of agricultural labour as a determinant of rural poverty ratio was 0.11, which implied that one per cent decline in the proportion of agricultural labour population led to 0.11 per cent fall in rural poverty ratio. In terms of proportion of agricultural labour population to total rural population, the districts of Karauli, Udaipur, Sawai Madhopur, Hanumangarh, Sri Ganganagar, Kota, Sirohi, Jhalawar, Tonk and Pali were among the top districts, which were also mainly among the top poor districts.

(c) Proportion of Scheduled Caste and Scheduled Tribe Population and Incidence of Rural Poverty

It is well known that scheduled castes and scheduled tribes form the socially most vulnerable group of population. It was therefore, intended to know the nature and extent of relationship between proportion of SC/ST population on the one hand and CHPI on the other. The elasticity co-efficient of proportion of SC/ST population, as a determinant of rural poverty was 0.52. This showed that 1 per cent higher in the SC/ST population would result in 0.52 per cent increase in rural poverty ratio. The districts like Banswara, Dangarpur, Chittorgarh, Baran, Dausa, Ganganagar, Karauli, Sirohi, Udaipur and Jalore are the top ten districts in terms of higher proportion of SC/ST population and half of these were relatively high poverty districts.

It may be mentioned that the composite index can take values between 0 and 100; 0 representing no deprivation and 100 representing highest deprivation all relating to the highest level achieved. The average value of the composite index for demography is 51.3. This indicates that the districts of Rajasthan on an average are at half the level as compared to the best achieved in the state. The 16 districts having composite index values higher than the average (i.e. with higher levels of deprivation in terms of demography indicator) are Banswara, Barmer, Bhilwara, Bikaner, Bundi, Chittorgarh, Dungarpur, Tonk, Jaisalmer, Jalore, Jhalawar, Nagaur, Rajsamand, Sikar, Sirohi and Udaipur. Out of these, 5 districts had even higher levels of C.Is which are Banswara, Bhilwara, Jaisalmer, Jalore and Sirohi.

Housing and Sanitation

Under this group, variables like percentage of families having own house, *pucca* house, proportion of houseless population, proportion of households having access to safe drinking water and toilet facilities were considered. All these variables turned out to be significant.

(a) Access to Pucca House

Percentage of families not having *pucca* house were found to be positively correlated with percentage of rural families below the poverty line. In other words, having a *pucca* house was an indication of not being poor. The top poorer districts of Rajasthan having highest head-count ratio were also those where percentage of families not having *pucca* house were high. In other words, in the absence of detailed statistical exercise, even the simple counting of number of *pucca* houses in a village could by and large be a reliable basis for estimating the proportion of people below or above the poverty line.

(b) Incidence of Houselessness and Rural Poverty

It is generally believed that those who do not have houses of their own are also the poor people. We therefore, included it in our analysis as one of the variables which could influence poverty. The elasticity coefficient of percentage of houseless families as a determinant of poverty was 0.20, which indicated that 1 per cent fall in the proportion of houseless families would result in the decline in poverty ratio by 0.20 per cent.

Table 7.2: Demography Population

	Population Nos.	*Urban Population (%)*	*SC+ST/ population (%)*	*Sex ratio 2001*	*Agricultural Labour as per cent of Rural Population*	*Living children (Male) number per household*	*Living children (Female) number per household*	*Composite Index*	*Rank*
Ajmer	1729207	40.09	19.1	932	2.92	1.4	1.3	48.6	21
Alwar	2296580	14.52	36.48	887	1.76	1.3	1.3	46.2	27
Banswara	1155600	7.13	86.49	976	2.34	1.3	1.3	59.1	4
Baran	810326	16.93	47.48	978	1.95	1.2	1.3	47.5	24
Barmer	1435222	7.39	34.32	896	0.85	1.6	1.4	54.8	11
Bharatpur	1651584	19.49	32.52	857	2.09	1.5	1.3	47.4	25
Bhilwara	1593128	20.66	37.13	964	2.58	1.2	1.1	59.8	3
Bikaner	1211140	35.51	23.17	889	1.19	1.4	1.4	53.1	14
Bundi	770248	18.63	42.53	908	3.41	1.4	1.4	52.3	15
Chittorgarh	1484190	16.04	48.15	966	3.32	1.2	1.1	57.4	6
Churu	1543211	28.62	34.53	948	1.11	1.3	1.3	48.4	23
Dausa	994431	10.33	50.68	899	1.59	1.4	1.3	44.2	29
Dholpur	749479	17.92	30.43	828	1.37	1.6	1.4	46.8	26
Dungarpur	874549	7.32	80.78	1027	3.26	1.3	1.2	56.3	7
Ganganagar	1402444	25.28	48.39	873	8.08	1.1	1.1	48.9	20
Hanumangarh	1220333	20.04	42.75	895	9.53	1	1.1	50.4	18
Jaipur	3887895	49.39	22.65	897	1.59	1.3	1.3	42.2	30
Jaisalmer	344517	15.19	22.21	821	1.66	1.3	1.3	61.0	2
Jalore	1142563	7.6	44.8	968	3.44	1.4	1.4	63.2	1
Jhalawar	956971	14.24	40.21	928	5.95	1.3	1.3	53.2	13

(Contd.)

(Contd.)

	Population Nos.	Urban Population (%)	SC+ST/ population (%)	Sex ratio 2001	Agricultural Labour as per cent of Rural Population	Living children (Male) number per household	Living children (Female) number per household	Composite Index	Rank
Jhunjhunu	1582421	33.75	26.83	946	1.56	1.2	1.2	38.6	31
Jodhpur	2153483	20.65	36.87	908	1.77	1.6	1.3	45.3	28
Karauli	927719	14.27	47	858	8.63	1.5	1.3	48.4	22
Kota	1220505	53.44	22.2	895	6.63	1.3	1.3	37.8	32
Nagaur	2144810	17.2	41	951	2.09	1.3	1.3	55.5	9
Pali	1486432	21.5	40.08	983	4.5	1.4	1.4	50.7	17
Rajsamand	822721	13.08	38.08	1002	3.70	1.2	1	52.0	16
Sawai Madhopur	875752	19.09	38.98	889	4.43	1.5	1.3	50.2	19
Sikar	1842914	20.64	38.81	951	2.29	1.2	1.2	56.1	8
Sirohi	654029	17.65	64.21	944	5.06	1.5	1.3	57.4	5
Tonk	975006	20.89	39.17	936	3.48	1.4	1.3	54.3	12
Udaipur	2066580	18.66	62.44	972	3.7	1.2	1	55.2	10
Rajasthan		20.1	40.01	896	3.11	1.3	1.23	51.3	

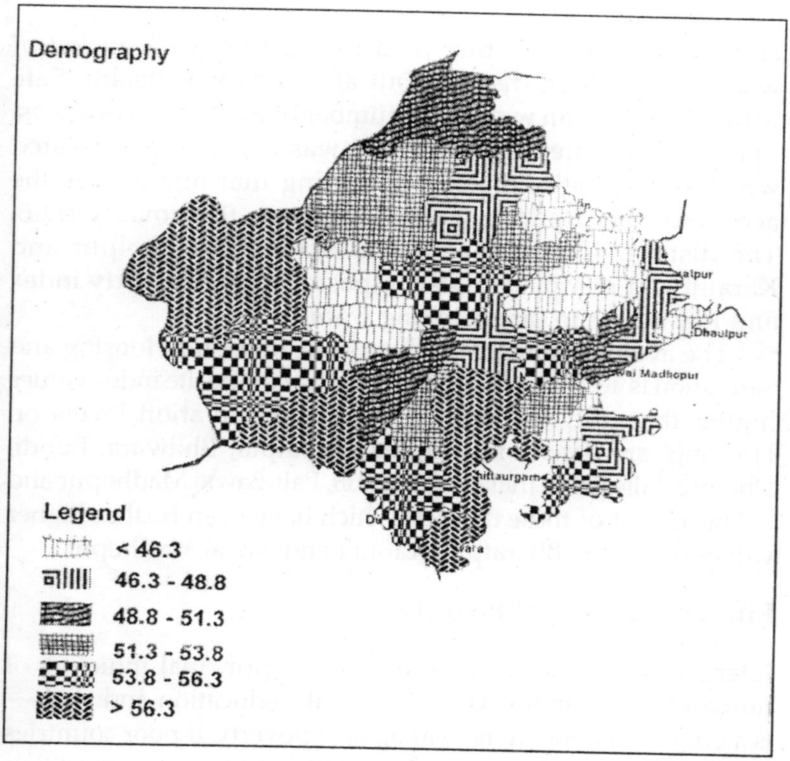

Table 7.2

(c) Access to Toilets

The districts of Ganganagar, Hanumangrah, Ajmer, Dausa and Jaipur had relatively low CHPI and more access to toilet facilities. Conversely, Banswara, Dungarpur, Bharatpur, Alwar, Jhalawar, Jalore, Sawai Madhopur, and Dholpur had relatively high or medium CHPI and low access to toilet facilities. Although toilet facilities may not necessarily influence consumption based poverty ratio directly, it improves sanitation and human health, thereby having influence on human poverty index.

(d) Access to Safe Drinking Water

Access to safe drinking water in the village helps in saving time for both men and women to either earn more income or enjoy leisure hours rather than toiling to fetch a bucket of water from a long distance but also improves health. Safe drinking water can ward off a number of water born diseases. The access to safe drinking water was negatively correlated with poverty ratio, thereby indicating that higher was the access to safe drinking water, lower was the poverty ratio. The districts like Barmer, Sawai Madhopur, Dholpur and Karauli had relatively high composite human poverty index and low access to safe drinking water.

The average value of the composite index for Housing and Sanitation is 40.1. The 12 districts having composite index values higher than the average (i.e. higher deprivation levels on Housing) are Banswara, Barmer, Bharatpur, Bhilwara, Bundi, Dholpur, Jalisalmer, Jhalawar, Karauli, Pali, Sawai Madhopur and Udaipur. Out of these districts which have even further higher values of C.I. are Bharatpur, Karauli and Sawai Madhopur.

Literacy and Rural Poverty

Literacy is considered to be one of the principal indictors of human poverty index. Human capital—education and skills—is a critical weapon in the war against poverty. If poor countries are to achieve faster economic growth—a necessary condition for reducing poverty—they will need a better educated workforce. Even primary education can pay off handsomely (table below). Investments in primary eduction have been shown to reap higher returns—estimates range from 11 per cent to more than 30 per cent—than investments in physical capital. Investment in the education of girls yields especially high returns.

Education in low-income countries yields high returns
(Per cent)

	Private Rate of Return	*Social Rate of Return*
Primary Schooling	26.4	20.6
Secondary Schooling	18.5	14.1
Higher Education	22.4	11.3

Source: George Psacharopoulos, cited in Alain Mingat and Bruno Suchaut, 2000, Les Systemes educatils africains: Une analyse economique comparative (Brussels: De Boeck University). Finance and Development March, 2002.

Table 7.3: Housing and Sanitation

District	*Pucca House (%)*	*Owned House (%)*	*House Less Population (%)*	*Having toilet facility (%)*	*Having Safe drinking water (%)*	*Index*	*Rank*
Ajmer	54.2	77	1.6	32.8	74.42	39.3	14
Alwar	74.2	94	1	11.7	50.24	38.2	24
Banswara	19.5	93	0.9	9.2	61.53	41.1	6
Baran	34.8	85.4	2.5	26.1	78.33	39.0	16
Barmer	27.6	89	0.8	83	38.25	40.8	9
Bharatpur	42.5	94	0.4	12.1	26.83	43.1	4
Bhilwara	43.2	83.2	1.7	18.4	62.31	40.9	8
Bikaner	55.1	87.5	1.4	35.1	60.94	38.6	21
Bundi	40.3	81.8	3.7	16.1	74.02	40.4	11
Chittorgarh	46.3	86.8	2.6	12.4	74.66	38.9	18
Churu	68.7	94.6	0.6	21.6	53.32	37.6	27
Dausa	64.9	89.1	1	30.3	68.65	36.8	31
Dholpur	67.4	88.4	0.4	11.8	39.62	41.0	7
Dungarpur	24.7	94.1	0.6	63	67.82	37.4	28
Gangnagar	35.4	90.9	2.2	54.8	62.44	38.4	23
Hanumangarh	29.1	90.9	1.4	54.8	62.44	38.8	20
Jaipur	59.6	89.1	1.3	30.3	68.65	37.3	29
Jaisalmer	32.1	77.5	7.2	14.2	65.63	43.3	3
Jalore	31.2	92.3	1.9	56	57.31	39.0	17
Jhalawar	34.4	90.8	1	11.7	53.62	41.3	5
Jhunjhunu	82.8	82.9	0.9	19.2	62.07	38.0	25
Jodhpur	62.7	90.5	0.5	25.9	70.47	36.6	32
Karauli	51.5	32.9	0.3	12.8	39.15	53.0	1
Kota	37.6	85.4	2.7	26.1	78.33	38.8	19
Nagaur	74.8	95.2	0.7	14.8	50.65	37.7	26
Pali	53.7	83.1	1.5	14.9	61.67	40.4	10
Rajasamand	57.9	85.8	2	16.1	66.38	39.0	15
Sawai Madhopur	53.5	32.9	0.8	12.8	39.15	53.0	2
Sikar	54.9	96.3	1.3	17.4	64.45	37.2	30
Sirohi	52.2	84.4	2.4	15.6	76.47	38.6	22
Tonk	33.3	93.5	1.3	13.5	60.47	40.0	13
Udaipur	41.5	85.8	1.7	16.1	66.38	40.2	12
OVERALL		84.9	1.6	25.3	60.5		

It remains to be said that building human capital will not, in and of itself, bring about economic growth and poverty reduction. Economic growth results from the interplay of

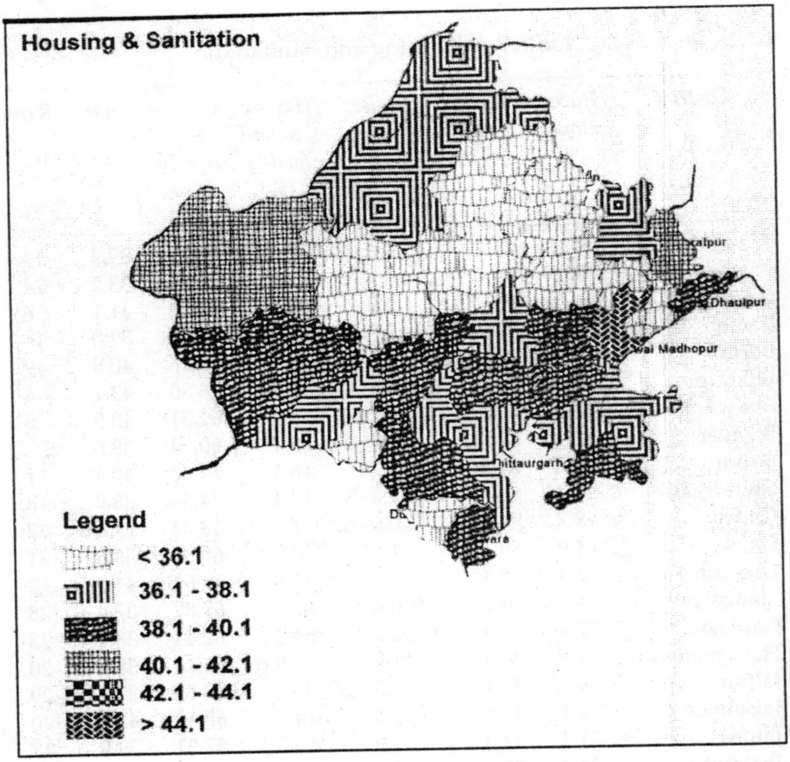

Table 7.3

investments in human, physical, and institutional development. The interaction of eduction with other investments—such as the construction of roads to markets, the establishment of microcredit schemes, and the provision of agricultural extension—is very important in ensuring that the returns to education are realized and the condition of the poor improved. Yet a country's provision of a quality primary education to all its citizens is a critical cornerstone in achieving economic growth with equity.

In our analysis, we considered a number of literacy related variables of which only female literacy rate turned out to be statistically significant. Women are the most vulnerable section of population in our traditional, and gender biased society. Therefore, women's access to education becomes important, not only for enhancing household income, but also for empowering women both socially and economically. The elasticity co-efficient of female literacy in influencing poverty turn out to be 0.7 per cent. The high CHPI districts like Banswara, Dungarpur, Karauli and Jalore had low levels of female literacy. Conversely, Ganganagar, Hanumangarh, Jaipur, Jhunjhunu and Sikar had comparatively high female literacy rate and low composite human poverty index (Table 7.4).

The average value of the composite index for Literacy is 61.1. The districts having composite index values higher than the average are Ajmer, Alwar, Baran, Bharatpur, Banswara, Barmer, Bhilwara, Bikaner, Bundi, Chittorgarh, Dungarpur, Tonk, Jaisalmer, Jalore, Jhalawar, Nagaur, Rajsamand, Sikar, Sirohi and Udaipur.

Access to Health Facilities and Rural Poverty

The health related variables included in this analysis were number of doctors per lakh population, average life expectancy, percentage of safe delivery, percentage of children having complete immunization, infant mortality rate, etc. Of these, infant mortality rate and percentage of children having complete immunization came out statistically significant. The financial health of a state, its rural infrastructure index, primary health facilities, poverty resulting in malnutrition and low levels of literacy appear primary determinants of mortality and morbidity in any society. In the context of India, it is persistent undernourishment of women and girl child in particular that is emerging as the critical factor responsible for infant mortality. Only 10 per cent of the higher socio-economic population of India records low birth weight infant mortality. Poverty thus appears as the major determinant of infant mortality in India. Medical interventions and nutrient supplements as local initiatives are likely to achieve limited results.

In the early eighties, experts were convinced that it is not the average per capita wealth of the country that influences IMR but the distribution and disposition of the wealth. To this,

Table 7.4: Literacy

	Literate (Male) (%) 2001	Literate (Female) (%) 2001	Children attending school (Male) (%) I-XII	Children attending school (Female) (%) I-XII	Drop-out rate (Male) (%) I-V	Drop-out rate (Female) (%) I-V	Primary school attendance (Male) (%)	Primary school attendance (Female) (%)	Composite Index	
									Index	Rank
Ajmer	79.96	49.10	76.32	49.22	52.29	59.92	96.59	63.90	50.2	24
Alwar	78.91	43.95	86.46	53.84	55.40	62.15	98.70	73.24	49.0	28
Banswara	60.24	27.86	79.72	45.15	73.38	77.03	100.00	68.96	62.6	3
Baran	76.86	42.18	82.67	57.22	54.75	64.99	100.00	90.75	50.3	23
Barmer	73.64	43.91	73.00	39.31	58.75	67.05	100.00	67.14	56.6	9
Bharatpur	81.39	44.12	82.04	51.57	53.96	64.89	95.98	74.52	50.1	25
Bhilwara	68.12	33.47	70.12	39.47	61.76	66.68	94.05	57.37	60.8	4
Bikaner	70.78	42.55	76.94	46.12	61.74	42.08	98.84	63.89	52.8	17
Bundi	72.17	37.76	79.85	50.10	48.81	54.10	100.00	75.90	52.1	18
Chittorgarh	71.82	36.45	69.46	43.51	64.88	70.65	91.48	66.47	59.7	5
Churu	79.52	53.87	75.31	46.05	58.74	49.00	94.99	68.41	49.6	26
Dausa	80.37	43.15	96.45	49.32	50.33	53.78	100.00	74.19	45.9	29
Dholpur	75.85	42.36	87.55	54.81	58.23	67.70	100.00	88.30	50.4	22
Dungarpur	66.19	31.22	78.33	48.72	62.21	65.33	100.00	71.76	58.0	8
Ganganagar	75.49	52.69	68.99	57.30	67.56	67.79	86.32	79.65	53.1	16
Hanumangarh	77.41	52.71	67.44	50.80	67.56	67.79	77.29	69.75	54.3	15
Jaipur	83.58	56.18	80.87	58.88	41.68	40.22	98.08	83.25	41.9	30
Jaisalmer	66.89	32.25	69.82	37.42	67.10	78.79	97.98	60.44	63.6	1

(Contd.)

(Contd.)

	Literate (Male) (%) 2001	Literate (Female) (%) 2001	Children attending school (Male) (%) I-XII	Children attending school (Female) (%) I-XII	Drop-out rate (Male) (%) I-V	Drop-out rate (Female) (%) I-V	Primary school attendance (Male) (%)	Primary school attendance (Female) (%)	Composite Index	
									Index	Rank
Jalore	65.10	27.53	75.33	28.42	56.99	70.15	100.00	47.56	63.2	2
Jhalawar	74.29	40.39	75.24	47.01	61.82	71.47	100.00	75.03	56.2	12
Jhunjhunu	86.61	60.10	81.57	65.62	47.41	31.28	84.14	82.89	38.8	32
Jodhpur	73.86	38.18	100.00	52.59	50.68	76.20	100.00	72.71	49.3	27
Karauli	80.93	45.44	82.47	45.62	53.96	64.89	100.00	70.97	50.8	21
Kota	86.25	61.25	82.67	66.78	48.81	54.10	99.25	90.67	40.8	31
Nagaur	75.33	40.45	70.07	42.27	64.31	70.68	87.32	66.89	58.2	7
Pali	73.06	36.70	89.09	45.74	56.10	56.99	100.00	69.99	52.0	19
Rajsamand	74.05	37.89	77.05	52.84	62.16	67.57	100.00	83.21	54.9	14
Sawai Madhopur	76.75	35.44	86.95	48.24	45.92	66.16	100.00	72.35	51.5	20
Sikar	25.20	56.70	81.41	55.90	55.07	57.73	92.84	81.60	56.2	11
Sirohi	70.58	37.37	74.53	37.00	55.80	68.63	96.81	56.48	58.5	6
Tonk	73.06	36.70	81.40	39.89	59.03	65.32	100.00	60.70	56.0	13
Udaipur	74.47	43.71	68.41	42.85	57.18	63.25	89.38	59.83	56.3	10
Rajasthan	69.08	40.11	74.34	45.58	53.95	58.95	90.59	67.32	55.4	

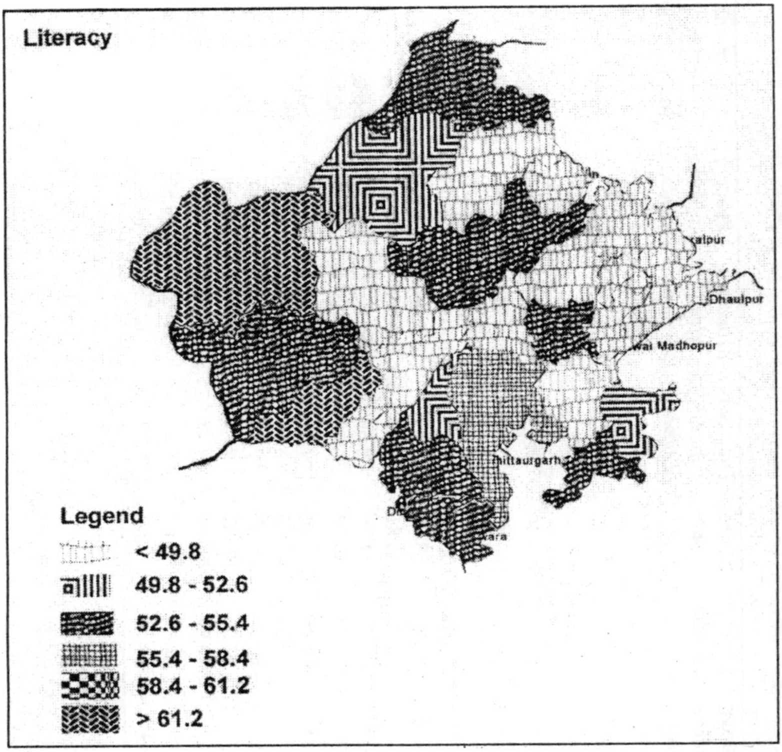

Table 7.4

we may add that our cultural diversity, political insecurity of some of our minority communities, religious orthodoxy and preference for a son become strong deterrents in our desire to reduce IMR. The critical failure of our IMR strategy is our inability to conceive an integrated health management programme that takes into account socio-economic, cultural and health issues in a holistic perspective. Nevertheless the role of overall life expectancy and percentage of safe delivery in poverty alleviation cannot be undermined. As poverty is reduced, the average life expectancy is likely to improve. Likewise, the percentage of safe delivery has a direct effect on the poor peoples access to health and maternity related facilities. The elasticity co-efficients of two significant variables, namely complete immunisation and infant mortality rate were 0.76 and 0.32 respectively, which indicated that 1 per cent rise in coverage under immunisation reduces poverty by 0.7 per cent and 1 per cent fall in infant mortality led to decline in poverty ratio by 0.32 per cent. Banswara, Chittorgarh, Dungarpur, Dholpur, Bhilwara, Barmer, Pali, Sirohi and Tonk (Table 7.5) had relatively higher infant mortality rates. Of these districts Banswara, Dungarpur Barmer, Dholpur and Tonk had also high CHPI and other districts belonged to relatively medium group of CHPI. In terms of complete immunisation, Baran, Bhilwara, Bundi, Ganganagar, Jaipur, Kota, Pali, Rajsamand, Sikar and Tonk were among the top districts, of which CHPI was relatively high only in Tonk and Rajsamand.

The average value of the composite index for Health is 54.5. The districts having composite index values higher than the average are Alwar, Banswara, Barmer, Bharatpur, Bundi, Chittorgarh, Churu, Dholpur, Jaisalmer, Jalore, Jhalawar, Karauli, Nagaur, Pali, Rajsamand, Sawai Madhopur, Sirohi, Tonk and Udaipur.

Nutritional Status and Rural Poverty

While the incidence of poverty affects the nutritional status of both adults and children, it is more so in the case of children. We considered nine nutrition related variables, namely, per capita availability of milk, number of Annapurna beneficiaries, access to anganwadi centres, protein deficiency, calorie deficiency, proportion of severely malnourished male child, and female child, chronic energy deficiency of male and female adult population. Milk being one of the main sources of nutrition, in the State of Rajasthan, per capita availability of milk is considered important for determining the level of poverty. Similarly, protein deficiency, calorie deficiency, chronic energy deficiency of male and female population indicate the poverty status. It was also intended to find out whether implementation of Annapurna scheme (which provided 10 kg of foodgrains per month per beneficiary) and access to anganwadi centres had made any significant difference in nutritional status and poverty situation.

Table 7.5: Health

	No. of Doctors/Lac population	No.of beds/ Lac population	Complete Antenatal Care (%)	Safe Delivery (%)	Complete Immunisations (%)	Current User of Family Planning Methods (%)	3rd & Higher Order Births (%)	Girls marrying after 18 yrs of age (%)	Infant Mortality Rate (IMR)	Expectation of life (Male) years	Expectation of life (Female) years	Composite Index: Index	Composite Index: Ranks
Ajmer	25.73	120.00	22.20	46.60	28.20	41.20	47.90	37.50	118.00	58.76	59.28	42.67	27
Alwar	8.75	56.00	10.20	29.30	33.20	45.90	56.10	46.60	106.00	57.46	58.26	67.20	4
Banswara	13.41	82.00	28.30	45.90	23.10	34.30	55.40	34.40	135.00	62.81	63.69	58.03	13
Baran	15.80	87.00	16.20	50.90	59.90	44.00	55.50	39.00	95.00	62.14	63.00	43.61	25
Barmer	11.73	59.00	5.30	41.90	11.50	20.40	56.30	42.00	121.00	68.88	69.82	76.80	2
Bharatpur	10.47	60.00	11.70	31.10	23.20	33.10	54.00	43.10	101.00	52.86	53.60	71.00	3
Bhilwara	15.38	84.00	19.20	33.80	58.70	35.70	50.60	23.80	125.00	55.38	56.14	58.68	12
Bikaner	13.90	114.00	17.90	42.50	39.20	41.90	50.60	36.30	69.00	74.87	75.91	36.04	31
Bundi	7.27	64.00	12.70	45.60	52.10	39.40	54.50	19.40	105.00	58.27	59.07	62.84	7
Chittorgarh	26.41	72.00	15.40	39.00	33.00	23.10	41.40	40.00	134.00	56.49	57.27	57.56	15
Churu	12.96	75.00	5.50	20.10	25.20	39.60	51.00	32.00	75.00	70.07	71.05	61.56	9
Dausa	7.44	119.00	18.30	36.00	35.20	34.60	53.40	28.40	78.00	61.79	62.65	52.16	20
Dholpur	9.34	60.00	16.30	30.20	33.40	21.50	62.20	43.60	127.00	52.86	53.60	77.79	1
Dungarpur	14.06	78.00	29.90	42.90	33.80	38.60	49.20	65.60	129.00	62.14	63.00	45.26	24
Ganganagar	7.63	56.00	12.90	31.90	42.70	62.90	40.50	52.20	64.00	69.31	70.27	40.21	28
Hanumangarh	7.46	56.00	6.10	24.90	38.20	61.90	42.10	48.40	64.00	69.31	70.27	47.91	23
Jaipur	10.67	119.00	11.70	46.10	42.50	50.80	49.00	56.00	78.00	61.79	62.65	37.21	30
Jaisalmer	16.54	96.00	6.90	18.30	24.30	21.50	58.60	49.40	97.00	69.30	70.26	64.73	6
Jalore	8.40	64.00	16.70	29.80	41.90	33.90	57.70	51.80	112.00	62.98	63.86	62.40	8
Jhalawar	13.27	75.00	20.80	40.40	29.10	43.00	52.60	25.80	111.00	59.10	59.92	59.39	11
Jhunjhunu	11.94	114.00	16.20	50.90	38.00	54.20	48.10	51.70	66.00	67.58	68.52	30.22	32
Jodhpur	22.10	69.00	15.80	37.00	34.50	35.70	55.80	42.70	75.00	68.37	69.31	49.63	21
Karauli	18.15	52.00	16.70	43.70	24.20	26.00	45.30	43.00	106.00	54.43	55.19	60.88	10
Kota	16.22	87.00	16.20	50.90	59.90	44.00	55.50	39.00	95.00	62.14	63.00	43.45	26

(Contd.)

(Contd.)

	No. of Doctors/Lac population	No.of beds/ /Lac population	Compl-ete Antena-tal Care (%)	Safe Delivery (%)	Complete Imm-unisations (%)	Current User of Family Planning Methods (%)	3rd & Higher Order Births (%)	Girls marrying after 18 yrs of age (%)	Infant Mortality Rate (IMR)	Expectation of life (Male) years	Expectation of life (Female) years	Composite Index	
												Index	Rank
Nagaur	10.91	64.00	12.40	38.80	33.90	35.30	53.00	32.80	89.00	68.58	69.54	58.00	14
Pali	14.13	85.00	19.90	36.50	42.80	35.00	53.20	49.40	128.00	57.79	58.59	56.36	18
Rajsamand	5.35	106.00	23.80	40.90	57.40	32.40	53.20	50.70	113.00	59.76	60.60	47.96	22
Sawai Madhopur	31.97	52.00	16.70	43.70	24.20	26.00	45.30	43.00	106.00	54.43	55.19	55.69	19
Sikar	9.93	70.00	17.50	47.70	55.60	42.50	56.10	57.80	70.00	68.40	69.36	39.92	29
Sirohi	13.30	78.00	19.10	44.50	35.10	30.10	54.10	52.40	126.00	59.60	60.42	57.00	16
Tonk	13.03	72.00	20.80	30.30	53.30	37.20	54.10	21.70	127.00	52.26	52.98	66.25	5
Udaipur	9.92	106.00	24.10	40.30	23.10	34.30	51.50	30.40	113.00	59.76	60.60	56.55	17
Rajasthan	18.22	75.03	15.39	36.25	35.01	35.29	49.02	39.64	95.82	58.23	59.03		

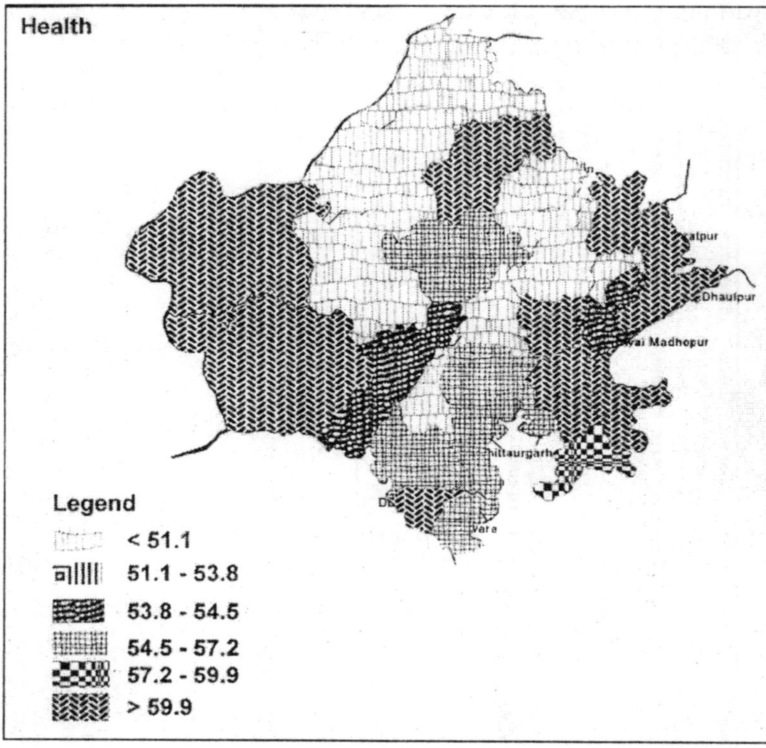

Table 7.5

Only two variables, namely, the proportion of severely malnourished male and female children turned out to be statistically significant. The elasticity co-efficients of these two variables were 0.31 and 0.30 respectively, which meant that 1 per cent rise in the proportion of severely malnourished children led to rise in poverty ratio by about 0.3 per cent. Banswara, Barmer, Dungarpur, Hanumangarh, Jaisalmer, Jhunjhunu, Nagaur, Sirohi, Ajmer and Alwar (Table 7.6) were having more number of severely malnourished children, of which only Banswara, Dungarpur, Jaisalmer, Barmer and Nagaur had relatively high CHPI. Box 2 indicates the action needed to reduce malnutrition and poverty.

The average value of the composite index for Nutrition is 51.4. The districts having composite index values higher than the average are Alwar, Banswara, Barmer, Bundi, Dholpur, Dungarpur, Jaipur, Jaisalmer, Jalore, Jhunjhunu, Jodhpur, Karauli, Kota, Nagaur, Rajsamand, Sirohi, Tonk and Udaipur. Of these 9 districts had still higher values of C.I. which are Barmer, Bundi, Dholpur, Dungarpur, Jhunjhunu, Kota, Sirohi, Tonk and Udaipur.

Box 2: Action against malnutrition and poverty

1. Concentrate resources on areas with the highest incidence of food insecure people.
2. Focus on the most insecure population (the hungry poor) within the identified areas.
3. Carry out activities that address community needs and root causes of food insecurity.
4. Support a range of self-help activities to develop community infrastructure.

Source: The State of Food Insecurity in the World, FAO 2001, p. 30.

Livestock Population and Rural Poverty

We considered six livestock related variables namely, number of cross bred cows, number of indigenous cows, number of buffalo, number of draught cattle and number of milk co-operatives of which number of cows and buffalo population per capita and number of milk co-operatives were found to be statistically significant. The roles of number of cross bred cows, and number of milk co-operatives are quite important to raise livestock productivity and hence important in the reduction of poverty in a livestock based economy. Districts which had relatively high per capita buffalo population and higher per capita cows population had low incidence of poverty and deprivation (Table 7.7).

The average value of the composite index for Livestock is 58.8. The districts having composite index values higher than the average are Banswara, Baran, Barmer, Churu, Dausa, Dungarpur, Jaipur, Jaisalmer, Jalore, Jhunjhunu, Jodhpur, Kota, Nagaur, Sawai Madhopur, Sikar, Sirohi, Tonk and Udaipur.

Table 7.6: Nutrition

	Per capita availability of milk kg/day	Annapurna Benificiaries/ lakh population	Access to Anganwadi Centres/lakh population	Protein Deficiency (%)	Calorie Deficiency (%)	Severly Malnourished Children (Male) (%)	Severly Malnourished Children (Female) (%)	Chronic Energy Deficiency (CED) (Male) (%)	Chronic Energy Deficiency (CED) (Female) (%)	Composite Index: Index	Composite Index: Rank
Ajmer	0.57	113.06	76.86	11.40	9.40	18.30	31.50	36.10	39.40	49.74	19
Alwar	0.41	176.18	90.53	12.00	13.00	21.30	33.40	36.30	38.30	52.74	16
Banswara	0.13	170.91	106.78	13.70	16.70	22.80	37.70	69.20	59.00	75.46	1
Baran	0.26	385.77	86.88	9.70	9.20	13.80	28.30	43.20	51.70	45.87	22
Barmer	0.23	69.47	88.70	16.70	10.40	21.00	33.60	59.70	49.20	70.00	2
Bharatpur	0.43	48.38	85.25	9.70	7.90	9.50	15.20	45.00	40.90	42.11	26
Bhilwara	0.34	202.18	84.36	5.40	7.90	13.00	26.10	25.30	26.70	32.92	31
Bikaner	0.55	246.05	68.94	6.30	9.70	8.00	17.60	44.50	38.00	35.98	29
Bundi	0.25	55.05	80.36	1.60	7.10	16.20	31.70	62.90	58.70	59.93	7
Chittorgarh	0.22	69.20	105.65	3.80	4.20	16.20	31.80	26.90	25.70	34.29	30
Churu	0.32	229.20	78.15	4.60	6.30	9.00	20.40	43.50	39.80	36.70	28
Dausa	0.32	318.47	86.98	1.90	5.70	8.10	23.50	36.80	32.30	26.44	32
Dholpur	0.22	14.68	70.32	13.10	15.60	10.70	20.60	37.60	37.30	58.21	10
Dungarpur	0.28	314.33	89.42	11.10	9.80	26.50	41.80	56.60	61.60	66.18	3
Ganganagar	0.75	39.50	87.56	2.30	10.80	14.60	28.50	33.70	36.60	36.81	27
Hanumangarh	0.58	61.79	68.01	2.50	8.60	19.10	28.30	37.60	35.00	44.49	24
Jaipur	0.37	27.73	58.28	14.80	11.10	12.70	29.60	33.60	34.00	58.04	11
Jaisalmer	0.40	285.33	94.92	8.80	9.40	29.80	42.40	53.90	43.60	57.27	13

(Contd.)

(Contd.)

	Per capita availability of milk kg/day	Annapurna Benificiaries/ lakh population	Access to Anganwadi Centres/lakh population	Protein Deficiency (%)	Calorie Deficiency (%)	Severly Malnourished Children (Male) (%)	Severly Malnourished Children (Female) (%)	Chronic Energy Deficiency (CED) (Male) (%)	Chronic Energy Deficiency (CED) (Female) (%)	Composite Index	
										Index	Rank
Jalore	0.38	44.37	87.44	11.70	12.40	11.00	26.60	43.80	43.50	53.27	15
Jhalawar	0.22	134.17	86.73	4.40	2.30	16.00	26.70	48.10	46.50	45.17	23
Jhunjhunu	0.21	175.55	91.44	13.30	10.00	19.80	33.90	39.90	46.60	57.68	12
Jodhpur	0.37	97.42	57.53	7.90	12.80	11.50	28.10	41.70	34.30	53.81	14
Karauli	0.32	146.92	84.83	9.54	9.70	15.37	28.82	44.78	43.26	51.32	17
Kota	0.27	104.22	69.48	17.70	6.00	7.20	24.70	56.90	50.00	59.45	8
Nagaur	0.26	312.57	85.79	17.80	14.10	18.30	35.70	50.90	49.00	63.74	4
Pali	0.35	103.20	86.78	8.60	7.40	12.20	26.70	48.90	47.10	49.24	20
Rajsamand	0.24	133.70	82.41	7.00	12.50	17.30	18.60	43.30	45.10	51.13	18
Sawai Madhopur	0.27	192.52	79.82	7.70	7.40	5.60	21.90	53.10	42.70	43.56	25
Sikar	0.32	105.86	81.88	12.90	10.00	15.30	30.60	27.50	30.30	48.18	21
Sirohi	0.29	113.91	94.80	10.70	9.40	20.70	36.90	45.30	59.30	62.11	6
Tonk	0.40	153.74	86.77	13.00	11.70	14.60	30.80	55.50	52.40	59.28	9
Udaipur	0.24	116.09	80.04	13.60	12.00	16.50	30.30	50.90	46.40	62.98	5
Rajasthan	0.32	158.56	92.69	8.98	9.13	14.47	27.13	42.15	40.71		

Table 7.7: Livestock

	Cows- Cross bred/ lakh population	*Cows- Indeginous/ lakh population*	*Buffalo/ lakh population*	*Drought cattle Above 3 yrs./Lakh population*	*No. of Milk Cooperatives/ lakh population*	*Composite Index*	
						Index	*Ranks*
Ajmer	174.99	5922.43	5802.37	4717.08	24.64	51.98	26
Alwar	29.39	2218.86	11438.66	1006.02	20.68	56.38	21
Banswara	22.41	5072.34	5825.98	26451.11	7.62	64.52	8
Baran	30.11	8579.51	6721.62	17304.76	2.22	62.31	11
Barmer	1.81	10022.21	2143.43	3041.90	0.00	64.35	9
Bharatpur	41.23	1815.35	11659.66	486.14	11.50	55.24	24
Bhilwara	340.90	7727.69	6696.89	10901.95	0.00	51.31	28
Bikaner	136.90	12701.01	2468.09	1993.25	44.34	40.61	31
Bundi	35.96	6259.28	8982.04	14965.44	11.81	51.94	27
Chittorgarh	93.18	6714.44	7727.78	16449.11	0.00	56.08	23
Churu	42.83	6109.66	4020.45	490.60	8.36	60.68	14
Dausa	43.64	3151.05	12078.46	2918.25	0.00	60.34	17
Dholpur	15.34	2097.06	12264.25	1939.21	8.81	56.12	22
Dungarpur	31.44	4037.74	5729.24	24610.28	7.78	69.94	2
Ganganagar	678.96	7292.41	7531.92	2950.78	0.00	31.07	32
Hanumangarh	339.50	7311.45	9021.88	1298.17	0.00	47.96	30
Jaipur	182.36	254.04	6999.65	1632.94	0.00	69.82	3
Jaisalmer	44.12	20495.36	114.36	5258.38	0.00	78.60	1
Jalore	4.90	5596.80	9236.16	4778.90	0.00	60.61	15
Jhalawar	12.12	7194.16	7242.54	14842.67	5.02	58.89	18
Jhunjhunu	335.18	11159.23	4187.95	1620.30	0.00	50.73	29

(Contd.)

(*Contd.*)

	Cows-Cross bred/ lakh population	Cows-Indeginous/ lakh population	Buffalo/ lakh population	Drought Cattle Above 3 yrs./lakh population	No. of Milk Cooperatives/ lakh population	Composite Index	
						Index	Ranks
Jodhpur	100.53	1809.39	5364.05	168.10	0.00	68.55	5
Karauli	4.42	3187.93	12334.12	4961.52	0.00	58.02	19
Kota	54.24	3818.34	4567.54	5901.82	4.51	67.33	6
Nagaur	37.63	5726.19	6170.38	767.95	0.00	60.99	13
Pali	44.94	6308.06	6859.51	4358.96	24.96	52.86	25
Rajsamand	240.06	5795.65	8093.51	11059.16	0.00	56.97	20
Sawai Madhopur	10.16	3688.94	9282.99	75998.11	0.00	68.75	4
Sikar	179.28	2976.75	7415.54	725.70	0.00	61.10	12
Sirohi	23.70	6142.24	6339.17	8328.38	0.00	64.83	7
Tonk	10.15	5972.17	7954.93	9757.68	0.00	60.58	16
Udaipur	154.80	5732.95	6312.36	19839.93	0.00	62.53	10
Rajasthan	136.62	6846	7694.22	8306.94	11.8		

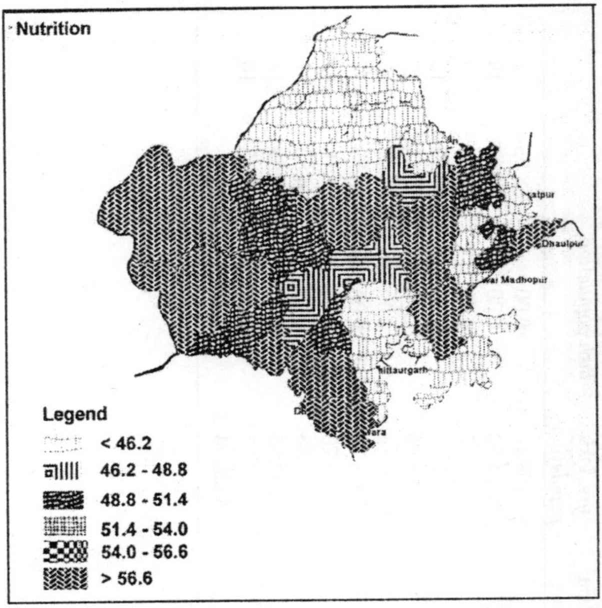

Table 7.6

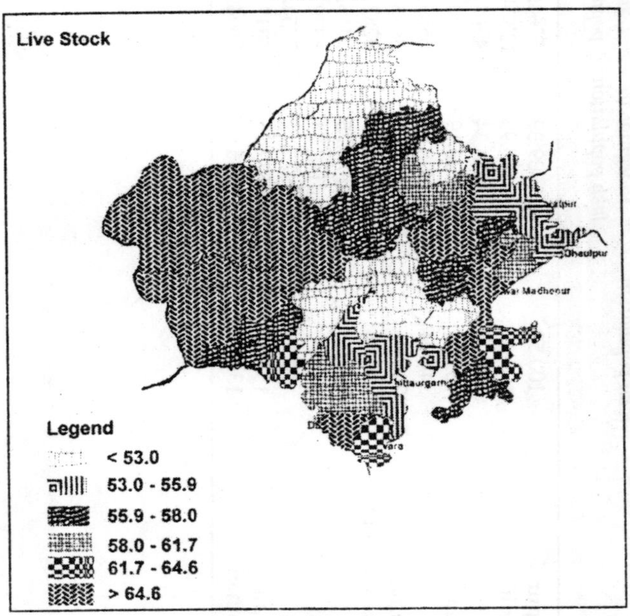

Table 7.7

Agricultural Production and Rural Poverty

Among agriculture related variables, we considered proportion of area irrigated, per capita output of cereals, oilseeds and other cash crops, average size of holdings, proportion of small holdings, out of which per capita output of cereals, oilseeds and cash crops turned out to be statistically significant. The proportion of area irrigated has an important role to play in influencing agriculture growth which was indirectly reflected in per capita output. Similarly, in arid and semi-arid conditions, size of farming did not matter much, as even the families with so-called large farmers stayed below the poverty line. The elasticity co-efficients of per capita output of cereals, oilseeds and other cash crops were 0.260, 0.0093 and 0.13 respectively. This meant that 1 per cent rise in per capita income of cereals, oilseeds and other cash crops led to reduction in poverty by 0.26, 0.009 and 0.13 per cent respectively. The districts which had per capita cereal production and relatively higher production of cash crops had poverty ratio as lower.

The average value of the composite index for Agriculture is 54.4. The districts having composite index values higher than the average are Ajmer, Banswara, Bharatpur, Bhilwara, Dausa, Dholpur, Dungarpur, Jhalawar, Jhunjhunu, Karauli, Pali, Rajsamand, Sawai Madhopur, Sikar, Sirohi, Tonk and Udaipur.

Access to Infrastructure and Rural Poverty

For the purpose of identifying the relative role of infrastructure variables in poverty reduction, we considered factors like number of branches of commercial banks, number of branches of co-operative banks, percentage of villages having access to *pucca* roads, percentage of villages having access to electricity, number of regulated markets, number of fair price shops and number of milk co-operatives. Of these variables, only number of branches of commercial banks, and access to *pucca* road and electricity were found to be statistically significant. The number of regulated markets is likely to help promote agricultural growth and thereby to reduce poverty. Since Rajasthan is a livestock based rural economy and cropwise also it is a subsistence economy, the role of regulated markets turned out to be statistically non-significant. Likewise in a food deficient state like Rajasthan, the role of PDS, as measured by the number of fair price shops should be significant, but it was not so.

The access to road turned out to be a very significant determinant of poverty. It is widely recognised that access to road and transportation enhances a person's capability to take up new enterprises or employment, as it increases the accessibility to market, bank and new places of work. The results of regression analysis show that one per cent rise in the number of villages having access to *pucca* road, tends to reduce rural poverty by 0.11 per cent. Table 7.9 shows that in terms of percentage of villages having access to *pucca* road, districts like Jhalawar, Tonk, Kota, Karauli, Chittorgarh, Bundi, Baran, Barmer, Bhilwara and Sawai Madhopur were among bottom ten, which were high or medium deprivation districts.

Access to electricity removes not only natural darkness but also the darkness of poverty. It enables the people to take new economic initiatives. Besides, it is an integral part of modern living. Districts like Banswara, Dungarpur, Barmer, Jalore, Jaisalmer, Sawai Madhopur, Dholpur, Tonk and Udaipur (Table 7.9) which inhabited highest proportion of poor households based on CHPI, had also less access to electricity. The over all elasticity co-efficient was 1.31 which was statistically significant, thereby indicating that one per cent rise in the coverage of villages under electricity reduced poverty by 1.31 per cent.

The average value of the composite index for infrastructure is 44.0. The districts having composite index value higher than the average are Banswara, Baran, Barmer, Bharatpur, Bhilwara, Bundi, Chittorgarh, Churu, Dholpur, Dungarpur, Jaisalmer, Jalore, Jhalawar, Karauli, Nagaur, Rajsamand, Sawai Madhopur, Sirohi and Udaipur.

Role of Anti-Poverty Programmes

Of all the direct anti-poverty programmes, percentage of women getting employment in Swarojgar Yojana/ JGSY and

Table 7.8: Agriculture

	Per cent of Irrigated Area	Cropping Intensity	Small Holding (%)	Marginal Holding (%)	Average area per holding (hectares)	Average area per holding SC (hectares)	Average area per holding ST (hectares)	Production Cereals/lakh population (in '000 tonnes)	Production of Oilseeds/ lakh (population '000 tonnes)	Production of Cash Crop/ lakh (population '000 tonnes)	Composite Index	Rank
Ajmer	29.30	140.60	20.80	44.20	2.33	1.87	2.09	12.69	2.1	0.1	78.23	4
Alwar	53.00	152.00	24.90	46.40	1.80	1.24	1.69	28.55	9.1	0.1	61.24	21
Banswara	36.80	152.30	23.10	50.70	1.63	0.89	1.71	23.28	0.5	0.1	78.55	3
Baran	65.40	151.40	23.60	29.80	2.81	1.93	2.80	22.84	23.0	0.3	62.04	19
Barmer	4.00	107.80	5.40	3.80	12.44	9.70	10.48	11.89	1.0	0.0	52.41	30
Bharatpur	45.30	140.90	12.70	49.90	1.76	1.17	1.78	25.67	11.1	0.0	66.30	14
Bhilwara	50.60	145.20	26.80	39.30	2.05	1.49	1.68	28.80	2.4	0.3	69.73	12
Bikaner	10.20	112.10	3.10	1.30	10.83	9.39	6.37	10.84	4.8	1.0	53.05	29
Bundi	70.40	149.20	25.60	33.60	2.42	1.85	2.72	50.20	12.5	0.3	61.80	20
Chittorgarh	57.80	156.80	27.20	34.10	2.31	1.62	1.90	31.53	11.6	0.0	62.59	18
Churu	3.20	123.90	4.80	1.50	9.56	7.58	6.90	14.06	1.7	0.0	55.76	27
Dausa	63.30	150.60	25.30	34.20	2.47	1.71	2.75	31.14	9.0	0.3	66.17	15
Dholpur	46.40	129.80	5.80	13.60	1.57	1.10	1.75	14.37	9.5	0.3	68.88	13
Dungarpur	26.40	154.30	21.20	56.50	1.37	0.73	1.41	14.99	0.1	0.0	84.90	1
Ganganagar	70.80	138.60	7.00	2.10	7.32	6.18	5.20	35.60	18.2	4.6	27.01	32
Hanumangarh	37.30	138.40	12.90	6.80	6.02	5.27	5.48	48.58	5.5	3.5	40.25	31
Jaipur	50.00	141.90	23.10	28.90	3.09	2.20	2.74	15.90	3.8	0.0	60.09	23
Jaisalmer	8.50	107.70	7.00	5.70	13.10	10.29	9.42	10.36	4.2	0.0	55.35	28

(Contd.)

(Contd.)

	Per cent Irrigated Area	Cropping Intensity	Small Holding (%)	Marginal Holding (%)	Average area per holding (hectares)	Average area per holding SC (hectares)	Average area per holding ST (hectares)	Production of Cereals/lakh population (in '000 tonnes)	Production of Oilseeds/ lakh (population '000 tonnes)	Production of Cash Crop/ lakh (population '000 tonnes)	Composite Index	Rank
Jalore	44.60	130.10	15.20	8.40	6.03	4.47	4.43	14.21	11.0	0.1	60.54	22
Jhalawar	54.20	161.90	23.80	33.50	2.61	1.73	2.47	23.33	16.7	0.0	65.26	17
Jhunjhunu	9.80	109.30	10.70	7.30	2.80	2.09	2.07	16.13	5.0	0.2	72.51	8
Jodhpur	37.10	170.70	28.50	19.70	8.73	6.56	7.75	9.91	2.9	0.0	56.67	26
Karauli	41.80	149.70	18.73	27.22	4.27	3.26	3.53	23.12	5.7	0.3	65.89	16
Kota	76.90	161.50	23.20	27.30	3.04	2.01	3.70	18.62	16.7	0.3	58.71	24
Nagaur	18.90	131.90	13.80	10.20	5.96	4.86	4.78	18.36	7.5	0.1	57.09	25
Pali	39.70	126.20	22.90	27.50	3.93	2.51	2.60	14.25	7.6	0.4	72.09	9
Rajsamand	49.40	142.90	22.00	52.10	1.68	1.17	1.31	18.63	0.5	0.0	81.82	2
Sawai Madhopur	40.50	125.60	23.90	43.20	2.06	1.57	2.35	23.84	16.4	0.3	74.41	7
Sikar	34.30	141.40	25.20	20.50	3.08	2.28	2.26	16.94	2.3	0.0	71.45	10
Sirohi	57.90	137.40	25.30	35.40	2.70	2.14	1.80	15.57	10.5	0.3	74.89	6
Tonk	32.80	124.60	21.10	26.30	3.39	2.52	3.48	25.30	12.5	0.0	69.76	11
Udaipur	37.60	147.00	24.60	49.90	1.62	1.06	1.49	17.29	0.6	0.3	76.64	5
Rajasthan	38.36	130.99	17.62	25.62	4.02	3.07	3.32	21.83	6.71	0.37	105.45	68.14

Table 7.9: Infrastructure

	No. of branches of co-operative bank/lakh population	No. of branches of commercial bank/lakh population	Access per cent of villages having pucca road (%)	No. of Regulated Markets/lakh population	No. of Fair Price Shop /lakh population	Electricity Avaliabiity (%)	Composite Index	
							Index	Rank
Ajmer	0.17	8.79	65.16	0.87	51.00	47.1	49.9	27
Alwar	0.09	7.18	51.97	0.61	36.00	28.6	72.4	3
Banswara	0.17	7.62	48.20	0.61	47.00	21.8	68.0	21
Baran	0.12	7.53	33.70	1.85	43.00	50.3	71.6	5
Barmer	0.14	5.16	41.86	0.84	53.00	14.9	74.1	16
Bharatpur	0.12	6.72	51.27	0.85	41.00	29.9	70.8	9
Bhilwara	0.13	7.53	42.03	1.13	39.00	37.3	76.2	4
Bikaner	0.17	10.90	57.68	0.66	46.00	49.1	46.6	22
Bundi	0.26	8.57	36.06	0.78	35.00	35.2	69.6	11
Chittorgarh	0.20	7.55	35.06	1.41	38.00	36.7	73.1	12
Churu	0.13	7.52	48.85	1.36	43.00	35.8	66.8	17
Dausa	0.00	15.89	48.42	1.51	36.00	48.4	67.6	18
Dholpur	0.13	5.07	58.39	1.87	55.00	20.6	57.0	29
Dungarpur	0.23	7.20	57.61	0.46	37.00	22.3	68.0	20
Ganganagar	0.21	9.55	61.55	2.50	37.00	43.2	52.8	31
Hanumangarh	0.08	7.21	61.55	2.87	41.00	43.2	58.8	28
Jaipur	0.10	9.59	48.42	0.95	68.00	48.4	59.1	26
Jaisalmer	0.29	11.03	40.90	0.58	42.00	16.1	65.0	25

(Contd.)

(Contd.)

	No. of branches of co-operative bank lakh population	No. of branches of commercial bank/lakh population	Access per cent of villages having pucca road (%)	No. of Regulated Markets/ lakh population	No. of Fair Price Shop /lakh population	Electricity Avaliabiity (%)	Composite Index	
							Index	Rank
Jalore	0.18	5.78	55.81	0.96	48.00	20	67.6	23
Jhalawar	0.21	7.31	28.16	1.46	44.00	29.2	70.5	15
Jhunjhunu	0.19	9.92	70.94	0.76	49.00	39.2	56.2	30
Jodhpur	0.09	4.23	73.16	0.51	44.00	41.7	73.0	10
Karauli	0.11	5.07	40.86	1.62	42.00	25.2	76.3	7
Kota	0.16	10.00	33.70	1.72	34.00	50.3	70.3	8
Nagaur	0.09	6.11	42.78	0.84	39.00	32.9	81.7	1
Pali	0.13	7.74	54.97	0.94	44.00	36.3	60.1	19
Rajsamand	0.00	7.17	45.35	1.82	44.00	33.1	75.1	6
Sawai Madhopur	0.23	7.88	40.86	1.83	42.00	25.2	64.2	24
Sikar	0.11	6.02	54.41	0.60	38.00	45.9	78.9	2
Sirohi	0.31	9.02	71.42	1.68	51.00	38.5	43.7	32
Tonk	0.21	7.08	28.29	1.23	44.00	28.6	74.4	13
Udaipur	0.10	7.65	45.35	0.82	51.00	33.1	72.6	14
Rajasthan	0.18	9.16	46.32	1.23	41.24			

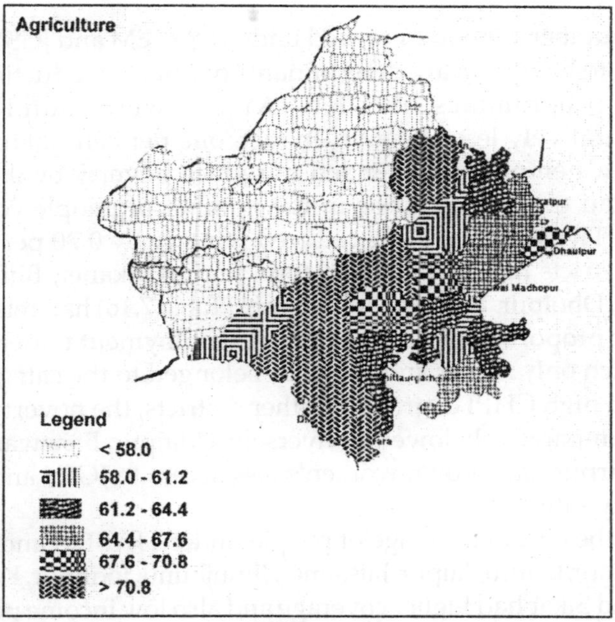

Table 7.8

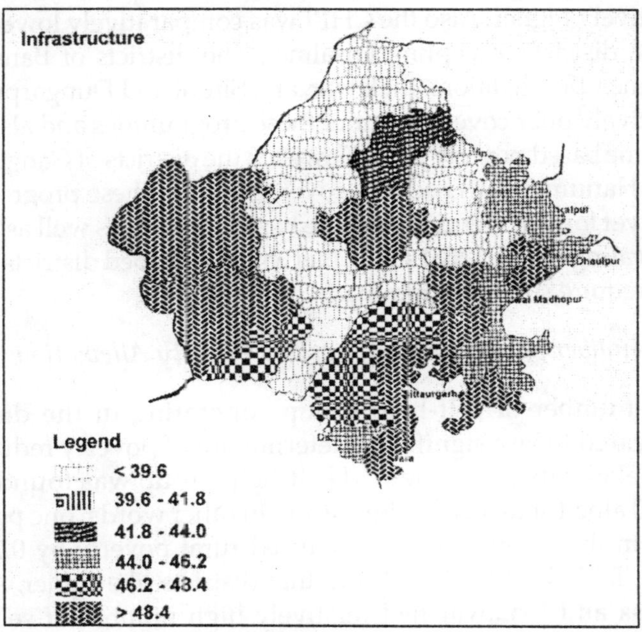

Table 7.9

total number of people covered under TRYSEM and JGSY were found to be significant determinants of poverty reduction. All other programmes like JRY, IAY etc. were found to be comparatively less effective. In fact, one per cent increase in women's employment tended to reduce poverty by 0.13 per cent and one per cent rise in the number of people covered under TRYSEM and JGSY reduced poverty by 0.20 per cent.

Districts like Alwar, Bharatpur, Jaipur, Bikaner, Bhilwara, Bundi, Dholpur, Pali, Sikar and Sirohi (Table 7.10) had relatively higher proportion of women getting employment under JGSY, of which only Alwar and Dholpur belonged to the category of top ten high CHPI districts. In other districts, the poverty ratio was comparatively lower. Conversely, Udaipur, Banswara and Dungarpur had shown women's less access to JGSY and high poverty ratio.

In the case of coverage of people under TRYSEM and JGSY, Bharatpur, Churu, Jaipur, Jaisalmer, Jhunjhunu, Jodhpur, Karauli, Pali and Sikar had higher coverage and also low income poverty ratio excepting in Karauli where the income poverty ratio was relatively higher. Also the CHPI was comparatively lower in all these districts, excepting Jaisalmer. The districts of Banswara, Bikaner, Bundi, Jalore, Jhalawar, and Sirohi and Dungarpur had relatively poor coverage under these programmes and also high income based poverty ratio. However, the districts of Ganganagar and Hanumangarh had low coverage under these programmes and yet low incidence of income based poverty as well as CHPI, indicating thereby that such otherwise developed districts might not require such programmes.

(a) Number of Self-Help Groups and Poverty Alleviation

The number of self-help groups operating in the districts appeared to be a significant determinant of poverty reduction. The elasticity co-efficient of self-help group was found to be –0.20 albeit statistically significant. In other words, one per cent rise in the self-help groups reduced rural poverty by 0.20 per cent. Table 7.10 further shows that districts like Ajmer, Alwar, Dausa and Jhalawar had relatively high number of self-help groups and also low income based poverty ratio, while districts of Banswara and Dungarpur had more number of self-help groups and high income based poverty ratio.

(b) Natural Disaster and Rural Poverty

Many parts of Rajasthan are subjected to frequent occurrence of drought, as a result of which there are loss of crops, livestock and also human life. More recently in 2000-2001, about 3.3 crore population of the state was affected by drought. In the absence of adequate data, crop loss due to drought was considered as a proxy variable here. It was observed that the elasticity co-efficient of this variable was–0.20, which meant 1 per cent rise in the incidence of drought resulted in the growth in rural poverty by 0.20 per cent. The intensity of crop loss was found to be more in districts like Barmer, Bikaner, Churu, Jaipur, Jalore, Jhunjhunu, Nagaur, Pali and Sikar.

(c) Average per Capita Income and Poverty Ratio

It would be seen from Table 7.10 that on the basis of per capita net domestic product, districts like Hanumangarh, Sri Ganganagar, Baran, Kota, Chittorgarh, Bundi, Alwar, Rajsamand, Jaipur and Tonk were high income districts which were expected to have low poverty ratio. But districts like Chittorgarh, Bundi, Baran, and Rajsamand had fairly high incidence of rural poverty. However, the composite human poverty index (CHPI) was relatively low in these districts, although comparatively higher than the income based poverty index. This could be partly due to unequal distribution of income and partly due to other factors including high level prices, low wages and so on. Based on composite human poverty index also, districts of Dungarpur, Barmer, Dholpur, Banswara, Jaisalmer, Jalore were high poverty districts. The elasticity co-efficient of per capita income, showing its role in poverty reduction, was 0.026, which meant 1 per cent rise in per capita income resulted in poverty reduction by 0.026 per cent. This also shows that non-income measures of poverty are probably more important.

Table 7.10: Development

	NDP per capita (1991-92) Rs.	Annual growth rate of NDP per capita (81-92)	BPL families/ rural population	BPL families engaged in Agriculture (%)	No. of BPL families Registered under I.A.Y/* (%)	No. of BPL families Registered under JGSY/ * (%)	No. of BPL families Registered under JRY/* (%)	No. of Women getting employment in Swarojgar/ JGSY/* (%)	No. of people regd. under TRYSEM / JGSY/* (%)	Average Market Price (Wheat) (Rs.)	Average Market Price (Cereals) (Rs.)	Crop loss Due to drought (%)	No.of Self-Help Groups	Persons covered under old age pension	Composite Index: index	Composite Index: rank
Ajmer	4400.00	3.38	0.26	68.05	0.00	3.05	52.56	264.26	0.47	700.00	395.00	2.72	61.88	9291.12	58.9	9
Alwar	5269.00	3.98	0.22	71.91	0.01	4.25	65.65	698.59	0.68	590.00	280.00	0.11	10.27	1765.17	50.2	30
Banswara	3739.00	3.81	0.73	86.30	0.01	6.42	63.45	39.10	0.04	630.00	400.00	1.64	18.86	1598.04	64.5	1
Baran	6415.00	3.22	0.33	72.14	0.02	1.00	32.57	60.00	0.20	651.00	390.00	0.00	0.38	419.39	55.1	21
Barmer	2828.00	2.93	0.29	90.54	0.02	2.43	56.12	213.99	0.00	538.00	385.00	12.09	0.21	1872.53	53.4	26
Bharatpur	3976.00	3.11	0.18	64.95	0.01	1.41	44.68	1767.38	0.50	580.00	280.00	0.00	2.06	1743.05	49.3	31
Bhilwara	4391.00	3.49	0.35	79.83	0.00	1.78	57.50	312.36	0.32	627.00	411.00	1.51	1.19	2041.31	59.0	7
Bikaner	4399.00	3.56	0.37	80.16	0.11	1.02	37.60	399.02	0.00	560.00	310.00	7.74	5.20	469.81	56.5	19
Bundi	5508.00	3.36	0.36	67.11	0.01	1.45	30.13	320.69	0.00	645.00	455.00	0.20	2.73	853.25	58.7	11
Chittorgarh	5806.00	3.47	0.49	79.60	0.00	2.26	57.88	242.48	0.16	670.00	690.00	1.20	2.22	1360.61	63.6	2
Churu	3175.00	2.74	0.29	84.17	0.03	2.52	47.44	105.95	0.49	590.00	370.00	5.96	5.18	1472.20	55.6	20
Dausa	4113.00	3.22	0.23	71.60	0.01	2.56	43.63	159.77	0.19	700.00	295.00	0.44	14.87	795.44	57.3	15
Dholpur	3404.00	3.22	0.35	68.05	0.01	1.50	27.82	340.67	0.27	570.00	271.00	0.00	0.00	1187.22	58.3	12
Dungarpur	2735.00	3.03	0.71	80.34	0.00	7.18	82.23	15.88	0.11	600.00	450.00	0.94	188.23	2174.63	58.2	13
Ganganagar	7386.00	3.29	0.21	76.82	0.01	2.14	47.46	270.56	0.00	665.00	400.00	0.11	1.83	519.34	58.8	10
Hanumangarh	7386.00	3.29	0.22	87.95	0.01	1.30	16.48	134.62	0.01	581.00	415.00	0.00	4.02	326.39	55.0	22
Jaipur	4794.00	3.22	0.16	47.37	0.02	2.34	64.84	698.72	1.28	600.00	325.00	3.66	0.55	451.79	48.5	32
Jaisalmer	3576.00	3.03	0.26	53.77	0.02	3.64	39.23	3.02	0.81	602.00	525.00	2.79	7.84	1858.54	50.4	29

(Contd.)

(Contd.)

	NDP per capita (1991-92) Rs.	Annual growth rate of NDP per capita (81-92)	BPL families/ rural population	BPL families engaged in Agriculture (%)	No. of BPL families Registered under I.A.Y/* (%)	No. of BPL families Registered under JGSY/ * (%)	No. of BPL families Registered under JRY/* (%)	No. of Women getting employment in Swarojgar/ JGSY/* (%)	No. of people regd. under TRYSEM/ JGSY/* (%)	Average Market Price (Wheat) (Rs.)	Average Market Price (Cereals) (Rs.)	Crop loss Due to drought (%)	No.of Self Help Groups	Persons covered under old age pension	Composite Index: index	Composite Index: rank
Jalore	3825.00	3.54	0.38	74.76	0.01	1.99	43.14	243.22	0.15	665.00	367.00	3.77	0.00	1060.19	59.2	6
Jhalawar	4181.00	3.52	0.33	80.94	0.01	1.02	43.14	65.69	0.10	567.00	415.00	0.00	10.45	632.83	59.0	8
Jhunjhunu	3467.00	3.16	0.14	76.51	0.02	2.45	46.80	170.61	1.14	610.00	400.00	9.16	5.37	1157.02	54.5	23
Jodhpur	3982.00	3.20	0.11	65.87	0.01	1.68	35.75	244.05	0.47	675.00	260.00	3.33	0.60	634.09	54.2	25
Karauli	4538.00	3.61	0.41	70.32	0.02	0.81	46.65	161.73	0.55	600.00	282.00	0.00	7.61	1383.83	59.3	5
Kota	5925.00	3.22	0.32	45.50	0.02	0.82	34.68	297.56	0.00	655.00	390.00	0.00	2.76	1325.41	54.5	24
Nagaur	4134.00	3.97	0.17	76.60	0.01	1.77	53.18	241.24	0.14	680.00	310.00	8.35	0.00	699.55	59.4	4
Pali	4496.00	3.54	0.24	60.60	0.01	1.52	50.32	360.53	0.70	683.00	386.00	3.84	26.51	1406.66	56.7	17
Rajsamand	5125.00	2.98	0.36	76.30	0.01	3.01	40.24	59.47	0.43	702.00	575.00	0.74	16.67	3313.99	61.4	3
Sawai Madhopur	4538.00	3.61	0.37	75.12	0.01	2.20	46.52	170.00	0.25	605.00	251.00	0.15	7.84	734.40	56.8	16
Sikar	2996.00	2.99	0.11	73.32	0.08	1.48	39.64	346.62	28.89	602.00	301.00	3.61	4.18	1218.88	50.6	28
Sirohi	4556.00	3.78	0.31	75.24	0.01	1.49	40.40	305.37	0.00	615.00	410.00	1.04	3.67	706.54	57.9	14
Tonk	4711.00	3.41	0.33	72.28	0.01	1.47	36.62	77.55	0.16	575.00	275.00	1.33	2.15	2197.44	52.6	27
Udaipur	4038.00	2.98	0.58	73.02	0.01	7.08	107.53	103.25	0.15	677.00	620.00	1.76	1.18	1372.34	56.5	18
Rajasthan	4229.76	8.23	0.3	68.44	0.02	2.27	45.06	261.59	1.14	588.53	361.44	2.3	12.25	1413.03		

* BPL families

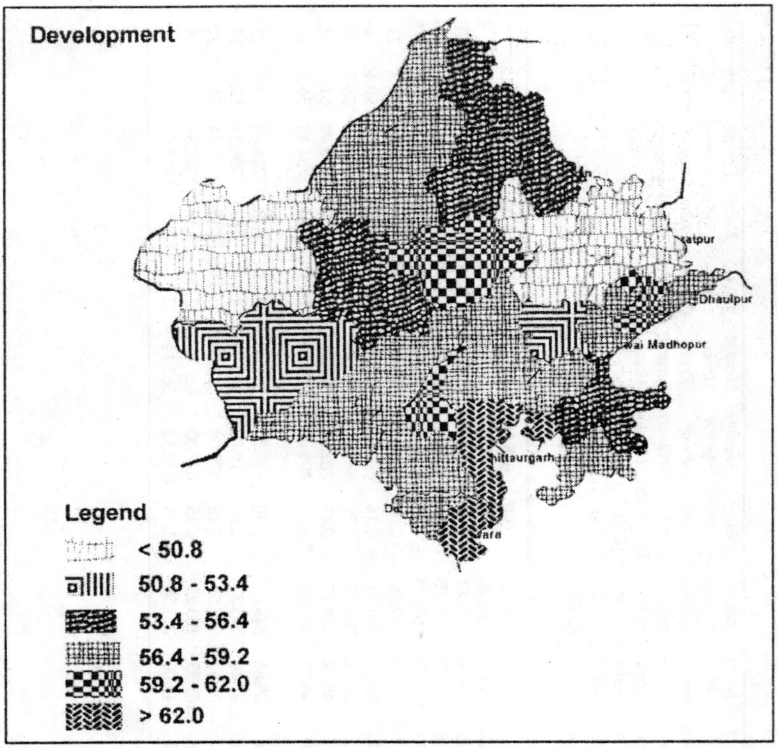

Table 7.10

The average value of the composite index for Development is 56.4. The districts having composite index values higher than the average are Ajmer, Banswara, Barmer, Bhilwara, Bikaner, Bundi, Chittorgarh, Dausa, Dholpur, Dungarpur, Ganganagar, Jalore Jhalawar, Karauli, Nagaur, Pali, Rajsamand, Sawai Madhopur, Sirohi and Udaipur.

Composite Human Poverty Index

Using the methodology, we developed a Composite Human Poverty Index (CHPI) for various districts of Rajasthan. Table 7.11 presents the values of composite indices (C.I.) for different indicator groups as well as CHPI along with the ranks of the districts according to CHPI. It may be mentioned that these CIs represent relative deprivation with respect to highest achievement, the value '0' representing no deprivation and '100' representing highest deprivation. It is observed that the overall CHPI value was about 53. Futher, it is seen that the relative deprivation (in districts) was lower for Housing (40) and Infrastructure (44) but higher for Agriculture (64) and Livestock (59). For other indicators the values of C.Is were in the range of 51.3 to 56.4.

The districts which had values of C.Is higher than the average for different indicators are indicated in Table 7.11(a). It would appear from this that the number of districts showing higher deprivations showed variation from indicator to indicator, the number ranging from 12 to 20. Also, the districts were not common always. On the basis of CHPI, Poverty and both the districts have been categorised and presented in Table 7.11 (b). It is observed that out of 12 districts with high CHPI, 5 were common with Poverty.

The criteria used is:

	Poverty	*Ratio*	*CHPI*
A	Poor	>37	>55.5
B	Good	<28	<50
C	Average	Others	Others

The CHPI had correlations with C. It is ranging between. 0.16 to 0.76 (Table 7.11a). The indicators whose C is influenced more the CHPI were Infrastructre, Health, Livestock, Nutrition and Agriculture,

KEY FINDINGS OF DISTRICT LEVEL ANALYSIS

Table 7.12 presents the values of Poverty Ratio and Human Poverty Index along with CHPI.

Table 7.11: Composite Index (C.I.) for Broad Indicator Groups

District	*Demography*	*Housing*	*Literacy*	*Health*	*Nutrition*	*Live-stock*	*Agriculture*	*Infrastructure*	*Development*	*CHPI value*	*Rank*
Ajmer	48.6	39.3	50.2	42.67	49.74	51.98	78.23	24.6	58.9	49.4	25
Alwar	46.2	38.2	49	67.2	52.74	56.38	61.24	45.7	50.2	51.9	20
Banswara	59.1	41.1	62.6	58.03	75.46	64.52	78.55	52.6	64.5	61.8	1
Baran	47.5	39	50.3	43.61	45.87	62.31	62.04	46	55.1	50.2	22
Barmer	54.8	40.8	56.6	76.8	70	64.35	52.41	61.5	53.4	59.0	3
Bharatpur	47.4	43.1	50.1	71	42.11	55.24	66.3	45.4	49.3	52.2	18
Bhilwara	59.8	40.9	60.8	58.68	32.92	51.31	69.73	47.7	59	53.4	17
Bikaner	53.1	38.6	52.8	36.04	35.98	40.61	53.05	29	56.5	44.0	31
Bundi	52.3	40.4	52.1	62.84	59.93	51.94	61.8	53.4	58.7	54.8	14
Chittorgarh	57.4	38.9	59.7	57.56	34.29	56.08	62.59	53.3	63.6	53.7	16
Churu	48.4	37.6	49.6	61.56	36.7	60.68	55.76	43.6	55.6	49.9	23
Dausa	44.2	36.8	45.9	52.16	26.44	60.34	66.17	36.2	57.3	47.3	28
Dholpur	46.8	41	50.4	77.79	58.21	56.12	68.88	45.8	58.3	55.9	10
Dungarpur	56.3	37.4	58	45.26	66.18	69.94	84.9	45.3	58.2	57.9	5
Ganganagar	48.9	38.4	53.1	40.21	36.81	31.07	27.01	29.7	58.8	40.4	32
Hanumangarh	50.4	38.8	54.3	47.91	44.49	47.96	40.25	29.7	55	45.4	29
Jaipur	42.2	37.3	41.9	37.21	58.04	69.82	60.09	36.2	48.5	47.9	27
Jaisalmer	61	43.3	63.6	64.73	57.27	78.6	55.35	61.5	50.4	59.5	2
Jalore	63.2	39	63.2	62.4	53.27	60.61	60.54	48	59.2	56.6	8
Jhalawar	53.2	41.3	56.2	59.39	45.17	58.89	65.26	62.9	59	55.7	11
Jhunjhunu	38.6	38	38.8	30.22	57.68	50.73	72.51	25.2	54.5	45.1	30
Jodhpur	45.3	36.6	49.3	49.63	53.81	68.55	56.67	22	54.2	48.5	26
Karauli	48.4	53	50.8	60.88	51.32	58.02	65.89	56	59.3	56.0	9
Kota	37.8	38.8	40.8	43.45	59.45	67.33	58.71	46	54.5	49.6	24

(Contd.)

(*Contd.*)

District	*Demography*	*Housing*	*Literacy*	*Health*	*Nutrition*	*Live-stock*	*Agriculture*	*Infrastructure*	*Development*	*CHPI value*	*Rank*
Nagaur	55.5	37.7	58.2	58	63.74	60.99	57.09	49.9	59.4	55.6	12
Pali	50.7	40.4	52	56.36	49.24	52.86	72.09	38.8	56.7	52.1	19
Rajsamand	52	39	54.9	47.96	51.13	56.97	81.82	47.8	61.4	54.8	15
Sawai Madhopur	50.2	53	51.5	55.69	43.56	68.75	74.41	56	56.8	56.7	7
Sikar	56.1	37.2	56.2	39.92	48.18	61.1	71.45	33.3	50.6	50.5	21
Sirohi	57.4	38.6	58.5	57	62.11	64.83	74.89	25.2	57.9	55.2	13
Tonk	54.3	40	56	66.25	59.28	60.58	69.76	63.2	52.6	58.0	4
Udaipur	55.2	40.2	56.3	56.55	62.98	62.53	76.64	47.8	56.5	57.2	6
Average	51.3	40.1	55.4	54.5	51.4	58.8	64.4	44.0	56.4	52.9	

CHPL—Composite Human Poverty Index.

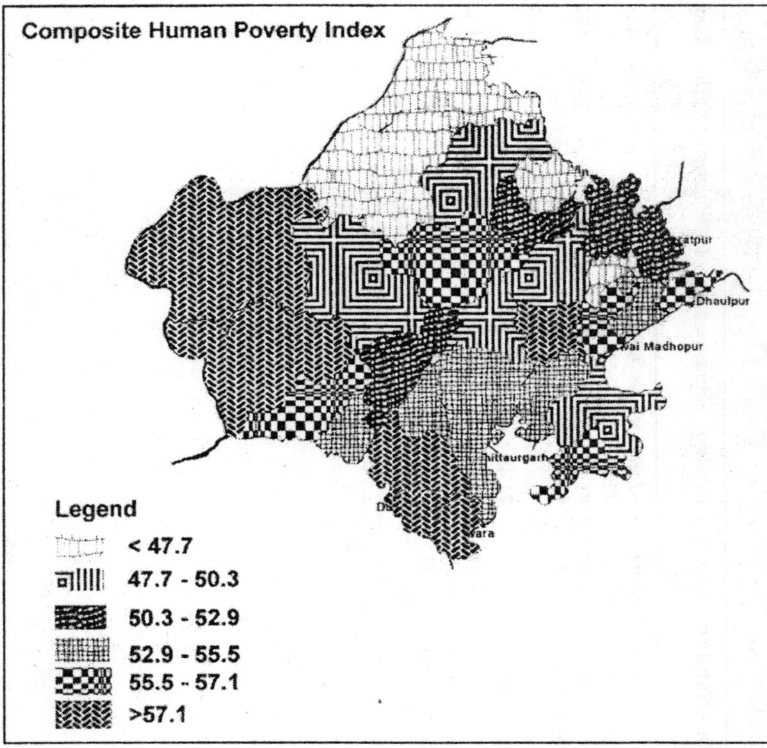
Composite Human Poverty Index
Dhaulpur
Legend
< 47.7
47.7 - 50.3
50.3 - 52.9
52.9 - 55.5
55.5 - 57.1
>57.1

Table 7.11

Table 7.11(a): Districts with Composite Index (C.I.) More Than Average

Indicator group									*No. of districts*	*Average*
Demography	Banswara	Barmer	Bhilwara	Bikaner	Bundi	Chittorgarh	Dungarpur	Tonk		
	59.1	54.1	59.8	53.1	52.3	57.4	56.3	54.3	16	51.3
	Jaisalmer	Jalore	Jhalawar	Nagaur	Rajsamand	Sikar	Sirohi	Udaipur		
	61	63.2	53.2	55.5	52	56.1	57.4	55.2		
Housing	Banswara	Barmer	Bharatpur	Bhilwara	Bundi	Dholpur	Jaisalmer	Jhalawar		
	41.1	40.8	43.1	40.9	40.4	41	43.3	41.3	12	40.1
	Karauli	Pali	Sawai Madhopur	Udaipur						
	53	40.4	53	40.2						
Literacy	Banswara	Barmer	Bhilwara	Chittorgarh	Dungarpur	Jaisalmer	Jalore	Jhalawar	13	55.4
	62.6	56.6	60.8	59.7	85.0	63.6	63.2	56.2		
	Nagaur	Sikar	Sirohi	Tonk	Udaipur					
	58.2	56.2	58.5	56.0	56.3					
Health	Alwar	Banswara	Barmer	Bharatpur	Bhilwara	Bundi	Chittorgarh	Churu		
	67.2	58.03	76.8	71	58.68	62.84	57.56	61.56	19	54.5
	Dholpur	Jaisalmer	Jalore	Jhalawar	Karauli	Nagaur	Pali	Sawai Madhopur		
	77.79	64.73	62.4	59.39	60.88	58	56.36	55.69		
	Sirohi	Tonk	Udaipur							
	57	66.25	56.55							

(*Contd.*)

(*Contd.*)

Indicator group									*No. of districts*	*Average*
Nutrition	Alwar 52.74	Banswara 75.46	Barmer 70	Bundi 59.93	Dholpur 58.21	Dungarpur 66.18	Jaipur 58.04	Jaisalmer 57.27	16	51.4
	Jalore 53.27	Jhunjhunu 75.68	Jodhpur 53.81	Kota 59.45	Nagaur 63.74	Sirohi 62.11	Tonk 59.28	Udaipur 62.98		
Livestock	Banswara 64.52	Baran 62.31	Barmer 64.35	Churu 60.68	Dausa 60.34	Dungarpur 69.94	Jaipur 69.82	Jaisalmer 78.6	18	58.8
	Jalore 60.61	Jhalawar 58.89	Jodhpur 68.55	Kota 67.33	Nagaur 60.99	Sawai Madhopur 68.75	Sikar 61.1	Sirohi 64.83		
	Tonk 60.58	Udaipur 62.53								
Agriculture	Ajmer 78.23	Banswara 78.55	Bharatpur 66.3	Bhilwara 69.73	Dausa 66.17	Dholpur 68.88	Dungarpur 84.9	Jhalawar 65.26	17	64.4
	Jhunjhunu 72.51	Karauli 65.89	Pali 72.09	Rajsamand 81.82	Sawai Madhopur 74.41	Sikar 71.45	Sirohi 74.89	Tonk 69.76		
	Udaipur 76.64									
Infrastructure	Banswara 52.6	Baran 46	Barmer 61.5	Bharatpur 45.4	Bhilwara 47.7	Bundi 53.4	Chittorgarh 53.3	Churu 43.6	20	44

(*Contd.*)

(Contd.)

Indicator group									No. of districts	Average
	Dholpur 45.8	Dungarpur 45.3	Jaisalmer 61.5	Jalore 48	Jhalawar 62.9	Karauli 56	Nagaur 49.9	Rajsamand 47.8		
	Sawai Madhopur 56	Tonk 63.2	Udaipur 47.8	Kota 46						
Development	Ajmer 58.9	Banswara 64.5	Bhilwara 59	Bikaner 56.5	Bundi 58.7	Chittorgarh 63.6	Dausa 57.3	Dholpur 58.3	19	56.4
	Dungarpur 58.2	Ganganagar 58.8	Jalore 59.2	Jhalawar 59	Karauli 59.3	Nagaur 59.4	Pali 56.7	Rajsamand 61.4		
	Sawai Madhopur 56.8	Sirohi 57.9	Udaipur 56.5							
CHPI	Banswara 61.8	Barmer 59.0	Bharatpur 53.4	Bundi 54.8	Dholpur 55.9	Dungarpur 57.9	Jaisalmer 59.5	Jalore 56.6	17	52.9
	Jhalawar 56.3	Karauli 57.3	Nagaur 55.6	Rajsamand 55.6	Sawai Madhopur 57.8	Sirohi 55	Tonk 58.4	Udaipur 57.4		
	Chittorgarh 53.7									

Table 7.11(b): Categorisation of Districts

Categorisation by CHPI					
More than > 55.5 (A) Poor	Tonk Jaisalmer Sawai Madhopur	Udaipur Jalore Dungarpur	Banswara Jhalawar	Barmer Karauli	Dholpur (12) Nagaur
Less than<50. (B) Good	Jodhpur Kota	Jhunjhunu Ajmer	Jaipur Bikaner	Hanumangarh Churu	Ganganagar (10) Dausa
Others (C) Average	Alwar Chittorgarh	Baran Pali	Bundi Rajsamand	Bharatpur Sikar	Bhilwara (10) Sirohi
Categorisation by poverty					
More than >37 (A) Poor	Banswara Karauli	Chittorgarh Sawai Madhopur	Dausa	Dungarpur	Jalore (7)
Less than <28.5 (B) Good	Ajmer Ganganagar Nagaur	Alwar Hanumangarh Pali	Barmer Jaipur Rajsamand	Bharatpur Jaisalmer Sikar	Churu (14) Jodhpur
Others (C) Average	Baran Jhalawar Udaipur	Bhilwara Jhunjhunu	Bikaner Kota	Bundi Sirohi	Dholpur (11) Tonk

(Contd.)

(*Contd.*)

Categorisation by CHPI		*No. of Dist.*		*No. of Dist.*		*No. of Dist.*
Cross categorisation:- CHPI & Poverty ratio	A Poor		B Good		C Average	
(A) Poor	Jalore Dungarpur Sawai Madhopur Karauli Banswara	5	Dausa	1	Chittorgarh	1
(B) Good	Jaisalmer Barmer Nagaur	3	Jodhpur Ajmer Hanumangarh Churu Ganganagar	5	Alwar Pali Sikar Rajsamand Bharatpur	5
(C) Average	Tonk Udaipur Jhalawar Dholpur	4	Kota Jhunjhunu Bikaner	3	Baran Bundi Bhilwara Sirohi	4

Table 7.11(c): Correlation Matrix of Indicators & CHPI

Indicator	*Demography*	*Housing*	*Literacy*	*Health*	*Nutrition*	*Live stock*	*Agriculture*	*Infrastructure*	*Development*	*CHPI Value*
Demography	1									
Housing	0.077007	1								
Literacy	-0.95763	-0.0388	1							
Health	0.352751	0.33614	-0.3048	1						
Nutrition	0.143466	-0.0113	-0.0813	0.19035	1					
Livestock	0.124618	0.1383	-0.0384	0.22864	0.47402	1				
Agriculture	0.14011	0.15209	-0.056	0.035	0.30098	0.39568	1			
Infrastructure	0.388635	0.48414	-0.252	0.6467	0.22597	0.37387	0.12935	1		
Development	0.354043	0.10028	-0.3097	0.01736	-0.0312	-0.2565	0.21674	0.110958	1	
CHPI Value	0.441967	0.42452	-0.3091	0.65861	0.61158	0.65413	0.56699	0.763036	0.1673103	1

A comparison of CHPI, HPI and Poverty Ratio had been attempted by

(i) studying the relationship of CHPI with poverty ratio and HPI with poverty ratio.
(ii) comparison of ranks of the districts by the 3 indices.

Table 7.12: Comparison of CHPI, HPI and Poverty Ratio

District	*CHPI*	*Rank*	*HPI*	*Rank*	*Poverty Ratio*	*Rank*
	(1)	*(2)*	*(3)*	*(4)*	*(5)*	*(6)*
Ajmer	49.4	25	54.89	32	26.4	20
Alwar	51.9	20	61.35	23	22	24
Banswara	61.8	1	65.01	9	72.9	1
Baran	50.2	22	58.39	28	32.5	15
Barmer	59.0	3	69.44	2	28.7	18
Bharatpur	52.2	18	61.22	24	18.3	27
Bhilwara	53.4	17	62.38	17	34.7	12
Bikaner	44.0	31	61.7	19	36.8	8
Bundi	54.8	14	63.69	12	25.5	22
Chittorgarh	53.7	16	64.13	11	49.1	4
Churu	49.9	23	61.66	20	28.5	19
Dausa	47.3	28	63.01	14	35.8	9
Dholpur	55.9	10	65.72	5	34.8	11
Dungarpur	57.9	5	62.67	15	71.3	2
Ganganagar	40.4	32	59.47	27	20.2	26
Hanumangarh	45.4	29	56.44	29	21.8	25
Jaipur	47.9	27	56.02	30	16.3	29
Jaisalmer	59.5	2	62.44	16	26.1	21
Jalore	56.6	8	69.71	1	37.5	6
Jhalawar	55.7	11	63.17	13	33.2	13
Jhunjhunu	45.1	30	60.22	26	10.5	31
Jodhpur	48.5	26	60.26	25	13.1	30
Karauli	56.0	9	65.6	6	40.8	5
Kota	49.6	24	55.04	31	32.1	16
Nagaur	55.6	12	66	4	16.5	28
Pali	52.1	19	61.53	21	24	23
Rajsamand	54.8	15	62.18	18	35.7	10
Sawai Madhopur	56.7	7	65.6	6	37.4	7
Sikar	50.5	21	61.48	22	10	32
Sirohi	55.2	13	67.07	3	30.9	17
Tonk	58.0	4	64.62	10	32.9	14
Udaipur	57.2	6	65.13	8	58	3
Average	52.9		61.7		31.7	

Note: HPI—Human Development Report, Rajasthan, 1999.

The results are as under:

(a) The relationship of CHPI with poverty ratio as well as that of HPI with poverty ratio is rather weak. The strength of relationship measured in terms of R square along with other cofficients is presented as under:

Regression Equations

(i) Composite Human Poverty Index (CHPI) and Poverty Ratio
Poverty Ratio = – 59.63 + 1.64 CHPI
$R^2 = .20$

(ii) Human Poverty Index (HPI) and Poverty Ratio
Poverty Ratio = – 7.28 + 1.43 × HPI
$R^2 = .12$

(b) An analysis of poverty and deprivation had been undertaken in order to analyse whether there is some commonality in categorisation of districts as high poverty districts by our methodology and conventional poverty ratio approach. By comparing the ranks of the districts by 3 indices it is observed that there has been somewhat close agreement in the ranks for half of the districts but large disagreement on about one-third of the districts (Table 7.13).

Table 7.13: Comparison of CHPI, HPI and Poverty Ratio

Difference in Ranks	*CHPI vs. Poverty Ratio*	*CHPI vs. HPI*
Upto 2	12	10
3-5	2	10
5-7	6	4
8-10	4	4
>10	9	4

Poverty ratio which is based on household income alone is not a sufficient indicator of deprivation. The composite human poverty index (CHPI) as calculated for various districts in Rajasthan in this study reflects a more realistic picture as it is based on 9 indicators influencing rural poverty. This also helps in better targetting of the districts having higher level of deprivation as reflected through high CHPI.

Let us first examine why some districts are poor according to CHPI and not as per other measures of poverty. The poverty ratio is based on income criteria alone. The HPI considers many indicators which are heavily loaded to capture income in addition to some aspects of Health and Nutrition. In CHPI the emphasis is more on outcome indicators having bearing on well-being as measured by Health and Nutrition. Rajasthan being a livestock based economy, the same has also being given due importance. In the analysis, Bikaner is an interesting case where Health, Nutrition and Livestock indicators are favourable taking the district to the top category. The factors contributing to CHPI are low levels of urbanisation, high proportion of agricultural labour population as well as SC/ST population, high proportion of houseless families, poor access to electricity and toilet, low levels of per capita cereal production, oilseed production, production of cash crops and per capita livestock. In terms of infrastructure facilities, factors are less number of bank branches, very poor access to *pucca* road, apart from less number of milk co-operatives. CHPI is also influenced by very low female literacy rates, high infant mortality rates, low levels of immunizations, doctor/population ratio, low average life expectancy and low level of safe delivery facilities. Proportion of severely malnourished children, population suffered most due to frequent occurrence of drought, etc.

An attempt has been made to estimate Poverty Ratio using CHPI by relating Poverty Ratio and CHPI through regression analysis based on districts data where ranks match by both methods. The results are presented in Table 7.14.

Table 7.14: Estimation of Poverty Ratio

District	*Income Approach*	*CHPI Approach*
Ajmer	26.4	32.2
Alwar	22.0	44.8
Banswara	72.9	72.4
Baran	32.5	37.7
Barmer	28.7	66.5
Bharatpur	18.3	43.6
Bhilwara	34.7	38.1
Bikaner	36.8	9.7
Bundi	25.5	53.6
Chittorgarh	49.1	42.2
Churu	28.5	35.5
Dausa	35.8	28.2
Dholpur	34.8	61.0
Dungarpur	71.3	59.1
Ganganagar	20.2	4.5
Hanumangarh	21.8	16.0
Jaipur	16.3	34.1
Jaisalmer	26.1	59.9
Jalore	37.5	48.8
Jhalawar	33.2	53.6
Jhunjhunu	10.5	25.9
Jodhpur	13.1	31.5
Karauli	40.8	57.3
Kota	32.1	44.4
Nagaur	16.5	51.8
Pali	24.0	42.2
Rajsamand	35.7	51.0
Sawai Madhopur	37.4	57.3
Sikar	10.0	30.4
Sirohi	30.9	47.0
Tonk	32.9	61.4
Udaipur	58.0	56.6

Regression of Poverty Ratio and CHPI

$$\text{Poverty Ratio} = -146.35 + 3.70\ \text{CHPI}$$
$$R^2 = 0.61$$

Thus, judged by various indicators of poverty, the district-wise profile of factors which tend to cause poverty could be summarised as follows:

1. Ajmer: Medium level of per capita income, coupled with medium level of agricultural labour population; low proportion of irrigated area, low average size of holding, low level of immunization, low life expectancy, low coverage under Indira Awas Yojana.

2. Alwar: Poor access to electricity, poor access to toilets, poor access to safe drinking water, low level of urbanisation, high proportion of agricultural labour population, high proportion of SC/ST population, high proportion of BPL families engaged in agriculture high proportion of houseless families. Low size of land holding, less number of bank branches, less number of regulated markets, less number of fair price shops, poor level of immunization facility, poor doctor-population ratio, poor average life expectancy, poor access to safe delivery, poor coverage under Indira Awas Yojana.

3. Banswara: Low per capita income, less number of *pucca* houses, poor access to electricity, poor access to toilets, poor access to safe drinking water, low level of urbanization, high proportion of SC/ST population, high proportion of houseless families, low proportion of irrigated area, low size of holding less number of regulated markets, low level of female literacy (despite large number of Primary School per population), highest infant mortality rate, low level of immunization facility, (despite high doctor-population ratio), high incidence of severely malnourished children, poor coverage under IAY, very low proportion of women getting self-employment under JGSY and overall very low coverage under TRYSEM/JGSY.

4. Baran: Poor access to toilet, relatively low level of urbanization, relatively high proportion of agricultural labour population, relatively high proportion of SC/ST population, low per capita cereal output (despite high proportion of irrigated area), less number of bank branches (both co-operative and commercial banks), poor access to *pucca* road, low Primary School-population ratio, low doctor- population ratio, relatively medium to high percentage of severely malnourished children, less number of self-help groups, poor coverage under JGSY, JRY, low proportion of women getting self-employment in JGSY/IRDP.

5. Barmer: Very low level of per capita income, less number of *pucca* houses, poorest access to electricity, very poor access to toilet facilities, very poor access to safe drinking water, very low level of urbanization, very high proportion of agricultural labour population, high proportion of SC/ST population, high proportion of houseless families, very poor access to irrigation water, low level of per capita cereal output, oilseed output, and also production of cash crops, less number of commercial bank branches, poor access to *pucca* road, high infant mortality rate lowest level of immunization facility, low level of life expectancy, high proportion of severely malnourished children, high intensity of loss due to drought, less number of self-help groups, relatively poor coverage under TRYSEM/JGSY.

6. Bharatpur: Low per capita income (despite low proportion of families below the poverty line due to better income distribution) relatively less access to electricity, low access to toilet facility, poorest access to safe drinking water, high proportion of agricultural labour population, high proportion of SC/ST population, low size of land holding, low per capita production of cash crops, relatively less number of commercial bank branches, relatively less number of fair price shops, low level of immunization, very low level of average life expectancy, poor access to safe delivery, high proportion of severely malnourished male children and highest proportion of severely malnourished female children, less number of self-help groups.

7. Bhilwara: Less number of *pucca* houses, relatively high proportion of SC/ST population, high proportion of houseless families, low average size of landholding, low average size of landholding, low per capita production of oilseeds, relatively less proportion of villages having access to *pucca* road, relatively less number of fair price shops, low level of female literacy. Low average life expectancy, relatively low access to safe delivery, relatively high proportion of severely malnourished children, less number of self-help groups very low coverage under IAY.

8. Bikaner: Poor income distribution, less number of *pucca* houses, relatively poor access to safe drinking water, low proportion of irrigated area, low per capita cereal production, less number of regulated markets, very high proportion of severely malnourished children, high intensity or damage due to drought, relatively poor coverage under JGSY, JRY and overall coverage under TRYSEM/JGSY.

9. Bundi: Relatively less number of *pucca* houses, relatively less access to electricity, relatively less access to toilet facility, high proportion or BPL families engaged in agriculture, very high proportion of houseless families, low size of holding, very poor access to *pucca* road, relatively less number of regulated markets, second lowest number of fair price shops per unit of population, relatively low level of female literacy, low doctor-population ratio, low average life expectancy, relatively high proportion of severely malnourished children, relatively very poor coverage under JGSY, JRY, IAY and overall TRYSEM/JGSY.

10. Chittorgarh: Less number of pucca houses, poor access to toilet facility, relatively low level of urbanization, high proportion of SC/ST population, high proportion of poor families engaged in agriculture, high percentage of houseless families, low size of land holding, low per capita production of cash crops, very poor access to *pucca* road, relatively less number of fair price shops, low level of female literacy, second highest infant mortality rate, low level of immunization (despite second best doctor population ratio), low average life expectancy, relatively high proportion of severely malnourished female children, relatively less number of self-help groups and low coverage under IAY,

11. Churu: Low level of per-capita income, poor access to safe drinking water, high proportion of BPL families engaged in agriculture, lowest proportion of irrigated area, low per capita production of cereals, oilseeds and cash crops, less number of primary schools per unit of population, high infant mortality rate, low level of immunization and low proportion of women getting employment in JGSY.

12. Dausa: Relatively low level of per-capita income, low access to toilet facility, low level of urbanization, high proportion of SC/ST population, relatively high proportion of BPL families engaged in agriculture, high proportion of houseless families, relatively low size of holding, less number of fair price shops, high infant mortality rate, low doctor- population ratio, relatively less access to safe delivery, relatively high intensity of damage due to drought, relatively less coverage under IAY, and low proportion of women getting employment in JGSY.

13. Dholpur: Low level of per capita income (although having better income distribution, poor access to electricity, poor access to toilet facility, poor access to safe drinking water, high proportion of houseless families, lowest average size of holdings, less number of commercial bank branches, high infant mortality rate, low level of immunization, low doctor-population ratio, low average life expectancy, low access to safe delivery, low number of self-help groups and relatively less coverage under JGSY and JRY.

14. Dungarpur: Lowest level of per capita income, lowest number of *pucca* houses, low access to electricity, low access to toilet, low level of urbanization, high proportion of SC/ST population, high proportion of BPL families engaged in agriculture, high proportion of houseless families, low proportion of irrigated area, lowest average size of land holding, low per capita output of oilseeds and cash crops, lowest number of regulated markets, less number of fair price shops, one of the very low levels of female literacy (despite having relatively more number of primary schools per unit of population), high infant mortality rate, second highest proportion of severely malnourished children, lowest coverage under IAY, very low proportion of women getting employment under JGSY/IRDP, and relatively low coverage under TRYSEM/JGSY.

15. Ganganagar: Relatively high proportion of agricultural labour population, relatively high proportion of SC/ST population, relatively high proportion of BPL families engaged in agriculture, relatively high proportion of houseless families, relatively less number of commercial bank branches, relatively less number of fair price shop, relatively less number of primary schools per unit of population, lowest doctor-population ratio, low access to safe delivery, less number of self-help groups and overall low coverage under TRYSEM/JGSY.

16. Jaipur: Relatively low per capita production of cereals, oilseeds and cash crops, less number of co-operative bank branches, less number of regulated markets, less number of primary schools per unit of population, low doctor-population ratio, relatively high proportion of severely malnourished male children, high intensity of damage due to drought, less number of self-help groups.

17. Jaisalmer: Low per capita income, low access to electricity, relatively low access to toilet facility, low level of urbanization, low proportion of irrigated area, low level of per capita production of cereals, oilseeds and cash crops, poor access to *pucca* road, less number of regulated markets, low level of female literacy (despite large number of primary schools per unit of population), relatively high infant mortality rate, low level of immunization (despite high doctor-population ratio), low access to safe delivery, highest proportion of severely malnourished children, low coverage under JRY, low proportion of women getting employment in JGSY.

18. Jalore: Low per capita income, less number of *pucca* house, low access to electricity, low access to toilet facility low access to safe drinking water, low level of urbanization, high proportion of houseless families, relatively low per capita output of cereals and cash crops, less number of commercial bank branches, lowest female literacy rate, less number of primary schools per unit of population, high infant mortality rate, low doctor-population ratio, low access to safe delivery, high intensity of damage to drought, less number of self-help groups and relatively less coverage under TRYSEM/JGSY.

19. Jhalawar: Less number of *pucca* houses, relatively low access to electricity, low access to toilet facility, poor access to safe drinking water, low level of urbanization, high proportion of agricultural labour population, high proportion of BPL families engaged in agriculture, relatively high proportion of houseless families, low per capita production of cash crops, poorest access to *pucca* road, low level of immunization, relatively high infant mortality rate, relatively low average life expectancy, poor coverage under JGSY, low proportion of women getting employment under JGSY, relatively low coverage under TRYSEM/JGSY.

20. Jhunjhunu: Low per capita income, low access to electricity, low access to toilet facility, low proportion of irrigated area, less number of regulated markets, high proportion of severely malnourished male and female children, high intensity of loss due to drought.

21. Jodhpur: Relatively low per capita income (probably better income distribution as income based poverty is lowest), poor access to electricity, poor access to toilet facility, low per capita production of cereals, oilseeds and cash crops, less number of branches of both co-operative and commercial banks, very few number of regulated markets, relatively low level of female literacy, less number of primary school per unit of population, relatively low access for safe delivery, high intensity of loss due to drought, less number of self-help groups, low coverage under JRY.

22. Karauli: Less number of *pucca* houses, poor access to safe drinking water, low level of urbanization, high proportion of SC/ST population, relatively low per capita output of cereals and oilseeds, very less number of branches of both co-operative and commercial banks, low access to *pucca* road, less number of primary schools per unit of population, low level of immunization, low average life expectancy, relatively high proportion of severely malnourished children, poor coverage under JGSY and relatively low proportion of women getting employment in JGSY.

23. Kota: High proportion of agricultural labour population, low per capita production of cereals (despite high proportion of irrigated area), relatively less number of branches of co-operative and commercial banks, very poor access to *pucca* road, lowest number of fair price shops, lowest number of primary schools, low doctor-populaiton ratio, very low coverage under JGSY, JRY and TRYSEM.

24. Nagaur: Relatively less access to electricity, poor access to safe drinking water, low level of urbanization, relatively high proportion of SC/ST population, relatively high proportion of BPL families engaged in agriculture, relatively low proportion of irrigated area, less number of branches of co-operative and commercial banks, relatively less access to *pucca* road, less number of fair price shops, less number of primary schools per unit of population, high proportion of severely malnourished male and female children, high intensity of loss due to drought, less number of self-help groups, less coverage under IAY and TRYSEM/JGSY.

25. Pali: High proportion agricultural labour population, relatively low per capita production of cereals, low level of female literacy, very high infant mortality ratio, low average life expectancy, relatively low access to safe delivery, high intensity of loss due to drought and relatively low coverage under JGSY.

26. Rajsamand: Less number of *pucca* houses, low level of urbanization, relatively high percentage of BPL families engaged in agriculture, high proportion of houseless families, low average size of holdings, low per capita production of oilseeds and cash crops, less number of co-operative bank branches, relatively low level of female literacy, high infant mortality, low doctor-population ratio, relatively high proportion of severely malnourished male children, relatively less coverage under JRY, and IAY, low proportion of women getting employment under JGSY.

27. Sawai Madhopur: Less number of *pucca* houses, poor access to electricity, poor access to toilet, high proportion of agricultural labour population, low average size of holding, low per capita production of cereals, less number of bank branches (both co-operative and commercial), low access to pucca road, relatively less access to regulated markets, low level of female literacy, less number of primary schools per unit of population, relatively high infant mortality rate, low level of immunization, low average life expectancy, high proportion of severely malnourished female children, relatively less coverage under IAY, low proportion of women getting employment in JGSY.

28. Sikar: Very low level of per capita income high proportion of households families, low proportion of irrigated area, low per capita output of oilseeds and cash crops, relatively less number of branches of co-operative and commercial banks, less number of regulated markets, less number of fair price shops, relatively less number of primary schools, relatively low doctor-population ratio, relatively high proportion of severely malnourished female children, relatively less coverage under JGSY, JRY and IAY.

29. Sirohi: High proportion of agricultural labour population, high proportion of SC/ST population, relatively low level of female literacy, less number of primary schools, high infant mortality rate, high proportion of severely malnourished male and female children, relatively low coverage under JGSY, JRY, and overall coverage under TRYSEM/JGSY.

30. Tonk: Relatively poor access to electricity, relatively poor access to toilet facilities, poor access to safe drinking water, high proportion of agricultural labour population, low proportion of irrigated area, low per capita production of cash crops, very poor access to *pucca* road, low level of female literacy, high infant mortality rate, low level of life expectancy, poor access to safe delivery, relatively high proportion of severely malnourished female children, relatively less number of self-help groups, less coverage under JGSY, JRY, IAY and low proportion of women getting employment in JGSY.

31. Udaipur: Relatively low level of per capita income, less number of *pucca* house, less access to electricity, high proportion of agricultural labour population, high proportion of SC/ST population, low size of landholding, low per capita production of cereals and oilseeds, less number of branches of co-operative banks and commercial banks, less number of regulated markets, low level of immunizations, low doctor-population ratio, relatively high proportion of malnourished children, relatively high incidence of loss due to drought, less number of self-help groups, less coverage under IAY, and low overall coverage under TRYSEM/JGSY and low proportion of women getting employment in JGSY.

32. Hanumangarh: Low level of urbanization, high proportion of SC population, less number of doctors per thousand population and less access to safe delivery facility.

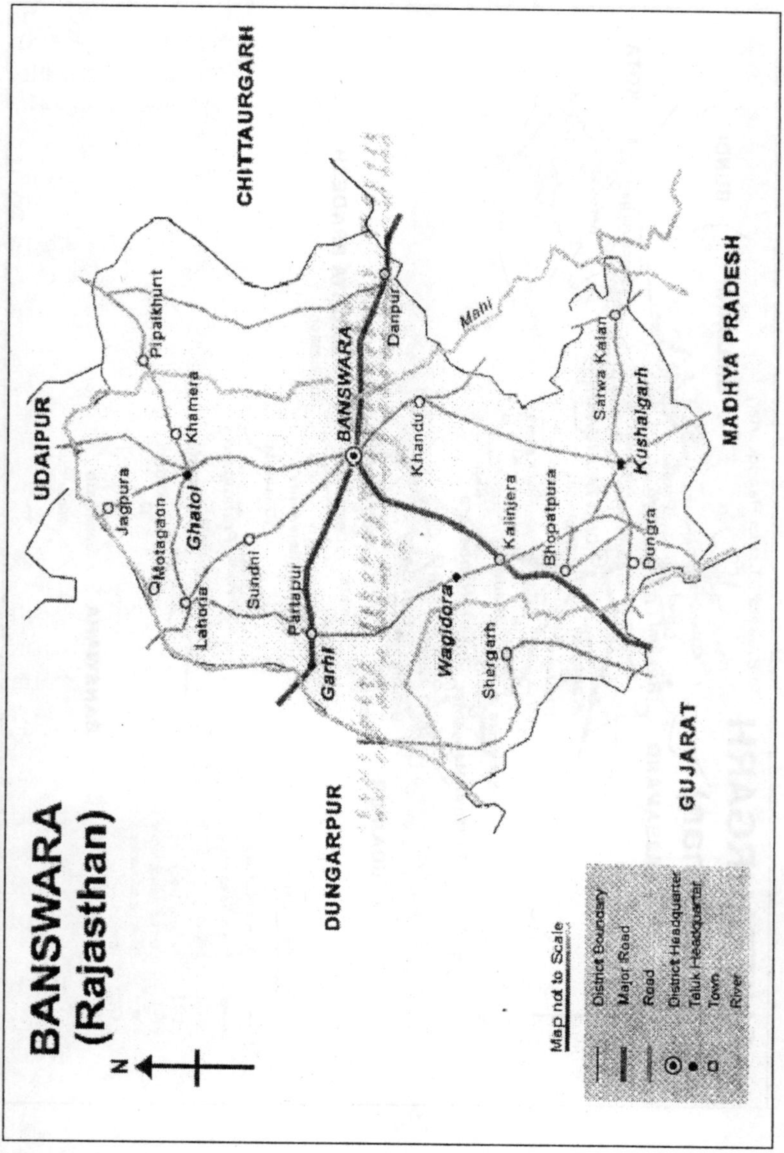

Source: www.mapsofindia.com

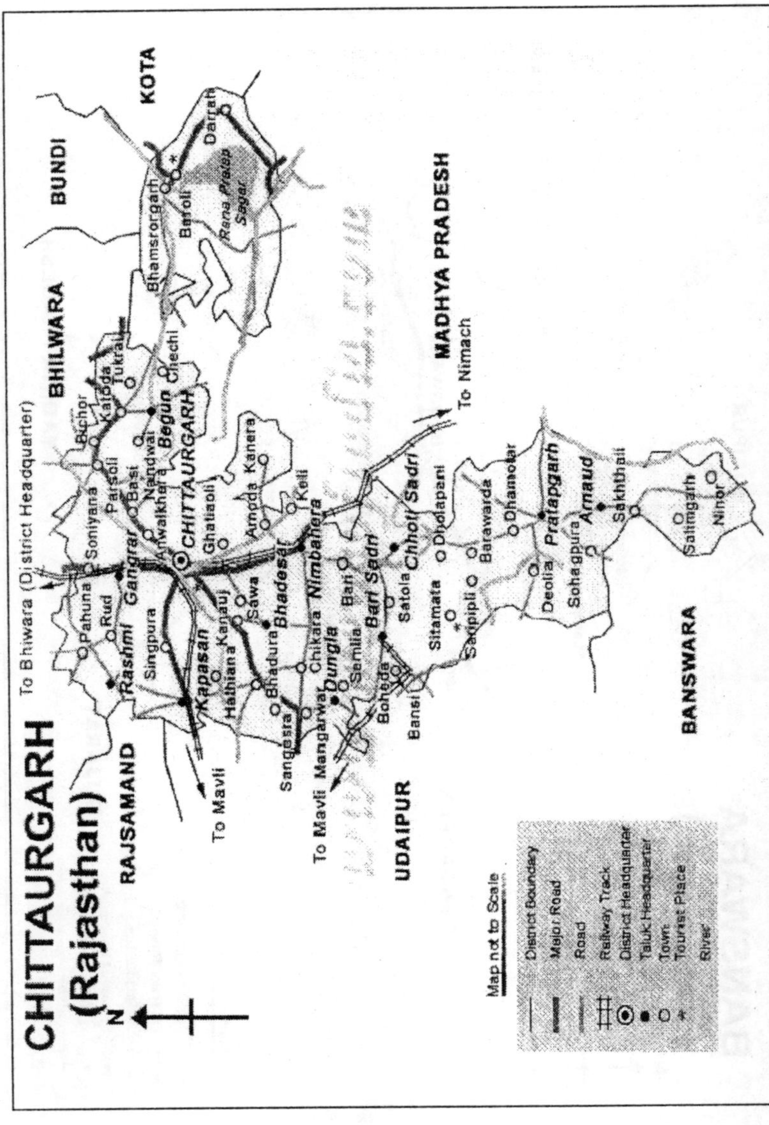

Source: www.mapsofindia.com

8

Rural Poor — Village and Household Levels Analysis

"Think of the poorest person you have ever seen and ask if your next act will be of any use to him".

—*Mahatma Gandhi*

With a view to supplementing and complementing the findings of district level analysis, an intensive survey at the village and household levels was conducted using structured questionnaires in one block each of of Banswara and Chittorgarh districts. The surveyed districts are relatively poor and underdeveloped. Further, the two blocks selected for this purpose, namely Sajjangarh in Banswara and Rushmi in Chittorgarh also had relatively high poverty ratio. The analysis of data in constructing composite index was carried out on the same pattern as that of the secondary data at the district level.

The number of villages covered in the survey were 186 and 81 respectively from Sajjangarh Block of Banswara and Rashmi block of Chittorgarh. The number of households covered were 21,032 from Sajjangarh and 9,146 from Rushmi blocks respectively. The distribution of villages in the two districts by poverty ratio is given as under (Table 8.1).

The overall poverty ratio was 85 per cent and 51 per cent in the selected villages from Sajjangarh block of Banswara and Rashmi block of Chittorgarh districts respectively. It would be seen that where as 95 per cent villages in the block from Banswara had poverty above 70 per cent, in Chittorgarh two-third of villages had poverty between 20-60 per cent. In the presentation of results the reference hereafter would be of districts only but based on the data of the villages from selected blocks.

Table 8.1: Distribution of Villages by Poverty (%)

Poverty (%)	*Banswara*	*Chittorgarh*
1-10	0.0	2.8
11-20	0.0	5.6
21-30	0.6	12.5
31-40	0.6	18.1
41-50	1.2	13.9
51-60	1.8	20.8
61-70	0.0	6.9
71-80	24.4	8.3
81-90	56.7	2.8
91-100	14.6	8.3
Average Poverty Ratio	**84.6**	**50.6**

Village Level Indicators

At the village level, sixty variables of rural poverty were considered. On the pattern of district level analysis, these variables were grouped under nine broad indicators.

The '**Demography**' group included variables such as sex ratio, population density, proportion of SC and ST population and workers as per cent of total population. The '**development**' related variables included proportion of beneficiaries of anti-poverty programmes, wrong identification of poor families, proportion of rural families crossing the poverty line, proportion of disabled receiving pension, incidence of drought and percentage of population affected by drought, incidence of flood and percentage of population affected by flood, access to self-help groups and DWCRA, wage rates of skilled and unskilled male and female workers and allocation of panchayat resources for development. Under '**Agriculture**' group, eleven variables were considered for analysis. These include per capita area under all crops, proportion of irrigated area, proportion of area under rice and wheat, proportion of rice and wheat area irrigated, proportion of dependable source of irrigation, use of diesel pump with available electricity, distance from *mandi/up-mandi*, distance from agriculture-service centre and panchayat resources allocated to agriculture. The '**Livestock**' related variables included per capita miltch buffaloes, per capita non-miltch buffaloes, per capita livestock population, distance from veterinary hospital and panchayat resource allocated for livestock development. The **'Health'** related indicators were number of Trained Dai (%) in a village, number of disabled persons, distance of Primary Health Centres, distance of sub-centre, access to private practitioner and panchayat resources allocated to health. The **'Nutrition'** related variables, were access to ICDS, distance from the ICDS and nutritional status (Grade III). The **'Housing and Sanitation'** included mainly safe drinking water. The **'Infrastructure'** related variables included, percentage of villages electrified, access to co-operative credit for seed, fertilisers, etc. distance from *pucca* road, distance from a ration shop, distance from railway station, distance from post office and panchayat resources allocated for infrastructure development. The **'Literacy'** related variables considered were literacy rate, availability of primary school for boys, availability of primary school for girls, availability of primary school for all children and panchayat resources allocated for education.

Household Level Indicators

The information collected at the household level had also been grouped under 9 broad indicators. Under the head **'Demography'** four variables were considered, namely, female headed household, percentage of SC population, percentage of ST population and sex ratio. Under the head **'Agriculture'** the variables considered were agricultural land: (i) total, (ii) irrigated, and (iii) owned: area under Kharif, total and irrigated; and under Rabi, total and irrigated; area under zaid, total and irrigated. The other sub-indicators are bonded labour, in agriculture-male and female and in non-agriculture—male and female. The wage rate of agricultural labourers, both—male and female as well as non-agricultural workers—male and female had also been included under this head. Under **'Development'**, the sub-indicators were income, training under TRYSEM, assistance under IRDP, increase in income due to IRDP, drought and floods, and losses in days and rupees due to both these natural calamities. The other variables included number of days in a year spent on economic activities (separately for males and females) under the head agriculture, non-agriculture and others. The information on migration in terms of duration and distance was also considered. Under the head **'Housing and Sanitation'**, the variables were availability of electricity, tap water for drinking, type of house—*pucca* or *kuccha*, owned, rented, free and from Indira Awas Yojana. Under the head **'Infrastructure'**, the information collected related to access to co-operative/Government agencies for agricultural and non-agricultural credit. Under the head **'Livestock'**, the information related to milch animals, namely cow, buffalo and total livestock population. Under the head **'Nutrition'**, the variables considered were per capita consumption of cereals, (rice, wheat and others) pulses, fruits, vegetables, milk and milk products, egg, fish etc.

General Characteristics of the Selected Villages

Demography

In order to understand the overall general profile, Table 8.2 provides information on important characteristics for two districts based on village level data. The population of Banswara is primarily tribal with STs accounting for more than 87 per cent and another 2 per cent were SCs. District Chittorgarh can be taken as an average district (demographically) as it had 20 per cent SC and 7 per cent ST population. Agricultural labourers account for nearly 40 per cent of the total population in both the districts. Banswara has very high population density of 4642 persons per sq kilometre as against 1767 in Chittorgarh.

Agriculture

Percentage of irrigated area is almost nil (1%) in Banswara but around 10 per cent in Chittorgarh. Area under rice and wheat together accounts for 47 per cent of total cropped area in

Banswara and 41 per cent in Chittorgarh. Of the area under two crops, irrigated area is only 4 per cent in Banswara but 33 per cent in Chittorgarh. Though irrigated area is low, the dependable source (other than canal) is 90 per cent in Chittorgarh as against 30 per cent in Banswara. Allocation of panchayat resources for agriculture was reported in 44 per cent villages of Banswara and in 38 per cent of Chittorgarh. Use of diesel pumps was significantly in the surveyed villages of the two districts being 88 per cent in Chittorgarh and 91 per cent in Banswara.

Table 8.2: Variables/Indicators at Village Level

Variables/Indicators	*Chittorgarh (Rashmi)*	*Banswara (Sajjangarh)*
Agriculture		
Per cent Irrigated Area	9.92	1.13
Per cent Area under Rice and Wheat	41.24	46.66
Per cent Irrigated Area under Rice and Wheat	35.38	4.04
Dependable source of irrigation (%)	92.56	29.53
Use of diesel pump (%)	88.00	91.00
Mandi Yard—Distance (km)	2.14	2.00
Up-Mandi Yard—Distance (km)	7.87	3.00
Agri Centre—Distance (km)	2.88	0.78
Panchayat Resources allocated to Agriculture (% villages)	38.00	44.00
Demography		
SC (%)	19.89	2.14
ST (%)	6.97	87.66
Agricultural Labourers (%)	41.33	40.08
Population Density	1767	4642
Development		
Per cent Beneficiaries Covered	10	2
Per cent Crossing Poverty Line	3	0
Receiving Pension (%)	25	12
Drought (%)	92	99
Self-Help Group (%)	32	25
DWCRA (%)	8	8
Wage Rate (Rs)		
Skilled Male	93.26	64.7
Unskilled Male	45.28	38.13

(*Contd.*)

(*Contd.*)

Variables/Indicators		*Chittorgarh (Rashmi)*	*Banswara (Sajjangarh)*
Skilled Female		34.31	0
Unskilled Female		34.03	33.45
Panchayat Resources allocated to Development (%villages)		19	29
Health			
Trained Dai (%)		58	25
Disabled (%)		3.35	5.23
Distance of PHC (km)		6.96	4.0
Distance of Sub-Centre (km)		2.33	3.1
Distance of Private Practitioner (km)		1.18	1.14
Panchayat Resources allocated to Health (%)		23	48
Housing and Sanitation			
Safe Drinking Water (%)		25	4
Infrastructure			
(%) Regular Supply of Electricity		10	5
	Village Electrified	89	40
Access to Cooperative (%)–	Seed	69	15
	Fertiliser	66	98
	Medicine	47	2
Pucca Road (Distance in km)		2.15	1.65
Distance of Ration Shop (km)		1.44	1.77
Distance of Railway Station (km)		18.71	*
Distance of Post Office (km)		3.24	3
Panchayat Resources allocated to Infrastructure (% villages)		85	100
Literacy			
Literacy (%)		10	32
Children Attending Primary School (%)		94	86
Panchayat Resources allocated to Literacy and Culture (% villages)		19	95
Livestock			
Buffaloes (Miltch)/Capita		0.02	0.07
Buffaloes (Non-Miltch)/Capita		0.05	0.10
Live Stock per Capita		0.03	0.82
Vaternity Hospital (Distance in km)		0.7	4.16
Panchayat Resources attached to Livestock (%)		51	7
Nutrition			
ICDS (villages %)		61	58

* Not in the District

The distance of Mandi Yard, Up-mandi Yard and Agriculture Centre (KVK) was less than a kilometre for Banswara. For Chittorgarh the distance of Mandi Yard and Agriculture Centre was over 2 kilometres, but that of Up-mandi Yard about 8 kilometres.

Infrastructure

About 90 per cent of the villages in the selected block of Chittorgarh district and 40 per cent of the villages in the selected block of Banswara district are electrified. On the contrary, percentages of villages electrified in these two districts are 78 and 63 respectively. The regular supply of electricity is 10 per cent in Chittorgarh and 5 per cent in Banswara. However, the use of Diesel Pump with this electrification was about 90 per cent in the concerned villages of both the districts. About 40 per cent of the villages had access to *pucca* road, the average distance being 2 kms. Ration shops were available within 1-5 kms and Post Office at 3 kms. The access to co-operative credit for seed was 5 per cent, in Banswara and 70 per cent in Chittorgarh and that for fertiliser was 98 per cent in Banswara and 70 per cent in Chittorgarh. The Panchayat resources was allocated for infrastructure in all the villages of Banswara and in 85 per cent villages in Chittorgarh.

Housing and Sanitation

Safe drinking water was accessible to only 4 per cent of villages in Banswara and 25 per cent in Chittorgarh.

Development Activities

The IRDP and other beneficiaries of BPL families accounted for only 10 per cent in Chittorgarh and 2 per cent in Banswara. This was because number of poor were much more in Banswara as compared to Chittorgarh. Those crossing poverty line were nil in Banswara and 3 per cent in Chittorgarh. Of disabled persons, 25 per cent of them received pension in Chittorgarh and 12 per cent in Banswara. Almost all villages in Banswara and 92 per cent in Chittorgarh were affected by drought. The percentage population affected was 85 per cent in Banswara and 55 per cent in Chittorgarh. Incidence of flood was negligible. Membership of self-help groups was reported by two-third villages in Banswara and one-third in Chittorgarh. DWCRA was reported by 8 per cent villages in both the districts. The wage rate was Rs. 93 for skilled males and Rs. 45 for unskilled males in Chittorgarh but Rs. 65 for skilled males and Rs. 38 for unskilled males in Banswara. For females (skilled and unskilled) the wage rate was Rs. 35 only. For development activities, nearly 19 per cent of the villages in Chittorgarh and 29 per cent of the villages in Banswara received allocation of resources from village panchayats.

Health Services

About 25 per cent of villages in Banswara and 58 per cent in Chittorgarh had Trained Dai. Disabled persons were 3 per cent in Chittorgarh and 5 per cent in Banswara. The distance of Sub-centre was 2 kms in Chittorgarh and 3 kms in Banswara. PHCs were at an average distance of 7 kms. in Chittorgarh and 4 kms. in Banswara. Private practitioners were accessible within one km. of the surveyed villages of both the districts. Panchayat allocation for health was in 23 per cent of villages in Chittorgarh and 48 per cent of villages in Banswara.

Literacy

Literacy rate is considerably high being 32 per cent in Banswara, but very poor being only 10 per cent in Chittorgarh. The reasons for proportionately higher literacy rate in Banswara is attributed to higher coverage of villages (95%) under literacy campaign with Panchayat resources. In both the districts proportion of boys attending the primary schools is marginally higher than that of girls.

Livestock

The livestock per capita was 0.03 in Chittorgarh and about 0.8 in Banswara. Maternity hospital was available at a distance of over 4 kms. in Banswara but less than 7 kms. in Chittorgarh. Panchayats allocated resources for livestock development in 51 per cent of villages in Chittorgarh district and 58 per cent of villages in Banswara district.

Nutrition

On nutrition, about 60 per cent of villages had ICDS Centres in both the districts.

Characteristics of Selected Households

Demography

Table 8.3 provides the results on the profile of the Districts on the basis of household survey. In Chittorgarh 4 per cent of the households were headed by females as against 6 per cent in Banswara. Household in Banswara district were mainly tribal (>90 per cent) but in Chittorgarh district SC and ST together accounted for about 47 per cent. These results indicate much higher share of SC/ST in surveyed households as compared to general population of the villages in Chittorgarh district (*vide* Table 8.2).

Housing

Availability of electricity was in 30 per cent of the households in Chittorgarh and only 8 per cent in Banswara. Tap water for drinking was available in 13 per cent of households in Chittorgarh and only 2 per cent in Banswara. *Pucca* houses of their own were available in 20 per cent of households in Chittorgarh as against only 3 per cent in Banswara. Further, 52 per cent of the households in Chittorgarh district and 27 per cent of the households in Banswara district were provided houses under Indira Awas Yojana.

Table 8.3: Variables/Indicators at Household Level

Variables/indicators		*Chittorgarh*	*Banswara*
Agriculture	Agricultural Land Owned (acres)	0.84	0.87
	Land cultivated Kharif Total (acres)	0.81	0.71
Demography	Female Headed Households (%)	4	6
	S.C.+S.T. (%)	47	94
Development	Training under TRYSEM (%)	1	1
	Help from IRDP (%)	10	9
	Increase in Income (Rs.)	26	98
	Loss in days due to drought	78	217
	Loss in Rs. due to drought	2437	6037
	INCOME (PER HH PER MONTH)	875	1006
	ECONOMIC ACTIVITIES (DAYS SPENT)		
	Agriculture Male	74	153
	Agriculture Female	58	144
	MIGRATION		
	Duration (days)	0.22	5.6
	Distance (km)	38.99	30.39
	WAGE RATE (Rs. per day)		
	Agricultural – Male	38.16	31.22
	Agricultural – Female	31.29	26.72
Housing	Electricity (%)	31	08
	Tap water (%)	13	02
	Own HOUSE *PUCCA* (%)	21	03
	Indira Awas Yojna	52	27
Infrastructure	SOURCE OF LOAN (%)		
	Govt./Cooperative for *Agriculture*	30	15
	Govt./Cooperative for *non-agriculture*	08	06
Livestock	Per capita		
	Miltch Cow	0.46	1.05
	Bullock	0.19	0.37
	Miltch Buffalo	0.61	0.98
	Others	0.16	0.19

(*Contd.*)

(Contd.)

Variables/indicators	*Chittorgarh*	*Banswara*
Nutrition (Consumption—kg month)		
Rice	4.82	5.2
Wheat	47.52	57.37
Other cereals	5.59	7.05
Fruits	2.0	1.2
Vegetables	4.23	4.36
Sweeterer	4.24	2.93
Egg	0.27	4.1
Fish/Meat	0.08	1.32

Agriculture

The owned land was 0.87 acres in Banswara and 0.84 acres in Chittorgarh. Almost the entire area was under Kharif crop in Banswara and Chittorgarh districts which was mainly unirrigated. Area under Rabi crop was negligible and that under Zaid was Nil.

Development

The wage rate for agricultural male workers was Rs.38 in Chittorgarh and Rs. 31 in Banswara and that for non-agricultural male workers Rs. 45 in Chittorgarh and Rs.40 in Banswara. For female workers, the wage rate in agriculture was Rs.31 in Chittorgarh and Rs. 27 in Banswara and that for non-agriculture Rs. 38 in Chittorgarh and Rs. 33 in Banswara. In Chittorgarh district, the number of days spent in a year by male on agriculture activities were 74 days, whereas the same in Banswara district was 153 days. Similarly, for females the days spent in a year on agriculture were 59 in Chittorgarh, while in Banswara it was 144 days. Thus, the number of days spent on agricultural activities both by males and females were much higher (more than double) in Banswara as compared to Chittorgarh. The duration of migration was on an average 12 days in Banswara but less then 1 day for Chittorgarh, the distance being over 300 kms. in Banswara and about 40 kms. in Chittorgarh. The loss of income due to drought was Rs. 133

in Banswara and 103 in Chittorgarh amounting to loss of days over 200 in Banswara and 78 in Chittorgarh with total loss over Rs. 6000 in Banswara and Rs.2500 in Chittorgarh per household. The average income was over Rs.1000 per household in Banswara and 876 in Chittorgarh. The access to loan from co-operatives for agriculture was 33 per cent in Chittorgarh and 40 per cent in Banswara and for non-agriculture, it was 8 per cent in Chittorgarh and 6 per cent in Banswara.

Livestock

The livestock per household were relatively more in Banswara as compared to Chittorgarh, the miltch cows and buffaloes together being 2 per household in Banswara as against 1 in Chittorgarh.

Nutrition

The cereals consumed (mainly wheat) were 84 gm. per day per capita in Banswara compared to 52 gm. in Chittorgarh. The consumption of milk and milk product was relatively more in Chittorgarh as compared to Banswara but that of edible oil and non-veg. other way round. Consumptions of all articles are much below the nutritional level.

Infrastructure

The availabilty of Credit for Agriculture from Government/ Co-operatives was 30 per cent in Chittorgarh as against about 15 per cent in Banswara. The same for non-agriculture activities was only about 8 per cent and 6 per cent respectively.

COMPARISON OF VILLAGES WITH EXTREME POVERTY RATIOS BASED ON INCOME

Criteria

In order to identify the village and household characteristics distinguishing high poverty villages and low poverty villages, a comparison was attempted by considering villages with extreme poverty levels, viz. very high and very low. For this in Banswara district villages with more than 90 per cent poverty and villages with less than 60 per cent poverty (average poverty ratio being 85) have been compared. Similarly in Chittorgarh villages with more than 70 per cent poverty and with less than 30 per cent poverty (average poverty ratio being 51) have been compared for various indicators. The results are presented in Tables 8.4 for village level data and 8.5 for household level data.

It would appear from these results that except for SC/ST population for almost all indicators there were no substantial differences between high poverty villages and low poverty villages. This puts a question mark on the basis of identification of poor and as a consequence estimates of poverty ratio. Hence, the need for a composite index as an alternative to income based poverty criteria.

Table 8.4(a): Comparison of Villages with Extreme Poverty Levels: Village Level Data—Banswara

Variables/Indicators	*> 90 per cent Poor*	*< 60 per cent Poor*
Agriculture		
Per cent Irrigated Area	0.89	0.51
Per cent Area under Rice and Wheat	52.71	46.96
Per cent Irrigated Area under Rice and Wheat	3.69	1.22
Dependable source of irrigation (%)	32.72	16.3
Use of diesel pump (%)	92	100
Mandi Yard—Distance (km)	2	2
Agri Centre—Distance (km)	0.63	0.22
Panchayat Resources allocated to Agriculture (% villages)	25	74
Demography		
SC (%)	0.58	2.43
ST (%)	99.37	16.61
Workers as per cent of total population (%)	48.29	13.13
Population density	4047	6314

(Contd.)

(*Contd.*)

Variables/Indicators	> 90 per cent Poor	< 60 per cent Poor
Development		
Per cent Beneficiaries Covered	2	1
Per cent Crossing Poverty Line	2	2
Receiving Pension (%)	17	0
Drought (%)	100	100
Per cent population effected	88.21	85.78
Self-Help Group (%)	21	24
DWCRA (%)	8	17
WAGE RATE (Rs.)		
Skilled Male	58.33	77.39
Unskilled Male	39.38	39.78
Skilled Female	NA	NA
Unskilled Female	34.79	34.78
Panchayat Resources allocated to Development (% villages)	25	23
Health		
Trained Dai (%)	17	35
Disabled (%)	5.54	5.26
Distance of PHC (Km)	3.46	5.13
Distance of Sub-Centre (Km)	2.67	2.61
Distance of Private Practitioner (Km)	0.33	0.3
Punchayat Resources allocated to Health (% villages)	42	26
Housing		
Safe Drinking Water (% villages)	0	17
Infrastructure		
Villages Electrified (%)	29	35
Regular Supply of Electricity (%)	0	13
Access to Cooperative (%)— Seed	8	13
Fertiliser	96	96
Medicine	0	9
Pucca Road (Distance in Km)	1.12	1.96
Ration Shop (Distance in Km)	1.21	3.13
Post Office (Distance Km)	3	3
Panchayat Resources allocated to Infrastructure (%)	100	100
Literacy		
Literacy (%)	31.67	16.3
Children attending Primary School (%)	86	75
Panchayat Resources allocated to Literacy and Culture (% villages)	83	100

(*Contd.*)

(Contd.)

Variables/Indicators	*> 90 per cent Poor*	*< 60 per cent Poor*
Livestock		
Buffaloes (Miltch)/Capita	0.08	0.02
Buffaloes (Non-Miltch)/Capita	0.12	0.03
Livestock per Capita	0.93	0.18
Vaternity Hospital (Distance in km)	3.67	5.39
Panchayat Resources attached to Livestock (%)	4	13
Nutrition		
ICDS (villages %)	50	52

Table 8.4(b): Comparison of Villages with Extreme Poverty Levels: Village Level Data—Chittorgarh

Variables/Indicators	*>70 per cent Poor*	*< 30 per cent Poor*
Agriculture		
Per cent Irrigated Area	16.79	4.44
Per cent Area under Rice and Wheat	44.49	42.1
Per cent Irrigated Area under Rice and Wheat	65	28
Dependable source of irrigation (%)	100	92
Use of diesel pump (%)	100	87
Mandi Yard—Distance (Km)	1.33	2.08
Up-Mandi Yard—Distance (Km)	4.67	7.28
Agri Centre—Distance (Km)	1.33	2.77
Panchayat Resources allocated to Agriculture (%)	33	29
Demography		
SC (%)	46.33	19.19
ST (%)	6.33	5.93
Workers as per cent of total population (%)	47.33	40.2
Population density	2169	1474
Development		
Per cent Beneficiaries Covered	3	12
Per cent Crossing Poverty Line	2	3
Receiving Pension (%)	33	28
Drought (%)	100	90
Per cent population effected	64	54.87
Self-Help Group (%)	10	38
DWACRA (%)	33	8

(Contd.)

(*Contd.*)

Variables/Indicators	>70 per cent Poor	< 30 per cent Poor
Wage Rate		
Skilled Male	126.67	90.74
Unskilled Male	46.67	45.41
Skilled Female	33.33	38.85
Unskilled Female	36.67	32.95
Panchayat Resources allocated Development (% villages)	33	5
Health		
Trained Dai (%)	33	56
Disabled (%)	1.67	2.7
Distance of PHC (km)	6.33	6.98
Distance of Sub-Centre (km)	2.33	2.34
Distance of Private Practitioner (km)	1.00	1.39
Panchayat Resources allocated to Health (% villages)	33	10
Housing		
Safe Drinking Water (%)	33	25
Infrastructure		
Village Electrified (%)	67	69
Regular Supply of Electricity (%)	5	11
Access to Cooperative (%)—Seed	67	68
Fertiliser	67	68
Medicine	33	54
Pucca Road (Yes) (%)	0	2
Pucca Road (Distance from village in km)	2.33	2.2
Ration Shop (Distance from village in km)	0.67	1.54
Railway Station (Distance from village in km)	30.67	17.9
Post Office (Distance from village in km)	1.67	3.46
Panchayat Resources allocated to Infrastructure (%)	100	83
Literacy		
Literacy (%)	10	11
Primary School Children (%)	47	97
Panchayat Resources allocated to Literacy (% villages)	33	10
Livestock		
Buffaloes (Miltch)/Capita	0.44	0.24
Buffaloes (Non-Miltch)/Capita	0	0.04

(*Contd.*)

(*Contd.*)

Variables/Indicators	*>70 per cent Poor*	*< 30 per cent Poor*
Livestock/Capita	0	0.04
Vaternity Hospital (Distance in km)	1	0.7
Panchayat Resources allocated to Livestock (%)	67	45
Nutrition		
ICDS Village (%)	67	59

Table 8.5(a): Comparison of Villages with Extreme Poverty Levels: Household Level Data—Banswara

Variables/Indicators			*Per cent*	*Poor*
			>90	*<60*
Agriculture				
Land owned			0.84	0.91
DEMOGRAHY				
Female Headed(%)			1	1
S.C.+S.T.(%)			91	92
Development				
Training under TRYSEM (%)			0	0
Help from IRDP			7	9
Increase in Income (Rs.)			44	184
Loss in Days due to drought			224	166
Loss in Rs. due to drought			5703	5592
INCOME			928	1050
ECONOMIC ACTIVITIES	MALE	Agriculture	131	147
	FEMALE	Agriculture	131	125
MIGRATION	Duration (days)		8.17	4.82
	Distance (km)		296	336
WAGE RATE	Agricutural	Male	31.5	34.64
	-do-	Female	27.06	30.36
	Non-agricultural	Male	41.28	31.77
	-do-	Female	33.5	29.91
Housing				
Electricity (%)			8	6
Tap (%)			3	3
Type of House *Pucca*	Own		3	3

(*Contd.*)

(Contd.)

	Variables/Indicators	Per cent > 90	Poor < 60
	Indira Awas Yojna	25	25
INFRASTRUCTURE			
SOURCE OF LOAN (%)	Cooperative for Agriculture	11	07
	Cooperative for non-Agricultural	06	04
Livestock			
	Miltch Cow	1.06	1.05
	Bullock	0.24	0.27
	Miltch Buffalo	1.06	1.05
	Others	0.12	0.09
Nutrition (Consumption kg per Month)			
Rice		4.06	5
Wheat		56.5	43.27
Other cereals		3.72	2.86
Pulses		2.36	3
Fruits		0.85	1.62
Vegetables		4.14	4.65
Sweetener		2.79	3.72
Egg		1.94	6
Fish/Meat		1.49	1.11

Table 8.5(b): Comparison of Villages with Extreme Poverty Levels: Household Level Data—Chittorgarh

Variables/Indicators	Per cent >70	Poor < 30
Agriculture		
Total Agricultural land owned	0.94	0.84
Demography		
Female Headed (%)	3	8
S.C.+S.T. (%)	71	44
Development		
Training under TRYSEM (%)	0	1
Help from IRDP	8	10
Increase in Income (Rs.)	74	22
Loss in days due to drought	95	69
Loss in Rs. due to drought	2528	2417

(Contd.)

(Contd.)

Variables/Indicators			*Per cent* >70	*Poor* <30
Income			848	845
Economic Activities	MALE	Agriculture	62	70
	FEMALE	Agriculture	59	54
Migration	Duration (days)		0.33	0.27
	Distance (km)		41.33	37.07
Wage rate (rs.)	Agricultural	Male	39.33	38.82
		Female	31.33	31.93
	Non-Agricultural	Male	45.67	46.03
		Female	37.67	39.25
Bonded Labour Housing				
Electricity (%)			25	32
Tap water (%)			13	11
Type of House (%) *(Pucca)*	Own		15	21
	Indira Awas Yojna		76	49
Infrastructure				
SOURCE OF LOAN (%)	Cooperative for Agriculture		31	27
	Cooperatve for non-Agricultural		20	08
Livestock				
	Miltch Cow		0.45	0.62
	Bullock		0.18	0.5
	Miltch Buffalo		0.55	0.7
	Others		0.08	0.37
Nutrition (Consumption in kg per month)				
Rice			5.03	10.14
Wheat			46.03	25.26
Other cereals			6.23	13.03
Pulses			2.01	0.92
Fruits			2.03	1.55
Vegetables			4.38	2.33
Sweetener			4.43	2.23
Egg			0.33	0.71
Fish/Meat			0.09	0.19

MISCLASSIFICATION OF POOR

In the study in addition to listing total families and families below poverty line information was collected on the following:

(i) Non-BPL families included in the list of BPL;
(ii) BPL families not included in the list of BPL families.

Based on this, an analysis of the misclassification of BPL, APL and both has been computed as under :

$$\text{Misclassification of BPL (\%)} = \frac{\text{BPL families not included in the list of BPL families}}{\text{BPL families + BPL families not included in the list of BPL families}} \times 100$$

$$\text{Misclassification of APL (\%)} = \frac{\text{Non-BPL families included in the list of BPL} \times 100}{\text{Non-BPL families + Non-BPL families included in the list of BPL families}}$$

$$\text{Misclassification of Both (\%)} = \frac{\text{BPL families not included in the list of BPL families + Non-BPL families included in the list of BPL families}}{\text{All families}} \times 100$$

The results are presented in Table 8.6. Following table summarises the results in misclassification.

Misclassification (%)	Banswara	Chittorgarh
BPL	8.0	8.0
APL	10.7	3.4
Both	9.0	6.0

The extent of misclassification was about 9 per cent in Banswara and 6 per cent in Chittorgarh. The misclassification of BPL was the same 8 per cent in both. The misclassification of Non-BPL families included in the list of BPL was over 10 per cent in Banswara and 3.4 per cent in Chittorgarh which results to non-poor availing the benefits meant for poor.

Table 8.6 (a): Misclassification of Poor—Banswara

Village	*No. of BPL families*	*No. of non-BPL families*	*No. of non-BPL families included in the list of BPL families*	*No. of BPL families not included in BPL families*	*Misclassification (%)*	
					BPL	*APL*
Agoriya	49	21	6	15	23.4	22.2
Amba	66	25			0.0	0.0
Andeshve	225	56		3	1.3	0.0
Ausaata	81				0.0	0.0
Baaldiya	42			5	10.6	0.0
Baallipa	66				0.0	0.0
Bagaapac	82			33	28.7	0.0
Bagayach	80			7	8.0	0.0
Bakaghut	33				0.0	0.0
Balasind	60			4	6.3	0.0
Basaliva	47	15		14	23.0	0.0
Bavripar	127	116			0.0	0.0
Beejalpu	69			8	10.4	0.0
Beraonat	85	29		26	23.4	0.0
Beraoodh	90	22		10	10.0	0.0
Bhamri	41	11		5	10.9	0.0
Bheelkuv	99			10	9.2	0.0
Bheemkho	69			8	10.4	0.0
Bhoolpar	39			4	9.3	0.0
Bhorajjo	61			5	7.6	0.0
Bhorajna	25			7	21.9	0.0
Bhuradau	135			24	15.1	0.0
Bhurakua	258	97		100	27.9	0.0
Bhurigha	34			2	5.6	0.0
Bichawar	79			15	16.0	0.0
Bilri	246				0.0	0.0
Biyapara	91	120			0.0	0.0
Bocharda	148			6	3.9	0.0
Boondika	108			4	3.6	0.0
Borkund	115			7	5.7	0.0
Bormatod	67				0.0	0.0
Chanawal	136				0.0	0.0
Charkali	37				0.0	0.0
Chhiyakh	35			11	23.9	0.0
Chhiyasa	72				0.0	0.0
Chitaura	24				0.0	0.0

(Contd.)

(*Contd.*)

Village	*No. of BPL families*	*No. of non-BPL families*	*No. of non-BPL families included in the list of BPL families*	*No. of BPL families not included in BPL families*	*Misclassification (%)*	
					BPL	*APL*
Chorpar	109				0.0	0.0
Choraka	80			4	4.8	0.0
Chorakh	74			6	7.5	0.0
Chotiya	15			8	34.8	0.0
Chowkid	40				0.0	0.0
Chtauram	54		7		0.0	100.0
Cunakhan	15	8		3	16.7	0.0
Daamaris	73				0.0	0.0
Damasath	125				0.0	0.0
Dharka	66				0.0	0.0
Dharki	45			15	25.0	0.0
Dhoteeki	28				0.0	0.0
Dungraba	83		6	34	29.1	100.0
Dungrach	68				0.0	0.0
Durala	547	61	14	95	14.8	18.7
Durgeniy	20	5		2	9.1	0.0
Ganeshpo	15			3	16.7	0.0
Garariya	182	69		69	27.5	0.0
Gariator	21				0.0	0.0
Ghatiya	105	14	26	14	11.8	65.0
Ghootach	102			8	7.3	0.0
Ghorwara	48				0.0	0.0
Godawara	92			6	6.1	0.0
Gora	137			6	4.2	0.0
Goykabar	137				0.0	0.0
Goykapar	95				0.0	0.0
Gundikh	23				0.0	0.0
Hagamogj	72	13		13	15.3	0.0
Hejabhav	52	5		5	8.8	0.0
Himmatga	30			6	16.7	0.0
Imlijhar	60			7	10.4	0.0
Jalimpur	214				0.0	0.0
Jaspoora	6				0.0	0.0
Jatlesat	46				0.0	0.0
Jeeracot	25	5		5	16.7	0.0
Jeevaboo	249	98	28	58	18.9	22.2

(*Contd.*)

(Contd.)

Village	No. of BPL families	No. of non-BPL families	No. of non-BPL families included in the list of BPL families	No. of BPL families not included in BPL families	Misclassification (%)	
					BPL	APL
Jhakoriy	156	27	4	21	11.9	12.9
Jhalkia	30			3	9.1	0.0
Jhamri	95	40		15	13.6	0.0
Jhandari	38	12			0.0	0.0
Jharvel	261			19	6.8	0.0
Jhoomki	67	21		21	23.9	0.0
Jogarima	8	7		4	33.3	0.0
Kabalaki	32			4	11.1	0.0
Kachala	115			7	5.7	0.0
Kala kho	135	43	8	40	22.9	15.7
Kalakhet	22			4	15.4	0.0
Kaliya	36				0.0	0.0
Karaimaa	26				0.0	0.0
Karmee	206				0.0	0.0
Kasarbar	481			7	1.4	0.0
Kasumba	52				0.0	0.0
Kawriya	82	9		9	9.9	0.0
Kharorch	100	32		10	9.1	0.0
Kheriya	150				0.0	0.0
Khootar	87				0.0	0.0
Kishenpa	41	2			0.0	0.0
Koondani	131			15	10.3	0.0
Koothlip	90				0.0	0.0
Kouidob	102			4	3.8	0.0
Kunda	111				0.0	0.0
Ladela	14	12		8	36.4	0.0
Lasoriya	168			14	7.7	0.0
Lohariya	91			15	14.2	0.0
Maatvad	129				0.0	0.0
Macha	114	17	10	9	7.3	37.0
Machhras	150				0.0	0.0
Machhuri	113	13	2	10	8.1	13.3
Madlibar	60	14		11	15.5	0.0
Madlicho	124			3	2.4	0.0
Magarda	62				0.0	0.0
Mahuree	220	59		59	21.1	0.0

(Contd.)

(*Contd.*)

Village	*No. of BPL families*	*No. of non-BPL families*	*No. of non-BPL families included in the list of BPL families*	*No. of BPL families not included in BPL families*	*Misclassification (%)*	
					BPL	*APL*
Malfomji	23			6	20.7	s
Maska ka	345			5	1.4	0.0
Maska kh	255			5	1.9	0.0
Matorith	34			3	8.1	0.0
Mepabat	79			6	7.1	0.0
Merana	117			12	9.3	0.0
Molna	15	1	1	1	6.3	50.0
Mooniya	345			7	2.0	0.0
Motapara	194				0.0	0.0
Motiya	120			40	25.0	0.0
Naalpara	124	48			0.0	0.0
Nawaagau	152			35	18.7	0.0
Paadala	75	20	3	20	21.1	13.0
Paatadiy	43			3	6.5	0.0
Palee kh	136				0.0	0.0
Pali kal	183			20	9.9	0.0
Parwalak	165				0.0	0.0
Parwallo	112				0.0	0.0
Patapor	125	41		15	10.7	0.0
Ranagee	110				0.0	0.0
Rathdhan	462			23	4.7	0.0
Ratnagho	34			5	12.8	0.0
Rautalim	82			6	6.8	0.0
Rawatasa	53				0.0	0.0
Renganiy	59	32			0.0	0.0
Rohanime	64				0.0	0.0
Rohaniya	160	56	7	27	14.4	11.1
Roopapar	47			8	14.5	0.0
Roopgarh	79				0.0	0.0
Rupa khe	74				0.0	0.0
Saalan	46			2	4.2	0.0
Saatsera	54			4	6.9	0.0
Sadriya	238			4	1.7	0.0
Sagawa	250	65	28	50	16.7	30.1
Sajjanga	124		2		0.0	100.0
Samlaser	90			2	2.2	0.0

(*Contd.*)

(Contd.)

Village	*No. of BPL families*	*No. of non-BPL families*	*No. of non-BPL families included in the list of BPL families*	*No. of BPL families not included in BPL families*	*Misclassification (%)*	
					BPL	*APL*
Sanidung	29	8		4	12.1	0.0
Sarendra	116				0.0	0.0
Sasa vad	32			7	17.9	0.0
Satserak	87			4	4.4	0.0
Seemalkh	103	36	1		0.0	2.7
Seemela	37			6	14.0	0.0
Sewaniya	61	10	6	10	14.1	37.5
Shakkar	180	9	18	9	4.8	66.7
Shambhup	54	6		6	10.0	0.0
Somjipar	106				0.0	0.0
Sookhera	69			15	17.9	0.0
Talaaipa	22			3	12.0	0.0
Tambsera	69				0.0	0.0
Tanda me	343			30	8.0	0.0
Tandarat	346			49	12.4	0.0
Tandi ba	236			12	4.8	0.0
Tandi ch	58			4	6.5	0.0
Thoothi	49				0.0	0.0
Tidiyade	135				0.0	0.0
Todikalo	76			2	2.6	0.0
Tombamac	242				0.0	0.0
Tori	59			4	6.3	0.0
Vadlipar	90				0.0	0.0
Vageri	132			6	4.3	0.0
Vagool	56			35	38.5	0.0
Vajwa am	96	17		17	15.0	0.0
					0.0	0.0
Total	17724	1447	177	1544	8.0	10.7

Table 8.6 (b): Misclassification of Poor—Chittorgarh

Village	*No. of BPL families*	*No. of Non-BPL families*	*No. of Non-BPL families included in the list of BPL families*	*No. of BPL families not included in BPL families*	*Misclassification of poor (per cent)*	
					BPL	*APL*
Araana.	63	73	16	22	25.9	27.9
Baaru.	244	109	11	20	7.6	8.8
Baavlas.	110	270	19	50	31.3	18.2
Bagtaava.	28	19		5	15.2	10.6
Balvantp.	8	35	3	4	33.3	16.3
Bassee.	49	43		1	2.0	1.1
Bhatt kh.	41	45		5	10.9	5.8
Bheemgar.	317	249		5	1.6	0.9
Bhopanai.	37	17	1	3	7.5	7.4
Charavat.	186	51		10	5.1	4.2
Chitauri.	73	42		20	21.5	17.4
Chmanpur.	50	21	2	5	9.1	9.9
Daulatpu.	30	8		5	14.3	13.2
Davipura.	62	114		6	8.8	3.4
Devpuri.	3	14		1	25.0	5.9
Dhangali.	61	147	2	2	3.2	1.9
Dindoli.	233	215	93	20	7.9	25.2
Ganeshpu.	43	14	2	11	20.4	22.8
Goodliya.	59	0	3	2	3.3	8.5
Haripoor.	63	73		4	6.0	2.9
Hirakher.	82	54		4	4.7	2.9
Jaalpura.	43	157		8	15.7	4.0
Jadana.	133	220		5	3.6	1.4
Javaan p.	38	27		4	9.5	6.2
Jugpura.	46	37	5	18	28.1	27.7
Karajiya.	68	0	1		0.0	1.5
Keeroka.	29	18		3	9.4	6.4
Laalpura.	64	101	2	1	1.5	1.8
Lasaariy.	80	235	0	5	5.9	1.6
Lukari.	16	73		2	11.1	2.2
Marmi.	86	168		8	8.5	3.1
Medakher.	29	45		1	3.3	1.4
Michayai.	61	31	4	10	14.1	15.2
Muroli	99	327	4	2	2.0	1.4

(*Contd.*)

Village	*No. of BPL families*	*No. of Non-BPL families*	*No. of Non-BPL families included in the list of BPL families*	*No. of BPL families not included in BPL families*	*Misclassification of poor (per cent)*	
					BPL	*APL*
Pahooni	138	20	3	40	22.5	27.2
Pahunee	250	686	3	2	0.8	0.5
Punavati	22	43	4	4	15.4	12.3
Raashami	349	356	6	8	2.2	2.0
Ragnaath	35	78		5	12.5	4.4
Rampurni	7	5		2	22.2	16.7
Ratnakaka	41	62		2	4.7	1.9
Revar	252	231	15	5	1.9	4.1
Roode	265	185		20	7.0	4.4
Saakhali	56	84		2	3.4	1.4
Shamvhup	80	235	4	2	2.4	1.9
Sihana	78	82		5	6.0	3.1
Somkhalo	99	168		25	20.2	9.4
Uprera	119	279	2	5	4.0	1.8
Sihama	206	218	0	6	2.8	1.4
	104	9	1	9	10	8.8
Total	4735	5793	206	414	8.04	3.4

COMPOSITE INDEX OF POVERTY

Following the methodology of composite Index used for the data at district level, the variables were first converted to indicators. Thereafter, group specific indices were worked out. Based on the values of group level indices and the group specific weights the composite index was worked out.

Composite Human Poverty Index (CHPI) have been computed separately for village level data and household level data as well as combining both with 50:50 weight.

The results on composite indices for above 9 groups are given in Tables 8.7 to 8.10.

Table 8.7: Block-wise Indicators and Composite Index—Dist. Banswara

Vill-age	*Demo-graphy*	*Housing*	*Liter-acy*	*Health*	*Nutri-tion*	*Live-stock*	*Agri-cul-ture*	*Infra-struc-ture*	*Devel-opment*	*CHPI*
CODE										
1	61	67	37	72	100	71	57	50	58	63
2	57	67	77	69	100	77	70	70	40	70
3	58	100	77	71	100	76	84	59	63	76
4	60	100	38	73	28	77	75	47	53	58
5	61	100	77	71	100	54	80	55	60	73
6	55	100	37	69	100	66	71	55	61	67
7	57	67	38	68	33	89	76	53	58	58
8	51	100	79	71	100	73	83	55	56	74
9	60	67	58	53	33	64	74	40	52	54
10	52	67	58	81	39	83	67	55	57	61
11	70	67	38	68	100	83	65	43	72	66
12	63	67	38	69	17	61	67	52	61	53
13	61	67	39	72	100	75	58	46	57	63
14	58	67	37	74	28	75	71	45	56	55
15	56	67	38	75	100	77	72	48	56	65
16	70	100	37	83	28	82	71	46	54	60
17	70	100	37	66	100	71	77	44	62	67
18	71	67	38	76	33	89	73	45	52	58
19	74	100	59	64	33	88	79	18	43	58
20	71	100	36	75	50	76	61	53	54	61
21	67	33	55	60	33	74	63	45	50	53
22	72	100	37	49	33	62	67	45	47	53
23	73	100	36	69	100	85	47	53	43	65
24	60	100	37	50	100	72	84	45	50	64
25	64	100	57	87	28	71	62	40	53	60
26	62	100	36	57	33	72	70	39	58	55
27	61	67	37	73	39	68	70	55	52	56
28	60	100	36	48	100	29	59	51	39	56
29	67	100	39	41	100	48	50	52	48	58
30	56	100	37	49	50	50	60	53	39	52
31	67	67	37	57	50	46	63	49	45	51
32	58	33	55	61	100	72	59	18	32	55
33	58	33	55	61	50	72	59	18	32	48
34	68	67	37	43	50	46	68	36	46	49
35	70	100	36	60	89	77	74	48	56	65
36	61	33	53	61	39	92	63	30	40	51
37	72	100	35	36	33	62	71	51	55	53
38	71	100	35	53	39	76	82	56	52	59
39	72	100	36	73	39	67	83	38	59	59

(Contd.)

(*Contd.*)

Village	*Demography*	*Housing*	*Literacy*	*Health*	*Nutrition*	*Livestock*	*Agriculture*	*Infrastructure*	*Development*	*CHPI*
CODE										
40	70	100	36	72	100	79	96	55	72	74
41	77	100	38	74	39	69	72	46	60	60
42	76	100	39	77	28	62	83	41	60	59
43	72	100	37	67	33	75	90	40	59	60
44	76	100	37	74	100	62	70	35	65	66
45	72	67	59	51	39	73	64	20	54	53
46	72	100	38	54	100	54	82	48	60	66
47	57	67	36	82	100	51	45	38	57	59
48	69	100	57	77	100	65	43	38	49	65
49	67	100	36	75	28	63	75	48	55	57
50	69	100	57	75	22	88	73	40	56	61
51	67	100	37	74	28	57	70	38	55	55
52	67	100	37	73	28	70	66	48	56	57
53	68	100	36	79	28	47	81	49	56	57
54	66	67	57	81	0	60	78	39	38	51
55	61	67	35	72	28	66	83	48	42	53
56	60	67	33	64	100	67	84	54	74	67
57	65	100	37	49	100	59	70	53	56	63
58	73	67	37	50	28	77	73	53	56	54
59	76	100	37	63	100	84	76	60	56	70
60	74	100	57	67	39	93	78	60	56	66
61	75	100	37	64	28	88	77	60	55	61
62	81	100	37	34	100	74	88	51	55	66
63	75	100	38	62	100	86	77	60	55	70
64	68	100	57	76	100	65	83	54	53	72
65	68	67	37	73	100	52	81	48	55	63
66	67	67	77	94	28	83	82	40	55	65
67	67	100	36	75	100	61	81	46	55	67
68	68	100	56	78	28	60	69	39	53	59
69	74	100	38	44	33	80	81	54	55	58
70	75	100	39	61	100	90	84	50	55	70
71	74	100	33	57	100	52	69	47	54	63
72	74	100	37	62	100	91	78	60	54	70
73	74	100	37	81	100	87	78	60	54	72
74	76	100	38	62	33	91	75	50	55	60
75	81	100	38	62	100	92	77	50	55	70
76	74	100	37	60	100	90	74	60	56	70
77	74	100	37	61	100	87	79	60	55	70
78	63	67	37	48	50	63	81	55	46	55
79	63	67	57	54	39	61	75	48	51	56
80	62	100	37	72	33	59	81	53	48	57
81	59	100	36	82	100	59	84	45	55	67

(*Contd.*)

(Contd.)

Village	*Demography*	*Housing*	*Literacy*	*Health*	*Nutrition*	*Livestock*	*Agriculture*	*Infrastructure*	*Development*	*CHPI*
CODE										
82	63	100	38	71	33	63	73	38	53	56
83	73	100	39	20	100	83	99	45	60	66
84	73	100	38	63	100	67	75	53	51	66
85	74	67	57	69	33	75	67	49	63	60
86	71	100	37	68	100	58	62	49	53	64
87	71	100	37	65	100	61	71	54	61	67
88	70	100	56	62	100	54	80	45	53	67
89	69	100	38	58	100	80	76	49	51	66
90	74	100	37	63	100	79	74	48	59	68
91	73	100	37	61	39	67	85	51	52	59
92	80	100	37	64	100	86	77	50	55	69
93	74	100	37	23	100	71	74	41	55	61
94	74	100	37	64	100	83	80	60	55	70
95	78	100	38	62	33	89	73	60	55	61
96	76	100	37	64	28	90	79	60	55	61
97	74	100	57	68	28	90	77	50	55	63
98	74	100	37	61	100	86	79	60	54	69
99	73	100	57	50	39	69	73	50	56	60
100	76	100	37	62	100	89	78	50	56	69
101	75	100	36	50	100	80	69	59	55	67
102	74	100	37	58	100	81	67	49	55	66
103	74	100	36	41	33	77	69	57	55	56
104	74	67	56	57	39	81	71	40	56	58
105	75	100	37	56	39	77	64	59	55	59
106	75	100	36	54	39	79	73	50	55	58
107	75	100	37	49	100	79	65	58	55	66
108	74	67	36	55	28	85	77	40	49	53
109	75	100	37	54	100	77	75	57	55	67
110	61	100	37	60	33	67	86	43	50	56
111	61	100	37	59	100	57	75	39	52	63
112	54	100	20	63	33	48	81	51	70	55
113	60	100	36	66	33	62	70	43	49	54
114	60	100	37	67	39	71	88	49	70	62
115	60	67	57	67	33	75	94	36	50	58
116	60	100	35	39	100	68	92	43	53	63
117	68	100	37	73	28	52	76	56	50	56
118	66	67	76	93	28	77	70	40	56	63
119	70	100	56	75	100	66	87	58	56	73
120	69	67	37	71	28	70	83	58	56	57

(Contd.)

(Contd.)

Vill-age	*Demo-graphy*	*Housing*	*Liter-acy*	*Health*	*Nutri-tion*	*Live-stock*	*Agri-cul-ture*	*Infra-struc-ture*	*Devel-opment*	*CHPI*
CODE										
121	69	100	37	75	28	67	85	49	56	59
122	74	100	56	91	28	72	84	50	56	65
123	68	100	36	79	28	72	84	56	56	61
124	58	67	37	59	39	76	87	49	60	57
125	73	67	37	61	44	81	73	40	48	55
126	73	100	37	56	28	66	73	40	54	54
127	74	100	56	66	28	88	75	50	54	62
128	71	100	37	57	100	83	78	58	53	68
129	72	100	37	53	100	82	73	39	55	65
130	75	100	36	52	100	78	69	55	56	66
131	81	67	37	53	33	79	62	39	55	53
132	79	100	37	51	33	82	59	44	52	55
133	77	100	37	65	39	87	69	48	46	59
134	79	100	57	58	83	79	68	48	55	67
135	73	33	57	72	39	85	76	40	55	58
136	58	100	37	51	28	77	74	55	47	55
137	63	100	38	61	33	74	75	46	55	57
138	64	67	55	66	28	63	64	40	49	53
139	55	100	34	58	28	74	64	39	55	53
140	63	100	36	68	28	66	92	51	58	59
141	63	100	56	61	39	63	82	46	65	62
142	64	100	38	66	33	87	83	28	56	58
143	61	100	57	45	33	62	63	48	43	54
144	76	67	37	63	39	83	78	59	55	59
145	33	0	56	68	44	99	65	40	49	52
146	74	67	37	56	39	77	82	54	55	57
147	60	100	40	76	33	82	87	54	57	62
148	60	100	40	67	100	80	86	54	57	70
149	60	100	40	68	33	84	79	54	57	61
150	60	100	40	67	100	80	85	48	57	69
151	60	100	40	65	100	84	84	50	57	69
152	60	100	40	74	100	80	74	50	57	69
153	60	100	60	74	100	84	85	56	57	74
154	55	100	37	76	33	76	75	39	46	56
155	56	100	37	47	33	67	64	56	54	54
156	53	100	39	69	100	61	75	48	40	63
157	60	100	37	57	100	63	73	43	50	63
158	63	100	57	67	33	81	78	50	43	61
159	54	100	39	74	33	80	70	50	42	57

(Contd.)

(*Contd.*)

Vill-age	Demo-graphy	Housing	Liter-acy	Health	Nutri-tion	Live-stock	Agri-cul-ture	Infra-struc-ture	Devel-opment	CHPI
CODE										
121	69	100	37	75	28	67	85	49	56	59
160	81	100	16	63	50	80	68	48	48	57
161	74	100	36	52	50	72	75	57	55	60
162	74	100	36	57	50	82	79	49	55	61
163	74	67	56	60	100	98	69	40	48	67
164	86	100	36	57	100	68	77	49	54	66
165	76	100	16	52	100	49	67	56	55	60
166	76	100	36	57	50	64	79	49	56	59
167	72	100	36	56	100	85	66	36	48	64
168	73	67	38	61	33	61	77	35	44	51
169	68	0	35	64	100	67	68	40	46	55
170	51	33	34	57	33	49	58	48	46	45
171	50	0	56	71	33	82	67	29	40	48
176	63	100	36	65	28	81	73	47	56	57
177	68	100	37	64	100	80	75	54	56	68
178	60	100	40	68	28	87	77	54	56	60
179	60	100	40	69	100	87	87	53	61	71
180	60	100	40	68	28	87	78	54	56	60
181	60	67	60	59	28	96	75	40	48	57
182	60	100	40	68	100	87	77	55	56	70
183	60	100	40	67	100	87	76	55	56	69
184	60	67	60	80	28	82	78	39	50	59
185	60	100	40	67	28	87	77	52	56	60
186	60	100	40	67	100	84	78	52	56	69
Average	67.2	88.9	42.1	63.7	61.6	73.7	74.3	48.0	53.7	61.2

Note : For village names against code, refer to Table 8.13.

Table 8.8: Block-wise Indicators and Composite Index Village Level Data—Chittorgarh Dist.

Vill-age	De-mogra-phy	Hous-ing	Liter-acy	Health	Nu-tri-tion	Live-stock	Agricul-ture	Infra-struc-ture	Devel-op-ment	CHPI
CODE										
132	42	100	96	64	3	96	84	71	53	67
200	30	66.7	49	82	3	97	75	68	58	57
201	35	66.7	71	99	3	97	65	47	59	63
202	41	100	72	100	100	89	72	71	83	82
203	45	66.7	65	100	100	76	76	77	58	78
204	61	66.7	80	82	3	100	62	33	84	62

(*Contd.*)

(Contd.)

Village	Demography	Housing	Literacy	Health	Nutrition	Livestock	Agriculture	Infrastructure	Development	CHPI
CODE										
205	61	100	100	100	100	100	84	100	69	92
206	61	100	100	100	100	100	83	100	69	92
207	61	100	100	100	100	100	84	100	69	92
208	61	100	60	83	100	100	74	57	59	76
209	40	66.7	74	80	3	90	57	35	37	52
210	55	100	55	100	100	75	73	41	47	71
211	63	100	78	92	100	86	75	55	59	78
212	51	66.7	98	81	3	95	77	48	51	66
213	47	100	98	52	3	94	76	48	54	58
214	47	66.7	100	78	3	87	55	41	54	54
215	48	66.7	73	96	100	62	74	45	58	66
216	53	66.7	59	83	3	48	56	28	53	48
217	61	33.3	60	73	100	80	65	71	43	67
218	54	100	74	100	100	86	74	82	58	81
219	49	66.7	100	79	3	85	78	42	55	61
220	57	66.7	98	100	100	100	100	82	69	91
221	50	33.3	72	65	3	98	61	71	67	64
222	68	66.7	80	100	100	98	75	61	51	81
223	53	66.7	47	58	50	45	50	53	60	56
224	22	66.7	74	53	0	61	46	43	57	51
225	31	100	74	53	0	54	45	56	56	52
226	29	66.7	54	49	3	77	44	47	57	50
227	20	66.7	72	29	3	52	36	42	56	42
228	50	100	68	73	50	46	55	47	61	61
229	46	100	75	75	100	53	67	43	61	70
230	45	100	75	71	50	61	63	42	61	63
231	40	100	80	52	50	69	52	45	76	59
232	51	100	92	63	3	77	57	64	53	57
233	60	100	49	71	3	78	71	36	53	51
234	54	100	55	57	3	69	57	48	53	52
235	50	100	75	63	100	79	51	44	53	69
236	46	100	76	69	100	63	63	56	53	70
237	50	100	75	66	100	75	63	47	53	70
238	41	100	83	89	3	62	67	41	71	58
240	56	100	80	68	3	91	71	83	51	65
241	43	66.7	51	74	100	62	43	45	50	63
242	32	66.7	74	59	100	76	40	49	58	67
244	33	66.7	64	54	3	95	63	52	53	52
246	44	66.7	72	72	50	66	64	35	58	62
247	49	100	72	74	3	70	55	67	53	59
248	47	100	74	64	3	81	49	48	53	56

(Contd.)

(Contd.)

Village	*Demography*	*Housing*	*Literacy*	*Health*	*Nutrition*	*Livestock*	*Agriculture*	*Infrastructure*	*Development*	*CHPI*
CODE										
249	44	100	95	78	100	62	62	84	53	77
250	50	100	71	77	3	97	56	37	49	54
255	55	66.7	53	89	3	54	61	68	51	57
256	49	100	55	92	3	46	61	81	56	59
257	43	100	65	72	50	29	55	66	62	60
258	48	100	92	51	3	33	63	57	52	55
300	66	100	58	81	100	85	78	91	83	82
301	48	100	58	80	100	82	76	82	58	76
302	45	66.7	75	83	100	95	79	76	59	80
303	49	100	80	70	100	94	74	79	57	75
304	44	66.7	96	71	3	99	73	53	78	68
305	42	66.7	95	77	3	79	75	34	73	64
306	51	33.3	79	100	100	94	74	57	53	79
307	61	100	80	66	3	89	75	36	54	56
308	55	66.7	77	68	3	90	70	30	65	60
309	61	33.3	40	62	3	80	68	36	58	53
311	89	100	80	83	100	65	77	52	53	76
312	59	100	80	84	100	76	64	42	73	72
313	61	100	80	56	50	80	58	27	73	60
314	53	100	57	83	3	87	63	64	59	61
315	48	66.7	76	100	100	83	77	74	58	80
316	50	100	70	81	3	79	62	16	59	52
317	41	100	91	79	3	95	74	70	59	68
343	36	66.7	44	50	3	70	56	62	59	47
345	41	66.7	22	53	50	64	60	33	57	47
Average	48.9	83.3	73.5	75.4	45.9	77.9	65.5	55.8	58.9	64.9

Note : For village names against code, refer to Table 8.12.

Table 8.9: Blockwise Indicators and Composite Index Household Data—Banswara

Village	*Demography*	*Housing*	*Literacy*	*Health*	*Nutrition*	*Livestock*	*Agriculture*	*Infrastructure*	*Development*	*CHPI*
CODE										
1	50.95	49.5	95.9	50	88.6	58.9	56.7	91.3	40.8	65
2	43.65	63.3	92.2	41.7	75.7	52.2	55	99.1	33	62
3	53.9	66.1	94.5	36	90.4	65.6	56.4	92.6	35.9	66
4	48.3	62.8	87.1	47.5	87.2	58.9	56.4	98.5	38.9	65
5	0	66.6	100	30.8	91.5	65.6	56.7	95.9	40	61
6	50	67.7	79.7	37.7	89.9	47.8	58.9	85	36.6	61
7	51.8	64	93.7	51.4	87.9	55.6	60.3	96.1	34.5	66

(Contd.)

(*Contd.*)

Vill-age	*Demo-graphy*	*Hous-ing*	*Liter-acy*	*Health*	*Nutri-tion*	*Live stock*	*Agri-culture*	*Infra-stru-cture*	*Develop-ment*	CHPI
CODE										
8	50	63	94.9	92.3	87	47.8	56.7	98.3	38.8	70
9	50	66.6	83.7	99.6	88.8	62.2	56	99.9	35.8	71
10	53.15	60.7	73.5	96.2	95.9	55.6	61.7	99.4	38.3	70
11	47.2	57.7	80.2	89.2	91.9	62.2	61.3	100	24.5	68
12	49	70.9	91.9	100	90.1	37.8	52.1	98.5	36.6	70
13	50	69.1	93.7	100	77.3	35.6	56.7	99	35.5	69
14	48.5	70.9	75.4	100	81.1	58.9	55.7	99.4	36	70
15	50.55	70.9	90.3	63.3	88	47.8	56.7	98.9	33.1	67
16	41.75	55	75.6	100	90.2	62.2	53.9	100	37.4	68
17	40.6	62.4	70.5	97.5	93.9	65.6	59.2	96.6	32.9	69
18	45.65	64.4	79.6	69	93	62.2	56	98.2	38.7	67
19	47.2	60.7	82.2	77.6	82.7	58.9	54.3	99.1	40.9	67
20	50	59.1	84.1	94.1	87.1	58.9	50.7	100	39	69
21	50.35	55.3	78.9	98.5	78.9	45.6	51.8	98.6	37.6	66
22	46.25	49.1	67.7	95.6	77.7	38.9	50	96.6	37.6	62
23	52.2	59.8	84.1	98.2	74.8	31.1	51.1	100	41.4	66
24	44.95	52.8	78.3	98.6	90.1	48.9	55.7	98.1	37.3	67
25	42.25	58.7	84.8	100	70.5	52.2	58.2	94.1	40.3	67
26	50	53.8	60.3	97.7	74	62.2	58.9	91.6	33.6	65
27	42.5	60.2	90.3	100	91.5	44.4	49.3	98.8	35.9	68
28	34.25	56	89.1	100	91.6	20	52.8	99.6	35.7	64
29	50	58.6	94.9	90.7	93.2	62.2	56	100	38.6	72
30	46.2	51.8	75.8	96.8	83.4	55.6	55	90.5	40.1	66
31	41.2	52.9	78.7	0.6	67.1	25.6	49.6	98.9	38.2	50
33	67.35	49.4	39.7	99.4	77.2	62.2	57.4	94.2	37	65
34	48.8	55.4	79.1	83.3	62.5	65.6	55.7	94.8	32.5	64
35	58.35	72.9	96.4	97	81.4	46.7	62.1	100	33.1	72
36	51.55	51.5	51.5	100	76.5	62.2	59.9	77.3	32.6	63
37	50	57.6	82.2	100	71.7	42.2	64.2	83.1	30.4	65
38	51.55	58.2	80.3	81.1	91.5	42.2	55.3	95.2	35.3	66
39	48.35	60.2	54.6	98.9	72.4	58.9	65.6	93.2	27	64
40	50	56.5	61.9	100	73.4	52.2	58.2	94.5	33.3	64
41	48.25	60.3	78.5	98.5	73.3	62.2	64.5	98.1	32.4	68
42	45.95	58.9	39	98.5	79.6	58.9	66.7	60	34.7	60
43	50.35	59.7	68.1	100	76.1	58.9	53.2	98.3	37.1	67
44	50	62.7	77.3	90.5	81	52.2	58.2	96.2	39.3	67
45	48.55	64.2	81.9	86	74.7	45.6	53.5	97.3	43.5	66
46	55.8	55.6	81.4	96.9	77.8	42.2	35.1	91.6	36.3	64
47	42.25	38.2	69	100	72.2	65.6	50.4	100	36.7	64
48	100	55.3	87	97.5	70.7	58.9	61	95.8	29.9	73
49	43.75	48.5	38.1	2.5	80.4	62.2	50	100	40.4	52
50	50.65	63.8	68.7	58.3	64.1	41.1	47.5	99.7	32.9	59

(*Contd.*)

(Contd.)

Village	Demography	Housing	Literacy	Health	Nutrition	Live stock	Agriculture	Infrastructure	Development	CHPI
CODE										
51	51.45	62.5	78.1	40.1	73.7	65.6	49.3	99.6	37.2	62
52	51.45	63.5	79.7	8.8	75.4	62.2	48.9	97.2	32.8	58
53	50	65.8	83.9	99	78.4	65.6	0	88.9	33.8	63
54	50	62.1	47.3	99	88.7	48.9	52.8	99.8	35	65
55	52.05	61.1	62.3	100	84	55.6	54.3	96	36.3	67
56	50	58.3	64.2	100	86.9	62.2	50.4	99.7	39.9	68
57	50	62.5	71.4	100	89.1	65.6	53.2	96.8	36.3	69
58	50	54.9	89	99.2	83.1	62.2	17	99	34.9	65
59	48	62.6	89.4	100	75.5	62.2	40.4	96.5	39.3	68
60	46.15	66	89.9	100	86.1	65.6	13.5	96.5	35.1	67
61	43.5	49.9	82.6	99.5	84.3	52.2	19.9	95.5	39.7	63
62	47	63.6	53.8	32.4	74.6	24.4	53.9	98.5	40.6	54
63	70.65	53.4	82.7	87.6	80.1	58.9	58.9	93.9	26.9	68
64	44.65	57.8	82.6	100	73.8	65.6	59.9	82.9	38.3	67
65	50.6	62.8	79.9	98.1	69.1	48.9	47.2	95.2	37.9	66
66	53.85	64.3	81.3	96	72.8	52.2	55	96.4	39.8	68
67	49	68.9	83	90.7	72.8	52.2	48.2	93.8	37.4	66
68	48.25	62.6	72	99.3	58.6	48.9	49.6	78.4	28.4	61
69	41.35	59.6	94.3	100	71.4	58.9	45.7	90.1	31.3	66
70	46	61.9	90	100	75.1	65.6	51.1	93	33.5	68
71	50	62	82.8	99	70.6	62.2	49.6	91.1	35.4	67
72	50	63.8	92.5	80.3	88.2	62.2	50.7	86.2	33.1	67
73	46	63.9	87	100	75.3	58.9	52.5	91.1	34.8	68
74	48.75	59.6	83.8	98.2	89.9	65.6	54.3	82.5	35.9	69
75	49.05	65.1	89.4	98.1	73.8	55.6	48.6	73.8	39.8	66
76	46.95	62.9	72.7	98.5	70.9	58.9	49.3	89.3	31	65
77	50.35	59.6	75.2	98.1	75.6	62.2	50.4	94.9	34.5	67
78	50.7	59	80.3	99.3	89.2	55.6	51.1	96.5	35.4	69
79	49.15	63.8	57.9	55.7	82.9	58.9	52.1	96.6	39.1	62
80	49.25	46.2	86.9	59.8	82	14.4	45.7	86	40.2	57
81	48.65	55	88.8	99.7	73.3	52.2	51.8	95.4	38.8	67
82	45.9	61.1	86	95.6	80.8	58.9	52.8	97.8	35.4	68
83	49.6	64.1	77.8	99	77.1	65.6	49.3	81.7	37.6	67
84	48.2	58.4	71.9	99.1	76	58.9	50.4	95.9	31.4	66
85	48.95	55	71.2	100	78.5	55.6	55	79.6	33.8	64
86	48.3	59.7	74	98.4	65.5	42.2	41.1	89	33.2	61
87	48.8	59.5	85.7	100	75.4	55.6	51.4	86.2	32.3	66
88	41.7	59.8	91.8	100	79.1	58.9	59.9	98.9	30	69
89	48.1	63	67.1	98.6	80.6	58.9	47.2	84.4	31.6	64
90	50.45	63.8	69.3	100	71.5	45.6	55	88.9	34.9	64
91	50.3	57.7	60.2	98.9	84.5	55.6	48.2	98.1	35.4	65
92	46.4	64.9	65.4	98	65.5	52.2	49.6	96.3	35.8	64

(Contd.)

(Contd.)

Village	Demography	Housing	Literacy	Health	Nutrition	Live stock	Agriculture	Infrastructure	Development	CHPI
CODE										
93	43	59.1	85.5	100	75.2	62.2	45.7	98.6	36.9	67
94	46	56.6	81.4	99.3	70.8	65.6	51.1	92.2	38.5	67
95	35.25	60.5	85.7	100	75.6	62.2	49.6	79.8	34.9	65
96	46.4	57.5	44.1	100	72.8	62.2	50.7	95	39.2	63
97	45.25	59.8	70	100	74.5	58.9	52.5	99.2	37.3	66
98	42.4	62	83.5	100	74.6	52.2	54.3	99.5	39.3	68
99	51.55	60.7	83.3	100	72.8	62.2	48.6	98	36.2	68
100	39.55	61.6	81.6	33.3	75.2	62.2	49.3	100	38	60
111	83.35	70.9	89.9	20	81.2	33.3	17	98.5	10.2	56
133	45.75	58	71.6	0	77.4	62.2	51.1	98.9	29.7	55
134	50.9	59.2	64.7	71.8	72.3	62.2	18.8	98.7	39.9	60
135	57.5	63.7	77.9	99.1	76.1	52.2	45.7	93.9	42.1	68
136	32.7	50.7	76.7	98.4	80.2	52.2	51.8	93.1	34.1	63
137	47.45	60.7	83.3	90.8	82.3	52.2	52.8	97.1	37.3	67
138	34.05	55.4	85.7	98.8	69.1	48.9	49.3	87.4	37.3	63
139	58	53	70.2	99.2	53.8	55.6	50.4	79.7	37.2	62
140	50.85	54.6	68	99.4	74.5	27.8	55	99.6	39.8	63
141	50.3	59.6	83.4	99.4	86.3	58.9	41.1	96.1	38.4	68
142	50.85	61.2	52.9	98.1	89.3	55.6	18.1	82.6	30.9	60
143	49	54	79.8	84.5	86.2	27.8	50.4	93.1	34.3	62
144	52.75	60.2	75.1	75	77.2	65.6	55	97.6	29.5	65
145	75.9	52.9	0	96.4	70.5	65.6	54.6	99.5	17.8	59
146	50.75	59.6	85.6	99.3	90.1	65.6	55.3	98.8	31.4	71
147	41.45	59.6	87.9	99.1	63.4	48.9	56.4	99.7	31.2	65
148	50	62.5	76.9	96.3	72.3	58.9	48.9	82.3	30.5	64
149	50	64.3	96.1	100	87.7	62.2	51.8	98.3	39	72
150	50.65	63.7	77.5	95.7	93.1	58.9	47.9	97.3	39.6	69
151	54.35	53.8	91.5	98.3	87.6	62.2	55.3	99	27.8	70
152	48.25	63.7	93.5	98	90.5	62.2	56.7	96.7	28.9	71
153	50	62.6	80	94.5	87.4	58.9	60.6	93.2	35.7	69
154	42.85	60	96.7	95.2	91.1	52.2	60.3	94.3	33.7	70
155	50	64.7	80.8	97.5	90.8	45.6	54.6	99.2	40.7	69
157	41.75	63.3	81.3	94.2	76.6	48.9	57.8	96.9	39.7	67
158	46.25	63.5	71.8	100	83.7	47.8	52.1	100	33.2	66
159	41.7	61.6	86.4	90.8	84.3	82.2	50.7	99.7	32.7	70
160	46.95	56.6	92.8	100	78.4	100	59.2	100	35.8	74
161	47.6	60.6	72.1	100	85.6	100	51.4	99.4	30.8	72
162	49.15	64.2	70	100	93.1	100	55	94.1	37.6	74
163	67.7	61.5	78.9	100	60.3	90	55	100	26.2	71
164	45.25	61.1	70.7	100	94	100	55.3	100	31.8	73
165	50	62.4	72.1	51.7	94.9	100	46.5	90.5	35.2	67

(Contd.)

(*Contd.*)

Vill-age	*Demo-graphy*	*Hous-ing*	*Liter-acy*	*Health*	*Nutri-tion*	*Live-stock*	*Agri-culture*	*Infra-stru-cture*	*Develop-ment*	*CHPI*
CODE										
166	49.25	66.9	78	98.7	79.8	68.9	49.3	99.2	38	70
167	43.55	61	66.5	63.5	92.4	62.2	56.4	85.9	29	62
168	46.4	63.3	58.4	37.5	92.3	48.9	52.1	94.8	36.2	59
169	59.8	58.4	76.9	100	80.4	65.6	56.7	73.9	31.6	67
170	44.5	58.4	79.5	97.2	78.6	65.6	61.7	87.9	38.1	68
171	43.7	59.9	83.5	98	80.4	65.6	58.2	96.3	30.1	68
172	51.75	59.7	62.9	69.5	72	62.2	44.7	99.6	33.2	62
173	52.4	59.5	70.6	66.5	76.7	62.2	46.8	96.1	31.9	63
174	63.6	65.4	23.1	100	49.6	62.2	61.7	98.9	27	61
175	72.55	67.4	83.4	97.1	53.9	62.2	25.9	97.9	23.9	65
176	51.45	62.1	92	100	82.6	65.6	50	99.9	29.8	70
177	50	54.3	92.9	100	84.6	65.6	49.3	100	36.1	70
178	50	61.2	77	97.2	85.8	65.6	51.1	99.4	38.7	70
179	52.75	71.7	90.5	100	81.4	65.6	27.7	100	26.4	68
180	50	58.6	87.7	100	53.9	37.8	52.1	99.7	27.5	63
181	43.95	60.9	90.3	100	52.2	45.6	49.6	100	32.6	64
182	50	58	74.8	100	86.1	62.2	56.4	100	37	69
183	44.5	64.8	81.5	100	56.9	65.6	54.6	99.9	32.3	67
184	47.4	67.8	32.3	100	67.6	65.6	53.5	100	39.9	64
185	50	59.5	80.3	100	88.3	62.2	54.3	100	40.3	71
186	52.25	74.1	70.2		67.7	45.6	53.5	94.7	32.6	61
Average	49.19	60.4	77.3	87.9	79.1	57.3	51.2	94.7	34.9	65.7

Note : For village neme against code, refer is Table 8.13.

Table 8.10: Block-wise Indicators and Composite Index Household Data—Chittorgarh

Vill-age	*Demo-graphy*	*Hous-ing*	*Liter-acy*	*Health*	*Nutri-tion*	*Live-stock*	*Agri-culture*	*Infra-stru-cture*	*Develop-ment*	*CHPI*
CODE										
132	100	59	67.4	50.1	90.2	97	42.2	49.6	37.1	65.8
200	96	75	61	50.5	67.1	71.7	35.2	66.5	32.9	61.8
201	100	75	78.8	50.5	50.7	85.9	25	71.7	32.6	63.4
202	56	87.5	68.1	0	60.1	100	41.2	52.6	36.4	55.8
203	45	56.5	58.6	49.9	83.8	93.9	39.9	88.1	45.9	62.4
204	73	62.2	77.8	50.5	49.4	93.9	48.5	59.5	43.4	62.0
205	63	65.1	55.7	50.5	42.3	97	42.5	55.9	49.7	58.0
206	52.3	64.6	76.9	50.2	62.1	100	41.9	49.4	40.3	59.7
207	100	64.4	68.2	49.8	71	100	41.9	60.6	35.8	65.7
208	92.7	68.2	70.3	50.5	70.8	97	47.6	68.5	37	67.0

(*Contd.*)

(Contd.)

Village	*Demography*	*Housing*	*Literacy*	*Health*	*Nutrition*	*Livestock*	*Agriculture*	*Infrastructure*	*Development*	*CHPI*
CODE										
209	47.7	64.7	55.4	50.5	67.6	90.9	44.2	66.7	22.4	56.7
210	73	62.1	62.2	50.5	62.6	97	42.2	53.9	35.3	59.9
211	86.7	65.8	73.5	50.5	73.3	90.9	42.5	54.2	37.3	63.9
212	51.7	65.6	91.6	50.5	66.3	87.9	42.5	47.6	45.4	61.0
213	50	71.3	85.4	50.5	67.3	93.9	48.6	55.5	33.4	61.8
214	79	75	83.5	50.5	76.5	90.9	46.5	55.7	38.5	66.2
215	100	66.5	63.2	50.5	71.9	97	34.2	63.8	38.2	65.0
216	100	69.7	87	50.2	65.8	93.9	42.2	50.5	46.8	67.3
217	100	71.2	98	49.4	70.9	100	48.5	47.7	35.5	69.0
218	100	66.7	53.8	50.5	72.6	100	49.5	49.6	37	64.4
219	86.3	75	76	50.5	72.6	100	49.5	47.1	36.3	65.9
220	66.7	55.6	62.3	50.5	75.1	100	41.9	49.9	33	59.4
221	60.3	66.1	91.2	50.5	73.6	93.9	37.6	49.7	40.5	62.6
222	69.7	62.7	41.1	50.5	71.6	90.9	41.6	42.1	43.4	57.1
223	0	67	55.3	50.5	68.5	93.9	48.2	50.6	47.1	53.5
224	75.3	58.2	79.1	50.2	66.9	93.9	40.2	54.2	33.5	61.3
225	41.3	68.3	73.3	50.5	70.3	97	40.2	59.6	43.1	60.4
226	73	65.5	66.6	50.5	71.6	73.7	46.9	61.8	37.1	60.7
227	71.3	70	81.2	50.5	73.2	78.8	48.9	68.1	36.8	64.3
228	83.7	71.3	14.2	50.5	66.4	93.9	41.9	66.9	38.5	58.6
229	58.3	74	72.4	50.5	69.4	76.8	41.6	48.4	45.1	59.6
230	68.7	60.2	56.3	50.5	69.2	67.7	43.6	39.9	40.2	55.1
231	66	72.1	62.3	50.5	67.9	87.9	45.2	64.5	34.5	61.2
232	66.3	70.4	44.2	50.5	62.4	87.9	47.9	67	32.1	58.7
233	43.7	72.3	53.3	50.5	62	93.9	48.6	42.7	34.5	55.7
234	86	60.4	72.6	50.5	71.3	93.9	46.2	48.7	34	62.6
235	36.7	53.2	71.1	50.1	68.8	87.9	30.1	62.1	32.9	54.8
236	62.3	52.8	76	50.5	68.7	79.8	27	58.9	39.6	57.3
237	70.3	52.8	73	50.5	70.8	90.9	35.3	53.5	37	59.3
238	28.7	71.2	65.4	50.5	65.2	90.9	41	51.2	37.5	55.7
239	83.7	51.5	79.1	50.5	68.9	76.8	28.1	50.9	34.5	58.2
240	55.3	57.5	62	50.5	65.8	73.7	23.2	57.8	41.8	54.2
241	72.3	57	53	50.5	62.4	93.9	42.5	63.7	32.3	58.6
242	65	59.4	40	50.5	60.2	100	48.2	52.4	30.2	56.2
243	72.7	40.1	34.2	50.5	70.8	93.9	41.2	75	36.3	57.2
244	78	59.4	74.8	50.5	61.8	65.7	44.2	71.1	41.3	60.8
245	84.7	54.6	54	50.5	64.4	34.3	32.9	56.1	43.1	52.7
246	76.7	52.2	79.5	50.5	60.2	39.4	39.2	52	40.7	54.5
247	34	46.8	89.7	50	65.5	68.7	47.2	56.7	43.4	55.8

(Contd.)

(*Contd.*)

Village	*Demography*	*Housing*	*Literacy*	*Health*	*Nutrition*	*Livestock*	*Agriculture*	*Infrastructure*	*Development*	*CHPI*
CODE										
248	43.7	58.5	77.8	37.6	58.6	56.6	43.2	40.6	42.4	51.0
249	44.3	60.9	36.6	49.8	69.6	59.6	43.3	75.2	46.1	53.9
250	62.7	44.4	80.3	50.5	62.3	0	24.3	60.9	37.6	47.0
251	63	44.6	89.5	50.5	71.3	51.5	45.8	74.7	39.4	58.9
255	57	60	59.2	50.5	65.3	31.3	40.7	53.9	47.4	51.7
256	71.7	54.8	65.4	48.7	60	48.5	34.2	50	42.7	52.9
257	85.3	49.9	85.2	50.5	70.5	34.3	35.9	45.9	34.7	54.7
258	81.7	58.7	55.6	50.5	59.1	100	37.6	50.6	16.2	56.7
259	76.7	60.9	15.9	50.5	61.7	100	39.9	47.1	25	53.1
260	67	56.3	94.5	50.5	58	50.5	21	52.7	31.7	53.6
261	68.3	56	88.4	50.3	68.9	71.7	17.7	61.5	36.8	57.7
300	75.3	57.2	100	50.5	62.3	93.9	40.5	57	40.7	64.2
301	100	48.1	83.8	50.5	63.9	79.8	31.8	50.5	43.6	61.3
302	100	50.4	63	50.5	64.2	90.9	37.7	45.6	58.4	62.3
303	90	62.5	54.7	50.5	73.1	65.7	49.8	48.3	42.1	59.6
304	89.3	62.5	95.4	50.5	71.6	68.7	45.9	52.3	41.9	64.2
305	94	60.1	89.9	50.5	68.9	71.7	48.6	60.2	39.2	64.8
306	100	62.1	82	50.3	69.1	65.7	41.6	55.1	41.1	63.0
307	100	55.3	65.8	50.5	67.9	62.6	43.9	51	49.4	60.7
308	100	55	45.4	49.6	67.2	68.7	44.5	50.7	48.4	58.8
309	93.7	55.2	62.3	50.5	69.4	59.6	44.6	45.5	40	57.9
310	94	55.2	50.3	50.5	63.8	59.6	46.8	55.4	39.9	57.3
311	82.3	59.5	58.5	49.1	64	68.7	43.2	60.7	30.2	57.4
312	81.3	55.4	52	50.5	68.5	65.7	32.3	57.1	38.9	55.7
313	82.3	47.1	46.9	50.4	67.7	62.6	29.6	67.7	31.8	54.0
314	61.3	55.1	35.3	49.8	67.5	62.6	43.2	66.1	34.9	52.9
315	74.3	66.1	67	49.8	68	50.5	44.2	52.6	31.5	56.0
316	77.3	55.1	67	50.5	76.9	71.7	42.9	54.6	41.3	59.7
317	80.3	58.7	67	50.5	68.7	42.4	31.6	55.2	39	54.8
341	100	51.7	67	50.5	68.5	59.6	27.9	52.5	42.1	57.8
342	68.2	45.7	67	50.2	63.1	62.6	33.4	28.3	55.7	52.7
343	68.2	46.3	67	50.5	67.4	50.5	45.2	61.8	32.6	54.4
344	68.2	75	67	49.6	58.7	85.9	40.4	55.9	29.1	58.9
346	68.2	60.7	67	49.6	67	77.7	40.4	55.9	38.5	58.3
347	68.2	60.7	67	49.6	100	77.7	40.4	55.9	38.5	62.0
348	68.2	60.7	67	49.6	100	77.7	40.4	55.9	38.5	62.0
Average	73.0	60.7	67.0	49.6	67.8	77.7	40.4	55.9	38.5	59.0

Note : For name of villge code, refer to Table 8.12.

Table 8.11: Correlation Matrix Village Level Data

Indicator	Demography	Housing	Literacy	Health	Nutrition	Live-stock	Agri-culture	Infrast-ructure	Develop-ment	CHPI
	Banswara									
Demography	1									
Housing	0.32	1.00								
Literacy	-0.22	-0.27	1.00							
Health	-0.24	-0.09	0.29	1.00						
Nutrition	0.10	0.19	-0.11	-0.16	1.00					
Livestock	0.16	-0.04	0.15	0.07	-0.02	1.00				
Agriculture	0.04	0.27	-0.01	0.05	0.00	0.17	1.00			
Infrastructure	0.13	0.39	-0.20	-0.04	0.22	0.10	0.22	1.00		
Development	0.17	0.32	-0.16	0.12	0.15	0.10	0.37	0.32	1.00	
CHPI Value	0.21	0.47	-0.06	0.03	0.44	0.39	0.41	0.40	0.30	1.00
	Chittorgarh									
Demography	1									
Housing	0.19	1.00								
Literacy	0.11	0.21	1.00							
Health	0.43	0.02	0.20	1.00						
Nutrition	0.34	0.12	0.05	0.46	1.00					
Livestock	0.21	-0.14	0.34	0.33	0.06	1.00				
Agriculture	0.50	0.07	0.38	0.63	0.33	0.55	1.00			
Infrastructure	0.15	0.16	0.20	0.39	0.40	0.23	0.45	1.00		
Development	0.09	0.11	0.20	0.15	0.12	0.17	0.22	0.13	1.00	
CHPI Value	0.54	0.35	0.44	0.70	0.76	0.45	0.72	0.64	0.32	1.00

(Contd.)

(Contd.)

Indicator	Demography	Housing	Literacy	Health	Nutrition	Live-stock	Agri-culture	Infrast-ructure	Develop-ment	CHPI
	Household	**Level data**								
	Banswara									
Demography	1.00									
Housing	0.04	1.00								
Literacy	-0.20	0.19	1.00							
Health	0.07	-0.06	0.01	1.00						
Nutrition	-0.19	0.04	0.20	-0.11	1.00					
Livestock	0.01	0.06	-0.08	0.12	0.14	1.00				
Agriculture	-0.10	-0.08	-0.09	0.04	0.06	0.03	1.00			
Infrastructure	0.02	0.10	0.11	-0.11	0.10	0.01	0.01	1.00		
Development	-0.42	-0.12	0.10	0.00	0.21	-0.13	0.10	0.03	1.00	
CHPI Value	0.08	0.16	0.42	0.65	0.36	0.46	0.25	0.20	0.10	1.00
	Chittorgarh									
Demography	1.00									
Housing	-0.06	1.00								
Literacy	0.05	0.02	1.00							
Health	0.13	-0.32	-0.02	1.00						
Nutrition	0.07	-0.04	0.04	0.12	1.00					
Livestock	-0.05	0.49	-0.10	-0.08	0.07	1.00				
Agriculture	-0.05	0.35	-0.13	-0.03	0.12	0.33	1.00			
Infrastructure	-0.07	-0.02	-0.14	0.08	0.07	0.01	0.01	1.00		
Development	-0.02	-0.17	0.13	0.02	0.02	-0.19	0.02	-0.21	1.00	
CHPI Value	0.49	0.43	0.37	0.13	0.34	0.59	0.36	0.12	0.04	1.00

The correlation of CHPI with other indicators has been worked out using village level data as well as household level data. The results are presented Table 8.11 using the village level data, for Banswara the highest co-relation of CHPI was observed with nutrition (0.75) followed by infrastructure (0.47), housing (0.47) and development (0.46). For Chittorgarh again the highest co-relation was observed with nutrition (0.79) followed by health (0.70), agriculture (0.69) and infrastructure (0.67). Other indicators contributing significantly was livestock (0.43), literacy (0.42) and demography (0.46).

Using household level data for Banswara the highest co-relation of CHPI was observed with health (0.64) followed by livestock (0.46), literacy (0.43) and nutrition (0.30). For Chittorgarh, the household level data indicated highest correlation of CHPI with the livestock (0.59) followed by demography (0.49) and housing (0.43).

The values of overall CHPI combined using the values of village and household level data for Banswara and Chittorgarh are given in Tables 8.12 and 8.13 respectively.

Table 8.12: Chittorgarh Composite Human Poverty Index (CHPI)

Code	*Name*	*CHPI*
132	Jadana	66.4
200	Marmi	59.4
201	Jaalpura	63.2
202	Lukari	68.9
203	Soliya	70.2
204	Somee	62
205	Davipura	75
206	Bagtaavar Pura	75.9
207	Keeroka Khera	78.9
208	Ghegpura	71.5
209	Pahoona	54.4
210	Bhopanai	65.5
211	Naarayan Pura	71
212	Kharitraa	63.5
213	Paavali	59.9

(Contd.)

(*Contd.*)

Code	*Name*	*CHPI*
214	Bassee	60.1
215	Devpuri	65.5
216	Balvantpoora	57.7
217	Savpoora	68
218	Rampurniya	72.7
219	Lasaariya	63.5
220	Shambhupoora	75.2
221	Sihaana	63.3
222	Medakhera	69.1
223	Haripoora	54.8
224	Araana	56.2
225	Ragnaath Pura	56.2
226	Javaan Pura	55.4
227	Charavati	53.2
228	Michayaikhera	59.8
229	Ratnakakhera	64.8
230	Punavati	59.1
231	Baavlas	60.1
232	Nangpura	57.9
233	Somkhalo ka-khera	53.4
234	Chitauriya	57.3
235	Kaanpura	61.9
236	Parmeshvarpura	63.7
237	Devpuriya	64.7
238	Uchha	56.9
240	Hirakhera	61.6
241	Chmanpura	58.6
242	Ganeshpura	62.8
244	Raashami	54.1
246	Jugpura	59.6
247	Depura	59.9
248	Gandark	54.4
249	Nalpura	65.8
250	Hernaathpura	54.9
255	Radarpura	54
256	Ganeshpura	56.5
257	Dadbaa	53.5

(*Contd.*)

(Contd.)

Code	*Name*	*CHPI*
258	Bhalotaki khera	57
300	Dhangaliya ka-khera	66.9
301	Daulatpura	64.5
302	Bhatt khera	67.4
303	Baaru	65.9
304	Bheemgar	60.6
305	Saakhalee	58.8
306	Karajiya	68.4
307	Laalpura	60.1
308	Maanyas	60.7
309	Revara	57.7
311	Karaas	67.8
312	Goodliya	68.1
313	Pahunee	62.4
314	Pukhariya	62
315	Pachakhera	70.4
316	Muroli	55.4
317	Uprera	63
343	Dindoli	52.2
345	Rood	52.2

Table 8.13: Banswara Composite Human Poverty Index (CHPI)

Code	*Name*	*CHPI*
1	Bhamri	64.6
2	Cunakhan	66.9
3	Durgeniya	71.5
4	Jhamri	62.5
5	Jogarimata	70.3
6	Ladela	64.9
7	Patapor	62.9
8	Sanidungari	73
9	Andeshver-tari	63.9
10	Bavripara	66.7
11	Jhandariya	68.3
12	Biyapara	62.5
13	Kishenpara	66.8

(Contd.)

(*Contd.*)

Code	*Name*	*CHPI*
14	Naalpara	63.4
15	Renganiya	66.7
16	Balasindoor	65.7
17	Baaldiya	69.5
18	Bichawara	63.9
19	Bilri	63.6
20	Bormatod	66.2
21	Chanawala	60.5
22	Dharka	58.5
23	Dharki	66.2
24	Beraonatha	66.8
25	Bhurakua	64.8
26	Basalivara	60.7
27	Kharorchatra	63.5
28	Shambhupura	61.8
29	Chitauraghalsa	66
30	Chtauramaphi	60.2
31	Damasath	51.2
32	Dungrabaratori	60.4
33	Dungrabara	60.8
34	Sarendragarh	56.4
35	Gariatori	65.6
36	Dungrachota	59.1
37	Motapara	59.6
38	Somjipara	62.5
39	Bheelkuva	64.8
40	Beejalpurgalia	67.9
41	Beejalpurhalia	64.3
42	Bhuradaur	64.2
43	Bhurighati	64
44	Godawaramanji	65.3
45	Godawaranareng	59.6
46	Motiya	67.9
47	Bagayacha	55.8
48	Bhoolpari	62.2
49	Boondikala	60.1
50	Himmatgarh	59.7
51	Kabalakichayana	59.6

(*Contd.*)

(Contd.)

Code	*Name*	*CHPI*
52	Sadriya	61.7
53	Satserakala	62.7
54	Durala	60.5
55	Macha	62.3
56	Molna	67.1
57	Bakaghuta	66.7
58	Goykabariya	61.4
59	Goykapargi	67.6
60	Jalimpura	60.6
61	Koothlipara	64.4
62	Rohanimehji	67.9
63	Roopgarh	68.6
64	Bhorajnayi	70.8
65	Bhorajjooni	65.6
66	Kasarbari	63.5
67	Thoothi	67.8
68	Tori	65
69	Ghootachatra	63.4
70	Jhalkia	69.7
71	Kalakhet	66.6
72	Kaliya	70.5
73	Shambhupura	69.9
74	Parwalakar	63.2
75	Parwallooja	69.3
76	Rautalimala	70.3
77	Ratnaghoota	66.6
78	Amba	56.3
79	Jeevaboota	62.6
80	Madlichori	63.9
81	Madlibari	67.9
82	Seemalkhera	61.8
83	Ganeshpoosh	65.9
84	Gora	64.4
85	Koondanitala	64
86	Koondaniroopa	68
87	Matorithapa	66.6
88	Malfomji	66.5
89	Merana	66.6

(Contd.)

(*Contd.*)

Code	*Name*	*CHPI*
90	Mepabat	66.9
91	Samlaser	64.5
92	Baallipara	69.1
93	Dhoteekitori	64.6
94	Karaimaal	67.5
95	Khoota rupji	64.9
96	Kunda	65.7
97	Machhrasath	66.5
98	Rawatasath	65.7
99	Ramgarh	60
100	Vadlipara	69
101	Charkali	67
102	Chowki dungari	66
103	Chor parnala	56
104	Daamarisath	58
105	Jatlesath	59
106	Magarda tori	58
107	Magarda machharasath	66
108	Palee khurd	53
109	Rupa khera	67
110	Garariya	56
111	Hejabhavaji	63
112	Hagamogji	55
113	Jhoomki	54
114	Jeeracot	62
115	Mahuree	58
116	Sewaniya	63
117	Karmee	56
118	Maska kala (bara)	63
119	Maska khurda	73
120	Kachala	57
121	Koui doban	59
122	Mooniya khoota	65
123	Vageri	61
124	Bagaapacha	57
125	Lohariya chhota	55
126	Nawaagauw	54
127	Pali kala (bari)	62

(*Contd.*)

(Contd.)

Code	Name	CHPI
128	Roopapara	68
129	Sasa vadala	65
130	Seemela	66
131	Sookhera	54.5
132	Vagool	57.9
133	Jhakoriya modar	63.8
134	Lasoriya	66.9
135	Rathdhanraj	63.6
136	Beraoodhuliya	60.5
137	Jhakoriyanatha	59.7
138	Rohaniya laxmamsingh	58.8
139	Rohaniya ram singh	61.6
140	Ghatiya	60
141	Kala khoota	62.8
142	Machhuriya vajja	62.4
143	Sagawa	55.7
144	Maat vadala	66
145	Sajjangar	60
146	Tidiyadeb	61.4
147	Bocharda	68.3
148	Bor kunda	70.7
149	Chora kala	66.4
150	Chora khurd	71.2
151	Gundi khurd	70.2
152	Imlijharn	70.8
153	Saatsera	72.7
154	Kawriya	62.7
155	Paadala Katara	63.6
156	Paadala Motala	70.2
157	Paadala Barakhiya	68.8
158	Shakkar Vara	68.7
159	Vajwa Ammba	64.2
160	Kheriya	66.6
161	Ausaata	64.5
162	Ranagee	66.5
163	Tambsera	65.7
164	Kasumba	63.1
165	Jaspoora	63.9
166	Tombamachhuri	64.8

(Contd.)

(*Contd.*)

Code	*Name*	*CHPI*
167	Todikaloo	67.6
168	Jharvel	56.9
169	Tanda Megala	59.3
170	Agoriya	53
171	Tandaratna	56
176	Bheemkhota	64.7
177	Chotiya	70.3
178	Chhiyakhoota	65.9
179	Chhiyasath	70.6
180	Ghorwara	62.2
181	Machhuri	61.6
182	Paatadiya	70.8
183	Saalan	69.1
184	Tandi bari	62.3
185	Tandi chauta	66.4
186	Talaaipara	68.4

COMPARISON OF VILLAGES BASED ON COMPOSITE INDEX

It may be mentioned that direct poverty ratio can not be estimated from composite indices. However, the CHPI which measures relative deprivation provides a basis for ranking of the villages. An analysis of indicators influencing the relative deprivation has been attempted in this sector.

The villages in the block were divided into four quartile categories according to their ranks as per the composite index as under:

	Per cent
First quartile	1-25
Second quartile	26-50
Third quartile	51-75
Fourth quartile	76-100

Thereafter a comparison of the villages falling into top 25 per cent category (fourth quartile) and bottom 25 per cent category (first quartile) has been attempted.

The results are presented in Tables 8.14 and 8.15.

Table 8.14: Comparison of Top Category and Bottom Category Villages According to Composite Index; Village Level Data

Indicator	*Banswara*			*Chittorgarh*		
	Bottom 25 %	*Top 25%*	*Ratio Top/Bottom*	*Bottom 25 %*	*Top 25%*	*Ratio Top/Bottom*
Agriculture						
Per capita area under all crops	0.05	0.27	5.4	0	0.50	
Per cent irrigated area	0	3.75		0	36.46	
Per cent area under rice and wheat	24.94	70.97	2.8	11.6	71.1	6.1
Per cent irrigated area	0	14.01		0	99.78	
Dependable source of irrigation (%)	0	78.33		70.26	100	1.4
Use of diesel pump	0.63	1	1.6	0.5	1	2.0
Mandi yard—distance	0.07	0		0	6.28	
Demography			0.0			
SC	8.33	0	0.0	43.61	1.13	0.0
ST	100	52.17	0.5	19.39	0	0.0
Wsorkers	17.37	62.33	3.6	9.78	65.81	6.7
Population density	10153	1114	0.1	3810	90	0.3
Development						
Per cent crossing poverty line	0	0.02	0.0	0	0.11	0.0
Receiving pension (%)	0	0.46	0.0	0	1	0.0
Drought	1	0.98	1.0	1	0.67	0.7
Per cent pop affected	93.48	73.78	0.8	72.56	25.44	0.4
Self help group	0	2.41	0.0	0	1.28	0.0
DWCRA	0	0.33	0.0	0	0.33	0.0
Wage-Skilled male	11.74	87.72	7.5	18.33	129.17	7.0
Unskilled male	32.39	40.22	1.2	12.78	61.11	4.8
Skilled female						
Unskilled female	27.5	36.35	1.3	6.67	52.78	7.9
			0.0			0.0
Health			0.0			0.0
Trained Dai	0	0.98		0	1	

(Contd.)

(*Contd.*)

Indicator	*Banswara*			*Chittorgarh*		
	Bottom 25 %	*Top 25%*	*Ratio Top/ Bottom*	*Bottom 25 %*	*Top 25%*	*Ratio Top/ Bottom*
Disabled	13.24	0.28		10.06	0	
PHC–distance	8.28	0.07	0.0	16.67	0	0.0
Sub–centre–distance	7.24	0	0.0	6.44	0	0.0
Private Practitioner–distance	4.13	0	0.0	4.72	0	0.0
Housing						
Is village electrified	0	1		0.56	1	1.8
Regular supply ?	0	0.2		0	0.39	
Safe drinking water	0	0.15	0.0	0	1	
Infrastructure			0.0			0.0
Cooperative loan for seed	0	0.2	0.0	0	1	
Ferti	0.93	1	1.1	0	1	
Medicine	0	0.09		0	1	
Pucca road (yes/)	0	1		0	1	
Ration shop (distance from village)	0	4.72		3.72	0	0
Literacy						
Lit	12.8	51.35	4.0	1.61	59.37	36.9
Boys primary	0	7	0.0	0	43	
Girls primary	0	0	0.0	0	0.29	
Children primary	48	100	2.1	0	100	
Livestock			0.0			0.0
Buffaloes (miltch)/capita	0.01	0.17	17.0	0.02	0.25	12.5
Buffaloes (non-miltch)/capita	0.01	0.2	20.0	0.01	0.23	23.0
Live stock per capita	0.26	1.42	5.5	0.05	0.85	17.0
Nutrition						
Village under ICDS (%)	0	100		0	100	

Table 8.15: Comparison of Top Category and Bottom Category Households According to Composite Index : Household Level Data

Indicator				Banswara Bottom 25%	Banswara Top 25%	Banswara Ratio Top/Bottom	Chittorgarh Bottom 25%	Chittorgarh Top 25%	Chittorgarh Ratio Top/Bottom
Agriculture	Wage rate	Agricultural	Male	16.54	41.91	2.5	29.82	46.38	1.6
			Female	13.46	36.14	2.7	23.18	38.5	1.7
		Non-agricultural	Male	23.66	53.58	2.3	36.88	50.63	1.4
			Female	18.73	45.88	2.4	28.88	45.63	1.6
	Total agricultural land			2.45	6.37	2.6	0.55	2.03	3.7
		Irrigated		0	0.42		0.05	0.93	18.6
		Owned		0.61	1.00	1.6	0.69	0.98	1.4
Demography	Female headed			0	0.04		0.17	0	
	S.C.+S.T. (%)			100	80	0.8	77	18	0.2
Development	Any training under TRISEM			0	0.02	0.0	0	0.04	
	Any help from IRDP			0.01	0.2	20.0	0	0.29	0.0
	Increase in income			0	309		0	86	
	Loss in Rs. Due to drought			9268	3459	0.4	3961	1020	0.3

(Contd.)

(*Contd.*)

Indicator				*Banswara*			*Chittorgarh*		
				Bottom 25%	*Top 25%*	*Ratio Top/ Bottom*	*Bottom 25%*	*Top 25%*	*Ratio Top/ Bottom*
	Income			752	1336.	1.8	635	1111	1.7
	Economic Activities	Male	Agri-cultural	42.3	261.71	6.2	70	151.36	0.0
		Female	Agri-cultural	30	255	8.4	50	129.	0.0
	Migration	Duration		1.61	33.65	20.9	0	1.06	0.0
		Distance		183.76	420.6	2.3	0	135.44	0.0
Housing	Electricity (%)			0	27		3	62	20.7
	Tap (%)			0	8		0	54	0.0
	Type of house (*pucca*)	Own		0	10		2	42	21.0
		Indira Awas Yojna (%)		0	0.8		0	100	
Infrastructure	Source of loan (%)	Cooperative for agri		1	45	45.0	2	90	45.0
			For non-agricultural	0	23		0	45	
Livestock	Miltch	Cow		0.83	1.36	1.6	0	1.25	0.0
		Bullock		0	1.26	0.0	0	0.69	
		Buffalo		0.68	1.24	1.8	0	1.44	
		Others		0	0.69		0	0.38	
Nutrition	Consumption of cereals			65	105	1.6	37	69	1.9

The proportion of scheduled caste and scheduled tribe is very high in the first quartile villages (bottom 25% category villages) as compared to the last quartile villages (top 25% villages). The workers as percentage of total population are much higher in top 25 per cent category villages as compared to bottom 25 per cent, the ratio being 3.6 in Banswara and 6.7 in Chittorgarh. Population density is much higher in the bottom 25 per cent category villages as compared to top 25 per cent category villages. The literacy level is much higher for the top 25 per cent category villages as compared to bottom 25 per cent and so are also children attending school.

In bottom 25 per cent category villages the population affected by drought is much higher. The wage rate (skilled as well as unskilled is much higher in top 25 per cent villages as compared to the bottom 25 per cent for both sexes.

Availability of Trained Dais is almost universal in top 25 per cent villages as against negligible in the bottom 25 per cent villages. The percentage disabled is much higher in the bottom 25 per cent villages as compared to the top 25 per cent villages. The distance of PHC, sub-centres and private practitioners is also much more in the bottom 25 per cent villages as compared to the top 25 per cent.

All the vilalges in the top 25 per cent category are electrified as against negligible in the bottom 25 per cent category. Regular supply of electricity is also higher in the top 25 per cent category villages so also the availability of safe drinking water. The connectivity with *pucca* road is better in top 25 per cent category villages as compared to bottom 25 per cent category.

In the infrastructure, the availability of cooperative loan for fertilizer was universal in top 25 per cent category villages as against relatively low percentage in the bottom 25 per cent category. Similar trend was observed for cooperative loan for medicine and seeds. Livestock, per capita (milch and non-milch) is 20 times higher in the top 25 per cent category villages as compared to bottom 25 per cent category.

The availability of ICDS is universal in top 25 per cent as against almost nil in the bottom 25 per cent.

As to the household information, scheduled castes and scheduled tribes together constitute 100 per cent in the bottom 25 per cent villages in Banswara and over 75 per cent Chittorgarh.

The wage rate for skilled male and female for agriculture as well as for non-agriculture is about 2 times in top 25 per cent category villages as compared to bottom 25 per cent category villages. The proportion of the bonded labour is higher in the bottom 25 per cent category as compared to top 25 per cent category.

The agricultural land per capita is much higher in the top 25 per cent category as compared to bottom 25 per cent and the differences are still higher for the irrigated land and owned land. The loss due to drought is much higher almost 10 times in the bottom 25 per cent category villages as compared to top 25 per cent category. The loss in rupees and days is $2\frac{1}{2}$ to 3 times in the bottom 25 per cent category villages to that in top 25 per cent category. The per capita income is about half in the bottom 25 per cent villages as compared to top 25 per cent category villages. Relatively very high proportion of villages had electricity in the top 25 per cent category as against bottom 25 per cent category. Very negligible proportion amongst bottom 25 per cent category had *pucca* houses. Availability of loan from cooperative, for agriculture and non-agriculture was better in the top 25 per cent category villages as compared to bottom 25 per cent. The availability of animals per capita was much higher in the top 25 per cent category as compared to the bottom 25 per cent category. As to the consumption of various items; for cereals alone, the ratio was 1.5 to 2 between top 25 per cent category and bottom 25 per cent category villages. For milk and milk products and other quality food the disparity showed wider range, the position being better in the top 25 per cent category villages as compared to bottom 25 per cent category villages.

Of these indicators, it may be mentioned that some are causes while some are consequences of poverty/deprivation. Thus, on the basis of above analysis the factors which influence composite index are the following:

Table 8.16: Significant Variables

Village level	*Household level*
Demography	**Demography**
Proportion of SC/ST	Proportion of SC/ST
Workers as percentage of total population	**Housing**
Population density	Pucca house
Housing	Electricity
Regular supply of electricity	Safe drinking water
Safe drinking water	
Literacy	**Literacy**
Literacy rate	Literacy rate
Primary school – children	**Agriculture**
Agriculture	Land per capita
Land per capita	Irrigated
Development	Owned
Drought	**Development**
Wage rate	Loss due to drought days
Health	money
Trained Dai	Wage rate
Disabled	**Health**
Distance of PHC, SC, private practitioner	Disabled drawing pension
Infrastructure	**Infrastructure**
Pucca road	Loan from cooperative
Cooperative loan	**Live stock**
Villages electrified	Per capita
Livestock	Miltch animals
Buffaloes per capita	Total animals
Livestock per capita	**Nutrition**
Nutrition	Consumption of cereals & other quality food
ICDS villages	

Using the CHPI values the estimates of poverty ratio are presented in Tables: 8.17 and 8.18.

Table 8.17: Estimates of Poverty Ratio—Banswara

Code	*Name*	*Poverty Ratio*	
		Income Based	*CHPI Based*
1	Bhamri	95	82.3
2	Cunakhan	92	86.8
3	Durgeniya	95	96
4	Jhamri	95	77.9
5	Jogarimata	90	93.5
6	Ladela	90	82.8
7	Patapor	90	78.7
8	Sanidungari	90	99.1
9	Andeshver-tari	90	80.8
10	Bavripara	52	86.4
11	Jhandariya	76	89.6
12	Biyapara	83	78
13	Kishenpara	95	86.6
14	Naalpara	72	79.9
15	Renganiya	65	86.4
16	Balasindoor	70	84.4
17	Baaldiya	90	91.9
18	Bichawara	80	80.8
19	Bilri	90	80.3
20	Bormatod	80	85.4
21	Chanawala	75	73.9
22	Dharka	85	69.9
23	Dharki	90	85.4
24	Beraonatha	60	86.7
25	Bhurakua	85	82.5
26	Basalivara	80	74.3
27	Kharorchatra	85	79.9
28	Shambhupura	62	76.7
29	Chitauraghalsa	80	85
30	Chtauramaphi	80	73.3
31	Damasath	80	55.3
32	Dungrabaratori	49	73.9
33	Dungrabara	34	74.5
34	Sarendragarh	80	65.8
35	Gariatori	85	84.2
36	Dungrachota	60	71.2

(Contd.)

(Contd.)

Code	*Name*	*Poverty Ratio*	
		Income Based	*CHPI Based*
37	Motapara	80	72.1
38	Somjipara	80	78
39	Bheelkuva	85	82.7
40	Beejalpurgalia	85	88.8
41	Beejalpurhalia	85	81.7
42	Bhuradaur	90	81.4
43	Bhurighati	90	81.1
44	Godawaramanji	90	83.5
45	Godawaranareng	90	72.2
46	Motiya	90	88.9
47	Bagayacha	83	64.7
48	Bhoolpari	90	77.4
49	Boondikala	80	73.1
50	Himmatgarh	72	72.5
51	Kabalakichayana	92	72.2
52	Sadriya	85	76.5
53	Satserakala	87	78.5
54	Durala	80	74
55	Macha	87	77.6
56	Molna	90	87.2
57	Bakaghuta	90	86.5
58	Goykabariya	85	75.8
59	Goykapargi	92	88.2
60	Jalimpura	85	74.1
61	Koothlipara	90	81.8
62	Rohanimehji	88	88.8
63	Roopgarh	92	90.2
64	Bhorajnayi	95	94.5
65	Bhorajjooni	90	84.1
66	Kasarbari	90	80.1
67	Thoothi	90	88.6
68	Tori	90	83
69	Ghootachatra	84	79.9
70	Jhalkia	92	92.4
71	Kalakhet	90	86.1
72	Kaliya	89	93.9
73	Shambhupura	62	92.8

(Contd.)

(Contd.)

Code	Name	Poverty Ratio	
		Income Based	CHPI Based
74	Parwalakar	95	79.4
75	Parwallooja	90	91.6
76	Rautalimala	90	93.6
77	Ratnaghoota	92	86.2
78	Amba	90	65.5
79	Jeevaboota	90	78.1
80	Madlichori	85	80.7
81	Madlibari	85	88.8
82	Seemalkhera	85	76.5
83	Ganeshpoosh	90	84.9
84	Gora	90	81.7
85	Koondanitala	83	81
86	Koondaniroopa	83	88.9
87	Matorithapa	85	86.2
88	Malfomji	80	85.9
89	Merana	90	86.1
90	Mepabat	85	86.7
91	Samlaser	90	82.1
92	Baallipara	89	91.1
93	Dhoteekitori	90	82.1
94	Karaimaal	87	88
95	Khoota rupji	89	82.7
96	Kunda	90	84.3
97	Machhrasath	89	86
98	Rawatasath	88	84.4
99	Ramgarh	90	73
100	Vadlipara	89	91
101	Charkali	92	87
102	Chowki dungari	90	85
103	Chor parnala	90	65
104	Daamarisath	90	69
105	Jatlesath	93	71
106	Magarda tori	90	69
107	Magarda machharasath	90	85
108	Palee khurd	85	59
109	Rupa khera	88	87
110	Garariya	85	65

(Contd.)

(Contd.)

Code	Name	Poverty Ratio	
		Income Based	CHPI Based
111	Hejabhavaji	91	79
112	Hagamogji	85	63
113	Jhoomki	76	61
114	Jeeracot	80	77
115	Mahuree	75	69
116	Sewaniya	86	79
117	Karmee	95	65
118	Maska kala (bara)	92	79
119	Maska khurda	90	99
120	Kachala	90	67
121	Koui doban	95	71
122	Mooniya khoota	96	83
123	Vageri	90	75
124	Bagaapacha	80	67
125	Lohariya chhota	84	63
126	Nawaagauw	90	61
127	Pali kala (bari)	80	77
128	Roopapara	80	89
129	Sasa vadala	80	83
130	Seemela	90	85
131	Sookhera	90	62
132	Vagool	83	68.8
133	Jhakoriya modar	88	80.7
134	Lasoriya	84	86.7
135	Rathdhanraj	83	80.3
136	Beraoodhuliya	80	74.1
137	Jhakoriyanatha	88	72.3
138	Rohaniya laxmamsingh	80	70.7
139	Rohaniya ram singh	80	76.2
140	Ghatiya	95	73
141	Kala khoota	98	78.6
142	Machhuriya vajja	50	77.7
143	Sagawa	92	64.4
144	Maat vadala	82	84.9
145	Sajjangar	92	72.9
146	Tidiyadeb	85	75.9
147	Bocharda	86	89.6

(Contd.)

(*Contd.*)

Code	Name	Poverty Ratio	
		Income Based	CHPI Based
148	Borkunda	86	94.5
149	Chora kala	86	85.7
150	Chora khurd	86	95.5
151	Gundi khurd	86	93.3
152	Imlijharn	86	94.6
153	Saatsera	90	98.5
154	Kawriya	70	78.5
155	Paadala katara	72	80.2
156	Paadala motala	72	93.5
157	Paadala barakhiya	72	90.6
158	Shakkar vara	80	90.4
159	Vajwa ammba	70	81.4
160	Kheriya	82	86.2
161	Ausaata	85	81.9
162	Ranagee	85	86.1
163	Tambsera	80	84.4
164	Kasumba	90	79.3
165	Jaspoora	92	80.8
166	Tombamachhuri	90	82.5
167	Todikaloo	80	88.2
168	Jharvel	75	66.8
169	Tanda megala	65	71.6
170	Agoriya	30	59
171	Tandaratna	40	65.1
176	Bheemkhota	90	82.5
177	Chotiya	85	93.6
178	Chhiyakhoota	86	84.7
179	Chhiyasath	86	94.2
180	Ghorwara	86	77.5
181	Machhuri	50	76.1
182	Paatadiya	86	94.5
183	Saalan	86	91.1
184	Tandi bari	86	77.6
185	Tandi chauta	86	85.8
186	Talaaipara	86	89.7

Table 8.18: Estimates of Poverty Ratio—Chittorgarh

Code	*Village*	*Poverty Ratio*	
		Income Based	*CHPI Based*
132	Jadana	32	57.8
200	Marmi	33.9	43.8
201	Jaalpura	38.8	51.4
202	Lukari	18	62.8
203	Soliya	33.3	65.4
204	Somee	40.3	49
205	Davipura	35.2	75
206	Bagtaavar pura	59.6	76.7
207	Keeroka khera	50.9	82.7
208	Ghegpura	55.4	68
209	Pahoona	26.7	33.7
210	Bhopanai	68.5	55.9
211	Naarayan pura	55.7	66.9
212	Kharitraa	48.1	52
213	Paavali	92	44.8
214	Bassee	53.3	45.2
215	Devpuri	17.6	56
216	Balvantpoora	18.6	40.3
217	Savpoora	25.4	61
218	Rampurniya	58.3	70.4
219	Lasaariya	14.2	51.9
220	Shambhupoora	25.4	75.4
221	Sihaana	48.6	51.6
222	Medakhera	66.3	63.1
223	Haripoora	46.3	34.5
224	Araana	39.7	37.3
225	Ragnaath pura	31	37.4
226	Javaan pura	58.5	35.7
227	Charavati	78.5	31.3
228	Michayaikhera	100	44.6
229	Ratnakakhera	100	54.6
230	Punavati	78.5	43.1
231	Baavlas	44.7	45.2
232	Nangpura	21.5	40.7
233	Somkhalo kakhera	48.8	31.7
234	Chitauriya	63.5	39.6

(Contd.)

(Contd.)

Code	Village	Poverty Ratio	
		Income Based	CHPI Based
235	Kaanpura	51.5	48.8
236	Parmeshvarpura	51.6	52.3
237	Devpuriya	73.8	54.3
238	Uchha	37.1	38.7
240	Hirakhera	46.6	48.2
241	Chmanpura	70.4	42.2
242	Ganeshpura	33.3	50.6
244	Raashami	49.5	33.2
246	Jugpura	55.4	44.2
247	Depura	35.2	44.8
248	Gandark	75.3	33.7
249	Nalpura	100	56.5
250	Hernaathpura	53.4	34.8
255	Radarpura	25.7	33
256	Ganeshpura	58.9	37.9
257	Dadbaa	29.3	32
258	Bhalotaki khera	42.9	38.9
300	Dhangaliya ka khera	100	58.7
301	Daulatpura	78.9	53.9
302	Bhatt khera	47.7	59.7
303	Baaru	69.1	56.7
304	Bheemgar	56	46.1
305	Saakhalee	40	42.6
306	Karajiya	48.1	61.7
307	Laalpura	38.8	45.2
308	Maanyas	32	46.3
309	Revara	67.6	40.3
311	Karaas	100	60.6
312	Goodliya	100	61.2
313	Pahunee	88.5	49.8
314	Pukhariya	28	49
315	Pachakhera	19.5	65.7
316	Muroli	23.2	35.8
317	Uprera	29.9	50.9
343	Dindoli	52.8	29.3
345	Rood	60.2	29.4

KEY FINDINGS OF VILLAGE AND HOUSEHOLD LEVEL ANALYSIS

The key finding of in-depth village and household level surveys in the districts of Chittorgarh and Banswara are summarised in Box 3.

Box 3: Key Findings of Village and Household Level Analysis

1. Poverty measurement identification of poor based on income criteria alone may not reflect the true picture of overall deprivation at the village/household level. Therefore, this needs household level indication.
2. In both Chittorgarh and Banswara, the demography related variables such as proportion of agricultural labour households, population density and proportion of SC/ST population influenced rural poverty quite significantly.
3. The impact of existing anti-poverty programmes on poverty alleviation was marginal, as very negligible proportion of the total number of beneficiaries crossed the poverty line.
4. The panchayat resources allocated to health services, access to safe drinking water, literacy, ICDS, Trained Dai and irrigation and per capita buffalo population turned out to be significant determinants of composite human poverty index in both Chittorgarh and Banswara districts.
5. Access to railway station, *pucca* road and panchayat resources allocated to infrastructure development helped influence rural poverty in Chittorgarh, while access to co-operative credit and *pucca* road turned out to be significant determinants of rural poverty in Banswara.
6. At the household level, per capita milch buffalo, incidence of bonded labour, per capita income and agro-based income generating activities were important.

9

Poverty Debate

In a country well governed, poverty is something to be ashamed of. In a country badly governed, wealth is something to be ashamed of.

—Confucius

The short-lived poverty of the benevolent wealthy man is like the temporary dryness of the rain cloud.

—Thiruvalluvar, The Kural

There are no two opinions that poverty is the biggest curse on earth and every effort to remove the same is most welcome. But unfortunately the efforts made and the resources spent are in the nature of chasing the mirage. An unending debate is going on whether the number of BPL families according to the latest NSSO Survey data is 26 per cent or more. Poverty, whatever its definition, is not the game of just abstract numbers, but something to do with the person who is poor—poverty being individual specific, we propose to examine how misplaced our research is in tackling the real issue of poverty—more so when it is realized that the only purpose of these numbers is to determine the level of aid to be provided to a State.

Since the very beginning, main thrust of the Indian Planning process has been the economic upliftment of the Indian milieu through all round economic and social development. India, like other developing countries was caught in structural poverty trap due to severe underdevelopment of their productive forces, compounded by an unfavourable international environment. The planners realized that despite these odds, the country had latent potential for a faster growth and eradication of the scourge of poverty. It was assumed that the programme of development incorporated in the successive five-year plans would strengthen the economy at the base and provide faster increase in production, in investment and in employment, which would ultimately banish poverty from the country.

Time and again, it has been argued that the economic betterment of the poorer sections cannot be achieved without social transformation involving structural changes, educational development, growth in awareness and change in outlook, motivation and attitudes. In order to meet this objective, direct attack on poverty through specific poverty alleviation programmes has been the strategy since the Seventh Five Year Plan. To adopt this strategy it was no doubt, necessary to have precise knowledge about the number of poor people. But for the planners as well as the implementing authorities it was also necessary to know who were these poor people and where they reside. Here lies the crux of the problem. Since poverty has not been properly defined, it has become the subject matter of hot political debate and contentious election issue for the political parties of all hues. Further, all through the post-independence period the focus of academic research as well as government policy reports in India have been on absolute poverty or the proportion of poor population.

Poverty Line and Poverty Ratios

The head-count measures, adopted for calculating the number of poor, have to depend largely on standardisation which is not very easy to achieve in a country where so much variation prevails. Even in food preferences due to regional, class, caste and other non-demographic factors, one has at least to take into account variations and fluctuations in prices. Here, again, the problems are not the same in rural and urban areas or in the different regions of the country. Dandekar (1981) in his paper 'On Measurement of Poverty' said that several criteria might be used to define the poverty line, and listed four:

"(i) the proportion of expenditure taken up by specified essential items such as food; (ii) caloric value of food; (iii) cost of balanced diet; (iv) cost of essentials of tolerable human existence." But he insisted that "whichever criterion we may choose, it is used to determine an expenditure level which meets that criterion; and ultimately, it is the expenditure level so determined and not the chosen criterion which defines the poverty line."

Majority of poverty studies using head-count measures have taken the individual or household as the unit. The 'Classes' with which these studies deal are statistical rather than sociological categories. But in many societies there are not only inequalities between individuals but also disparities between groups based on race, caste and ethnicity. The continuing and sometimes increasing disparities between such groups are more a potent source of political conflict in a democracy than the movements across a line dividing the poor and the non-poor.

We have mentioned earlier that the most widely used database for poverty studies is the household consumer expenditure data collected by the National Sample Survey Organisation (NSSO). Suryanarayana (1996) rightly points out that consumer expenditure includes all the non-productive expenditure incurred by the households. It includes consumption out of home-grown produce, gifts, loans, etc. There is often under estimation of foodgrains consumption when a poor family, like landless household gets food in the employer's home as wage payment in kind. The NSS also does not take into account the imputed rental value of owner occupied houses. This would affect estimates of consumer expenditure inequality measure and hence any estimation of poverty based on the inequality parameter. Further, there is also allegation of seasonality bias into the data and method of valuation of consumption data. Poverty estimates based on such data using conventional statistical deflators may be valid in a given stationary context but lose their meaning and relevance when the context itself undergoes a change.

When consumer expenditure data comes to empirical verifications, it bristles with many problems. Empirically, conclusions from comparison of real consumer expenditure levels would vary depending upon how different items of consumption are valued. In a country where income distribution is not optional, market price is not a proper welfare measure. In addition, in respect of the NSS database, there are a number of queries regarding its reliability. There are other issues like sample data presentation, tabulation and institutional parameters which have been ignored in the poverty studies and thereby leading to wrong inferences.

Official estimates published by the Planning Commission (2001) suggested that India recorded one of the developing world's fastest reduction in poverty. However, there has been an active and acrimonious debate regarding the accuracy of the official numbers, as well as the accuracy of the various alternative estimates offered challenging the official numbers. According to official estimates, poverty fell from 36 per cent of the population in 1993-94 to nearly 26 per cent at the end of the decade (1999-2000). Needless to reiterate that these estimates were derived from successive rounds of the National Sample Survey on household consumer expenditure, which has been collecting household level data for over 50 years. The NSS provides the basis for one of the longest continuous time series of poverty estimates in the world. But, of late, concerns have been raised regarding the comparability of the latest poverty estimates (based on the NSS 55th round, 1999-2000) with estimates based on earlier rounds of the NSS. Changes in the survey methodology to calculate household welfare (measured in terms of per capita consumption) are stated to have rendered the most recent official poverty estimates not comparable to the earlier official estimates.

The main issue of the debate about poverty trends in India across the 1990s is about the comparability of the quinquennial 50th and 55th rounds of the Consumer Expenditure Survey (CES) carried out by the National Sample Survey Organization in 1993-94 and 1999-2000. It has been argued that because of these problems, the 55th round survey for 1999-2000 might have overstated consumer expenditures. Sundaram and Tendulkar (2003), however, are of the view that poverty in India did decline in 1990s – in all dimensions. They point out that "the primary and most widely debated problem is that information in the 55th round CES concerning household spending on a frequently purchased group of food items—comprising 'food, paan, tobacco and intoxicants' and henceforth referred to as 'the food group' – was canvassed on two alternative reference or recall periods of 30 days and 7 days, among the same set of households, and recorded on the schedule of enquiry in blocks juxtaposed side-by-side. While only 30-day based reporting was published in the 50th round CES, critics maintain that this reporting may have been biased if households were first canvassed on the 7-day reference period, and subsequently extrapolated this to the 30-day entry by rough multiplicative adjustment. If this was indeed true, then there would be strong grounds to believe that the 55th round overstated consumer expenditures.

Sen (2000), however, held a view that the 55th round was unlikely to provide any conclusive indication of the trend in poverty. According to him, initial analysis of the partial data released by the NSSO from the 55th round in fact showed a large decline in the incidence of poverty during 1999-2000 as compared to 1993-94. However, he pointed out that this comparison was vitiated by differences in reference periods used. The reference periods used in the 55th round made its results conceptually non-comparable to all previous official released estimates from the NSSO.

Sen further opines that "the only conceptually valid comparison possible of the 55th round results from the one-week recall is with those obtained from the alternative experimental schedule canvassed during rounds 51st to 54th. On this basis, the presently available results from the 55th round show higher poverty than during each of the previous four 'Thin Sample' NSS rounds. Since rural poverty in at least three out of these four rounds was earlier found to have been higher than during 1993-94 by using the mutually comparable 30 day recall, there is greater validity to the opposite claim: that poverty during 1999-2000 was significantly higher than in 1993-94. However, the real problem at this stage is the threat posed by such highly contradictory conclusions to the credibility of the country's statistical system."

The root of this problem of credibility, Sen also identifies, lies in differences between NSS estimates of household consumption and those available from the National Accounts Statistics (NAS). And, particularly, in a perception that these differences had increased so markedly during the 90s that he suggests an immediate review of the NSS methodology.

Datt, Kozel and Ravallion (2003) have also expressed their concern about the gap between aggregate private consumption as measured by the national accounts and mean consumption from the NSS. Depending on the precise measures used, the latter accounts for 60-70 per cent of the measure of private consumption implied by the national accounts. They, therefore, assert that since there are differences in definitions and coverage between these two data sources one cannot expect that they will agree. They agree with Sen (2000) that the divergence has been widening over time since 1970s which is a matter of concern.

The other and less widely recognised problem is stated to be that in the 55th round, information on certain infrequently purchased items – namely 'clothing', 'footwear', 'durables', 'education' and 'health care', (institutional) – was collected only on a 365-day reference period. The published results for all remaining items were based on a 30-day reference period. Accordingly, in the published results the size-distributions of Per Capita Total Expenditure (PCTE) as per the NSS 55th round consumer expenditure survey for 1999-2000 were based on a Mixed Reference Period (MRP). In contrast, the published size-distributions of PCTE from the NSS 50th round survey were based on data collected with a Uniform Reference Period (URP) of 30 days for all items of expenditure. This was also true for the published results of all earlier quinquennial surveys in 1972-73, 1977-78, 1983 and 1987-88.

Ray and Lancaster (2005) point out that much of the theoretical debate on the measurement of poverty has been on the poverty measures rather than on the poverty line. While there has been considerable discussion on whether the poverty line should reflect an 'absolute' or 'relative' view of poverty, the literature is relatively thin on how to update the poverty line to account for inflation and changing consumption patterns and ensuring its accuracy in terms of the original definition. The 'absolute' poverty views the poverty line as the expenditure required to purchase a 'subsistence' bundle of items by the individual. In the Indian context, the 'subsistence' bundle was derived from a recommended minimum calories or energy requirement that was considered necessary for subsistence. However, with inflation and changing consumer preferences, the 'official poverty line' in India, that was anchored on the minimum energy requirements three decades ago, according to them, has ceased to be an accurate or even a reasonable, indicator of the cost of acquiring the minimum energy requirement. In our country, therefore, the debate on the 'relative' *versus* 'absolute' poverty line has given way to a debate on whether the poverty line should be money metric and expenditure based, as the official poverty line is, or whether it should be specified directly in terms of the minimum calories requirements.

Last, but not the least, agreeing to the controversy over the magnitude of Indian poverty Bhalla (2003) in his paper on 'Recounting the Poor: Poverty in India, 1983-99' analyses the trends in the survey capture ratio, i.e. the ratio of what household surveys indicate is the level of per capita consumption, to that corresponding estimate provided by an alternative source such as the national accounts. He also points out the possible sources and magnitude of errors contained in both the household surveys and national accounts. Bhalla then estimates poverty in India in 1999-2000 according to different methods, emphasizing in particular a method which uses information about increases in NSS household survey-measured real wages between 1983 and 1999. According to him the former is the year of an 'uncontaminated' survey and the latter is that of a problematical expenditure survey and in neither year the national sample survey containing wage information was 'contaminated'. He concludes, arguing in particular that in the light of data from the national sample surveys, it is almost incontrovertible that poverty in India was less than 15 per cent in 1999-2000, which is some conceptual distance away from the 35 to 40 per cent World Bank estimate for the same year, and is nearly half of the official government of India estimate of 26 per cent.

The controversy boils down to the fact that the Planning Commission's official 55th round poverty estimates were based on its 30-day food recall ignoring 7-day food recall and accepting its 365-day recall for clothing, etc. This implied apparently that All India poverty incidence had declined by 10 percentage points and the number of poor reduced by about 60 million since 1993-94 (i.e. the previous 'large sample' 50th round). Though, while releasing these, the commission drew attention to 'changes in methodology of data collection' and qualified that 'estimates may not be strictly comparable to earlier estimates of poverty', the results are being challenged by the economists, sociologists, planners as well as the World Bank. In fact, since the publication of the estimates, volumes of literature have grown upon the 55th round. The debate hovered mainly around the fact that accepting non-comparability of the estimate based on 55th round with previous rounds, to what extent official figures had over estimated poverty decline.

Thus, the debate on the extent of poverty in India has become too serious a matter. There is in fact, a 40 per cent divergence between the poverty estimates of the National Accounts Statistics (NAS) and those of the National Sample Survey Organisation (NSSO). As is known, the Planning Commission's poverty estimate of 26 per cent is based on the 55th round conducted by NSSO in 1999-2000. If one were to believe in National Accounts Statistics (NAS) our poverty levels are down to 15 per cent. The problems do not end here. The divergence between NAS and NSS data remains. The NSS samples are such that they under-report consumption at the upper end. This anomaly should be addressed, and the change explained in a transparent manner, so that the data is not open to political misuse. The four thin rounds suggested a stagnation in average per capita expenditure, or poverty levels, between 1993-98. How does this square with high growth? The economy seems to have grown impressively in the 90s, but that growth caused a concentration in consumption in the upper reaches. The World Bank, in 2000, observed that Indian reforms had deepened in equality. Meanwhile, one needs to go beyond expenditure data to other indices, such as literacy, health achievements and nutrition levels. The government, while worrying about the embarrassment of low consumption, should also include in its poverty line consumption norm a range of non-food items that are essential to decent living. Addressing data anomalies is fine, but let us not lose sight of the big picture.

The issue being raised by us is not with regard to refinements in the methodology, but the very purpose and utility of the whole concept of 'Poverty line'. So far as we understand the only purpose of these exercises (whatever be the numbers) is apolitical–distribution of funds to the States. This number plays an important part for fund allocation to States whether under the Gadgil formula or Ministry of Rural Development Programmes for a particular State. This number gets further importance when it is realized that this is the only bench mark to determine the level of poverty for the country as a whole and respective States. Although States have no role to play in determining this number, the higher it is, the happier they are. If so, one has the right to ask the question whether it is worth the resources spent (wasted) on all such efforts to determine the number of BPL.

In this context, it may be stated that we have also the income poverty ratios on the basis of Purchasing Power Parity (PPP) at 1 US $ per day and according to this we have 34.7 per cent of the population at this level. Further, as per UNDP's Human Development Report (HDR) of 2003, for the period 1990-2001, our rank is lowly placed at 53 amongst 91 countries ranked for constructing Human Poverty Index. It is, however, important to note that the UNDP's Human Poverty in India is based on non-food indicators – probability at birth of not running to age 40 years (15.3%), adult literacy rate (42%), population not using improved water sources (16%) and under weight children under the age of five years (47%).

Thus, we observe that country has three sets of figures of poverty ratios. The country's official figures are at large variance with the two other figures generated by the Ministry of Rural Development after a field survey and another generated by UNDP as part of their HDR. Interestingly the latter two figures came out rather close, yet they find no acceptance by the system. To overcome this problem, many have suggested alternative models. We also agree that there is a need to improve the official methodology hitherto used to measure poverty in India, including the approach used to calculate official poverty line and strongly feel that other 'very essential' indicators such as, housing, sanitation, literacy, health, nutrition level, etc. may also be considered for more realistic approach to identification of poor. In this study we have endeavoured to do so in Rajasthan State.

Other Anomalies

The issue becomes all the more important when it is realized that the very base from which these calculations are derived is flawed. The available corroboratory data would raise serious doubts on the validity of these results – whatever the number. Number of the persons below the poverty line is calculated by the Planning Commission on the value attached to an average consumer basket at average unit price, providing specified number of calories for rural and urban population. It would be appreciated that there is some sort of arbitrariness in this calculation at every stage. A study by Subramanian and Deaton (Table 9.1), shows that there is a big difference in unit value per 1000 calories consumed by the bottom and top 10 per cent households in rural Maharashtra. If so, the calorie criteria and the values attached to determine the number of those below the specified level would not appear to be correct.

Table 9.1: Expenditure Patterns, Calorie Consumption, and Prices per Calorie, Rural Maharashtra

	Expenditure Share %			*Calorie Share (%)*			*Price/calories (Rs. 1000 calories)*		
	Mean	*Bottom 10%*	*Top 10%*	*Mean*	*Bottom 10%*	*Top 10%*	*Mean*	*Bottom 10%*	*Top 10%*
Food Groups									
Cereals	40.7	46.0	31.0	70.8	77.3	57.3	0.64	0.51	0.79
Pulses	8.9	10.2	7.8	6.8	6.2	7.2	1.51	1.44	1.60
Dairy	8.1	4.9	11.8	2.8	1.3	4.9	3.69	3.59	3.92
Oils and fats	9.0	9.2	9.2	5.9	4.8	7.6	1.74	1.67	1.81
Meat	5.1	3.4	6.4	0.7	0.4	1.0	11.7	11.0	12.2
Fruits and vegetables	10.5	8.5	12.0	3.5	2.3	5.4	3.90	3.83	3.85
Sugar	6.5	7.4	5.9	7.2	7.0	8.0	1.01	0.94	1.09
Other food	11.3	10.4	16.1	2.5	0.8	8.6	17.4	16.8	15.9
Cereals									
Rice	11.6	9.0	10.9	15.2	10.1	16.5	0.95	0.89	1.02
Wheat	5.6	3.8	7.9	8.5	4.7	14.4	0.79	0.73	0.82
Sorghum	18.2	27.4	9.3	37.8	52.9	21.6	0.50	0.43	0.55
Pearl millet	3.0	2.7	1.3	6.6	4.9	3.2	0.48	0.48	0.50
Other coarse cereal	1.2	2.8	0.3	2.2	4.5	0.6	0.66	0.58	0.99
Cereal substitutes	1.1	0.5	1.3	0.6	0.2	0.8	2.23	2.22	2.22
Total food (or total calories)	**67.4**	**73.4**	**54.1**	**2.120** **2.098**	**1.385** **1.429**	**3.382** **3.167**			

Mean refers to mean over the whole sample, bottom 10 per cent to mean over households in the bottom decile of per capita household expenditure, top 10 per cent to mean over households in the top decile of per capita household expenditure. The figures in the last row of the middle panel are unadjusted and adjusted total calories respectively, where the adjustment corrects for meals given to others or not received from others. Shares of calories and of expenditures are calculated on an individual household and are averaged over all appropriate households. Calorie prices are averages over consuming households.

Let us take the case of an answer to a straight question to the same person who is being interviewed under NSS survey. According to the latest survey, it is hardly 3 per cent of the total population in the country which does not get 'two square meals' throughout the year or a part of the year (Table 9.2). There is no logic for a 'hungry person' to say that he is having 'two square meals', when poverty *per se* is being treated as a medium to partake the aid (loot) by nations, states, districts, villages and even individuals. In an atmosphere, like this, one would wonder why a hungry man will say that he is well fed. There is actually a greater possibility of the reverse—a well fed person saying that he remains hungry. It would then seem that if poverty line is intended to define those suffering from hunger, there is something wrong somewhere down the line. Our calculations are from the same source as an answer to a direct question and Planning Commission calculations represent a derived number from the same source with a number of assumptions. Certainly, we should depend more on a direct answer.

Again, in keeping with the Engel's Law of Consumptions not only per capita consumption of coarse cereals, but foodgrains as a whole is consistently declining both in rural and urban India (Tables 9.3 and 9.3A). This is not enough, consumer basket of those in the lowest docile is also changing by substituting cereals by fruits, vegetables and livestock products (Tables 9.4, 9.5 and 9.5A Graphs I and II). These two derivatives referred to above have also NSS as the source. No hungry person will say that he is having 'two square meals' and no rationally thinking person will ever diversify his consumer basket to replace cheaper cereals for costlier horticultural and livestock products particularly so if the total calories consumed are even less than 1500 as revealed by the NSSO data. One possible answer to this riddle is that in respect of most of these persons falling in the category of BPL, the NSS questionnaire are not in a position to catch their total consumer basket.

Table 9.2: Proportion of Household Getting Two Square Meals a Day – Urban Hunger

(*Per cent*)

State/ Union Territory	*Response Type*															
	Throughout the year					*Only some months of the year*					*Not even in some months of the year*					*Not Repo-rted*
	1983	*1991*	*1993*	*1994*	*1998*	*1983*	*1991*	*1993*	*1994*	*1998*	*1983*	*1991*	*1993*	*1994*	*1998*	*1993*
Andhra Pradesh	92.94	96.4	99.0	98.3		6.93	2.7	1.0	0.9		0.04	0.9	0	0.7		.1
Assam	90.77	93.8	98.0	98.1		7.23	1.3	2.0	1.2		1.79	4.9	0	0.6		.1
Bihar	87.60	94.4	96.8	97.0		9.14	5.0	2.7	1.1		2.89	0.6	0.5	0.9		.9
Gujarat	98.18	98.5	98.3	98.4		1.05	1.5	1.5	0.8		0.09	–	0.2	0.7		0
Haryana	99.47	98.1	100.0	99.4		0.53	1.9	0	0.6		0.00	–	0	0.0		0
Karnataka	88.65	96.4	97.4	98.6		10.37	2.8	2.6	0.1		0.58	0.8	0	0.3		.1
Kerala	86.05	95.2	92.5	93.9		11.67	4.8	5.5	4.8		1.85	–	2.0	1.1		.2
Madhya Pradesh	94.21	97.7	98.8	98.8		4.86	1.8	1.2	0.9		0.37	0.5	0	0.3		0
Maharashtra	94.50	98.7	98.6	98.5		5.00	1.1	1.1	1.1		0.42	0.2	0.3	0.4		0
Orissa	87.41	88.7	93.2	95.8		11.33	11.3	6.6	1.3		5.00	–	0.2	0.7		.2
Punjab	96.80	99.8	99.5	99.8		1.80		0.5	0.1		0.84	–	0	0.1		.1
Rajasthan	96.98	98.0	99.4	99.2		1.18	2.0	0.4	0.2		0.82	–	0.2	0.0		.7
Tamil Nadu	91.28	96.6	95.8	97.7		7.15	2.8	4.0	0.1		0.27	0.2	0.2	0.6		.7
Uttar Pradesh	95.17	97.6	99.1	98.5		3.86	2	0.9	0.8		1.05	2.2	0	0.2		.5
West Bengal	91.88	95.9	94.0	96.0		6.14	3.3	5.4	0.2		0.71	0.7	0.6	1.5		.5
All India	93.25	96.9	97.7	98.1		5.56	2.1	2.1	1.1		0.77	0.9	0.2	0.5		.3

Source: NSSO and Bansil P.C., *Agricultural Statistical Compendium*, Vol. 1 and Supplement, 1997.

Table 9.3 : Consumption Pattern of Cereals by Period in Rural and Urban India (Monthly Per capita in kg)

NSS round	*Year*	*Rice*	*(%)*	*Wheat*	*(%)*	*Coarse cereals*	*(%)*	*Total cereals*	*(%)*
				Rural					
17	1961-62	8.77	50	2.63	15	6.15	35	17.55	100
	1970-71							15.35	100
27	1972-73	8.56	56	3.83	25	4.84	32	15.26	100
28	1973-74	6.90	46	3.52	23	4.67	31	15.09	100
32	1977-78	7.12	45	4.05	26	4.51	29	15.68	100
38	1983	6.63	45	4.46	30	3.71	25	14.80	100
42	1986-87	7.11	49	4.77	33	2.49	17	14.37	100
43	1987-88	7.04	49	4.94	34	2.49	17	14.47	100
44	1988-89	7.07	49	4.73	32	2.76	19	14.56	100
47	1991	7.10	49	4.60	32	1.70	12	13.8	100
48	1992	7.20	49	4.50	31	1.70	12	13.8	100
49	1993	7.20	49	4.50	31	1.60	11	13.6	100
50	1993-94	7.00	52.2	4.40	32.8	2.00	15	13.4	100
51	1994-95	7.10	49	4.30	30	1.40	10	13.2	100
52	1995-96	7.00	48	4.20	29	1.50	10	12.9	100
53	1997	6.70	46	4.50	31	1.40	10	12.8	100
54	1998	6.80	47	4.30	30	1.20	8	12.5	100
55	1999-00	6.78	53.3	4.55	3.58	1.39	10.9	12.72	100
				Urban					
17	1961-62	6.16	50	4.10	33	2.09	17	12.35	100
	1970-71							11.36	100
27	1972-73	4.94	43	4.82	42	1.61	14	11.37	100
28	1973-74	5.38	48	4.32	38	1.62	14	11.32	100
32	1977-78	5.48	47	4.87	42	1.27	11	11.62	100
38	1983	5.32	47	4.82	43	1.16	10	11.30	100
42	1986-87	5.33	49	4.82	44	0.83	8	10.98	100
43	1987-88	5.35	48	4.98	45	0.86	8	11.19	100
44	1988-89	5.35	48	4.81	43	0.90	8	11.06	100
47	1991	5.20	47	4.90	44	0.40	4	10.70	100
48	1992	5.20	47	4.90	44	0.40	4	10.70	100
49	1993	5.30	45	4.50	41	0.60	5	10.50	100
50	1993-94	5.28	49.7	4.72	44.4	0.63	5.9	10.63	100
51	1994-95	5.10	46	4.90	44	0.60	5	10.70	100
52	1995-96	5.30	48	4.70	42	0.40	4	10.60	100
53	1997	5.20	47	4.60	42	0.40	4	10.30	100
54	1998	5.30	48	4.70	42	0.40	4	10.40	100
55	1999-00	5.22	50.0	4.77	45.8	0.43	4.13	10.42	100

43rd Round : July 1987-June 1988
47th Round : July 1991 - December 1991
48th Round : January 1992 - December 1992
52th Round ; July 1995-June 1996
53rd Round : January 1997- December 1997
49th Round : January 1993- June 1993
50th Round : July 1993- June 1994
51st Round : July 1994- June 1995
54th Round : January - June 1998
5th Round : July 1999 - June 2000

Note: Percentage of total cereal consumption.

Source: NSSO. Survey on Consumer Expenditure, Various Rounds.

Table 9.3A : Per Capita Consumption of Cereals from 1970-71 to 1997-98 and 1999-2000

(*kg./month*)

State	*1970-71*	*1972-73*	*1973-74*	*1977-78*	*1983-84*	*1986-87*	*1987-88*	*1989-90*	*1990-91*	*1991-92*	*1997-98*	*1999-2000*
Urban												
Andhra Pradesh	13.31	12.68	13.07	12.83	11.95	11.37	11.70	11.74	11.70	11.57	11.30	10.94
Assam	11.91	12.55	12.31	13.44	12.78	11.89	12.39	12.34	12.08	11.53	11.00	12.26
Bihar	13.68	13.49	13.22	14.06	13.44	12.90	13.37	13.50	12.85	13.66	13.28	12.70
Gujarat	10.35	10.77	10.71	10.17	9.61	8.81	9.44	9.48	9.55	8.88	9.06	8.49
Haryana	11.90	11.86	12.23	12.24	11.59	10.61	10.98	10.24	10.11	9.90	11.14	9.36
Himachal Pradesh	11.30	11.97	12.57	11.62	11.79	11.44	13.28	NA	NA	NA	NA	10.33
Jammu & Kashmir	14.62	14.16	14.31	13.16	13.80	14.62	14.09	NA	NA	NA	NA	12.84
Karnataka	11.91	11.32	11.24	12.68	11.69	10.37	11.06	10.71	10.40	10.44	10.38	10.21
Kerala	7.55	8.17	7.93	8.91	10.12	9.55	9.60	9.88	9.60	9.73	9.68	9.25
Madhya Pradesh	12.88	12.88	12.53	12.61	12.32	11.70	11.89	11.63	11.54	11.46	10.72	11.09
Maharashtra	9.75	8.95	9.24	9.92	9.90	9.23	10.18	10.18	9.74	9.42	8.86	9.35
Orissa	13.22	13.77	13.42	13.96	14.19	13.98	13.74	14.39	13.94	13.36	13.35	14.51
Punjab	11.25	10.71	11.03	10.80	9.94	10.25	9.74	9.40	9.06	8.85	9.67	9.25
Rajasthan	13.03	13.21	12.97	12.55	12.95	13.32	12.73	11.76	12.03	11.62	10.35	11.56
Tamil Nadu	10.63	11.12	11.39	11.05	10.39	9.93	10.14	10.26	10.14	9.98	9.48	9.65
Uttar Pradesh	11.79	12.24	12.48	12.27	11.66	11.77	11.63	11.33	11.14	11.42	11.34	10.79
West Bengal	10.88	10.53	10.92	11.92	11.80	12.75	11.71	12.12	11.78	11.30	10.95	11.17
All India	11.36	11.24	11.32	11.62	11.30	10.94	11.19	11.04	10.87	10.68	10.42	10.42

(*Contd.*)

(*Contd.*)

State	1970-71	1972-73	1973-74	1977-78	1983-84	1986-87	1987-88	1989-90	1990-91	1991-92	1997-98	1999-2000
						Rural						
Andhra Pradesh	16.05	15.25	15.80	15.85	15.37	13.99	14.35	14.31	13.62	13.60	13.02	12.65
Assam	15.70	14.81	15.33	14.38	14.23	13.24	14.23	13.93	13.63	13.20	12.56	12.63
Bihar	16.39	15.58	14.99	16.16	15.77	15.25	15.39	15.14	16.45	15.00	14.08	13.75
Gujarat	15.00	13.32	13.87	13.44	12.56	11.05	12.00	12.22	11.75	11.10	9.27	10.19
Haryana	18.13	17.57	16.56	15.22	14.54	14.84	15.02	13.74	14.55	10.20	11.48	11.37
Himachal Pradesh	17.64	18.06	16.30	15.47	16.06	14.32	16.06	NA	NA	NA	NA	12.86
Jammu & Kashmir	20.14	18.72	19.09	17.99	17.59	17.82	17.26	NA	NA	NA	NA	14.68
Karnataka	15.71	15.63	15.61	15.01	15.03	13.16	13.75	12.11	11.62	12.30	11.21	11.53
Kerala	7.99	7.97	7.69	9.18	10.01	10.28	10.36	9.75	10.73	10.00	9.90	9.89
Madhya Pradesh	16.51	17.28	17.12	16.08	15.83	15.14	15.39	16.60	15.22	14.30	12.51	12.94
Maharashtra	12.83	12.60	13.45	13.52	13.79	11.84	13.03	11.89	11.48	11.70	10.45	11.32
Orissa	16.12	15.22	15.88	15.97	15.61	16.02	15.72	16.52	15.98	17.10	15.87	15.09
Punjab	15.46	15.38	14.89	14.35	13.52	11.86	12.41	12.29	11.69	12.00	9.77	10.58
Rajasthan	17.91	18.17	18.76	18.18	17.19	16.69	16.62	15.54	15.75	14.90	12.72	14.19
Tamil Nadu	13.95	14.53	14.72	13.85	13.05	12.27	12.24	12.43	12.20	11.60	11.28	10.66
Uttar Pradesh	16.32	16.83	16.24	16.57	15.17	15.48	15.32	14.77	14.79	13.70	12.83	13.62
West Bengal	13.35	13.64	12.97	14.74	14.28	15.41	15.12	15.44	15.06	14.20	13.74	13.59
All India	15.35	15.26	15.09	15.25	14.80	14.28	14.47	14.00	14.06	13.5	12.47	12.72

Source: R. Radhakrishnan, *Indian Journal of Agricultural Economics*, January-June 1996 and Bansil, P.C., *Agricultural Statistical Compendium*, Vol.1 and Supplement, NSS 55th round, level and pattern of consumer expenditure in India, 1999-2000.

Table 9.4: Per Capita Annual Food Consumption for Bottom and Upper Income Groups in India, 1983–2000

(in kg)

	Bottom Income Group			*Upper Income Group*		
	1983	*1999-2000*	*% Change*	*1983*	*1999-2000*	*% Change*
			Rural			
Rice	70.9	84.3	+18.9	102.3	93.4	-8.6
Wheat	40.0	41.2	+3.1	74.3	61.2	-17.8
Coarse cereal	44.5	13.7	-69.3	42.7	13.7	-67.9
Cereals	155.4	139.2	-10.4	219.3	168.3	-23.2
Pulses	7.2	6.5	-10.2	18.0	15.0	-16.8
Edible oil	2.1	4.1	+94.7	6.0	10.5	+73.8
Vegetables	36.6	56.3	+53.6	60.9	86.8	+42.7
Fruits	1.6	3.3	+107	5.3	15.2	+188
Milk	12.4	15.9	+28.3	82.9	105.1	+26.7
Meat, fish & eggs	2.4	3.4	+41.0	6.3	9.2	+45.1
Sugar	5.6	5.7	+1.2	20.0	17.7	-11.7
			Urban			
Rice	56.2	60.1	+6.8	82.2	75.5	-8.2
Wheat	51.9	51.4	-1.0	65.8	58.1	-11.7
Coarse cereal	19.7	8.7	-56.0	7.0	2.7	-62.2
Cereals	127.8	120.1	-6.0	155.0	136.2	-12.1
Pulses	8.7	7.8	-9.6	17.3	18.8	+8.2
Edible oil	3.7	5.3	+42.7	9.2	18.0	+95.8
Vegetables	37.7	49.7	+43.2	72.0	96.2	+33.5
Fruits	1.6	5.8	+261	8.2	22.2	+171
Milk	23.4	29.0	+24.1	100.3	133.5	+33.1
Meat, fish & eggs	0.7	4.49	+556	2.4	12.6	+430
Sugar	8.1	8.15	+1.0	16.7	20.4	+22.1

Bottom group: Below poverty line.
Upper group: Above 150% of poverty line.
Source: Courtesy Prof. Praduman Kumar, IARI.

Table 9.5: Per Capita Consumption of Different Livestock Products (kg/capita/annum)

Products	*Year*	*Income Class*				
		Very poor	*Poor*	*Non poor*	*Rich*	*All*
Milk	1983	9.36	22.03	40.16	89.68	43.04
	1987-88	12.42	23.77	43.76	97.89	54.37
	1993-94	13.42	26.54	48.01	99.01	58.56
	1999-2000	13.83	23.47	46.68	115.61	73.54
Goat meat and mutton	1983	0.31	0.63	1.06	2.12	1.09
	1987-88	0.34	0.57	0.89	1.89	1.10
	1993-94	0.32	0.56	0.79	1.55	0.97
	1999-2000	0.45	0.40	0.83	1.30	0.96
Beef and buffalo meat	1983	0.48	0.55	0.58	0.83	0.62
	1987-88	0.59	0.56	0.60	0.95	0.71
	1993-94	0.51	0.63	0.63	0.81	0.69
	1999-2000	0.69	0.63	0.78	1.00	0.85
Pork	1983	0.05	0.05	0.14	0.33	0.16
	1987-88	0.06	0.08	0.14	0.36	0.19
	1993-94	0.05	0.11	0.18	0.47	0.26
	1999-2000	0.07	0.10	0.14	0.37	0.24
Chicken	1983	0.11	0.22	0.31	0.60	0.32
	1987-88	0.09	0.17	0.28	0.67	0.37
	1993-94	0.08	0.16	0.26	0.72	0.39
	1999-2000	0.18	0.26	0.47	1.09	0.71
Total meat	1983	1.04	1.62	2.26	4.18	2.38
	1987-88	1.17	1.46	2.00	4.05	2.49
	1993-94	1.03	1.54	1.95	3.66	2.39
	1999-2000	1.43	1.43	2.35	4.37	3.10
Eggs (Numbers)	1983	1.92	4.09	7.25	21.31	9.22
	1987-88	2.78	4.95	8.02	23.33	12.05
	1993-94	3.33	6.10	9.70	22.52	12.97
	1999-2000	5.62	8.85	13.55	28.74	19.48
Fish	1983	1.35	1.98	2.43	3.73	2.45
	1987-88	1.32	2.01	2.55	4.02	2.78
	1993-94	1.14	1.84	2.64	4.34	2.93
	1999-2000	1.32	2.16	3.11	4.44	3.47

Courtesy Dr. Parduman Kumar, IARI.

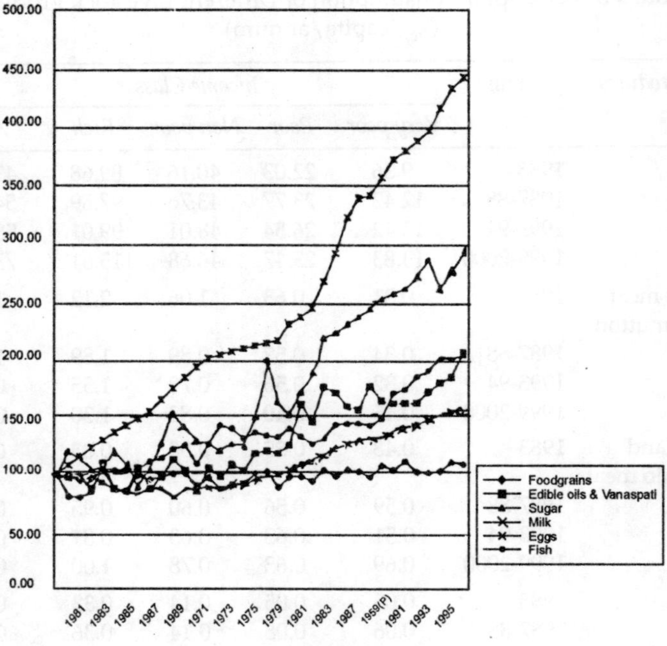

Graph I

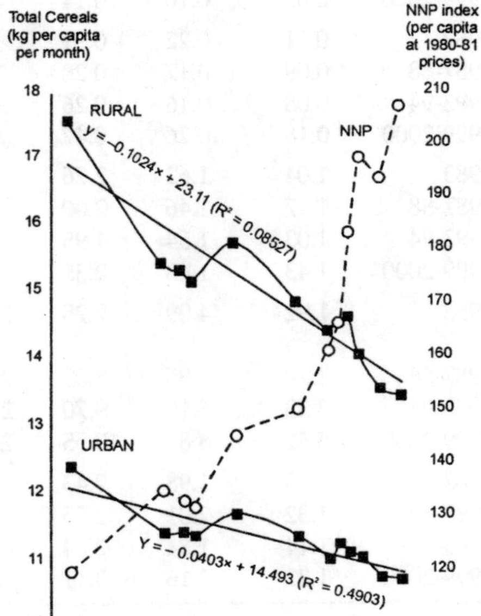

Graph II

We give here an extract of an interview by a correspondent of *Hindu* (October 1, 2004) Newri village, falling under the Badauni Panchayat of Datia tehsil, which was in the news recently after a television news channel projected the villagers eating chapattis made of grass due to extreme poverty and food shortage. However, a trip to Newri by this correspondent revealed an entirely different story. Newri is predominantly a tribal village. Most of those living here belong to the Saharia tribe. Inquiries revealed that 92 of the 114 families in this village have the Antyodaya cards that entitles them to a monthly quota of 30 kg of wheat at Rs. 2 per kg and rice at Rs. 3 per kg Halku, the village patel, who was minutely studying the crop when the *Hindu*'s correspondent met him, said that there was a below average crop due to shortage of rain this year. He said that any food shortage due to crop failure was taken care of by what could be purchased at subsidized rates under various government schemes. When asked whether the villagers were even being forced to eat chapattis made of grass, he responded in the negative saying it was not grass but some herbs, roots and plants growing in wild like Sama seeds and Kodo that were part of their traditional eating habit.

Such examples, particularly among the tribals, majority of whom constitute the BPL numbers, would be many. Further, according to a study of the National Council of Applied Economic Research, the Wealth effect is growing and increasingly percolating down to the middle income group in the country. The NCAER finding is based on a sample of 4,50,000 households. The study shows that in the rural segment the percentage of households in the low income category (below Rs. 45,000) is projected to dip to 20.6 per cent by 2009-10 against a high of 42.7 per cent in the review period. A similar fall is observed in the urban low income category. On the back of this trend, the overall percentage of low income households on a nationwide basis will dip to 15.6, against 34.6 for the review period. If compared with data from 1989-90, the improvement is even more startling. For the lower-middle category (Rs. 45,001-Rs.90,000), the change is also substantial with 21.4 per cent households remaining in this slot, against 31.7 per cent in the review period.

The Indian middle class is not just growing at a rapid pace, it has also become the segment driving consumption of "luxury" goods like cars and air-conditioners, according to a survey by the National Council for Applied Economic Research. While the middle class, which the survey defines as households with annual incomes between Rs. 2 lakh and Rs. 10 lakh at 2001-02 prices accounted for barely 5.7 per cent of all Indian households in 2001-02, it already owned 60 per cent of all the cars and ACs in the country and 25 per cent of all TVs, fridges and motorcycles. Read that with the projection that the middle class will account for 13 per cent of India's population by 2009-10 and one can very well see why the NCAER sees huge growth potential in the market for cars and mobiles. The study predicts that the market for cars will grow at 20 per cent a year, while bikes will clock growth of 16 per cent per annum till 2009-10. Fridges and colour TV makers can hope to cash in on the boom too, with projected growth rates in the range of 10 per cent to 11 per cent. The market for radios, electric Iron, bicycles and wrist watches too will grow, though by a more modest 7-9 per cent a year.

The projected consumption boom isn't just restricted to urban India. On the contrary, the survey suggest that the urban market for some relatively low-end products will be saturated by the end of the decade, while rural demand picks up. As a result, 80 per cent of radios, 65 per cent of colour TVs, 48 per cent of mobiles, 40 per cent of scooters and 33 per cent of fridges will be owned by the rural populace by 2009-10. Indeed, the projection is that with rural incomes rising, even the demand for cars will grow in the villages to the point where the country side will account for 11 per cent of all cars by the end of the decade. The survey – The Great Indian Middle Class – categorises the population into four income groups. The "deprived" are those with household incomes below Rs. 90,000 a year and they constituted just under 72 per cent of all households in 2001-02. By 2009-10, that share will be down to 51.6 per cent, says the survey.

The next step up the income ladder consists of the "aspirers" those with annual household incomes between Rs. 90,000 and Rs. 2 lakh. This category constituted a little under 22 per cent of all households in 2001-02, but is likely to rise to 34 per cent by the end of the decade. The "middle" class households numbered 10.7 million in 2001-02; by 2009-10, they are expected to rise to 28.4 million. "The rich too are growing in numbers", according to NCAER. From 0.8 million in 2001-02, they are expected to grow to 3.8 million by the end of the decade.

"While the number of *crorepati* families was 5,000 in 1995-96, they increased to 20,000 in 2001-02. By the end of the decade, there will be 1.4 lakh such households". Also, most of the deprived (85%) and the aspirers (60%) will be concentrated in rural areas by the end of the decade, while three-fourths of the rich and two-thirds of the middle class will be found in cities. The report is based on extensive surveys covering three lakh households across 858 villages and 660 towns and cities all over India. It covered a list of 20 durables, seven consumables, and a host of services including mediclaim, life insurance and credit cards.

Again rural India's consumption patterns seem to be undergoing a rapid shift. Consumer expenditure has risen by more than 9 per cent or Rs. 544 on a per capita basis in two and a half years. Annual per capita consumption expenditure has increased to Rs. 6,378 from Rs. 5,834 two years ago. Not only has the absolute level of consumption risen, the composition also seems to be changing. At the broadest level, there is an increasing move towards non-food articles, as seen from its increasing share in consumer expenditure.

Non-food expenditure's share in the rural consumer expenditure has risen from 40.6 per cent to 45 per cent, according to the latest (58th) NSS round data, compared to the 55th round data. On the other hand, the expenditure on food has declined from 59.4 per cent to 55 per cent over the same period. Thus, of the Rs. 544 per capita rise in consumption expenditure, non-food articles contributed Rs. 502, while the food segment contributed Rs. 42 only.

Under the non-food segment the heads of 'fuel and light', and consumer durables' have shown a particular rise. 'Fuel and light' has shown an increase of 31 per cent while 'consumer durables' have grown by 35 per cent. For consumer durables, this could be attributed to the low base, since it accounts for just about 3.2 per cent share in overall consumption expenditure. But it is a significant increase for fuel and light, which had a 7.5 per cent share in overall expenditure even earlier. At present it accounts for 9 per cent of total expenditure (Table 9.6).

Table 9.6: Share of Major Items in the Rural Consumption Basket

	Share During	
	55th Round	*58th Round*
Cereals	22.2	18.2
Milk and Milk Products	8.8	8.5
Edible Oil	3.7	4.0
Vegetables	6.2	6.6
Beverages etc.	4.2	4.6
Food Total	59.4	55.0
Fuel and Light	7.5	9.0
Clothing	6.8	7.1
Miscellaneous Goods and Services	19.6	12.4
Durable Goods	2.6	3.2
Non-Food Total	40.6	45.0

Source: NSSO.

However, the head of 'miscellaneous goods and services', which includes rent and taxes paid, has shown a drastic drop in both absolute as well as percentage terms. In absolute terms, it has shown a decline of Rs. 352, which amounts to a 31 per cent decline on the segment. Under the food category, there seems to be a move away from traditional consumption goods like pulses and cereals in favour of vegetables, eggs etc. This is evident from the fact that only, four items have shown a rise in share in consumption expenditure. These are edible oil, eggs meat and fish, vegetables and beverages. On the other hand, cereals, the biggest item of consumption has shown a decline in percentage share to 18 per cent as well as an absolute decline of Rs. 132.

If according to NCAER, the number of those in the lower middle class and below is decreasing, rural India is attracting multinationals as a 'consumer paradise' even for. white goods and rural India is witnessing these fast changes in its consumption patterns, one would be forced to conclude that there is something wrong somewhere on poverty results. The studies referred to above are a sufficient proof of the fact that those having income less than Rs. 90,000 is declining fast and their expenditure on non-food (out of total PCE) is increasing. The composition of the food basket is changing in favour of non-cereals. No wonder then that number of those having 'two square meals a day' is increasing.

Poverty Redefined

Poverty must be seen as the deprivation of basic capabilities rather than merely as lowness of incomes, which is the standard criterion of identification of poverty. However, the perspective of capability – poverty does not involve any denial of the sensible view that low income is clearly one of the major causes of poverty, since lack of income can be a principal reason for a person's capability deprivation. But policy debates have indeed been distorted by overemphasis on income poverty and income inequality, to the neglect of deprivations that relate to other variables, such as unemployment, ill health, lack of education, and social exclusion.

There is no dispute that to be poor is to be unable to manage the basic elements of human subsistence. No per capita income figures, no indices of calorie consumption can capture the wretchedness that is the lot of the poor, whether destitute amidst the dust of rural India or begging on the side-walks of its teeming cities. To be poor is to be born of a malnourished mother in conditions where ones survival is uncertain; to survive with inadequate food, clothing and shelter, without the stimulation of learning or play; to grow unequipped intellectually or physically to be a productive member of a striving society.

We all know that man does not live by bread alone. Of course, we must end poverty, and give men and women enough bread to live on. But music, dance, art and the telling of stories are indispensable to humanity's ability to cope with the human condition. After all, why does man need bread? To survive. But why survive, if it is only to eat more bread. To live is more than just to sustain life – it is to find meaning in life. And the poorest men and women in the developing world feel the throb of culture on their pulse, for they tell stories to their children as their fires are lit at dusk and the shadows fall – stories of their land and its heroes, stories of the earth and its mysteries, stories that have gone into making them what they are.

It is necessary, too, to tackle poverty on broad front. After all, what is the use of providing a farmer with high yielding varieties if his crop cannot fetch a fair price? What is the point to providing development aid when poor countries lose more to trade barriers and declining commodity prices? What could be more cruel than immunizing a child only to see it dies of starvation? What is the use of education if unemployment is the only reward awaiting the educated. Indeed, there are broader questions too, that one would tend to ask whenever poverty is discussed – questions of sustainable development and of good governance, what is the merit of economic growth if it benefits only the rich? Who can sustain creative energy under conditions of instability or corrupt institutions.

For whom, after all, is development ? It is not an abstract endeavour of states, a set of figures on GNP tales. Development is about people – human beings with needs and rights. Without culture, development becomes mere materialism, a subject for economist and planners rather than a matter of people. And if people are to develop, it is unthinkable that they would develop without culture, without song, and in turn, without expressing their views on their present lot and their future hopes. Development implies dynamism, requires freedom – the freedom to create.

Let us not forget that there exist, around us, many societies whose richness lies in their soul and not in their soil, whose past may offer more wealth than their present, whose culture is more valuable than their technology. We must strive to eradicate poverty, but we must also ensure that poverty of the spirit that ultimately is as harmful to humanity as lack of food or medicine. Let us work for a world in which we can fill both stomachs and souls at the same time. There is an example of a small country Bhutan where the ruling King, Jigme Singye Wangchuk opined that his country's "gross national happiness" was more important to him than its gross national product.

It must be a appreciated that poverty is no longer inevitable. For the first time, long-cherished hopes of eradicating poverty seem attainable, because the world has the material, natural and technological resources to do so within a generation – provided that concerted political will and sufficient resources are brought to the task. This is not just rhetoric: over the last three decades, more than 20 industrial states, have eliminated absolute poverty. Others can do it too.

The wealth of nations has increased seven-fold since 1945. The astonishing proliferation of billionaires is not the only indication of that. Overall, the proportion of people living in poverty has declined, yet thanks to population increases, the number of poor has risen considerably. Almost one-quarter of the world's population still lives in poverty. Income disparities between the richest 20 per cent and the poorest 20 per cent of the world's population have doubled since 1960 from 30:1 to 61:1. The statistics point to the increasing number of people (1.5 billion today) with incomes of less than $ 1 a day; about three billion people, half the world's population, live on less than $2 a day.

There are 750 million people unemployed and another 750 million underemployed. Some 160 million children are moderately or severely malnourished. About 110 million do not attend school. Another 1.5 billion are without clean drinking water, 800 million have no health services whatsoever, 35 million people suffer from HIV/AIDS. And poverty in old age remains the most common human experience around the world.

We may conclude that whatever the definition of Poverty Line it fails to catch the poor. But a most critical part of the whole game is that the effort made and energy spent by various top experts to come to any refinement in these numbers is certainly not worth the effort made – more so when it, is of little value to determine 'who, why and where' of the real poor.

Who, Where and Why

None of these exercises to determine the number of persons below the poverty line is thus hardly of any relevance to tackle the problem of poverty. For poverty alleviation what is important is to ascertain who is poor, where is he and why he is poor. This is precisely what we have tried to do in the Rajasthan Study.

Identification of Poor by the Ministry of Rural Development

At the all India level, the exercise made by the Planning Commission based primarily on NSSO consumption surveys provides a comparative picture of BPL families at the State level, for estimating the magnitude of poverty or to be precise about the numbers involved. This was of little use for implementing poverty alleviation programmes at the ground level where we need to identify the actual poor. In the initial stages, during the seventies, various schemes were implemented on an adhoc basis through village panchayats by the Ministry of Rural Development (MRD) responsible to eradicate poverty. After launching the IRDP programme in 1980-81, it became necessary to create a machinery at the District level to identify the BPL families at the village level and draw up various programmes for each individual who falls into the BPL category.

To achieve this objective a new organisation, called District Rural Development Agency (DRDA) was created at the District level in 1980-81 to co-ordinate various programmes for rural development and poverty alleviation. Initially an adhoc system of village level census was introduced which was controlled by the State Governments, primarily based on income criteria as determined by the Planning Commission and BPL families were identified by completing a structured questionnaire (Annexure I). However, lot of complaints were reported about the inclusion of non-BPL and exclusion of BPL families. There being a lot of criticism about leakages in the programme, an organised system of village level census based on a questionnaire was developed for the first time in 1992 under the control of the Ministry of Rural Development (MRD). Problems relating to identification of the BPL families still persisted. Our own study as discussed in Chapter 8 where survey was carried out in two Blocks in the State of Rajasthan—shows misclassification in a Block having 73.9 per cent BPL families. While the number of APL families included in the list of BPL families was 220, number of BPL families not included in the BPL list was 1561. In the second Block corresponding figures were 233 and 424 respectively. This evidence should negate the possible, assumption of relying upon the figures generated by MRD. What is found to be more galling is that the Ministry generates this data from the States but when it comes to deal with the poor, States are left free to pick and chose when required to limit the number of BPL families as arrived at by Planning Commission. It is here that the mischief takes place but then the powers that be have never concerned themselves with such details. Ministry of Rural Development, Government of India, constituted an 'Expert Group on Identification of Households Below Poverty Line (BPL Census 2002)' with the following terms of reference:

(i) To advise the Ministry of Rural Development on the methodology to be adopted for the BPL Census 2002 for the Tenth Plan period,

(ii) To advise the Ministry of Rural Development on the modifications required in household survey schedule of the BPL Census 1997 and finalization of survey schedule for the BPL Census 2002, and

(iii) To advise the Ministry on the analysis, interpretations of data/information collected during the census and any other related matters from time-to-time.

In their report, the Expert Group sought to make a distinction between 'Poverty incidence' as estimated by the Planning Commission and the poor as they emerged from BPL Census by the Ministry of Rural Development.

The difficulty rightly encountered by this Expert Group was that the Planning Commission had estimated State specific poverty ratios for 17 States only for the year 1999-2000. This has a very strong bearing with the critical recommendation made by this Group. Despite State's specific demand, this Expert Group went on to recommend fixing the number of poor, on the basis of poverty ratios determined by the Planning Commission. This is purely arbitrary and could be a clear case of injustice to the poor.

While it is encouraging to see use of Socio-Economic Index for identifying the poor and also arriving at an 'Exclusion criterion', two points need to be made with regard to the Questionnaire (Annexure II) developed by the Group and adopted by the Ministry. One, food security has been perceived solely in terms of cereal security and limited to hunger criteria. There is not a word on Nutrition Security, data for which is available in anganwadi centres. Secondly, there is no reference to the critical point as to, for how many days a person is getting work/employment from wage employment/employment generation programmes? Group recommendation is also unfair to the poor on the point, that if a person is included/excluded from BPL at the time of Census, next chance to redeem is only at the time of next such census. It is painful to note, that while Review of this census has been found to be in order with regard to mid-term deletion if he crosses to APL, it could not be the other way round. Currently, validity of BPL Survey generally holds good for five years – or till the next survey. Anomaly is that 'exit' from the group for the families crossing the BPL marker is provided for, but no provision exists for including a family in the BPL which has either missed the bus included in the previous census or has fallen into this category during the intervening period.

Another anomaly perceptible in our view is that there is no coherence or coordination in the timing of data generated by different agencies. First time household data was generated by MRD in 1992 whereas Planning Commission did it for 1993-94. Subsequently, MRD again generated poverty ratios for 1997 and Planning Commission did it for 1999-2000 and now MRD is collecting Poverty ratios based on a new Questionnaire (Annexure-III) for the year 2003 supposed to correspond to the Xth Plan period which commenced in April 2002, leaving inconsistencies unattended. The report of this BPL survey is not yet (2005) available.

It is appreciated that the Planning Commission bases its data on NSSO's quinquennial survey (last available for 1999-2000 called 55th round) and MRD does it at the commencement of Plan period. It is regretted that no efforts has so far been made by the arms of the same Government to rationalise the period and figures consistent with or relating to the same timeframe (Table 9.7). It leaves the poor in the cold as they have to wait for five years to come within the fold of BPL relating to a percentage determined few years earlier, thus completely missing the spatial context.

Table 9.7: Estimation of Poverty Ratios (%)

	1992	*1993–94*	*1989–94*	*1997*	*1999–00*	*1990–2001*
Planning Commission	–	35.37	–	–	26.1	–
Ministry of Rural Development	52.5	–	–	41.05	–	–
UNDP						34.7

Nevertheless, on account of large element of subjectivity and outside influences in all these censuses, there are complaints galore that APL families are still being included and BPL being excluded at the village level. Therefore, we may have to look for a new method for identification of the poor families in rural areas. As against the 'exclusion criteria' developed by the ministry during the IXth Plan, we would propose an 'inclusion criteria'. Discussion in Chapter 10-Targeting the Poor-is aimed at refining the system further. It provides a method to concretize the 'inclusion' indicators at the 81 sub-regions and also identify the Districts/Talukas where majority of the hungry people (37 million according to 55th round) are living.

We would like to highlight the issue that while there is so much of discussion by the Research Community about the Planning Commission methodology to determine the number of poor in the country, (this really is a non-issue in so far as the identification of the poor is concerned) hardly any effort is made to comment on the Ministry of Rural Development methodology on which all the poverty alleviation programmes are based. Chapter 10 is aimed to fill this gap.

The other-and much more important-issue relates to the arbitrary reduction of poverty ratios of the Ministry of Rural Development by the Planning Commission methodology. As shown in Table 9.7, poverty ratio according to Ministry of Rural Development was 41.05 per cent in 1997. This has to be reduced to 26.1 per cent as determined by the Planning Commission in 1999-2000. How this 15 per cent reduction is being made at the village level will be any body's guess. All those BPL families who come under this arbitrary cut have to suffer for at least 5 years before they can be considered for inclusion in the BPL list even after 5 years when the new MRD census is undertaken. From what is stated above, we may conclude:

(1) First and foremost issue relates to defining poverty. Does it only mean food or income poverty as defined by the Planning Commission or as what we have discussed in this study.

(2) There are no doubt a number of snags in the methodology of the Planning Commission to arrive at the number of poor even according to the limited scope of poverty. This, all the same, is not an area which should call for so much of heat, because this after all has a limited role – being unable to identify the poor whatever the definition.

(3) For purposes of identifying the poor, the number arrived at by the MRD is being arbitrarily reduced according to Planning Commission figure derived from NSSO data.

These data are not only flawed, but are also based on different definitions and relate to different periods. Justification for such reduction calls for further debate.

(4) An attempt has been made in Chapter 10 how to go about 'Targeting the Poor'. While we do not claim any finality in the process, this is the best one could think of.

REFERENCES

1. Bhalla, Surjit S. (2003), 'Recounting the Poor: Poverty in India, 1983-99'; *Economic and Political Weekly*, January 25, 2003.
2. Dandekar, V.M. (1981), 'On Measurement of Poverty', *Economic and Political Weekly*, XVI (30): 1241-50.
3. Datt, Gaurav, Valerie Kozel, Martin Ravallion (2003), 'A Model-Based Assessment of India's Progress in Reducing Poverty in the 1990s'; *Economic and Political Weekly*, January 25, 2003.
4. Planning Commission (2001), *Official Poverty Estimates for 1999-2000*, Government of India, Planning Commission Press Release, February 22, 2001.
5. Ray, Ranjan and Geoffrey Lancaster (2005), 'On Setting the Poverty Line Based on Estimated Nutrient Prices'; *Economic and Political Weekly*, January 1, 2005.
6. Sen, Abhijit (2000), 'Estimates of Consumer Expenditure and Its Distribution – Statistical Priorities after NSS 55th Round', *Economic and Political Weekly*, December 16, 2000.
7. Sundaram, K. and Suresh D. Tendulkar (2003), 'Poverty Has Declined in the 1990s'; *Economic and Political Weekly*, January 25, 2003.
8. Suryanarayana, M.H. (1996), 'Poverty Estimates and Indicators – Importance of Data Base'; *Economic and Political Weekly*, Special Number September 1996.

ANNEXURE I

Guidelines for the Survey of the IRDP Beneficiaries Assisted During the Earlier Five Year Plans

1. The survey should cover every family assisted under IRDP during the earlier Five Year Plans. The information with regard to each of the families is to be collected in the enclosed proforma.
2. In order to ensure objectivity in survey, the staff engaged in the direct implementation of the programme may not be assigned the survey work, to the extent possible. The work may be assigned to teachers, N.S. Volunteers and other available officials/ agencies in the field.
3. The appointed surveyors will require some training to expose them to the methodology of survey in general and assessment of income in particular. A team of the District Collector, Project Director, DRDA and the Manager of the Lead Bank of the district may be constituted at the district headquarters to explain the methodology to a training camp at the district headquarters or some other central place in the district. Similar teams consisting of SDO wherever possible, BDO and the Bank Manager may be constituted at block level training camps to be organised for the surveyors. The preparatory work, the constitution of the teams, appointment of Surveyors and the training camp should be so organised as to be over by the end of the month of April.
4. The survey should commence from the month of May. This would be necessary if the teachers are involved as they would be available for the work only for the months of May and June. The efforts should be to complete the survey by the end of the month of June.
5. During the currency of the survey the district level team which had been constituted for the purpose of

imparting training should undertake some test checks of the surveys. In addition, BDOs should carry out sample checks to the tune of 5 per cent, the SDOs 2 per cent and the other project authorities 1 per cent.

Survey Schedule for IRDP Beneficiaries Assisted During the Earlier Plan:

1. State
2. District
3. Block
4. Village
5. Date of survey
6. Name of the head of family
7. Name of the beneficiary
8. Annual income at the time of the identification as per household survey
9. Number and name(s) of scheme(s) provided
10. The size of the unit supplied
11. Financial assistance provided:
    (a) Loan
    (b) Subsidy
    (c) Total
12. Date of provision of asset
13. Whether asset is insured Yes/No
14. Whether the asset is existing Yes/No
15. If the asset is not existing or partly existing, the reasons thereof:
    (i) Perished
    (ii) Disposed of
16. Annual Income of the family at the time of verification:
    (i) Income from asset provided under IRDP
    (ii) Income from other sources
    (iii) Total income
17. The income slab to which the beneficiary belongs:
    (a) Income between Rs. 0-2265
    (b) Income between Rs. 2266-3500
    (c) Income between Rs. 3501-4800
    (d) Income between Rs. 4801-6400

18. The Total loan (Principal repaid till date)
19. The date and the amount of last instalment paid
20. If the beneficiary is a defaulter, the reasons for default:
    - (i) Wilful default
    - (ii) Inadequate repayment period
    - (iii) Own investment resulting in low income generation
    - (iv) Failure of the asset
    - (v) Lack of infrastructure support
    - (vi) Lack of marketing support
    - (vii) Other reasons, if any
21. Does the beneficiary possessing full/part asset has any plan of expansion:
    - (i) If yes, what?
    - (ii) Financial resources he has in mind for this
22. Does the beneficiary who is no longer in possession of the asset want to take up any other Project?
    - (i) If yes, why?
    - (ii) What project does he want?
    - (iii) What financial resources does he have in mind?

ANNEXURE II

Schedule for the BPL Census for the Ninth Plan

Explanatory Notes

1. Use of Exclusion criteria and Multiple Criteria for identifying BPL household:
   The BPL Census Schedule is divided into two parts. The field investigator will visit all the households of the village and fill up Part A of the Schedule. If (Y) is indicated for any of the items in Part A of the schedule that household will be excluded from the BPL list and the investigator need not fill up Part B of the Schedule. However if (N) is indicated for all the items of Part A of the Schedule, the investigator would go to Part B of the Schedule.
2. If the total expenditure of the household is higher than the poverty line, the household will be excluded from the BPL list. Details of assets asked for in items 4, 5 and 6 of the schedule should be in broad consensus with the expenditure of the household.
5. For the purpose of *pucca* house, the definition of these terms of Population Census may be used.

Definitions

1. *Small Farmer*: Those operating land more than one hactare. But less than 2 hectares.
2. *Marginal Farmer*: Those operating land less than one hectare.
3. *Landless*: Those operating land less than 0.05 hectare or not operating any land.
4. *Agricultural wage labourer*: Those deriving more than 50 per cent of income from agricultural wages.
5. *Non-Agricultural worker*: Those deriving more than 50 per cent of income from non-agricultural wages.
6. *Contractual labour*: Those deriving income from contracts agreed to with the employer.

7. *Salaried worker*: Those deriving fixed monthly income in the form of a salary.
8. *Business man/trader*: Those deriving more than 50 per cent of their income from purchase and sale of goods with the object of earning profits.

Part–A of the Household Schedule

General Information/Identification Particulars

(i) State
(ii) District
(iii) Block
(iv) Village
(v) House No.
(vi) Name of Head of household

Whether operating more than 2 hectares of land* | Yes | No |

Whether having a *Pucca* House** | Yes | No |

Whether any resident member of the household has Annual income from salary/self-employment exceeding Rs.20,000 per annum (Rs.1,700 per month) | Yes | No |

Whether the household owns the following consumer durables:

(a) T.V. | Yes | No |
(b) Refrigerator | Yes | No |
(c) Ceiling fan | Yes | No |
(d) Motorcycle/Scooter | Yes | No |
(e) Three wheeler | Yes | No |

Whether the household owns the following farm implements.

(a) Tractor | Yes | No |
(b) Power Tiller | Yes | No |
(c) Combined thresher/harvester | Yes | No |

Note: Any household for which Y has been indicated under any of the above criteria should not be considered for Part-B of the Schedule.

* The land limits of DPAP/DDP areas for small and marginal farmers as defined by the State Government will be considered for this.

** *Pucca* house as defined in the Population Census or by the State.

Part—B of the Household Schedule

1. Block/ Household data

Name	Sex	Age	Whether Physically Disabled	Educational Status	For Household as a whole			
	Male [1] Female [2]	(Completed Yrs.)	(Y/N)	Illiterate [1] Studied upto Class V[2] Class VIII[3] Beyond Class VIII[4]	*Social Group (a)*	*Religion (b)*	*Occupation (c)*	*Priority Category *** (d)*
					SC-1 ST-2 OBC-3 Others-4 *(based on the list of castes to be provided to enumerators)			

(i) (Head of the household)
(ii)
(iii)
(iv)
(v)
(vi)
(vii)

** Occupation		
	Agricultural labour	[1]
	Other rural labour	[2]
	Self-employed in agriculture	[3]
	Self-employed in non-agriculture	[4]

	Artisan	[5]
	Others	[6]
*** Priority category	Women	[1]
	Assignee of Surplus Land	[2]
	Freed bonded labourer	[3]

2. *Housing Status*

(i) Ownership: Owned[1] Rented [2]
(ii) Type : Semi *Pucca*[1] *Kutcha*[2] Houseless [3]

3. *Ownership of Land in Hectares (Ha.)*

(i) Landless[1] Small Holdings[2] Marginal Holdings [3]
(ii) Size of landholding in ha.
  (a) Irrigated
  (b) Un-irrigated
  (c) Total (a+b)

4. *Ownership of Livestock Assets in Nos.*

Milch Animals
Bullocks
Camels
Sheep
Goat
Pigs
Poultry Birds
Others (please specify)

5. *Formal training for skill development of the members*

Name	*Sex* Male [1] Female [2]	*Age (Completed Yrs.)*	*Training Received (Y/N)*	*Training under TRYSEM Institutional [1] Mastercraftsmen [2]*	*Type of skill (code)*	*Any other training govt. [1] Private[2]*
(i)						
(ii)						
(iii)						
(iv)						
(v)						
(vi)						

6. *Expenditure of the household in Rs. during the last 30 days unless otherwise specified*

A. Food
  (i) Cereals
  (ii) Pulses
  (iii) Edible Oils/Vanaspati/Ghee
  (iv) Milk & Milk products
  (v) Meat, fish & eggs
  (vi) Fruit & vegetable
B. Beverages/Drinks/Pan/Tobacco
C. Clothing (expenditure incurred last year divided by 12)
D. Shelter
  (i) Cost of maintenance/repair of house (Rs. per annum divided by 12)
  (ii) Rent
E. Fuel & light
F. Education
G. Travel
H. Medical
I. Entertainment
J. Total Expenditure of the household during the last 30 days (A to I)

K. Per Capita Expenditure per month (J divided by Total members of the Household)

7. *Receipt of assistance to household under different programmes during last 365 days preceding date of survey*

Sl. No.	*Scheme*	*Amount of Assistance (Rs.)**	*No. of @ mandays of employment recd. during last year*	*If assistance received for any asset, status of asset (in tact-1) (not in tact-2)*	*Wage rate received per day (Rs.) @*
1	*2*	*3*	*4*	*5*	*6*
1.	IRDP				
2.	TRYSEM				
3.	DWCRA				
4.	TOOLKITS				
5.	JRY				
6.	EAS				
7.	IAY				
8.	MWS				
9.	CRSP				
10.	NSAP				

* applicable for IRDP, TRYSEM, TOOLKITS, DWCRA, IAY, MWS, NSAP, CRSP, etc.
@ Applicable for JRY, EAS, etc.

8. *Migration*

Whether any member in the village went outside the village/ District for wage employment during the last month

Yes –1 No–2

If yes,

1. Name of the member
2. Kind of employment pursued

JRY/EAS [1]
Agriculture [2]
Non-farm [3]

3. Daily wage rate (Rs.)
4. Work outside village but within the block [1]
   Work outside the block but within district [2]
   Work outside district [3]
5. Reason for going out for employment
   For higher wages [1]
   No employment in the village [2]
   Other reasons [3]
9. Perception of the household regarding sufficiency of food. Do all members of the household get two square meals (enough food) in a day?
10. Indebtedness of the household

	Year of Taking Loan	*Principal Amount (Rs.)*	*Amount Outstanding (Rs.)*
Bank			
Moneylenders			
Relatives			
Total			

11. Comments of the Enumerator

ANNEXTURE III

Schedule for BPL Census 2002

Name of Head of Household:
House Number and Name, if any: Total Score:
Name of Village:
Name of Gram Panchayat: Sub-category:
Name of Block:
Name of District:

A. Profile of the household

(a) Educational Status

Sl. No.	*Name*	*Age (in years)*	*Sex: Male (M)/ Female (F)*	*Relation to head of household*	*Educational status (Use code$)*

$: Illiterate-1 Passed Class V-2 Passed Class VII-3
Passed Class X-4 Passed Class XII-5 Graduate and above-6

(b) Average Monthly Income of the household in Rupees [Only one column, which is the most appropriate, to be ticked (✔)]

Less than 250	*250-499*	*500-1499*	*1500-2500*	*More than 2500*

(c) Type of operational holding of land [only one column, which is the most appropriate, to be ticked (✔)]

Owner	*Tenant*	*Both owner and tenant*	*None*

(d) Drinking Water Facility [only one column, which is the most appropriate, to be ticked (✔)]. Only one row (either 'for plain areas' or 'for hilly areas') to be used.

(for Plain areas)	No source of drinking water within distance of 1.6 kilometre	Source of drinking water at a distance of 1.00 – 1.59 kilometre	Source of drinking water at a distance of 0.50-0.99 kilometre	Source of drinking water within a distance of less than 0.50 kilometre Source available within the house	Source available within the house
(for hilly areas)	No source of drinking water within elevation of 100 metres	Source of drinking water within elevation of 50 – 100 metres	Source of drinking water at elevation of less than 50 metres		

(e) Social Group of the household* only one column to be ticked (✓)

ST	*SC*	*OBC*	*Others*

* Not to be included in the Total Score.

B. Identification and Sub-categorization of Poor

[(Only one column, which is the most appropriate, to be ticked (✓) against items at Sl. No.1 to 13]

Sl. No. Characteristics	Scores				
	0	1	2	3	4
1. Size group of operational holding of land	Nil	Less than 1 ha. land (or less than 0.5 ha. of irrigated land)	1 ha., 2 ha. of un-irrigated land (or 0.5-1.0 ha. of irrigated land)	2 ha., 5 ha. of un-irrigated land (or 1.0 – 2.5 ha. of irrigated land)	More than 5 ha. of un-irrigated land (or 2.5 ha. of irrigated land)
2. Type of house	Houseless	*Kutcha*	Semi-*pucca*	*Pucca*	Urban type
3. Average availability of normal wear clothing (per person in pieces)	Less than 2	2 or more, but less than 4	4 or more, but less than 6	6 or more, but less than 10	10 or more
4. Food Security	Less than one square meal per day for major part of the year	Normally, one square meal per day, but less than one square meal occasionally	One square meal per day throughout the year	Two square meals per day with occasional shortage	Enough food throughout the year
5. Sanitation	Open defecation	Group latrine with irregular water supply	Group latrine with regular water supply	Clean group latrine with regular water supply and regular sweeper	Private latrine

(*Contd.*)

Sl. No.	Characteristics	Scores				
		0	*1*	*2*	*3*	*4*
6.	Ownership of consumer durables: do you own (tick √) - TV - electric fan - kitchen appliances like pressure cooker - radio	Nil	Any one	Two items only	Any three or all items	All items and/or ownership of any one of the following - Computer - Telephone - Refrigerator - Colour TV - Electric Kitchen appliances - Expensive furniture - LMV/LCV - Tractor mechanized two-wheeler/ three wheeler - Power Tiller - Combined thresher/ harvester [@4 wheeled mechanized vehicle]

(*Contd.*)

Sl. No.	Characteristics	Scores				
		0	1	2	3	4
7.	Literacy status of the highest literate adult	Illiterate	Upto primary (Class V)	Completed secondary (Passed Class X)	Graduate/Professional Diploma	Post Graduate/Profession Graduate
8.	Status of the household labour force	Bonded labour	Female and Child labour	Only adult females & no child labour	Adult males only	Others
9.	Means of livelihood	Casual labour	Subsistence cultivation	Artisan	Salary	Others
10.	Status of children (5-14 years) [any child]	Not going to School and working	Going to School and working			Going to School and not working
11.	Type of indebtedness	For daily consumption purposes from informal sources	For production purpose from informal sources	For other purpose from informal sources	Borrowing only from institutional agencies	No Indebtedness and possess assets
12.	Reason for migration from household	Casual work	Seasonal employment	Other forms of livelihood	Non-migrant	Other purposes

(Contd.)

Sl. No.	*Characteristics*	*Scores*				
		0	*1*	*2*	*3*	*4*
13.	Preference for Assistance	Wage Employment TPDS (Targeted Public Distribution System)	Self Employment	Training and Skill Upgradation	Housing	Loan/Subsidy more than Rs. one lakh or No assistance needed

@ Including Non-formal Education.

Note: The Total Score for a household will vary between 0 and 52

10

Targeting the Poor

Articulated in the Atlantic Character 'as Freedom from Want' it failed to find entrenchment in the character of United Nations in San Francisco, and has been the most critical ... unmet need in the post war period.

—Sir Shridhar Ramphal

Identification of poor has been a major challenge before all developing societies, which is a *sine qua non* of successful 'Targeting'. As discussed earlier, to identify the poor, India adopted a hazy undetermined criteria of family income as the divide, Below Poverty Line (BPL) and Above Poverty Line (APL) families except that during the last survey an 'exclusion' criteria was also introduced. Global experience is that the criteria being subjective and the machinery for identification being susceptible to local influences, the outcome is always suspect. In order to streamline the system, we give below a new methodology based on this Rajasthan study.

Methods of Targeting

Broadly speaking there could be five kinds of individual assessment:

(i) Means Test
(ii) Social Worker Evaluation
(iii) Proxy means test
(iv) Gender of Household 'Head'
(v) Nutrition status or Risk.

Our recent primary data collected in order to 'Map' the poor on 'Nine' indicators reveal a different value judgment as also the fact that many APL families get added at the cost of poor and many BPL families are left out of the fold thus literally non-entitling them on the threshold, for getting benefits otherwise available to BPL families.

The Development Hypothesis demands that such postulates are put in place, so that the quotient does not leave out the real poor.

Suggested 'Stepwise' approach could be as follows:

1. Using 'Inclusion' criteria—identify the poor; then
2. Using 'Exclusion' criteria—weed out any APL families which have crept in (Table 10.1)
3. (i) Using a Nine Point Scale/Indicators, identify the factors having a bearing on poverty at the household level (Table 10.2). (ii) Identify factors having a bearing on poverty at the Administrative unit level-village/village Panchayat, Block/Mandal and then at District level (Table 10.3).
4. The Manager of the Programme attaches 'Weight' to each of the indicators within two Identifiable Groups (i) Household level, and (ii) Gram Panchayat level. For example a Weight of 70:30 under each.
5. Weight is attached, intra-Group, for each indicator.
6. Totalling the weights of both–Inter and Intra-Group weights gives a quotient.
7. Village/Village Panchayats are then classified—Bottom 1-20 per cent, then 21 per cent, 50 per cent and then 51-100 per cent.
8. 'Map' these for a Block/Mandal, i.e. indicating the poverty status, on broad group basis of a village within a Block, the same can then be developed for the Block, District and for the whole State.
9. Tabulate for each Block a Format as per Table 10.4 or feed it in the computer with a special software with 'Querry' system to respond to a specific querry to ascertain the major factors having a bearing on Poverty

to help the Policy Makers, Programme Administrators/Managers to devise appropriate Intervention, either adopting an Area Development Approach or a Household Development Approach or a combination of both to make them cross over the poverty line.

Poverty Alleviation/Eradication

Taxonomy of Poverty

Poverty ratios emanating from the Census/Survey could throw up several groups vying for attention in different scales/proportions:

(i) Landholders—small and marginal under rainfed conditions.
(ii) Semi-skilled labour
(iii) Rural artisans
(iv) Women headed households:
  (a) With assets
  (b) Without assets
(v) Old Age/Handicapped persons
(vi) Landless Agricultural/Non-Agricultural Labour
(vii) Others

This broad classification could have its dimension in terms of caste/tribe etc. Broadly the stratification is two fold.

Group 'A' Households with assets—Physical or in terms of skills and Group 'B' without assets.

While the effort to address the Group 'A' would be to upgrade their exposure to technology and marketing support, the effort for the Group 'B' would focus on to upgrade their skills.

For Group 'B' a special effort shall also have to be made to ensure them food and nutrition security, access to drinking water, literacy, health, anganwadi and in the short to medium term, wage employment openings. While disparate efforts are perceptible on ground but what one also sees is everyone is working in its own turf largely unmindful of the efforts of others—thus missing the concept of Convergence of efforts on the Target Group. The way out perhaps could be to go on 'Mission-Mode'.

Mission Mode Approach

At the National, State and District level 'Mission on Poverty Alleviation' could be constituted, making one person as a Mission Leader. Each Mission Leader would head an Inter Ministerial/Departmental Group and assisted by certain number of specialized Group(s), say on Transfer of Technology, Access to Health, Drinking Water, Literacy, Infrastructure like Road/Marketing yard, on forming Self-Help Groups, Credit and Employment Generation, Skill Upgradation etc.

While the policy framework would be the job of the Mission at National level, Flexibility to adopt the programme(s) to local conditions shall be the job of the Missions at State/District/Sub-District Level.

Prioritization of activity to be undertaken and resources allocation for such activities shall be guided by the relevant factors having a bearing on poverty as thrown up by the 'Poverty Mapping' based on given Indicators/Factors as a result of a any special Survey/Census of Poor.

While leadership/convergence of co-ordination role would be with one agency but the main job of the Mission shall be to ensure total Governmental/Non-Governmental effort to alleviate the pangs of the poor to make them decent partners of the civil society.

This Expose is fundamental to breaking away from the largely 'Food Security' based income criteria to determine the Poverty Ratios. Imperative is to factor in other indicators led inputs having a bearing on poverty so as to fully appreciate both the poverty ratios and poverty intensity as well as the factors having a bearing on poverty and then go on to evolve appropriate response Matrix to respond to specifics—given the situation of a household, geographical area or an administrative unit.

Table 10.1: Household Schedule

A.

1. Village: ______________________ Panchayat Samiti/ Block:____________ District:________State ________
2. Head of the Household______________________
3. Sex: M/F
4. Age in years: ______________________
5. Total Members of family:______________________
6. Caste:

S.C.	S.T.	O.B.C.	Others

B. Inclusion Criteria

1. Whether illiterate — Yes/No
2. Whether Houseless — Yes/No
3. Whether the household headed by a lady with no adult support — Yes/No
4. Whether a landless Agriculture/ Non-Agriculture Labour — Yes/No
5. Whether beneficiary of Old Age Social Security of the Government — Yes/No
6. Exempted from house/chula tax (wherever applicable) — Yes/No
7. If children going to Anganwadi (wherever there is one) and is below grade III of Nourishment/Nutrition levels/mother held to be anaemic — Yes/No
8. Unemployed for major part of the year — Yes/No
9. Children instead of going to school are engaged in any type of child labour — Yes/No
10. Sleeps hungry at night or depends on the mercy of neighbours etc. for good — Yes/No
11. Village artisan. — Yes/No

C. Exclusion Criteria

(a) Whether a household owns a colour T.V., Two Wheeler, Refrigerator — Yes/No

(b) Owning more than 2 hectares of unirrigated or one hect. of irrigated land — Yes/No

(c) Whether a household owns a Tractor or Power Tiller Yes/No
(d) Has *Pucca* House Yes/No
(e) Income more than Rs. 2000 per month Yes/No

Table 10.2: Nine Point Indicator Schedule

1. Main Economic Activities

(A) Monthly Family Income (in Rs.) Rs.

(B) Source of Income

(C) Wage Rate

Agriculture		Non-Agriculture	
Male	Female	Male	Female

(D) Typical Migration Patterns:

Location	Season	Duration	Distance	Activity

2. Access to potable drinking water: Yes/No

If Yes, source of supply

Tap	Tubewell		Well		Any Other (please specify)	
Yes/No	Yes	No	Yes	No	Yes	No

3. Assets

(a) Livestock (in No.):

	Cow	Bullock	Buffalo	Pig	Poultry	Others
Milch						
Draught						

(b) Agricultural Land (in Hect.):

Total Agricultural Land	Irrigated	Unirrigated

Owned	Leased in	Leased out	Share Cropper

4. Natural Calamity
   (a) What was natural calamity in recent years:

Drought	Food	Both

   (b) Was there any loss in employment ?

Yes/No

   (c) If yes, for how many days:

   (d) What was your loss/effect on the family as a result of: (Please convert in Rs. the physical losses)

Rs.

5. Food Consumption per month:
   (a) Do you get sufficient food
   Cereals Yes/No
   Milk Yes/No
   Oils Yes/No
   Pulses Yes/No
   (b) Do you have two square meals a day Yes/No
6. Source of Lighting:

Electricity	Kerosene	Any Other (Please specify)
Yes/ No	Yes/ No	

7.
   (a) Any training under TRYSEM

Yes/No

   (b) Whether assistance received under IRDP

Yes/No

   (c) Income gained as a result of above

Rs.

8. Your suggestions in order of priority for the help you need.

Explanations

'Illiterate' is to be understood, who has done formal schooling not beyond 'Primary' level.

'Houseless' does not have a *pucca* house (other than under Indra Awaas Yojana) as defined in the population census.

'Landless': Those operating land less than 0.5 ha. or not operating any land.

'Non-Agriculture Worker': Those deriving more than 50 per cent of income from non-agriculture wages.

Methodology

1. For conducting the Census, village teachers, doctors (if any), some elders, previous Sarpanch, any NGO and some youth leaders should also be involved. The idea is to avoid all types of bias and jealousies at any level.
2. In order to provide checks and balances and introduce an element of transparency, the final list must be displayed in the Panchayat for at least 7 days inviting comments or objections, if any. The list should be accessible to every family members in the village who will have the right to make representation to Village/Block/District Panchayat.

Any objection thus received shall be dealt with in a meeting of Gram Sabha specifically convened for this purpose. A record of proceedings shall be kept and BPL Schedule finalized.

Any person aggrieves by the decision of the Gram Sabha shall have the right to appeal in writing to Block/Mandal/Gram Panchayat, within 15 days of the meeting of Gram Sabha referred to above where it will be dealt with by a committee constituted for this purpose, by the Collector of the District comprising members from different sections/groups one of which shall be a lady member of the block/mandal panchayat. Their decision shall be final to include or exclude such names from the list finalized by the Gram Panchayat.

The final list thus arrived at shall constitute the BPL group in the Panchayat.

Table 10.3: Village Infrastructure

1. Revival of small water bodies. Create irrigation, water shed, soil conservation and rainwater harvesting facilities.
2. IRDP–Assistance
3. Connectivity to *Pucca* Road
4. School—Primary, Middle, Secondary
5. Anganwadi
6. Establish and Strengthen Primary Health Centre having Doctors, Dais and other required personnels.
7. Create:
   (a) Marketing facilities
   (b) (i) Irrigation facilities, (ii) Revive small water bodies, (iii) Undertake soil/water conservation measures, (iv) Operationalize village johads, etc.

Table 10.4: Cumulative Poverty Index

Sl. No.	*Name of Village*	*Weighted Average for Each Indicator*									*C.P.I* Total 1 to 9*
		1	*2*	*3*	*4*	*5*	*6*	*7*	*8*	*9*	

* CPI = Cumulative Poverty Index.

1. This Appendix is to arrive at a CPI for each village or Block.
2. While developing Poverty Map for each District 'Name of Village' will be substituted by 'Name of the Block'

and in case of developing Poverty Map of the State, the column shall show 'Name of the District' and at the National level it shall show 'Name of the State'.

Identifying Hungry Districts

Planning Commission calculation of BPL is based on the NSSO consumption data. NSSO also collects information from each household on another 24 major indicators (each divided into a number of sub-indicators (Table 10.5). TERI undertook a study sponsored by the Planning Commission for Bihar, Maharashtra, Himachal Pradesh, Orissa, Punjab and Tamil Nadu for the 50th (1993-94) NSS Round. There being wide variations from region to region, the result showed that significance of poverty indicators varied from not only State to State, but also between the sub-regions. We would then suggest the following steps:

(a) A study from the NSSO data on visible indicators of poverty for the 81 sub-regions in the country (Table 10.6) will provide a profile of those who are counted as 'poor' according to the official calculation.
(b) Separate questionnaires can then be drawn for each sub-region highlighting the prominent indicators to be investigated.
(c) Questionnaires thus prepared should be field tested and then finalized for the field survey.

Analysis of data on two square meals a day.

(d) Analyse the available data of 55th round for those not having two square meals a day upto the sub-regional level. This will give a rough idea of the magnitude of poverty at least in the concerned pockets. At the State level, major part of the hungry (over 68 per cent) are concentrated in Bihar, Orissa, U.P., West Bengal, Maharashtra and Madhya Pradesh (Table 10.7).
(e) Those regions like Kalahandi (Orissa) where majority of people do not have two square meals, the whole district should be taken up and Developmental programmes drawn up combined with Schemes like 'Food for work'. In addition to the normal programme, Tenth Plan should

concentrate on these selected Districts—some 40-45—each district being handed over to one NGO/MNC etc. who must ensure complete poverty eradication in the district.

Table 10.5: List of Indicators and Categorisation

Indicators	*Category*
Demographic	
1. Caste	VI
(a) ST	
(b) SC	
(c) Others	
2. Religion	VI
(a) Hindu	
(b) Muslim	
(c) Others	
3. Activity	VI
(a) Self-employed Non-Agricultural	
(b) Agricultural Labour	
(c) Other Labour	
(d) Self-Employed Agricultural	VI
(e) Others	
4. Sex of head	
(a) Male	
(b) Female	
5. Female Size	VI
Adult Total	
(a) Male	
(b) Female	
Children Total	
(a) Male	
(b) Female	
Dependency	
House	
6. Homestead Type	V
(a) Owned	
(b) Others	
7. Type of Dwelling	VI
(a) Chawl/basti	
(b) Independent house	
(c) Flat	

(Contd.)

(*Contd.*)

Indicators	*Category*
(d) Others	
8. Type of House	VI
(a) Kuccha	
(b) Pucca	
(c) Semi-Pucca	
(d) Other	
9. Floor type	
(a) Mud	VI
(b) Wood, Bamboo	
(c) Brick, Cement	
(d) Others	
10. Condition of House	
(a) Excellent	VI
(b) Good	VI
(c) Bad	
(d) Other	V
11. Source of Energy	
(e) Coke, Coal	
(f) Chips	
(g) Gas (coal, oil & natural)	
(h) Dung coke	
(i) Charcoal	
(j) Others	
12. Source of Lighting	
(a) Kerosene	
(b) Other oils	
(c) Electricity	
Possessions	
13. Milch animals	VI
(a) None	
(b) Cow	
(c) Buffalo	
(d) Both cow & buffalo	
(e) Others	
14. Draught animal	
(a) None	VI
(b) A pair of more	
(c) Single	
15. Land	
(a) Owned	VI
(b) Rented	

(*Contd.*)

(c) Others	
16. Land Possessed Categories	
(a) No land	VI
(b) Marginal	
(c) Small	
(d) Medium	
(e) Large	
17. Cops grown (last year)	
(a) Rice	VI
(b) Wheat	
(c) Jowar	
(d) Bajra	
(e) Maize	
(f) Barley	
(g) Ragi	
(h) Grain	
18. Income from	
(a) Cultivation	VI
(b) Fishing/Other Agricultural enterprise	
(c) Wage/Salaried enterprise	
(d) Non-agricultural enterprise	
(e) Pension	
(f) Remittances	
(g) Interest and dividends	
(h) Others	
19. Any Member Working on public works (at least 60 days last year)	O
20. Assistance during the last five years under IRDP	
(a) Miltch animal	O
(b) Draught animal	
(c) Sheep/Goat	
(d) Pump set	
(e) Sewing Machine	
(f) Others	
21. HH Purchases from ration shop	O
22. Consumption of Alcoholic Beverages during last 30 days	O
23. Consumption of fruits last 30 days	O
(a) Banana	
(b) Mango	
(c) Citrus	
(d) Apple	
(e) Grapes	

(Contd.)

(*Contd.*)

Indicators	*Category*
(f) Others	
24. Journey undertaken last 30 days	
(A) By train for	
(a) Domestic Work	
(b) Education	
(c) Other (not related to economic activity)	
(B) By Bus for	
(a) Domestic Work	
(b) Education	
(c) Other	

VI – Visible
V – Varifiable
O – others

Table 10.6: NSSO Regions

Big States	*Small States*	*Non-comparable States/Regions*
Andhra Pradesh (4), Assam (3), Bihar (3), Gujarat (5), Haryana (2), Karnataka (4), Kerala (2), Madhya Pradesh (7), Maharashtra (6), Orissa (3), Punjab (2), Rajasthan (4), Tamil Nadu (4), Uttar Pradesh (5), West Bengal (4)	Arunachal Pradesh, Goa, Himachal Pradesh, Jammu and Kashmir (3), Manipur (2), Meghalaya, Mizoram, Nagaland, Sikkim, Tripura, Andaman and Nicobar Islands, Chandigarh, Dadra and Nagar Haveli, Daman and Diu, Delhi, Lakshadweep, Pondicherry	Goa, Jammu & Kashmir (3) Nagaland, Dadra and Nagar Haveli, Daman and Diu
per cent Population = 96.74 Total States = 15 Total Regions = 58	per cent Population = 3.23 Total States = 17 Total Regions = 19	per cent Population = 0.31 Total States = 5 Total Regions = 4

Note: Population proportions have been computed leaving out J & K. Figures in parentheses are the number of regions in each State.

Table 10.7: Number of Hungry in Rural India

States	*Population Number (million)*				*Extreme Hunger*				*Partial Hunger*				*Total Hunger (per cent)*			
	1983	*1991*	*1993*	*1998*	*1983*	*1991*	*1993*	*1998*	*1983*	*1991*	*1993*	*1998*	*1983*	*1991*	*1993*	*1998*
Andhra Pradesh	44.02	48.6	50.1	54.2	0.36	0.15	0.10	0.65	6.47	1.94	1.80	0.92	6.83	2.09	1.90	1.57
Assam	18.55	19.9	20.8	22.8	0.66	0.92	0.12	0.07	3.32	2.17	1.87	1.39	3.98	3.09	1.99	1.46
Bihar	63.60	75.0	78.3	84.3	3.45	0.38	0.63	1.26	20.23	6.08	6.42	4.30	23.68	6.46	7.05	5.56
Gujarat	24.41	27.1	27.8	30.9	0.02	0	0.12	0.68	0.43	0.22	0.28	0.70	0.43	0.22	0.40	
Haryana	10.48	12.4	12.8	14.8	0.01	0.05	0.10	0.00	0.08	0.11	0	0.12	0.09	0.16	0.10	0.12
Karnataka	27.44	31.1	32.1	35.2	0.26	0.16	0.10	0.28	4.89	2.99	1.89	0.95	5.15	3.15	1.99	1.23
Kerala	21.49	21.4	22.0	23.4	0.79	0.73	0.13	0.09	3.29	2.29	1.80	1.73	4.08	3.02	1.93	1.82
Madhya Pradesh	43.22	50.8	52.8	59.4	0.74	0.61	0.16	0.18	5.77	2.69	1.85	1.48	6.51	3.30	2.01	1.66
Maharashtra	42.39	48.4	49.8	54.8	0.29	0.24	0.10	0.22	5.69	1.36	1.20	2.25	5.98	1.60	1.30	2.47
Orissa	24.17	27.4	28.3	30.6	1.21	0.66	0.23	0.15	7.69	5.18	4.44	4.56	8.90	5.84	4.67	4.71
Punjab	12.61	14.3	14.6	16.3	0.03	0	0	0.17	0.04	0	0.02	0.20	0.04	0.0	0.02	
Rajasthan	28.11	33.9	35.7	40.1	0.19	0	0	0.87	0.44	0.14	0.24	1.06	0.44	0.14	0.24	
Tamil Nadu	33.73	36.8	37.7	40.1	0.46	0	0.36	5.42	2.58	1.92	0.60	5.88	2.58	1.92	0.96	
Uttar Pradesh	94.52	111.5	116.2	131.5	0.59	0.33	0.23	0.66	9.82	3.68	1.39	3.81	10.41	4.01	1.62	4.47
West Bengal	41.70	49.4	51.0	56.0	3.59	0.59	0.61	0.17	12.93	7.31	8.87	6.22	16.52	7.90	9.48	6.39
All India	546.06	628.7	651.6	721.4	12.83	4.40	5.21	6.49	88.41	40.24	35.19	30.30	101.24	44.64	40.40	36.79

Source: NSSO, Various Rounds.

11

Conclusion and Recommendations

"People with vision do not wait for the events to happen – they prompt the events to happen".

Though the main thrust of this innovative study has been Poverty Mapping in Rajasthan State, it has also dealt with the general poverty situation in the country—various estimates of the poverty ratio, the controversies prevailing about the methodologies adopted by the different schools of thought in estimating poverty and the challenges which the official estimate has to confront from different quarters. The study also highlights the innumerable programmes, both centrally sponsored and State Governments' own, which are being implemented in the country to alleviate poverty. Many of these programmes are similar in nature with same objectives. In fact, there are around 360 Centrally Sponsored Schemes (CSS) and the amount transferred is not insignificant as the states, it is estimated, received nearly Rs. 25,000 crore during 2001-02 for implementation of CSSs.

As has been stated, the problem with CSS is that they are numerous, mostly stand alone and designed as if each scheme is meant for different sets of individuals. Very often, they promote the same cause. Let us take for instance, employment generation schemes. A rural unemployed person can either participate in a wage employment scheme or the self-employment scheme, or may be both. There are similar schemes for the urban folk. If a person is not able to benefit from any of these, he can participate in the self-employment scheme run by the Ministry of Human Resource Development. There is the Prime Minister's Rozgar Yojana under the Ministry of Agro

Rural Industries. Similarly for the women, there are several schemes for their betterment.

In this abundance of schemes, one can claim a house under the Indira Awas Yojana, even before one acquires any means of livelihood. In point of fact, there are schemes for every conceivable needs and contingency, be it nutrition, relief, rehabilitation, housing, child care, health, education, counselling or training. There are schemes even for those who run these schemes! And the target group includes everybody who is vulnerable: poor, women and children, the elderly, destitutes, orphans, disabled, victims of physical violence, drug addicts, widows, slum dwellers, tribals, and so and so forth. The agencies involved are diverse, ranging from the Ministry of Agriculture to the Ministry of Tribal Affairs.

Further, often the same person is a beneficiary of several schemes. It is difficult to identify who is benefiting from how many schemes. Similarly, when it comes to evaluation and monitoring, each scheme is evaluated on a stand alone basis as if there is no relation between the benefits received under different schemes. In trying not to follow "one size fits all" we move to the other extreme: we ensure some size definitely fits everybody.

In this mess of CSSs, it is perhaps too much to expect illiterate beneficiaries or even the schemes' implementors to know of them. One would lose count of the coverage and even purpose of various rural development programmes starting with Community Development Programme launched immediately after Independence. The list would be infinite – one programme overlapping the other or substituting the previous one with or without any specific reason. Therefore, a holistic approach is needed whereby genuinely needy persons are identified and their basic needs are attended to. However, it is gratifying to note that UPA Government have entrusted a task to the Planning Commission to bring order to the tangle of CSSs. Hopefully, the Planning Commission will be able to design such an approach.

Present Study

The aim of this study—Poverty Mapping—was to highlight the specific areas in Rajasthan at districts level where concerted actions are needed to eradicate poverty and prepare development planning of a district keeping in view the inter-district variations in growth indicators, resource availability and status of capacity building strategies. Similarly, the purpose of constructing district-wise segmental stratum index and summative total index is to put emphasis on the urgency of planning at the grassroots level in terms of specific deprivation which varies significantly from district to district and need for formulation of different strategies for each component.

The primary objective of this innovative study was, therefore, to make an assessment in a comparative framework at inter-district level regarding the extent of deprivation in each segment of the selected indicators. Raw data often gives a picture at the level of generality, and more so, disadvantaged areas within a district and disadvantaged social categories often become invisible. But when component and indicators are taken separately, deprivation for each stratum (component) and segment (indicator) can be understood meaningfully. Hence, a serious thought has been devoted to the choices of number of components for each indicator and giving weights to them so that the values could be logically assigned.

The composite index which has been constructed raises certain other issues like relationship between different components of indicators and of index, and index which comprises of all the indicators. Inability to relate otherwise logical interlinkages, no doubt, necessitates causalty, which however was beyond the scope of this study. However, our ability to identify the areas where there are concentration of poorer people and the reasons thereof will help immensely the policy makers to frame proper policies for removal of poverty.

The main driving force, which drove us to provoke this study was to emancipate the poor from being identified largely on income/consumption expenditure criteria. Man, yes he survives, but does not live on or for 'bread' alone. Being a social animal he has aspirations and expectations which run beyond more survival. His other requirements be it of personal nature or infrastructural, its assessment and its bearing on poverty were the reasons of this study.

Based on Triple 'A' approach of

- Assessment,
- Analysis, and
- Action.

This study substantially helps emerge a whole new approach to assess poverty, adopting a given set of indicators.

Following the methodology adopted in this study, our findings/conclusions could succinctly be put, as follows:–

Conclusions

1. There are much larger number of poor than estimated hitherto – either by the Planning Commission based on consumption expenditure criteria or on detailed survey basis – carried out by MRD.
2. Income alone may not be the correct basis for estimation of poverty. There are other influencing factors – both personal and infrastructural – which have a direct bearing on poverty.
3. Many of the factors having a bearing on poverty need to be seen in the context of local conditions.
4. Under the current approach to assess the poverty ratios – there are genuine BPL families who are left out and APL families making inroad to BPL. Resources being limited, application of funds on APL crowd out availability of funds for the BPL. This leads to imprecise targeting, bring cost benefit ratios under stress.
5. Irrigated areas offered less number of poor.

6. People with 'assets' and 'skills' managed to escape the poverty net.
7. Social Safety Net cover for the poor is inadequate.
8. Employment opportunities offered for the poor would appear to be an apology for the poor.
9. Empowerment is the name of the game – absence of which directly affect their opportunity to make over to the other side.
10. ST, SC and Women held households are in general, form the core of this poor.

The results of this study clearly show that every district does not have similar nature and extent of poverty and also the causes of poverty differ from district to district. Hence district specific strategies for poverty alleviation would be important. The key components of poverty alleviation strategy in different districts may be as follows:

Development

- Improve access to income generating activities in Banswara, Barmer, Bharatpur, Churu, Dausa, Dholpur, Dungarpur, Jaisalmer, Jalore, Jhunjhunu, Jodhpur, Sikar and Udaipur.
- Develop urban growth centres in Dausa, Jhalawar, Nagaur and Sirohi.
- Develop small towns and growth centres in Alwar, Banswara, Baran, Barmer, Chittorgarh, Dausa, Dungarpur, Jaisalmer, Jalore, Jhalawar, Karauli, Nagaur and Rajsamund.
- Enforce minimum wages and wage employment programme effectively in Alwar, Baran, Barmer, Bharatpur, Bikaner, Churu, Dausa, Dholpur, Jaipur, Jaisalmer, Jhunjhunu, Jodhpur and Rajsamund.
- Strengthen special component development programme for SCs and STs in Ajmer, Alwar, Barmer, Bharatpur, Bhilwara, Bikaner, Churu, Dholpur, Jaipur, Jaisalmer, Jhunjhunu, Jodhpur and Kota.

- Emphasize land based anti-poverty strategy in Ajmer, Alwar, Bharatpur, Bundi, Dausa, Dholpur, Jaipur, Jaisalmer, Jodhpur, Karauli, Kota and Pali.
- Provide homestead-*cum*-garden (of a little bigger size than small size constructed house under IAY) which is less cost effective to each household family in Ajmer, Alwar, Barmer, Bharatpur Bhilwara, Hanumangarh, Jaisalmer, Jhunjhunu, Jodhpur, Karauli, Nagaur, Sawai Madhopur and Tonk.
- Improve Watershed Development and Irrigation facility in Ajmer, Banswara, Barmer, Bikaner, Churu, Dungarpur, Hanumangarh, Jaisalmer, Jhunjhunu, Jodhpur, Nagaur, Sikar and Tonk.
- Increase number of regulated markets in Alwar, Banswara, Barmer, Bikaner, Bundi, Dungarpur, Jaipur, Jaisalmer, Jhunjhunu, Jodhpur, Sawai Madhopur, Sikar, Udaipur.
- Increase number of fair price shops in Alwar, Bharatpur, Bhilwara, Bundi, Chittorgarh, Dausa, Dungarpur, Ganganagar, Hanumangarh, Kota, Nagaur and Sikar.
- Increase number of milk co-operatives in Baran, Barmer, Bhilwara, Chittorgarh, Dausa, Ganganagar, Hanumangarh, Jaipur, Jaisalmer, Jalore, Jhunjhunu, Jodhpur, Karauli, Nagaur, Rajsamund, Sawai Madhopur, Sikar, Sirohi, Tonk and Udaipur.
- Launch short term and long term drought mitigating programme in Alwar, Baran, Bharatpur, Bundi, Dausa, Dholpur, Karauli, Kota, Rajsamund and Sawai Madhopur.
- Encourage formation of self-help groups in Baran, Barmer, Bharatpur, Bhilwara, Chittorgarh, Dholpur, Ganganagar, Jaipur, Jalore, Jodhpur, Nagaur, Tonk and Udaipur.
- Improve coverage under JGSY in Baran, Bharatpur, Bikaner, Bundi, Dholpur, Hanumangarh, Jhalawar, Karauli, Kota, Pali, Sikar, Sirohi and Tonk.
- Improve coverage under JRY in Baran, Bikaner, Bundi, Dholpur, Hanumangarh, Jaisalmer, Jodhpur, Kota, Rajsamund, Sikar, Sirohi and Tonk.

- Improve women's share in employment under JGSY in Banswara, Baran, Churu, Dausa, Dungarpur, Hanumangarh, Jaisalmer, Jhalawar, Karauli, Rajsamund, Sawai Madhopur, Tonk and Udaipur.

Infrastructure

- Improve access to electricity in Alwar, Banswara, Barmer, Bharatpur, Dholpur, Dungarpur, Jaisalmer, Jalore, Jhalawar, Nagaur, Sawai Madhopur, Tonk and Udaipur.
- Increase number of bank branches in Baran, Barmer, Ganganagar, Dholpur, Bharatpur, Jalore, Jodhpur, Karauli, Kota, Nagaur, Sawai Madhopur, Sikar and Udipur.
- Connect more number of villages with *pucca* road in Baran, Barmer, Bhilwara, Bundi, Chittorgarh, Jaisalmer, Jhalawar, Karauli, Kota, Nagaur, Sawai Madhopur and Tonk.

Housing

- Improve access to toilet facility in Alwar, Banswara, Barmer, Bharatpur, Chittorgarh, Dholpur, Dungarpur, Jaisalmer, Jalore, Jhalawar, Sawai Madhopur and Tonk.
- Improve provision for safe drinking water in Alwar, Banswara, Barmer, Bharatpur, Bikaner, Churu, Dholpur, Jalore, Jhalawar, Karauli, Nagaur, Sawai Madhopur and Tonk.

Agriculture

- Improve per capita cereal output in Baran, Barmer, Bikaner, Churu, Jaipur, Jaisalmer, Jalore, Jodhpur, Karauli, Kota, Pali, Sawai Madhopur and Udaipur.
- Improve per capita production of cash crops in Barmer, Bharatpur, Chittorgarh, Churu, Dungarpur, Jaipur, Jaisalmer, Jalore, Jhalawar, Jodhpur, Rajsamund, Sikar and Tonk.

Literacy

- Launch female literacy campaign in Banswara, Bhilwara, Bundi, Chittorgarh, Dungarpur, Jaisalmer, Jalore, Jodhpur, Pali, Rajsamund, Sawai Madhopur, Sirohi and Tonk.

Health

- Improve health care for reduction in infant mortality rate in Baran, Bikaner, Churu, Dausa, Ganganagar, Hanumangarh, Jaipur, Jaisalmer, Jhunjhunu, Jodhpur, Kota, Nagaur and Sikar.
- Strengthen immunization programme in Ajmer, Alwar, Banswara, Barmer, Bharatpur, Chittorgarh, Churu, Dholpur, Jaisalmer, Jhalawar, Karauli, Sawai Madhopur and Udaipur.

Nutrition

- Strengthen Nutrition Development programme for children in Baran, Bharatpur, Bhilwara, Bikaner, Churu, Dausa, Dholpur, Jodhpur, Jalore, Kota, Pali and Sawai Madhopur. In addition to the districts whose both male and female children need attention, female children would need special attention in Jhalawar and Rajsamund.

Livestock

- The economy in Rajasthan being Livestock based, initiate and strengthen programmes to improve the availability of Livestock in the districts where it is lacking.

Besides there is need for concentrated efforts first in high poverty districts then the districts the middle range which would also need location specific strategies for poverty alleviation. The key components to be addressed for poverty alleviation strategy in these districts are indicated in Table 11.1.

Table 11.1: Development Priorities in Various Districts

District	*Priorities*
Ajmer	Watershed development, female literacy
Alwar	Safe drinking water, female literacy, mid-day meal in schools
Banswara	Growth centres, homestead-*cum*-garden plots for the houseless, safe drinking water, literacy for both male and female
Baran	Female literacy, *pucca* road, improved coverage of women under JGSY, improved health care facilities
Barmer	Growth centres, female literacy, *pucca* road, safe drinking water, self as well as wage employment programmes
Bharatpur	Safe drinking water, female literacy, *pucca* road
Bhilwara	Self and wage employment programmes, female literacy, anganwadi, *pucca* road, electricity
Bikaner	Female literacy, anganwadi, safe drinking water
Bundi	Growth centres, female literacy, *pucca* road, homestead-*cum*-garden plots for the houseless
Chittorgarh	Female literacy, *pucca* road, growth centres, self and wage employment programmes, homestead-*cum*-garden plots for the houseless
Churu	Safe drinking water, watershed development, *pucca* road, improved health care facilities
Dausa	Growth centre, female literacy, homestead-*cum*-garden plots for the houseless
Dholpur	Female literacy, anganwadi, growth centres, self and wage employment programmes
Dungarpur	Female literacy, growth centres, homestead-*cum*-garden plots for the houseless
Ganganagar	Health care facilities, anganwadi, electricity
Hanumangarh	Health care facilities, anganwadi
Jaipur	Health care facilities, anganwadi
Jaisalmer	Female literacy, *pucca* road, growth centres
Jalore	Female literacy, growth centres, homestead-*cum*-garden plot for the houseless, improved health care facilities.
Jhalawar	*Pucca* road, growth centre, improved coverage of women under JGSY
Jhunjhunu	Watershed development, safe drinking water
Jodhpur	Female literacy, anganwadi centre, electricity, watershed development

(Contd.)

(Contd.)

District	*Priorities*
Karauli	Growth centre, *pucca* road, safe drinking water
Kota	*Pucca* road, anganwadi centre
Nagaur	Electricity, growth centres, watershed development
Pali	Female literacy, *pucca* road, electricity
Rajasmund	Female literacy, growth centres, homestead-*cum*-garden plots for the houseless, improved coverage of women under JGSY
Sawai Madhopur	Female literacy, safe drinking water, anganwadi
Sikar	Electricity, homestead-*cum*-garden plots for the houseless
Sirohi	Growth centres, female literacy, self as well as wage employment programmes
Tonk	Female literacy, *pucca* road, improved coverage of women under JGSY
Udaipur	Watershed development, growth centre, wage employment programme.

Recommendations

In the state as a whole, the key components of poverty alleviation strategy, as revealed by the detailed district, village and household level data would be to reduce infant mortality rate, illiteracy among women, incidence of malnourishment among children and to increase per capita buffalo population. Next in order of importance would be improving the accessibility of the villages to *pucca* road, access to electricity, access to safe drinking water, promotion of income generating activities, special development schemes for agricultural labourers and SCs and STs and drought mitigating programmes. The analysis of village level and household level data also revealed that agricultural labourers and SC/ST families would require special attention for poverty alleviation. Besides access to safe drinking water, irrigation, *pucca* road, railway station, credit, livestock development and agro-based income generating activities would form the key components of strategy for poverty alleviation. Main recommendations would be the following:

- Assess the poor correctly based on a multi-contour approach, monetise this cost of all these factors—add all of them to form the basis of BPL/APL divide.
- Promote Block as a unit of Development along with allocation of resources.
- Accountability of the people administrating the separate core and non-core issues and address them in that order in an integrated manner through a single agency programme.
- Better targeting of the poor and resources.
- Improve the level of skills and asset of the target group with specific/special reference to ST/SC and Women headed households.
- Better Social Safety Net cover for the disadvantages.
- In the interregnum period, better targeting of the employment generation/poverty alleviation programmes.
- Monitor progress and prepare report on all the factors.
- Family cases—current status.
- Fix a time frame.
- Go on to Mission mode, and leave out programme approach (*See* Chapter 9). Adopt both inclusion and exclusion criteria to identify the poor to ensure that no real BPL family is left out (*see* Chapter 9).

Index